MISSION
AND
MINISTRY

A HISTORY OF THE
VIRGINIA
THEOLOGICAL SEMINARY

MISSION
AND
MINISTRY

A HISTORY OF THE
VIRGINIA
THEOLOGICAL SEMINARY

JOHN BOOTY

MOREHOUSE PUBLISHING
Harrisburg, PA

Produced by Morehouse Publishing for
The Protestant Episcopal Theological Seminary in Virginia

Morehouse Publishing
P.O. Box 1321
Harrisburg, PA 17105

Published by:
The Protestant Episcopal Theological Seminary in Virginia
Seminary Post Office
Alexandria, VA 22304

Design and Composition: John Reinhardt Book Design

Library of Congress Cataloging-in-Publication Data
    Mission and Ministry: A History of the Virginia Theological Seminary/John Booty
       p.   cm.
    Includes bibliographical references and index.
    ISBN 0–9644169–1–3
    1. Protestant Episcopal Theological Seminary in Virginia (Alexandria, VA.)—History
    2. Alexandria (Va.)—Church History.   I. Title
    BV4070.P86B66   1995   95–7419
    207'.755296—dc20   CIP

Printed in the United States of America

CONTENTS

v

CONTENTS

FOREWORD

In October 1994, I dedicated a new window in Immanuel Chapel at the seminary. The window depicts women dancing with joy at God's liberating power, a visual representation of the Song of Miriam in Exodus 15:21, "Sing to the Lord for he hath triumphed gloriously." The window was the gift of students and friends of the seminary, honoring teachers of the Old Testament. It is the only window in the chapel in which all the persons depicted are women, and it is the only window that remembers a specific event in the Old Testament story.

This history of the seminary is another window that opens into the life of the Virginia Theological Seminary. Both the Miriam window and *Mission and Ministry* symbolize the best traditions of Virginia Seminary. Ours is a tradition deeply rooted in the biblical narrative, in which learning and piety are linked. Ours is a tradition that focuses on the liberating power of what God has done in Jesus Christ, a power available to all people who are justified by God's grace that is apprehended through faith. Ours is a deeply personal story. Generations of twentieth century students remember with thanksgiving the dynamism of those who have taught Old Testament and made those ancient stories come alive for us. Who can forget the experience of learning, in Hebrew, the beginning of the Song of Miriam, "Sing to the Lord . . ." The other window, this book, is also deeply personal. It tells of men and women whose learning and piety have been transmitted not so much by rote as through relationships. John Booty's history, then, is deeply faithful to the best traditions of Virginia Seminary: It is biblically grounded, joining learning and piety, celebrating relationships in community, and affirming across the generations the centrality of God's grace.

As this book makes clear, the Virginia Seminary is faithful when it maintains the vision of its founders in a dynamic relationship to the present. The Miriam window clearly seeks to celebrate the important place of women in the biblical narrative and in the life of God's people today. Virginia Seminary, at its best, is unafraid to engage the issues of a particular generation with the enduring and liberating gospel of Jesus

Christ. This book is published at a time of new beginning in the life of the seminary. The Very Rev. Martha Horne was elected Dean and President of the seminary in May 1994. A new chapter of fidelity, and change required by that fidelity, has begun. The seminary will look to new ways to equip God's people for mission and ministry, and will wrestle with questions unimagined by the founders. The seminary will take risks because risk-taking, as this story demonstrates, is part of what it means to be faithful.

The Virginia Seminary continues to train men and women to open the windows of people's souls to the light of the gospel of Jesus Christ. We do that by standing firm on the faith once delivered to the saints, a faith that requires us to launch into deep waters, into the tumult of our times. We pray that as this history tells of others, we, too, may be faithful and zealous in our service to the liberating gospel of Jesus Christ.

PETER JAMES LEE
Bishop of Virginia
Chairman, Board of Trustees

1994 Faculty: Martha Horne, Dean and President
First Row: (l to r) Judith McDaniel, Allan Parrent, Martha Horne,
Mary Lewis Hix, Anne Katherine Grieb, Amelia Gearey, Murray Newman
Second Row: Mitzi Jarrett Budde, Burton J. Newman, Walter Eversley,
Jane Anderson Morse, David Scott, Raymond Glover, Churchill Gibson
Third Row: William Stafford, Richard Jones, Jacques Hadler, James Ross,
Howard Hanchey, Edward Kryder, Richard Busch, Robert Prichard
Missing: Edward Gleason

PREFACE

This history of Virginia Theological Seminary was prepared with two objects in mind. First, every effort was to be made to present the history as objectively as possible. Second, recognizing that all historical narratives reflect the times in which they are written and the person doing the writing, it was my intent to be as conscious and open concerning the present historical setting and my own particular perspectives as possible.

For the sake of objectivity this history is largely based on official records, such as the minutes of board of trustees and faculty meetings. Archival materials, such as letters, lecture notes, and autobiographical sketches were considered and widely used. Undeniably more needs to be done in this regard. My hope is that this history will inspire further research and writing.

As to the subjective aspect, this history emphasizes the evolution of the institution, with certain assumptions concerning religious institutions, institutions in general, and theological seminaries in particular, gained through more than forty years of involvement in several seminaries of the Episcopal Church. In addition, my own understanding of problems involved in curriculum building and revision, certain perspectives on the changing theological scene, and the ways in which professors of apologetic and systematic theology in the history of Virginia Theological Seminary are to be viewed all contribute to the end product. Thus, as I have tried to convince my students through the years, neither this nor any such book is to be taken as altogether accurate or true. This is not the definitive history.

One issue is highlighted that to my mind is of critical importance, and that is the way in which theology has been fragmented, partly through the increasingly narrow specialization of its teachers. One of the great tragedies has been the growing separation of theory and practice, most dramatically encountered in the separation of biblical, theological, and church history departments from pastoral theology and all that it involves, including field education and spiritual formation. Some may think that I am overly concerned with this issue.

Many alumni will correctly discern that I have not included everything that might justifiably have been included—some things, some events, or some people of great importance to them and to others. The writing of history is very much concerned with setting themes and selecting what should be included and what reluctantly not included in historical narrative. If I have offended any, I apologize. The spouses of faculty and students do not receive the recognition due to them. Staff members who became personal friends and mentors are seldom mentioned. During my time as a student and then as a teacher at Virginia Theological Seminary, I felt the influence of Paul ("You may not have time to read it, but you do have time to buy it!") Sorel, bookstore manager extraordinaire. Many others beside myself benefited from knowing Paul. But to the historian he is an elusive person. Information concerning the details of his life is not readily available; the seminary records barely mention him.

Let us here pay tribute to all those saints in times past who contributed so much to this seminary, although the memory of them fades. I am thinking here of Paul and of others who have worked with the bookstore through the years and also of matrons of the seminary, office personnel of all sorts and degrees, cooks and dishwashers, maintenance staff and ground crews, janitors, and those in the past who cleaned the rooms of seminarians and waited on them in the dining hall, as well as postmasters, male and female.

The discerning reader will discover that, as the table of contents reveals, the chapters cover particular periods of time and scrutinize the wider setting in the church and in American society as background for the seminary's history, the functioning of the institution, its administration and finances, the constantly changing faculty, student body, and curriculum, and the theological scene in general though more particularly in the seminary itself. It is possible, depending on the reader's interests and needs, to pursue any one of these topics independently by reference to the section titles given in the table of contents. This arrangement unavoidably results in some repetition and some chronological rearrangement, but this has been avoided as much as possible. The book thus differs greatly from the previous two-volume history edited by W.A.R. Goodwin. That history was composed of assorted essays by different authors. It has been of great value to me along the way, and this fact leads me to pay tribute to my predecessors and in particular to W.A.R. Goodwin, a man deeply steeped in history, devoted to this seminary, whose dream of a restored Williamsburg came true with the assistance of John D. Rockefeller.

This work could not have been done without the assistance of many people. The Very Reverend Richard Reid, dean and president, friend and colleague, has supported this venture throughout. The board of trustees, until this year chaired by classmate the Right Reverend Robert Atkinson, initiated the project some five years ago and made it possible for me to do the necessary work. Dr. Allan Parrent, associate dean and vice president, has watched over the project with care and fidelity. The Reverend Edward

Stone Gleason, director of development, did much to initiate the project, convinced of its need. Jack Goodwin, librarian and professor emeritus, my good and faithful friend, has done all in his power to make archival and other materials available and to give sound advice along the way. Mitzi (Jarrett) Budde, the present librarian, has carried on from Jack Goodwin, making the library a very user-friendly place in which to labor. After the project was well under way, Julia Randle became archivist of the seminary and in a short time revealed hitherto "hidden" — at least hidden to me — resources, which have been invaluable.

Present members of the faculty and administration — such as the Reverend Professors Frank VanDevelder, David Scott, Christopher Hancock, Walter Eversley, Robert Prichard, and the Reverend Churchill J. Gibson — have helped in various ways. The Reverend Professor Murray Newman has convinced me of the importance of Reuel Keith in this history. I hope that I have not disappointed him. I have benefited from communications with previous faculty and spouses, including the Reverend Professors Clifford Stanley and Charles Price. Helen Reid, who knows more about the seminary houses than anyone else, has saved me from repeating errors in Goodwin's history. And there have been other persons, many others. I am deeply grateful to my wife, Kitty Lou, not only for putting this manuscript on disk but for detecting errors, grammatical and other, and for discussing with me various episodes in the history.

Finally, I am grateful for all that Virginia Theological Seminary has done for me since the day in September 1950 when I first set foot on the Holy Hill and for all that it means to me now. Years ago a professor of sociology brought home to me the obvious fact that institutions are by their very nature fallible and in need of reform over and over again. Writing this history has further convinced me of this insight. It has also made clear that by God's grace this seminary has been reformed again and again, in the light of its founders' purposes and in the light of present needs, to be a place where women and men are well prepared for mission and ministry, to go out into all the world, preaching the gospel and baptizing in the name of God, Father, Son, and Holy Spirit. Pray that it may ever be so.

JOHN BOOTY
December 1993
Center Sandwich, New Hampshire

CHAPTER ONE

FROM
NEAR DEATH
TO
NEW BIRTH

1. THE CONDITION OF THE CHURCH

The Protestant Episcopal Theological Seminary in Virginia came into being when the Episcopal Church in Virginia was at a low ebb. When James Madison, the first Bishop of Virginia, died in 1812, the Episcopal Church in the commonwealth seemed moribund. After a hopeful beginning in 1790, Madison had seen the church withering, its wealth diminished, the final blow coming with the sale of glebe lands for public benefit.[1] For years no delegates were sent to General Convention, and no diocesan conventions were held between 1799 and 1803, nor between 1805 and 1813. The number of clergy steadily declined, and all too many who remained or were newly ordained were deemed to be unworthy of their high calling.

The process of decline had its roots in the past. William Meade, writing in a time of revival, not decline, lamented the sad condition of the colonial church in Virginia. He attributed this condition in part to the difficulties involved in obtaining a sufficient supply of ministers of any character, "and of those who came, how few were faithful and duly qualified for the station!" Earlier in 1655 "many places were destitute of ministers, and likely to continue so, the people not paying their 'accustomed dues.'"[2] Of the fifty parishes in the colony only ten had ministers. Fifty years later only half of the parishes then established had ministers, "the rest being served by layreaders." He commented on the want of a bishop to lead the church and the insufficiency of the commissary representing the Bishop of London.[3]

Wesley Gewehr, writing of the church in colonial Virginia during the Great Awakening of the eighteenth century, concludes, "It is generally admitted that the Virginia Establishment as a spiritual factor in the life of the colony . . . was a failure," in part because "it contented itself with serving only one social group, namely the planter class." The depressed condition was observed by one Fithian, writing after the Great Awakening, who when he returned to New Jersey from Virginia compared the church in both places. In New Jersey, he writes, "I went to meeting. How unlike Virginia, no rings of Beaux chatting before and after Sermon on Gallantry; no assembling in crowds after Service to dine and bargain; no cool spiritless harangue from the Pulpit; Minister and people here seem in some small measure to reverence the Day, there neither do one or the other."[4] John Woolverton, a former professor in the seminary, remarks on the loss of prestige experienced by the church in Virginia as a result of the Great Awakening, the awakening causing a heightening of seriousness in religion among the common folk. "Despite the later Evangelicalism of Virginia's Randolphs and Meades, the church increasingly lost whatever hold it had maintained on the common run of humanity. The poor left the church of the aristocracy and formed distinct religious communities, an entire alternative society. That society was characterized by prudence and biblical sobriety."[5] The colonial church's loss was reflected in the rapid growth first of the Presbyterians and then of the Baptists and Methodists.

The decline was not altogether explained by the religious conditions of the time. It was due at least in part to social and economic factors: the waning of the all-important tobacco trade and the unresolved struggle between laity and clergy for the leadership of the church between 1740 and 1760, followed by the adversities of the Revolutionary War and the disestablishment of the church in Virginia from 1776 to 1785, culminating in the sale of glebe lands in 1802.

Taking all such matters into account, William Meade's report on his ordination at Williamsburg in 1811 does not seem exaggerated, although it does represent the perspective of one who viewed the church in Virginia as an Evangelical opposed to the Enlightenment and all of its effects. The report is in his manuscript autobiography, as well as in his *Old Churches, Ministers and Families of Virginia*.[6] In his autobiography he wrote,

In February 1811 I went to Williamsburg and received Deacon's orders on the 24th at the hands of Bishop Madison after a very slight examination in which I remember the Bishop made the Holy Spirit's operations and con-

The Right Reverend William Meade
Third Bishop of Virginia

science one and the same thing. Sad was the condition of things in Williamsburg at the time. During breakfast on Sunday morning at the Bishop's it was mentioned that one of his neighbours was engaged in filling his ice house, which the Bishop said was allowable, as perhaps there might not be another opportunity. As we went down to the Church companies of students with guns on their shoulders and dogs at their sides met us on their way into the country, the frosty morning being favourable for hunting. The Church was cold and comfortless. Only two ladies were present and about sixteen students with two professors, each of whom were infidels. The ordination service and communion were performed before the sermon and then I was put up into the pulpit, as it were to preach my own ordination sermon. During the service some of the students left the Church and drove off in the Bishop's carriage, which had not returned when the Bishop wanted it at the close of the service.[7]

3

In *Old Churches*, Meade denies that Madison "became an unbeliever in the latter part of his life." But the College of William and Mary at Williamsburg, Virginia, of which Madison was president while serving as bishop, was another matter. Meade admitted that the bishop's "political principles, which at that day were so identified in the minds of many with those of infidel France, may have subjected him to" the suspicion of infidelity. "His secular studies, and occupations as President of the College and Professor of Natural Philosophy, may have led him to philosophize too much on the subject of religion, and of this I thought I saw some evidence in the course of my examination."[8] Of the College, Meade said that at the time of his ordination the place was so irreligious "that not too long before two questions had been debated in the literary society of the young men—1st Whether a God existed. 2d Whether the Christian religion had been a blessing or a curse. One of them was decided in the affirmative by one vote only."[9] In *Old Churches* he concluded, "I can truly say, that then, and for some years after, in every educated young man of Virginia whom I met, I expected to find a sceptic, if not an avowed unbeliever."[10]

The nadir was reached for Meade when in 1812, after Bishop Madison's death, a convention was held in May at the request of Meade and his fellow clergyman William H. Wilmer, a man who was to play an important role in the founding of the seminary. Only fourteen clergy and fourteen laity attended. At that convention Dr. John Bracken, Rector of Bruton Parish, who had been present at Meade's examination in Williamsburg in 1811, was elected bishop, although opposed by Meade and others. Another convention was held the following spring with only seven clergy attending, meeting around a table at the committee room in the state capitol.[11] There they received Dr. Bracken's refusal of his election and such were the proceedings that, when he left, Meade was under the impression that he had attended the last convention to be held in the diocese. He wrote, "As I rode back to my home over the mountains, having just read the Lay of the last Minstrall by Walter Scott, I found myself often, involuntarily, exclaiming with the Elfin Page of that poem, *Lost, Lost, Lost.*"[12]

At that dark hour, however, the name of Richard Channing Moore was mentioned by the Reverend Mr. Dashiell of Baltimore as a possible candidate for Bishop of Virginia. As Meade reports, Dashiell "had become acquainted with Dr. Moore at a recent General Convention, heard him eloquently advocate the introduction of more hymns into the Prayer Book, and preach the Gospel with zeal and power in several large churches."[13] The suggestion was seized upon by Meade and his colleagues William Wilmer and Oliver Norris, who constituted an informal committee of concern and action. Moore was elected and accepted his election. With

The Right Reverend Doctor
Richard Channing Moore
Second Bishop of Virginia

the coming of Moore in 1814 the revival of the Episcopal Church in Virginia began. The founding of the seminary was to be an important part of that revival.

2. RAISING UP
A LEARNED MINISTRY

The dire straits of the Episcopal Church in Virginia—and also in North Carolina, Maryland, and elsewhere—was focused for many on the shortage of clergy and especially dedicated and learned clergy. The necessity of having a dedicated and learned clergy was emphasized by the Reformation churches of the sixteenth century, both on the European continent and in Tudor England. There was a world of difference between the ideal priest described by John Myrc in pre-Reformation England (a man of prayer who said the canonical hours and the Mass daily) and the ideal minister of the gospel as portrayed by John Reynolds, the Elizabethan "Puritan," in a letter to a young man preparing for ordination. Reynolds stressed godliness and learning. The priest needed far more than the ability to read services. He had to be skilled in preaching, teaching, and the administration of godly discipline. The Book of Common Prayer required such learned

5

ministers, students of Scripture and of the sound exposition of Scriptural truth, such as that of Calvin's Institutes and his many commentaries. To do so he must know Greek and Hebrew. A knowledge of Latin was taken for granted.[14]

The ideal of a learned ministry was carried over to the American colonies. Here, if it could be, candidates were to study at some such college of higher learning as William and Mary, chartered in 1693 "that the Church in Virginia may be furnished with a seminary of ministers of the Gospel." Samuel Seabury pursued his studies first at Yale and then at Harvard, intending to enter the ministry of the Congregational Church.[15] Richard Channing Moore studied at King's College (later Columbia University) in New York, studying English literature and the classics under Alexander Leslie,[16] but was not at first aiming at the ordained ministry. William Meade studied at Princeton and graduated with the intention of being ordained.[17]

In addition, it was customary for those aspiring to the ordained ministry to study under some neighboring clergyman or to travel some distance to join the household of and study with a learned minister. Moore, when he decided on ordination, returned to King's College for further study under Alexander Leslie.[18] Meade, upon leaving Princeton, studied under the Reverend Walter Addison, who lived on the Maryland side of the Potomac River opposite Alexandria. There Meade lived and read until his weak eyes made him give up such study for a time. In his autobiography he wrote that it was while reading under Addison's

> direction that the first clear and satisfactory and delightful view of the necessity and reasonableness of a propitiation for sin by our blessed Lord was presented to my mind. I shall never forget the time, or the instrument, or the happy effect and how I rose up again and again to give thanks unto God for it. The book which was instrumental to it, was Soame Jennings on the internal evidences of Christianity. Mr. Wilberforce's work about the same time was put into my hands, and gave me the cast and coloring of my religious views.[19]

In his *Old Churches*, Meade remembers as well reading Bishop Porteus's lectures on the Gospel of Matthew.[20]

When the tutors were excellent, such as Meade believed Addison to be or such as Samuel Johnson of Yale and King's College was reputed to be, the results were altogether satisfactory. But as Powel Dawley says, the weaknesses of this system were evident to many: "Candidates were subject not only to the intellectual limitations of their mentors, but to their theological idiosyncrasies as well. The result was that for many students, perhaps even for most, preparation was minimal if not woefully inadequate." Dawley cites Samuel Turner, ordained in 1811, who studied under William White and wrote,

> My theological studies were pursued under the direction of Bishop White, whom I regularly visited in his study, at first once in two weeks, and afterwards once a month, for upwards of three years. The Bishop never subjected me to any examinations; indeed, I do not recollect that he ever questioned me in reference to any theological point except at my examination for orders. If the plan of my recitations had been pursued with some regularity, my studies would, no doubt, have been more thorough, and my knowledge more accurate. As it was, I read a great deal, but thought and studied little. To use common language, I crammed so fully that I had neither opportunity nor ability to digest anything intellectually.[21]

Attempts were made from 1789 on to guide and control the process of theological education, and thus the tutors were not alone responsible. The 1789 General Convention enacted a canon requiring knowledge of the New Testament in Greek and the ability to give an account in Latin of the candidate's faith. Such requirements were quietly modified to allow dispensation from language requirements when necessary. A 1792 canon required "a competent knowledge of moral philosophy, church history, and the belles lettres." The General Convention continued to wrestle with language requirements and in 1808 passed a canon declaring the desirability of acquaintance with Hebrew.[22]

In 1801 the General Convention suggested the necessity of a theological syllabus, or course of study, which was produced in 1804, we believe under the guidance of Bishop White, and authorized by the House of Bishops. The "Course of Ecclesiastical Studies" as printed in the *Journal of General Convention* is composed of three parts. The first is a long list of books under the headings of "proof of divine authority of Christianity" (evidences), the Scripture of the Old and New Testaments, ecclesiastical history (with polity), systematic divinity, homiletics, liturgics, pastoral care, and the constitution and canons of the Protestant Episcopal Church. Second is a short list of "essential" books: "*No Student* is to be *ordained* without being fully prepared to *answer* on them." Third is appended a "Library for a Parish Minister, Prefixed to 'Elements of Christian Theology,' published by the Right Rev. the present Bishop of Lincoln." This is Sir George Pretyman Tomline, Bishop of Lincoln (1787–1820), later Bishop of Winchester, author of *Elements of Christian Theology* (London, 1799), a work included in the long list of the House of Bishops.

The general impression given by these lists is that the focus is on works of English divines from Hooker to Pearson and Butler, but there are works by important continental divines in English translation, such as Grotius and Mosheim. No mention is made of the writings of Luther and Calvin, nor of Cranmer and Jewel. The biblical works represent some of the best scholarship of the time and are basically conservative. Lowth's *Lectures on the Sacred Poetry of the Hebrews* professes to be "purely critical" but insists on the historicity of the Job narrative.[23] A detailed view of the syllabus is provided by Blackman[24] and Dawley.[25] Here it seems most important to pay particular attention to the divisions of the theological syllabus as presented in the lists and especially the short list of "essential" books. The divisions were taken seriously, helping to form the theological curricula of seminaries, leading, as we shall have cause to note, to a fragmentation of that which was the one subject of "theology." The short list conforms to the divisions:

1. William Paley's *View of the Evidences of Christianity* (1794). The distinct subject here is that of evidences or apologetics, later to be included in departments of theology.
2. Holy Scriptures. No particular secondary texts were specified in this list. It was explained, "Allowing in the *Study of Scriptures*, a latitude of choice among approved *Commentaries*; it being understood, that if the Student cannot on the grounds contained in some good commentary, *give an account* of the *different books*, and *explain* such *passages* as may be *proposed* to him, this is of itself a *disqualification*." In the long list there are suggested "Patrick and Lowth on the *Old Testament*, and Hammond or Whitby, or Dodderidge on the *New*."
3. Johann Lorenz von Mosheim (1694?–1755), *Ecclesiastical History*, a six-volume history of the church, which reached its final form in 1755. The standard history, it was intended to be nonpartisan but in fact is critical of the Roman Catholic Church. This was supplemented with Richard Hooker's *Of the Laws of Ecclesiastical Polity*, specifically for Hooker's teaching concerning episcopacy.
4. Thomas Stackhouse (1677–1752), *Complete Body of Divinity in Five Parts from the Best Ancient and Modern Writers* (1729). Systematic theology.
5. An edition of the Book of Common Prayer, with preface and notes by John Reeves (1801). Liturgics.
6. The constitution and canons of the Protestant Episcopal Church.

No books in the fields of homiletics nor pastoral care were listed in this course of study designed to provide the "lowest requisition."

The importance of the House of Bishops' syllabus is evident to any who scan the lists of required texts in the earliest seminary curricula, including

8

that of Virginia. From 1804 on, students studying for orders, and their mentors, had specific guidance and might begin with the short list, move on to the much longer one, and supplement that with books from the Bishop of Lincoln's bibliography. Of course, they might ignore all three lists, and, even if they did follow the advice of the House of Bishops, the old problems still remained. Much depended upon finding an adequate tutor, and, if a tutor was found, there was the danger inherent in relying upon one teacher whose personal and/or doctrinal idiosyncrasies would most likely be passed on to the student. John McVicker, ordained in 1811, complained that the theological student, with but limited direction from the church canons, "was left to grope his way, vaguely, if not blindly, through the most voluminous, intricate, and perplexing of all professional studies, without aid or guidance, beyond the casual counsel of some friendly parochial minister."[26] The need was to be met with the establishment of theological seminaries. For this beginning we must turn to the wider scene in America.

3. ANDOVER: THE FIRST AND MODEL SEMINARY

In his careful historical study of seminary education in this country, Robert Wood Lynn divides his history into periods of development toward a more and more elaborate, specialized, and pastorally oriented theological curriculum.[27] The first period is that of beginnings, from 1820 into the 1830s. General Theological Seminary and the Protestant Episcopal Theological Seminary in Virginia belong to that earliest and most innovative period. Bexley Hall dates its beginnings from 1824, but its inception was dominated by the early development of Kenyon College, of which it was a part. Bexley Hall's historian, Richard Spielmann asks, "Was there any Theological Seminary in the proper sense during the early years?" He writes, "The answer must be 'yes,' but not very much." The Kenyon College catalogue of 1831 makes no mention of a seminary, "except to list three theological students in the student body."[28] The suggestion must be made that in those early years Kenyon was not unlike other colleges with theological students receiving special instruction along the way, reading for orders under such faculty as William Sparrow and Marcus Wing. Thus it is true to say that General and Virginia were not only the first of the Episcopal Church seminaries but were among the first seminaries of any denomination in this country.

The first seminary, *per se*, not a part of a college, was Andover in Massachusetts. Andover was to have direct influence on Virginia Seminary through Virginia's first professor, Reuel Keith, who studied there prior to his ordination by Richard Channing Moore in 1817. In addition, Keith's close friend

9

Joseph Packard began his long teaching career at Virginia Seminary after studying at Andover. Founded in 1808 by orthodox Congregationalists in reaction to the Unitarian conquest of Harvard College in 1805, Andover was dominated by that old Calvinism that had established itself in the town of Andover. The founders included Hopkinsians from not-too-distant Newburyport. As Daniel Day Williams says, "Conservatism and dogmatic Calvinism were written into the very structure of the new institution; for its founders believed that they were defending the truth of God against evil and error."[29] This was the theological orientation from the beginning, an orientation that was to experience the effects of and give way to theological liberalism in the course of the nineteenth century.

What was the theological center at Andover? Williams summarizes;

> To these Calvinists the essential fact underlying all doctrine and all religious practice was man's status as a moral being who either has a primary affection for God or who does not have it, and whose eternal blessedness or damnation is to be determined by his primary choice. The religious enterprise consisted therefore in proclaiming to sinful men this fact of their moral status and doing what could be done to prepare the way for the work of regeneration which God can perform upon the human heart. The ultimate standard for judging every doctrine and every practice of Christianity was thus first, Will it help or hinder the salvation of men? and second, Will it help or hinder the increase and prosperity of the church upon whose work most men are dependent for salvation?[30]

Conversion (with perseverance in holiness) was thus uppermost in the minds of those at Andover, a theme and doctrine quite naturally associated with revivalism and missions. Andover men were prominent participants in the revivals of 1837 and 1857. It is well known that "for the first ten years all the missionaries sent out by the American Board except one were Andover men."[31]

Joseph Packard recognized the formative importance of Andover and its innovative approach to theological education, saying, "Here first was realized the idea of gathering students within college walls for three years for the study of Divinity in the departments of Doctrinal Theology, Biblical Study and Sacred Rhetoric, with every possible advantage for mutual incitement and mutual helpfulness."[32] It was also important, to his mind, for its staunch defense of "orthodox Christianity" against such enemies as the Unitarian William Ellery Channing. On the faculty, which included Leonard Woods, one of the founders, there was Moses Stuart, called "the Father of Biblical Science in America,"[33] a man Packard viewed with awe. Stuart's many writings on the Scriptures were widely read by seminarians and others during the nineteenth century and were a conduit through which much German scholarship reached the American scene.

Of Stuart, who began teaching sacred literature at Andover in 1810, Packard said that he "exerted a greater influence upon my life and character than any other man I have ever known."[34] He reports on Stuart's defense of the Trinitarian faith against the attacks of the Unitarian Channing, citing Stuart as concluding,

> When I behold the glory of the Saviour, as revealed in the gospel, I am constrained to cry out, with the believing Apostle, "My Lord and my God!" And when my departing spirit shall quit these mortal scenes, and wing its way to the world unknown, with my latest breath I desire to pray, as the expiring martyr did, "Lord Jesus, receive my spirit."[35]

Such a Christ-centered piety as that expressed by Stuart, grounded upon exhaustive biblical and historical studies, was in keeping with the Calvinist orientation of the seminary and deeply influenced Keith and Packard and through them others in the early days of Virginia Seminary. There is no indication that either understood the liberalizing tendencies in Stuart's theology, his disagreement with the Congregational Church catechism's doctrine of imputation and his sympathetic attitude toward the theology of Nathaniel Taylor, with its attack on "the extreme Calvinist doctrine of total depravity," its contention "that man can be held morally accountable only for those acts which he is truly free to perform," and its "holding that God permits sin because it is impossible for him not to permit it." Williams contends that, with Stuart's embracing Taylorism, "Andover took another step in its capitulation to liberalism."[36] If indeed such was the case, here is another example of how Andover paved the way for Virginia Seminary, if not in capitulation to liberalism then in that modification of Calvinism inherent in Anglican tradition from Hooker to Wilberforce and Simeon.

In addition to theological orientation, Andover, chiefly through Reuel Keith, influenced the evolving structure of the Virginia Seminary. As Packard suggests, the basic idea of three years study of divinity in departments was learned from Andover, although the divisions could have been learned from the House of Bishops' syllabus as well. It is significant that Packard speaks of doctrinal theology, biblical study, and sacred rhetoric but not of ecclesiastical history. As Lynn remarks, church history was not included in the first Andover curriculum, and its eventual inclusion required considerable effort. He writes, "Although the original plan for the seminary called for coverage of 'Ecclesiastical History,' no instruction in this field was offered in the first decade. The subject was finally allowed in the curriculum, but only after a bitter struggle that stretched over eleven years." The pattern eventually involved sacred literature in the first year, "Christian theology" in the second, and sacred rhetoric and ecclesiastical history in the third. It is significant that Leonard Woods referred to these as "departments," as did Packard. And it should be noted that sacred rhetoric, speaking and writing effectively, was not what we think of as "pastoral theology" or "practical theology," although it maintained a place in the curriculum for an emphasis on *practica*, such as that developed by William Meade at Virginia Seminary.

In addition there was the influence of the Andover teachers as pastors and men of prayer. Of greatest importance were the weekly gatherings of faculty and students begun by President Woods "for the fostering of personal piety. All the students were expected to attend, and either Woods or Stuart met them, and prayed and conversed for an hour in a practical way on the whole range of Christian Doctrine."[37] Packard remarked on how Stuart

> delighted in the Wednesday evening conference of professors and students, very much like our [Virginia Theological Seminary] faculty meetings on Thursday evening. Here the great principles of practical and experimental religion, and all matters of religious experience, duty, and comfort were fully treated; the work of the Saviour and the Spirit was glorified, and counsel and aid were given to the students as to their particular duties and dangers. Professor Stuart said: "If there is any part of my duty which I can remember with pleasure on a dying bed, it is what I did in the Wednesday Conference."[38]

Finally, we must note the "anniversaries," which helped to inspire and inform the concluding exercises held each year at Virginia Seminary. As Henry Rowe says, the end of the academic year at Andover came with "the Anniversaries, when every class was examined publicly before the assembled Trustees, Visitors, and the public, both lay and clerical, who packed the available space in Bartlet Chapel."[39] In the presence of this gathering the junior or first-year class was examined in "Hebrew and Old Testament and New Testament criticism, the Middle Class exhibited essays on theological subjects, the Seniors exhibited similar essays and were examined in sacred rhetoric." The examinations were detailed, could last an entire day for one subject, but did not cover all that had been dealt with in class during the year. At the end of the "anniversaries" there was an address by a member of the senior class.[40]

In various ways, thus, Andover Seminary was the parent of Virginia Seminary, and the latter was among the first representatives of that style of theological education that was pioneered at Andover and provided a solution to the problems inherent in the earlier alternatives. In turn, the new style produced its own problems to be faced in the years ahead.

4. EVANGELICALISM IN ENGLAND AND AMERICA

In a sense the revival of the Episcopal Church in Virginia during the episcopacy of Richard Channing Moore, together with the founding of the Virginia Theological Seminary, was a part of what historians call the Second Great Awakening, dated by McLaughlin as occurring between 1800 and 1830, associated with camp meetings and frontier revivals, especially in the South, and with Lyman Beecher and Nathaniel Taylor in New England. "The first phase of the awakening in New England," writes McLaughlin, "is best characterized as a nativist movement—an effort to call America back to the old-time religion and traditional way of life that were inevitably fading."[41] Albright believes that indeed the awakening did loosen the grip of Deism on America, transforming "the postwar secular and irreligious spirit into a nationwide religious atmosphere by 1835."[42] McLaughlin shows that the awakening involved a revision of Calvinism, exemplified by the teachings of Beecher and Taylor, a subversion of the old doctrine of predestination, and a transformation of Calvinism in the direction of Arminianism, focused on the question of freedom of the will.[43] The aim was revival, which to Nathaniel Taylor required allowance of freedom in the human will.

> Taylor allowed for the moral suasion of the preacher, assuming first that this suasion was God's Spirit at work, and, second, that *every soul had the ability to "choose right."* The help man needed came in the work of the Holy Spirit upon the religious affections. Choice "can be exercised by the sinner if he is aroused to action by appeal to the proper functions of the mind." God arouses the heart, and man responds by a clear decision to accept God's offer. The key to conversion lay in the manipulation of human "sensibilities," or, as evangelical preachers preferred to say, "in an appeal to the heart."[44]

That the founding of the Virginia Theological Seminary should be influenced by the Second Great Awakening is a reasonable assumption, but that influence was secondary to and informed by the tradition of English Evangelicalism very much alive in the minds and hearts of the founders of the seminary. Here, while considering background, we therefore need to examine the character of Evangelicalism in the Church of England in the last years of the eighteenth century and the beginning of the nineteenth.

William Meade testified to the great importance of William Wilberforce in his life, saying, "Mr. Wilberforce's work . . . was put into my hands, and gave the cast and coloring to my religious views."[45] He was referring to Wilberforce's popular and influential *A Practical View of the Prevailing System of Professed Christians, in the Higher and Middle Classes in this Country, Contrasted with Real Christianity* (1797). Here was a call to seriousness in religious profession, describing "real Christians" as those who "relying on the promises to repenting sinners of acceptance through the Redeemer . . . have renounced and abjured all other masters, and have cordially and unreservedly devoted themselves to God."[46] They aim at "vital religion," and their doctrines can be summarized simply as "the depravity of man, the conversion of the sinner, and the sanctification of the regenerate soul." Here, as Ian Bradley says, we have represented "virtually the sum total of the theology of early nineteenth century Evangelicalism."[47] William Romaine (1714–95), the scholarly London preacher, emphasized "the corruption of our nature by the fall, and our recovery through Jesus Christ." These, he said, "are the two leading truths in the Christian religion."[48] Conversion involved "conformity to Jesus" and an intensely active life reflecting the perfection of the Master.[49]

The doctrine of conformity to Jesus was the basis for introspection, that self-examination and soul-searching which was characteristic of Evangelicals. Henry Thornton, the banker whose house was the center for the Clapham sect, reported in his diary the details of his own self-examination. "First, I lie idly in bed often . . . 2. I am not steady and punctual enough in reading the Scripture. 3. In my prayers I am idle. 4. In my secret thoughts and imaginations I am far from having learnt self-denial. 5. I am not self-denying in my business."[50] As Romaine and Thornton indicate, there were grounds in this theology for action as well as introspection. Bradley writes, "Evangelicals had no sympathy with those who hid themselves away in the hermitage or cloister. 'Action is the life of virtue' wrote Hannah More . . . 'and the world is the theatre of action.'"[51] The Evangelicals were involved in moral crusades against gin and prostitution, against slavery and the exploitation of women and children in factories, and they were at the forefront of modern missions, actively involved through the Church Missionary Society (1799).[52]

There was much in this that was in agreement with Calvin and Calvinism, but the nineteenth century Evangelicals were inclined to what can be called a moderate Calvinism. Romaine was the consummate Calvinist Evangelical whom Wilberforce found wanting. Samuel, William Wilberforce's son who became Bishop of Oxford, wrote in his diary, "Father reading some of Romaine in the evening exclaimed, 'Oh how unlike this is to the Scriptures! He writes as if he had sat at the Council Board with the Almighty!' He then mentioned Mr. Newton's having told him that more of Romaine's people had become Antinomians than any other he knew."[53] Henry Venn objected to George Whitfield's views on predestination; "A false, libertine Calvinism stops up every avenue: sin, the law, holiness, experience are all nothing. Predestination cancels the necessity of any change, and dispenses at once with all duty."[54] Alexander Zabriskie, dean of the seminary during the 1940s, wrote of the Charles Simeon he so much admired that in him, as in Thomas Scott, "there is more stress proportionately on the love of God and less on his severity than in Romaine, for they had parishioners who had been aroused to a sense of sin and needed to be assured of His forgiveness."[55]

In part the moderation of Calvinist doctrine in Simeon was due to his Anglicanism and in particular to his love of the Prayer Book liturgy, which he preferred to extemporaneous devotions that tended to be "dry, dull, tedious repetitions."[56] Speaking of the spirituality of the Prayer Book, Simeon affirmed "that the whole scope and tendency of our Liturgy is to raise our minds to a holy and heavenly state, and to build us up upon the Lord Jesus Christ as the only foundation of a sinner's hope."[57] He furthermore appreciated the "*Moderation and Candour*" of Prayer Book worship and said that its compilers "kept back no truth through fear of giving offence; yet they were careful so to state every truth as to leave those inexcusable who should recede from the Church on account of any sentiments which she maintained." They did "not dwell on doctrines after the manner of human systems, but" introduced "them incidentally, as it were, as occasion suggested and" brought "them forward always in connection with practical duties."[58] In this view one can detect the influence of Richard Hooker and also the roots of William Meade's doctrine of proportion.

Hugh Evans Hopkins reports that Simeon maintained an independence of outlook and an objective attitude toward the issues commonly debated among Christians. "He refused to pigeonhole his theology or to ally himself with any of the current 'isms' of the day."[59] Behind this attitude was Simeon's commitment to Scripture and his suspicion that Calvinists and Arminians emphasized only that in the Bible which agreed with their *a priori* convictions. As Zabriskie said, this led Simeon "on to an insistence that the truth is not to be found in the logical conclusions of any one point of view but in the interaction between the two positions which are logically irreconcilable yet which are both true."[60]

Having said this we must now affirm that Simeon was most definitely Evangelical. In a sermon entitled "*Evangelical Religion Described*," he began "by acknowledging that God can speak and has spoken to man in various ways in the past, but it is mainly through the written word expounded by authorized teachers that men can come to recognize the will of God." As Hopkins says of Simeon,

> When he came to deal with the crucifixion, he pointed out how much more Paul dwelt on the doctrine about the cross than on the event itself. The death of Christ, he explained, is firstly the ground of all our hopes and secondly the motive of our obedience. There is no other way in which sinful men could be reconciled to a holy God, and it is the love of Christ dying for us which is the driving force that leads a man to forsake sin and seek forgiveness. This, says Simeon, is the heart of the Gospel, the evangel, and it is when "viewing its transcendent excellency we must rejoice and glory in it ourselves, and show forth its fruits in a life of entire devotedness to God; we must call upon our hearers also to rejoice and glory in it, and to display sanctifying effects in the whole of their life and conversation."[61]

This, then, was that English Evangelicalism which so influenced Meade and others of the founders and was a major influence in the founding of Virginia Theological Seminary.

5. THE THEOLOGICAL SETTING IN THE TEACHING OF THE *WASHINGTON THEOLOGICAL REPERTORY* AND WILLIAM MEADE

In quest of the inspiration of the founders of the seminary, we turn next to the *Washington Theological Repertory*, whose chief editor was William H. Wilmer, rector of St. Paul's Church in Alexandria from 1812 to 1826, co-worker in the revival of the church in Virginia with William Meade, and first president of the Education Society, which W.A.R. Goodwin calls "the Seminary in embryo."[62] Of the *Theological Repertory*, which commenced publication in August 1819, Goodwin says, "Its pages express the theological and religious convictions which the Education Society and subsequently the Seminary were designed to express and propagate through a well-trained ministry."[63]

In the first issue the editors explained that the principles for the conduct of the journal were to be "those of the Bible, as illustrated in the Articles, Liturgy, and Homilies of the Protestant Episcopal Church." Furthermore, the editors, being members of the Episcopal Church, "will feel bound to support the Apostolical character of her institutions, the pious tendency of her rites and ceremonies, and the evangelical nature of her doctrines." Thus they declared themselves to be "Evangelical Churchmen." And the spirit in which they would work was indicated, as they said that "they hope never to lose sight of that great law of charity which teaches us to 'preserve the unity of the spirit in the bond (sic.) of peace.'"[64] This last point was further emphasized as they began a detailed exposition of their theology, saying, "Discarding all party or sectarian views, they [the editors] will direct all their exertions to the furtherance of pure and undefiled religion, and endeavour faithfully to declare as far as opportunity is afforded the whole counsel of God."[65]

The theology then expounded was that which they shared with the English Evangelicals. "God is omnipotent . . . and consequently foresees, foreknows, governs and directs all things, yet so as not to be the Author of Sin." Man is "endowed with volition and power to act according to that volition" but being fallen is "'dead in trespasses and sins' . . . totally destitute of holiness," and justly condemned to punishment by God for his sins. The way out of this doom was provided by God in Jesus Christ "who offered himself a willing sacrifice for the sins of men, and poured out his blood upon the Cross for a satisfaction to that justice which required the punishment of a violated law." Thus, man "is saved from death through faith in Jesus Christ, which faith worketh by love, and necessarily produceth good works." And so, in part, we find the "outline of faith" to which Wilmer and his colleagues were dedicated.[66] Toward the end, saying that the outline contained that faith necessary to salvation, they added,

> Not that each of the foregoing articles, in every particular, is positively required, but that the substance of them, comprehending the perfections of the Deity, the fall of man from original rectitude, his present sinful nature and ruined condition, the atonement and mediation of Jesus Christ, a change of heart by Divine Grace, and a life conformable to the gospel, are indispensable prerequisites for admission into heaven.[67]

Such is the epitome of the outline which, they declared, cannot rightly be charged with "adopting the opinions of Calvin or Arminius." And like the English Reformers,[68] they modified Luther's doctrine of justification in order to emphasize human responsibility for the moral life, that is, a life lived in conformity to Christ and the gospel. "Justification . . . by faith without works, yet so as not to make void the law of moral obedience, will form a leading feature in the character of this work [i.e., the *Theological Repertory*]. The necessity of personal holiness through sanctification of the Spirit, and a life of piety and virtue, as the only evidence of our Christian character, will also be asserted and maintained." Lastly, they will not exclude the "affections" from their considerations, "the love of Christ acting upon and directing the affections to their proper object, being the first and moving cause of man's embracing the Saviour."[69]

There follows the first of what was to be a series of articles on the great doctrines. They might have begun with the doctrine of creation, but they chose to begin, as Evangelicals might be expected to begin, with human depravity, which they spoke of as "in some senses, the fundamental article of Christianity; for it is that which brings all her other doctrines, as well as her precepts, home to our hearts and our practice."[70] The salvific work of God in Christ depends upon this doctrine, affirmed in the Anglican formularies, such as the Articles of Religion and the Book of Common Prayer, and by Anglican divines from Cranmer to Hooker. The editors indicated the evidence for the reality and pervasiveness of human depravity, writing, for instance, that "in London, only, a very corrupt, but far from being the most corrupt city in Europe, 115,000 human beings, among whom are 50,000 abandoned females, according to Colquhoun, live either partly or wholly by customary fraud; and annually plunder their fellow citizens of two millions sterling."[71] Paris is worse, with its illegitimate births, divorces, and death in the streets. And in the United States murder and suicide, fraud and robbery, are rampant. "How many families are at open war with each other, or carrying on a secret work of jealousy, ambition, hatred, and revenge!"[72]

Here was the Evangelical perspective on the world, widely shared in the early part of the nineteenth century. It was a perspective gained by those who heralded the gospel. Here was the inspiration for preaching the good news of salvation through Jesus Christ and for calling, educating, and commissioning young men for the ministry of reconciliation. The darkness of the corrupt world was closing in, the time was short, the need was great.

William Meade, in a sermon preached before the professors and students of the Virginia Theological Seminary on February 15, 1840, affirmed the primacy of Scripture and the scriptural doctrine that he found focused in the doctrine of justification. He expressed his appreciation of the Episcopal Church and of the Book of Common Prayer for their fidelity to Scripture, their not equating church and Scripture, recognizing that the church is imperfect and the liturgy "a human writing," as he affirmed elsewhere.[73] In his sermon he lauded the English Reformers and spoke "of the acknowledged soundness of that system of doctrine which they set forth, and which we have in our book of Common Prayer." That doctrine is, he avers, universally conceded, even by those who differ from us. And those who judge in this way further "admire the wisdom with which our Reformers either avoided all doubtful and provoking subjects not essential to piety, or else spoke of them with that studied latitude, which allowed all due liberty to the human mind, at the same time that with the utmost fidelity they adhered to God's word, whenever it was necessary to declare essential and certain truths, and thus by a happy mixture of wisdom and fidelity, brought forth a system which at the same time frowns indignantly upon all needless and petty disputations, or metaphysical niceties, yet boldly protests against all false doctrine, heresy and schism."[74]

Here Meade was most Anglican, going on to emphasize doctrine as rooted in liturgy, in that worship of the community that as Aidan Kavanaugh has said, "is the primary place at which the Church does theology."[75] Thus Meade said, "It must be admitted that in the constant repetition of the creed each Sabbath, in the constant recitation of God's holy word, in the use of such prayers and offices, as are provided, we have the most effectual method for deeply impressing sound and wholesome doctrines upon the minds and hearts of both ministers and people, and producing an happy uniformity of sentiment." And he was deeply appreciative of what he saw as "a spirit of truest charity" breathing in all the Episcopal Church's articles and prayers. "Not only does she seek to promote love and unity among her own children, and within her own borders, but desires to follow peace with all men. She professes to believe in one Catholic and Apostolic Church, embracing all who profess to believe in Jesus Christ, and in the communion of saints; that is, the union of the hearts of all true believers, one with another, and with their divine Head. . . ." Meade concluded, "She never dogmatizes—never in the spirit of infallibility anathematizes those who differ from her, casting them out of the covenant, and leaving them to the unpromised mercies of heaven."[76] In this way she differs from the Church of Rome from sectaries, and is at odds with dogmatizing Anglo-Catholics.

Concerning predestination, Meade referred favorably to Bishop Burnet on the *Thirty-Nine Articles* (one of the books on the House of Bishops' long list) discussing the seventeenth of the Articles of Religion, admitting that he had not set forth his own opinion, "since the Church has not been peremptory (sic), but that a latitude has been left to different opinions, I thought it became me to make this explanation thus. And I leave the choice as free to my reader as the Church has done."[77]

This was the faith of an Anglican Evangelical, shared by many, including Wilmer and, as we shall have cause to note, William Sparrow.[78] It should be noted that for all of the emphasis placed by the *Theological Repertory* and William Meade on Scripture, without any dependence upon dogmatic, confessional additions, the Anglican Evangelical took the church seriously but subordinate to God's Word in Scripture. The church (fallible as they knew it to be) was an instrument of the gospel. The Book of Common Prayer, as Thomas Cranmer believed, was scriptural through and through.

Bishop Moore, writing in 1828, warned William Meade against the devices and manipulations of revivalists.[79] "If Christianity is a system founded on truth, the work of grace must be God's work; and I cannot believe that the Almighty stands in need of the cunning craftiness of man to promote his designs." Instead of relying upon human ingenuity, or "human management" as the bishop said, "we must use the means God has appointed; prayer, reading the Scriptures, and the faithful preaching of the Gospel." These "constitute the ordinances of heaven for the conversion of sinners. . . . If we wish to see the work of grace prosper in our hands, and a lasting and permanent effect produced, we must observe order and decency in our worship." This was not said by a staid and stodgy prelate but by one who loved "feeling in religion,"[80] whose preaching was fervent. What he feared was the manipulative arousing of the affections by the wily revivalists, exciting the passions of people only to allow them to relapse when the excitement of the moment had passed.

Bishop Moore reminded Meade that the fervent prayers of the faithful had been answered without recourse to manipulative revivalism. "Direct your attention to the state of things in this diocese when you first entered your ministry. Could you, at that dreary hour, have promised yourself the success with which a merciful God has blessed us? Did you expect to see, in fifteen or sixteen years, upwards of fifty churches built and repaired? Did you expect to see, instead of three or four men to help you, fifty clergymen disposed to do their duty? . . . Had the Almighty promised you that we should have a Seminary for the instruction of our youth, of so flattering a description as that with which we are now favoured, would you not have called on all the powers of your soul to bless His Holy Name?"[81]

The Protestant Episcopal Theological Seminary in Virginia was founded as a vital element in the revival of the church on Anglican principles as taught and exemplified by the editors of the *Washington Theological Repertory*, by Richard Channing Moore, and most importantly by William Meade.

NOTES

1. W.A.R. Goodwin, ed., *History of the Theological Seminary in Virginia and Its Historical Background* (New York: Gorham, 1923), 1:20–21.

2. William Meade, *Old Churches, Ministers, and Families of Virginia* (Philadelphia: J.B. Lippincott & Co., 1861), 1:14.

3. Ibid. 1:15.

4. Wesley M. Gewehr, *The Great Awakening in Virginia, 1740–1790* (Durham, N.C.: Duke University Press, 1930), 32–33.

5. John Frederick Woolverton, *Colonial Anglicanism in North America* (Detroit: Wayne State University Press, 1984), 203.

6. Meade, *Old Churches* 1:29.

7. Meade, MSS, Virginia Theological Seminary archives (VTSA), autobiography, 18–20; edited by J.E. Booty, *Seminary Journal* 14/2 (December 1962):35–36.

8. Meade, *Old Churches* 1:28–29.

9. Meade, MSS, autobiog., 20–21; *Seminary Journal* 14/2:36.

10. Meade, *Old Churches* 1:29; John Johns, *A Memoir of the Life of the Right Rev. William Meade* (Baltimore: Innes, 1867), 53.

11. Meade, *Old Churches* 1:37.

12. Meade, MSS, autobiog., 31; *Seminary Journal* 14/2:38.

13. Meade, *Old Churches* 1:38.

14. John Booty, "The Bishop Confronts the Queen. John Jewel and the Failure of the English Reformation," *Continuity and Discontinuity in Church History: Essays Presented to George Hunston Williams*, ed. F. Forester Church and Timothy George (Leiden: Brill, 1979), 215–31.

15. Bruce E. Steiner, *Samuel Seabury, 1729–1796, A Study in the High Church Tradition* (Athens: Ohio University Press, 1971), 7–8.

16. J.P.K. Henshaw, *Memoir of the Life of the Rt. Rev. Richard Channing Moore* (Philadelphia: Stavely, 1843), 19.

17. Johns, *Meade*, 26–37.

18. Henshaw, *Moore*, 38.

19. Meade, MSS, autobiog., 13–14; Johns, *Meade*, 38–39.

20. Meade, *Old Churches* 1:26.

21. Powell Mills Dawley, *The Story of General Theological Seminary . . . 1817–1967* (New York: Oxford, 1969), 16–17; see George L. Blackman, *Faith and Freedom. A Study of Theological Education and the Episcopal Theological School* (New York: Seabury, 1967), 6–7.

22. See Dawley on this, *General Theological Seminary*, 17–18.

23. See Robert Lowth, Bishop of Lincoln, *Lectures on the Sacred Poetry of the Hebrews* (London: S. Chadwick, 1847), 22, 354.

24. Blackman, *Faith and Freedom*, 7–15.

25. Dawley, *General Theological Seminary*, 1822.

26. Ibid., 23, citing John McVicker, *The Early Life and Professional Years of Bishop Hobart* (Oxford, 1838), 279.

27. Robert Wood Lynn, "Notes Toward a History: Theological Encyclopedia and the Evolution of Protestant Seminary Curriculum, 1808–1868," *Theological Education* 17/2 (Spring 1981): 118–44.

28. Richard M. Spielmann, *Bexley Hall: 150 Years. A Brief History* (Rochester: Colgate, 1974), 15.

29. Daniel Day Williams, *The Andover Liberals: A Study in American Theology* (New York: King's Crown, 1941), 7.

30. Ibid.

31. Ibid., 9.

32. Joseph Packard, *Recollections of a Long Life*, ed. Thomas J. Packard (Washington, D.C., 1902), 53.

33. See John H. Giltner, *Moses Stuart: The Father of Biblical Science in America*

(Atlanta: Scholars, 1988), title page, and Williams, Andover Liberals, 17.

34. Packard, Recollections, 55.

35. Ibid., 57.

36. Williams, Andover Liberals, 18–19.

37. Henry K. Rowe, History of Andover Theological Seminary (Newton, Mass.: n.p., 1933), 50.

38. Packard, Recollections, 59.

39. Rowe, History, 60.

40. Ibid., 61.

41. William G. McLaughlin, Revivals, Awakenings, and Reform: An Essay on Religion and Social Change in America, 1607–1977 (Chicago and London: Chicago University Press, 1978), 108.

42. Raymond W. Albright, A History of the Protestant Episcopal Church (New York and London: Macmillan, 1964), 161.

43. McLaughlin, Revivals, 113.

44. Ibid., 118.

45. Meade, MSS, autobiog., 14; Seminary Journal, 14/2:35.

46. William Wilberforce, A Practical View of the Prevailing Religious System of Professed Christians, in the Higher and Middle Classes in this Country, Contrasted with Real Christianity (Boston: Crocker and Brewster, 1829), 148.

47. Ian Bradley, The Call to Seriousness: The Evangelical Impact on the Victorians (London: Cape, 1976), 22.

48. William Romaine, The Life, Walk, and Triumph of Faith, new ed. (London: G. Routledge, 1856), 20–21.

49. Ibid., 481.

50. Bradley, Call to Seriousness, 23.

51. Ibid., 30.

52. Alexander C. Zabriskie, ed., Anglican Evangelicalism (Philadelphia: Church Historical Society, 1943), 15.

53. David Newsome, The Wilberforces and Henry Manning. The Parting of Friends (Cambridge, Mass.: Harvard, 1966), 47–48.

54. Standish Meacham, Henry Thornton of Clapham, 1760–1815 (Cambridge, Mass.: Harvard, 1964), 10.

55. Zabriskie, Anglican Evangelicalism, 14.

56. Charles Simeon, The Excellency of the Liturgy (New York: Easburn, Kirk, Co., 1813), 54.

57. Ibid., 79; see page 80 for an elaboration with particular reference to elements in Prayer Book worship.

58. Ibid., 89–90.

59. Hugh Evans Hopkins, Charles Simeon of Cambridge (Grand Rapids, Mich.: Eerdmans, 1977), 173.

60. Zabriskie, Anglican Evangelicalism, 14.

61. Hopkins, Simeon, 180.

62. Goodwin, History 1:122.

63. Ibid., 123.

64. *The Washington Theological Repertory. Conducted by Clergymen of the Protestant Episcopal Church* 1/1 (August 1819), prospectus.
65. Ibid., 3.
66. Ibid., 3–4. Note this statement: "the sufferings, death, and obedience of Jesus Christ satisfied divine justice and the demands of the law for the sins of the world, and procured for every believer Redemption from the curse, and a right and title to eternal life; which satisfaction and obedience, through faith, is imputed to us."
67. Ibid., 4.
68. See William A. Clebsch, *England's Earliest Protestants*, 1520–1535 (New Haven and London: Yale Publications in Religion, 1964).
69. *Wash. Theol. Rep.* 1/1:5.
70. Ibid., 7.
71. Ibid., 10.
72. Ibid., 11.
73. John E. Booty, "William Meade: Evangelical Churchman," *Seminary Journal* 14/2 (December 1962): 13.
74. See H.R. McAdoo's discussion of the way in which the Caroline Divines "maintained that a Church was truly Catholic only when 'lawful authority' and 'just liberty' by a permanent tension saved the faith from the unequilibrium of doctrinal additions or substractions," *The Structure of Caroline Moral Theology* (London: Longmans, 1949), 4.
75. Stephen Sykes and John Booty, eds., *The Study of Anglicanism* (London and Philadelphia: SPCK, Fortress, 1988), 63.
76. William Meade, "The Wisdom, Moderation, and Character of the English Reformers, and of the Fathers of the Protestant Episcopal Church in the United States" [An address to the students of our Theological Seminary at Alexandria], *Southern Churchman* 6/13 (April 3, 1840).
77. Ibid. In a footnote to the sermon.
78. See William Sparrow, "The Right Conduct of Theological Seminaries. An Address delivered at the Twenty-first annual commencement of the Theological Seminary of the Protestant Episcopal Church, in the Diocese of Virginia, July 13, 1843," *Southern Churchman* 9/31 (August 25, 1843).
79. Henshaw, Moore, 97–99.
80. Ibid., 100.
81. Ibid., 99.

CHAPTER TWO

---◦∽◟◯◞∽◦---

THE
FOUNDING
OF THE SEMINARY
1814–1823

i. GENERAL THEOLOGICAL SEMINARY
AND VIRGINIA THEOLOGICAL SEMINARY:
BEGINNINGS

For William Meade the beginning of the seminary in Virginia was related to an incident in 1814 on a street in New York. This is his account:

> As Bishop Moore was about leaving New York for Virginia, in the summer of 1814, Dr. Augustine Smith, a native of Virginia, who had been for some years a Professor in a Medical School in New York and who was about to take charge of William and Mary College, met him in the street and proposed that the Church in Virginia should establish a theological professorship in Williamsburg, and thus make the College, what its royal patrons designed, a School of the Prophets. Bishop Moore encouraged the proposal, and a deputation of one of the Professors was sent to the Convention of 1815 for the purpose of promoting the plan. The Convention approved it, and the Rev. Dr. Keith became the minister of the Episcopal congregation in Williamsburg, and was prepared to instruct any candidates for the ministry who might be sent there.[1]

Here, to use J.P.K. Henshaw's words, was "the germ of the Theological Seminary of Virginia."[2]

From the beginning Richard Channing Moore was a vital player in the drama that eventuated in the founding of the seminary. Moore was the first president of the board of trustees. He "felt a warm interest in this favourite institution of his Diocese. At its annual examinations he uniformly attended, and was deeply solicitous that all who received its honours should be scribes well prepared in the Kingdom of God, 'workmen that need not be ashamed, rightly dividing the word of truth.'"[3] Henshaw, who knew the bishop well, was correct in his estimate of Moore's commitment to the seminary. But Dr. Goodwin is right in saying that initially Moore was somewhat reluctant to give assent to the founding of a separate seminary in Virginia, chiefly because of his involvement in the proposal to found a general seminary for the entire Episcopal Church.[4] Meade indicates that Moore received threatening letters "calling upon him as a Bishop of the General Church bound to guard its unity, to interpose and prevent the establishment of the Seminary at Virginia."[5] The letters ceased when a large sum was provided for the General Theological Seminary in New York and Bishop Hobart of New York indicated his approval of diocesan seminaries. Moore was then at liberty to support the founding of the Virginia seminary, and he did, enthusiastically.

As this suggests, in the immediate background was the movement to found a national seminary, begun with Christopher Gadsden's motion passed by the convention of the Diocese of South Carolina in February 1814, just months before the conversation between Moore and Smith on a street in New York. The idea was seized upon by Theodore Dehon, Bishop of South Carolina, and taken to General Convention in May. There it was defeated in the House of Deputies, but those from Virginia voted with South Carolina in support of such a seminary. Prior to this General Convention, Bishop Hobart addressed his diocesan convention in 1813 concerning the need for a theological institution to prepare young men for ordination. A week before General Convention in 1814, Hobart issued a prospectus for a *grammar school and theological seminary*. Hobart had in mind a diocesan institution and thus opposed the founding of a national seminary.[6] By the end of the 1814 Convention it seemed that the cause was lost. But on the last day Bishop Dehon engaged Hobart in debate and with the support of Bishop Moore proposed an inquiry by the dioceses into the advisability of a general seminary. The proposal was approved by the House of Bishops; the Deputies concurred. And at the Convention of 1817, a favorable report having been received, the General Theological Seminary was approved.[7] As Professor Dawley says, "Although it would be more than a year before the Theological Committee [of General Convention] determined 'to carry into immediate operation the theological school' and appointed its first professors, and nearly two years before the first small class was assembled for instruction, the date of the convention resolution has the best claim to be the birthday of the Seminary."[8]

There is no need for us to pursue the history of the General Theological Seminary here, save to note that at the General Convention of 1820 it was determined to locate the seminary in New Haven, Connecticut, a place too distant to the minds of many in the South. Also the Convention agreed that the establishment of a national seminary did not preclude the founding of other, local seminaries, the House of Bishops saying "that they do not mean . . . to interfere with any plan now contemplated, or that hereafter may be contemplated, in any Diocese (sic) or Dioceses, for the establishment of theological institutions or professorships."[9] The way was clear for the founding of such a seminary as that proposed for Virginia.

2. RICHARD CHANNING MOORE:
THE MAN AND HIS THEOLOGY

Here it is appropriate to consider something of the character and religious convictions of the man who was Bishop of Virginia at the founding of the Virginia Theological Seminary and was the first president of its board of trustees. He was, as has already been indicated, an Anglican Evangelical. Moore came from New York, where he had the reputation of being an "enthusiastic and methodistic" preacher, comparable to George Whitefield, using extravagant gestures and being criticized for using extemporaneous prayer and for supporting religious societies. Hobart was said to criticize him "for deviating from the strict letter of the law in the performance of divine service." The extent to which such an accusation was true is open to debate. We have observed how Moore directed Meade to avoid the examples of manipulative revivalists and to "observe order and decency in . . . worship." We must allow for change in the fervent preacher as he becomes the responsible prelate, but we must also consider the possibility that Moore, a devoted churchman, was influenced by the revivalism associated with the Second Great Awakening. Lawrence Brown argues that the Second Great Awakening had its influence on some leaders in the Episcopal Church, saying that this church raised "up a leadership capable of riding the back of the Second Great Awakening, capturing its zeal, yet shaping it by the stabilizing power of the liturgy and the apostolic and sacramental structure of the Church in order to naturalize the Church to the America of its time without losing its essential marks."[10] This seems to be an adequate way of characterizing Moore as priest and then as bishop.

Moore taught the Reformation doctrine of justification, as is evident, for instance, in his sermon on Acts 24:25,[11] and made it central to his evangelistic ministry. Diocesan conventions under him became times of renewal, fervent worship being intended to inform the conduct of diocesan business. In this he was a leader of the Evangelicals in America. But he was no party man in the strict sense. On baptismal regeneration he sided with the High Church Hobart, citing Hooker, Beveridge, and other divines, objecting to Calvinism on this issue, writing, "The *Calvinist* says, that all who receive grace shall infallibly persevere; of course, those who fall into sin after baptism, and die impenitent, never had grace. As I do not subscribe to the doctrine of perseverence to the extent maintained by the followers of Calvin, as I believe that man may resist grace, and finally perish; the dilemma in which the strict Calvinist is involved, does not bear upon my opinions, and leaves me at liberty to believe that the sacraments of the Lord are no nullities, but gracious and holy means, worthy of their Divine Author, and consistent with the dispensation of mercy revealed in the Gospel."[12]

This outwardly stern man was at heart affectionate. As Henshaw said, "While . . . he denounced God's wrath against the impenitent, and assured them that they must repent or perish; he delighted to announce 'the faithful saying and worthy of all acceptation, that Christ Jesus came into the world to save sinners.'"[13] He was a pastor, rector of Memorial Church in Richmond while serving as bishop of the diocese, the former role informing him in the execution of his episcopal duties. In his letter on baptism, dated December 7, 1823, he wrote,

> When God tells me that he delights not in the death of the wicked, why should I not believe my Maker? When he tells me that the Saviour is the propitiation for the sins of the whole world, why should I discredit the assertion? When he says, that we will not come unto him, that we may have life, why should I endeavour to exonerate the offender, by saying that he cannot go, and charge the fault to my heavenly Father? With my latest voice I hope to proclaim the riches of redeeming grace, and to assert in my last moments that "God is love."[14]

It was in this light that Moore viewed and highly valued the Holy Communion, saying in a sermon on 1 Cor. 11:23–26, "To perpetuate in our minds this instance of divine love [the crucifixion] we are enjoined to meet around his table, to eat the bread and drink the cup in remembrance of him! Yes, when we behold the sacramental bread broken at his altar, we are to call to view the scourgings of the Lord Jesus; to reflect upon the agonies of the cross, when his hands and feet were lacerated with nails, and his side pierced with a spear."[15] The sermon proceeds in the meditative style so prominent in the preaching of John Jewel and Lancelot

Andrewes.[16] The emphasis is on remembrance, but more than remembrance. "The ordinance of the Last Supper is not only commemorative of the sufferings of the Lord Jesus, but it is to be viewed also as a means of grace—a channel through which we derive strength and ability to perform our religious duties. The intelligent communicant, in this holy sacrament, receives Christ, and feeds upon him; his body, which is represented by the bread, proves to him *meat indeed* . . . the sacramental elements, when received by the faithful, nourish the soul . . . animating us with gratitude to heaven, and inspiring us with a desire to love and serve the God of our salvation."[17] Like Hooker, Moore believed the sacrament was intended to change people, not things,[18] the bread and the cup (with the remembrance of divine love on the cross) being means instrumental to that end. The Holy Communion (with preaching) was the great evangelical ordinance, the sacrament of divine judgment and love. To neglect it was to manifest "a contempt of the greatest blessings."[19]

Such was the man who, encountering Dr. Smith on a street in New York City in 1814, began to think of the possibility of promoting in concrete ways the theological education of young men.

3. THE SOCIETY FOR THE EDUCATION OF PIOUS YOUNG MEN, 1818

The conversation with Dr. Smith, the discussions going on at General Convention and in diocesan conventions, and the success of the plan launched by Meade and Wilmer to persuade Moore to accept the rectorship of Memorial Church, Richmond, and to be Bishop of Virginia,[20] together with the strong signs of revival in the first year of the new episcopate—all of these factors contributed to the founding of the seminary. But one more factor of vital importance is the creation of the "Society for the Education of Pious Young Men for the Ministry of the Protestant Episcopal Church in Maryland and Virginia."

This voluntary society began in June 1818 at a meeting in Washington, D.C., at which a constitution was adopted and officers elected.[21] Wilmer, rector of St. Paul's Church, Alexandria, Virginia, a distinguished presbyter in the Diocese of Virginia and in General Convention, was the first president and remained in that position until he left Alexandria in 1826 to become president of William and Mary College. It is of interest to note, as does Dawley, that Wilmer had been enlisted by the theological committee established in 1817 to found a general seminary as one of three men to solicit funds, Wilmer being chosen to do so in the southern dioceses. It was reported to General Convention that "some circumstances occurred which prevented Mr. Wilmer's engaging in this work." These circumstances were not specified, but Wilmer, president of the House of Deputies in 1820, was already engaged in raising funds for the newly founded Education Society. As Dawley comments, "Wilmer's loyalties must have been at least strained."[22]

Among the managers beside Wilmer were William Meade; Oliver Norris, who was to succeed Meade at Christ Church, Alexandria; and Reuel Keith, rector of Christ Church, Georgetown. These men were to teach at the nascent seminary in Virginia. Other managers of note were John Johns, Stephen Tyng, J.P.K. Henshaw, and Charles P. McIlvaine as presbyters, and Dr. Thomas Henderson and Francis Scott Key as laymen.

In the December 1819 issue of the *Washington Theological Repertory* two facts were emphasized. The first was the "vast and increasing disproportion between the whole number of qualified ministers of the gospel, of all denominations among us," compared to the number of laity. The second was that "since the year 1799, or during the last twenty years, the actual number of Episcopal clergymen in Maryland and Virginia has diminished more than one third—in the state of Virginia, within that short period, nearly one half. The diminution in those states south of Virginia is still greater."[23] The society therefore set out to raise funds to enable candidates for the ministry to prepare themselves under competent tutors. At the first annual meeting of the society, in October 1818 at St. John's Church, Georgetown, Wilmer reported that they had received one hundred and five dollars from Meade, collected at church services, fifty dollars from Dr. Balmain for a life subscription, and fifty dollars "from the Church at Winchester."[24] At a subsequent special meeting of the board of managers the first two recipients of the society's funds were named: H. Nelson Grey of Middlebury College, Vermont, and James Thompson of Alexandria, each being awarded one hundred dollars for the year beginning July 1, 1819.[25] From then on the society was steadily involved in raising funds and awarding grants to young men "deserving of assistance."

Next the society turned its attention to the necessity of providing the means for adequate education, focusing attention upon those who should teach their young men. At its meeting held at Christ Church, Georgetown, on October 26, 1820, a resolution was passed, saying "that it is expedient to establish a Theological Professorship, to be located at William and Mary College or elsewhere as the Society may from time to time order and direct."[26] On November 8, 1820, in response to this resolution, Wilmer sent out an address stating that the managers of the society "deem it their duty to take advantage of the peculiar circumstances which in this case present themselves in favor of the attempt to establish a local Seminary in the southern country." These circumstances involved (1) the offer made by William and Mary to establish a theological professorship for the sake of theological students and (2) the conviction "that the public will give more liberally and cheerfully to an object thus brought home to them, and identified with their local interests and associations than the remote though equally important institution at New Haven [the General Theological Seminary]."[27]

4. THE FAILURE OF THE ATTEMPT TO FOUND A REGIONAL SEMINARY

From this point on the story of the Society for the Education of Pious Young Men and that of the Diocese of Virginia converge in their efforts to found a seminary. The society was representative of interests in both Virginia and Maryland, as well as the District of Columbia. The managers, many of them active in both the society and their own dioceses, began to think of the theological professorship in Williamsburg as the first step in the creation of a theological seminary for the South, and they sought to obtain the broadest possible support. The society certainly was dedicated to the idea of at least Virginia and Maryland cooperating in the venture. They would have been pleased to welcome North Carolina to the venture, but the latter was altogether unresponsive. On May 15, 1821, the board of managers of the society met, discussed the matter, and adjourned to await the outcome of diocesan conventions in Virginia and in Maryland.[28] Their intention was that the board should meet after the conventions, but a note of June 26, 1821, in the society book of minutes indicates that "the two dioceses not agreeing to the proposition of a union in the prosecution of this plan, no meeting of the Board took place."[29]

In fact on May 17 and 18, 1821, the Virginia convention met in Norfolk and pledged its support, approving the recommendation of the committee on the state of the church that a seminary be established in Williamsburg where the professorship was already a reality, that this be done with the cooperation and support of the college, and that to this end a board of trustees, clerical and lay, be appointed to found a seminary, raise funds, and select "one or more professors." This board was to be subject to the convention. An attempt was to be made, even as the convention moved on in its planning, to involve Maryland and North Carolina.[30]

The first board of trustees, as appointed by the convention, consisted of Bishop Moore, John S. Ravenscroft, William H. Wilmer, William Meade, and Reuel Keith as presbyters, and Dr. Augustine Smith of William and Mary, Burwell Bassett, Bushrod Washington, Col. Hugh Mercer, and William Mayo as laymen. John Nelson, Jr., of St. James Parish,

Mecklenburg County, was appointed to solicit funds. The first meeting of the board took place on May 15, 1822.[31] Meade reports,

> The Convention of Virginia had appointed Col. Edward Colston and myself a Committee to correspond with the Bishop of Maryland and some leading laymen in North Carolina, proposing a union with Virginia in the establishment and management of the Seminary at Williamsburg. From North Carolina we received no answer. From the Bishop of Maryland we received a prompt and decided refusal, accompanied with such severe strictures on the religion and morals of Virginia that we did not present it to the Convention, but only reported our failure.[32]

Meade's report does not reveal the extent of the struggle that developed in Maryland. In June 1821, the Maryland convention seriously entertained a motion to support the Diocese of Virginia in the establishment of a seminary at Williamsburg but after discussion agreed to postpone action until the next convention. At that convention, which met in June 1822, it was decided that, rather than cooperating with Virginia, Maryland should found its own seminary.[33] A committee was appointed, a constitution drafted and accepted,[34] and the convention elected a board of trustees with the bishop as president.[35] All of this was done knowing that the bishop, James Kemp, was not favorably disposed to the founding of any such seminary, declaring the convention's action to be "unconstitutional in its nature, disorganized in its tendency and indigested and ill-formed in its character."[36] After much discussion the Maryland board, "with a view to promoting harmony and union in the church," agreed to suspend operations, urging, however, that further consideration be given to the plan. But its action taken on June 11, 1822, effectively marks the end of the matter.[37] It is important to realize that among the board members were prominent participants in the Education Society, including Henshaw, Hawley, McIlvaine, Johns, Dr. Henderson, and Francis Scott Key.[38]

The issue did, however, come before the Maryland convention on May 28, 1823. A certain "Sampson," reporting in the *Theological Repertory*, tells of political maneuvering. Those supporting the seminary were confident of having the votes needed to sustain their plan in spite of the bishop's opinions but wary of "causing more serious division in the diocese than would be compatible with the peace and prosperity of the church." A resolution was passed suspending action on the seminary until there could be greater unanimity in its planning. No mention was made in this report that the bishop was the chief stumbling block. "Sampson" concluded his report with the hope "that the same holy cause will prosper in His good time."[39]

J.P.K. Henshaw, rector of St. Peter's Church, Baltimore, and a member of the board of the Education Society and of the trustees of the unborn Maryland seminary, noted that the failure in Maryland "was a sad trial" to those promoting the plan but that it had a positive outcome. "The friends of theological education in Maryland and Virginia . . . thus strangely prevented from accomplishing their end by separate action, were enabled to combine their efforts in the promotion of a common cause, through the medium of the Education Society."[40] And thus, although the institution that came to be was very definitely tied to the Diocese of Virginia, through the Education Society it did involve the cooperation of persons outside Virginia, at the beginning most importantly from the Diocese of Maryland.

5. FROM WILLIAMSBURG TO ALEXANDRIA, 1820–1823

The first beginnings in Virginia were not promising. Reuel Keith left Christ Church, Georgetown, in January 1820 to become rector of Bruton Parish, Williamsburg, and to teach at William and Mary College. To accommodate him, Alexander Smith, president of the college, had the visitors create a professorship of humanity and universal history. According to college records, Keith taught classes in history and classics; no mention is made of his teaching theology. As the most recent history of the College of William and Mary states, the intention to create a seminary through Keith's presence at the college was "a perfect failure. His classes of any sort were always small, and at length he had no class at all. During his years at the Col-

Reputed to be a likeness of
Reuel Keith. Photo of a portrait by
Madeleine W. Anschutz, c. 1858.

Courtesy of the Rev. Dr. and Mrs. Mark S. Anschutz

lege, he may have had one or two ministerial students."[41] By 1823 the experiment was abandoned. Keith left Williamsburg and returned to his native Vermont. [42] Although Meade was reported to be fully supportive of the attempt to found a seminary at Williamsburg, he retained his suspicions concerning a place that represented "infidelity." Meade had reason to suspect that President Smith held "atheistical" views. Moore did not believe that he was an atheist but believed the president "was not orthodox and might be Socinian or Unitarian."[43]

The failure at Williamsburg was not to stop either the Education Society nor the Diocese of Virginia in pursuit of their common goal. Indeed, the society had supported the placing of Keith at the college, but in their resolution of October 26, 1820, the board of managers added "or elsewhere."[44] At their meeting of July 2, 1823, the managers formally rescinded their action of October 1820 and agreed that the professorship should be established "at the town of Alexandria in the District of Columbia." It was further agreed that beneficiaries of the society "be placed under the care" of the institution in Alexandria when the seminary began operation" and that in the meantime the Reverend Mr. Keith, who is to reside in the city of Alexandria, be appointed to take charge of "the Society's beneficiaries at a salary of six hundred dollars for one year, beginning July 1, 1823."[45] It is apparent from this that Keith had been persuaded to return from Vermont to try again, now with greater prospects of success. Key figures in the society's work at this point were Meade, McIlvaine, Henshaw, and Wilmer.

In the meantime, the trustees of the seminary, appointed by the Virginia convention in 1821, were not idle. At their meeting on May 15, 1822, a constitution prepared by Meade, Keith, and Col. William Mayo was approved. It was adopted by the convention on May 16. This document directed that membership of the board should consist of the bishop and thirteen members elected by convention; that the bishop of the diocese should be ex-officio president; that the board appoint its own vice president, treasurer, and secretary; and that the board be responsible to collect funds pledged and to raise further funds. It also directed that there be an annual meeting the day preceding convention in the place where the convention was to meet; that special meetings be "called by the Bishop, on the application of any three of the Trustees"; that eight members constitute a quorum; that a majority of those present be required to approve any action; and that vacancies be filled by convention. Finally, it directed that funds for the operation of the seminary be managed by the board, which would report annually to the convention and be subject to the convention in all financial matters. There followed a singularly important article:

11. The management of the Institution shall be vested in the Board of Trustees, who shall have power to choose a professor or professors, and to prescribe a course of study agreeable to the canons of the Church, and in general make rules and regulations for the government and good management of the Institution.

The board was thus to maintain close control of the seminary, its teachers, its course of study, and all its regulations and to do this as representatives of the diocesan convention. The seminary was to be a diocesan institution with the bishop as its president. The final articles concerned keeping records, reporting to convention, and changing the constitution, which was to be done by a two-thirds vote of convention.[46] At the convention on May 17, 1822, Wilmer reported for the Board of trustees that John Nelson, Jr., had raised $10,268.33 for the seminary, all from within Virginia.[47]

The board met again on July 10 and 11, 1822, at a special meeting with Moore in the chair. At that meeting, Meade was elected vice president, the Reverend Edward C. McGuire, secretary, and John Gray, of Traveller's Rest, treasurer. These men provided stability through the first formative years, Moore remained as president until his death in 1841, when he was succeeded by Meade. McGuire continued as secretary, according to one reckoning,[48] until 1858. And Gray was treasurer, according to Goodwin, until 1865.[49] Plans were made to raise more funds.[50] Wilmer reported on the situation in Maryland, concluding that he had learned from private conversations that some members of the Maryland convention would co-operate with Virginia if the seminary could be located in Maryland.[51] And provisions were made to pay Keith, then at Williamsburg, two hundred dollars a year, with certain further provisions specified.[52]

Between the board meetings of July 10, 1823, and May 21, 1824, a dramatic change in plans occurred. All hopes of founding a seminary in Williamsburg having been abandoned, attention was fixed on Alexandria, where the powerful and energetic threesome of Meade, Wilmer, and Norris were located and where the Education Society was planning to locate Keith to instruct its beneficiaries. At its 1823 meeting the board appointed Keith as professor in the seminary at Alexandria and instructed him to hold himself in readiness "to take charge of" the seminary "whenever it should go into operation." The convention in 1824 was asked to approve the plan for a seminary at Alexandria rather than at Williamsburg ("too remote and inaccessible to justify the hope that students can be obtained for a Theological Institution at that place").[53] The board ordered that "the Treasurer be directed to pay to the Rev. Reuel Keith the sum of two hundred dollars as his salary for the year beginning 10th July 1824" and then, somewhat mysteriously, "that hereafter he be entitled to receive the interest of the funded principal of the debt due to the school as his salary."[54] A library for the new school was being assembled. Wilmer received a donation of books from the Reverend Mr. Andrus,[55] and at the 1824 meeting the board ordered that two hundred dollars be given to Keith "to be laid out by him and the Rev. Dr. Wilmer for the purchase of such books as they deemed necessary to the Institution."[56] Lastly, Meade,

Norris, Keith and Wilmer were appointed a committee to draw up "a system of rules for the government of the school."[57] Wilmer was thanked for "his services in the department of Theology" and was "requested to continue to act as Professor in that department."[58] Keith was the first of the seminary's professors; Wilmer, the second.

On July 11, 1822, at the board meeting, Meade was authorized to assist in fund-raising and to compose a circular, which was sent to every agent of the board. The circular emphasized the great shortage of clergy, especially in the South and in relation to overall population growth. To meet this need, seminaries were being founded. The board held up "as a noble example to the members of our communion, the school at Andover . . . where more than one hundred pious youths are continually preparing themselves for the sacred office. Nearly four hundred thousand dollars have been expended on the buildings, libraries, and professorships of this school, within a few years," a sum contributed "almost entirely . . . by the members of six families." On the basis of the pressing need and in the light of the example provided by Andover, the appeal was made. Furthermore, it was contested that "a personal faith in Christ—an honest desire for the welfare of others—a zeal in the cause" are not sufficient. Human learning, which is not to be overvalued, is "necessary for the preparation of a Christian for the clerical office. Scripture was cited in defense of the necessity for literary and theological learning. The circular also cited Moses, the schools of the Prophets, Paul, and others in Scripture, along with the learned of church history—" Irenaeus, Clemens, Tertullian, Cyprian, Eusebius, Jerome, Chrysostom, and Augustine," and, after a period of darkness, "Wickeliffe . . . Luther, Melanchthon, Calvin, Latimer, Ridley, Cranmer and Knox and others" of the age of Reformation, followed by "Tillotson, Chillingworth, Hooker, Hammond, Baxter, Doddridge, Watts, Horseley, Porteus, Buchanan, Faber and Chalmers." Thus went their plea for the maintenance of a learned ministry through the nascent Virginia Seminary.[59]

6. THE SEMINARY AT ALEXANDRIA:
KEITH AND WILMER, 1823–1827

The address of the Education Society, sent out in the same year as the board circular (1823), is clearly aimed at gaining support for the seminary in Alexandria. It explains that Alexandria was chosen as the site for several reasons: access "to an excellent library," obtainability of lodging and board "on the most reasonable terms," proximity to the wealth of resources available in the District of Columbia, adequate supervision "to guard" students "from the dangers incident to their youth and circumstances,"

Site of the Original Seminary
King and Washington Streets, Alexandria

and availability of "opportunities of much practical instruction in the several particulars of private and parochial duties," that is, the possibility of
what is now called "field education." Finally, they argue that "no where
south of Philadelphia is the Episcopal interest so concentrated and powerful
as in Alexandria." Thus they appealed for support of the seminary and of
Keith its first professor, "a Clergyman well known, and very highly prized
for his talents, learning, and piety."The seminary, they reported, was to
begin October 15, 1823.[60]

The seminary began on that date principally at St. Paul's Church in
the schoolroom where John Thomas Wheat, graduate in 1825 of the seminary, taught children. It was there, or in St. Paul's vestry room, that Wilmer,
the rector and now strong guide and benefactor of the institution, taught
classes in theology. Another larger space was obtained when the board
rented the house of Sally Griffith, daughter of the Reverend Dr. David
Griffith, elected bishop in 1786 but not consecrated. This brick building
was at the southeast corner of King and Washington streets. There "Keith
and four of the students lived and all of his recitations were in that building."[61] Two students lived with Dr. Wilmer, others lived elsewhere. Some,
for instance George Smith, lived at a house on the corner of Washington

and Duke streets "kept by Miss Peggy Ashton, who was a kind of mother to the students."[62]

The seminary opened with "twelve to fourteen students, thirteen of whom were candidates for holy orders." By the time of the board meeting in May 1824, there were eleven students.[63] When the 1824–25 session began, there were twenty-one. The board report to convention stated that

> during the present term the students have been instructed by the Professor of Biblical literature and criticism, the original languages of the Bible, Prideaux's connections, Horne on the inspiration of the Scriptures, Jahn's Archeology, Butler's Analogy, and Magee on the atonement. The more advanced class has recited to the Rev. Wm. H. Wilmer, who has charge of the department of systematic Theology, Pearson on the Creed, Burnet on the Articles and such other authors as the time admitted, and the course of study prescribed by the house of Bishops required.[64]

The report was referring to *Historical Connections of the Old and New Testaments* by Humphrey Prideaux (1648–1724), Dean of Norwich. Horne was Thomas Hartwell Horne of St. John's College, Cambridge. In all likelihood Keith learned of Jahn from Moses Stuart.[65] William Magee, Archbishop of Dublin 1822–31, was author of *Discourses and Dissertations on the Scriptural Doctrines of Atonement and Sacrifice*. John Pearson published a work entitled *An Exposition of the Creed* (1659). And Gilbert Burnet (1643–1715) was the author of an influential commentary on the Thirty-Nine Articles of Religion. Prideaux, Pearson, and Burnet were on the House of Bishops' list of approved texts and were British scholar-divines. An exception was John Jahn, who also wrote *An Introduction to the Old Testament*, translated by Samuel Turner, the first professor of the General Theological Seminary.[66] Significantly or not, nothing was said in the report about church history, an omission also noted in the beginning of the Andover Seminary.

Church history is mentioned in Joseph Packard's discussion of the course of studies in 1824. He reported approvingly,

> The four Gospels and the Acts of Apostles were critically studied in Greek, and eighteen chapters of Genesis and thirty Psalms in Hebrew by the Junior Class, besides the usual English studies. The Senior Class studied all the Epistles, and twenty chapters of Isaiah in Hebrew, with Systematic Divinity and Church History, &c. Each member of this class, as now, had in his turn to prepare a thesis, a sermon, and to read the service. On these occasions the students were permitted to offer their criticisms and remarks on the performances, which must have made things lively and interesting, and the next week each of the professors criticized them.[67]

No mention was made of a middler class.

At the board meeting on May 18, 1825, "a system of rules for the government of the" seminary was adopted. There were four chapters. The first concerned "the course of theological learning"; the second, the faculty; the third, the students; and the fourth, the course of study. The first chapter named the departments into which the course of learning was divided, reflecting the influence of the House of Bishops' syllabus and of the curriculum of Andover Seminary but with a larger number of departments. There were departments of the following:

1. Oriental and Greek literature (embracing the study of Hebrew and Greek)
2. Bible, "comprehending whatsoever relates to the criticism of the sacred text"
3. "Interpretation of the Scriptures, exhibiting the principles of Scriptural interpretation, and the meaning and practical application of the sacred writings"
4. "Evidences of Revealed Religion; establishing the genuineness, authenticity and credibility of the Scriptures, and a view of the character and effects of Christianity, of the various objections of infidel writers, with a refutation of them, and of moral science in relation to Theology"
5. "Systematic Divinity, presenting a methodical arrangement and explanation of the truth contained in the Scriptures, with the authorities sustaining these truths; a statement and refutation of the erroneous doctrines attempted to be adduced from the sacred writings; and a particular view and defense of the system of faith professed by the Protestant Episcopal Church"
6. "Ecclesiastical History; displaying the history of the Church in all ages, and particularly of the Church of England and the Protestant Episcopal Church in this country"
7. "The Nature, Ministry, and Polity of the Church, comprising a view of the nature of the Christian Church, and of the duty of preserving its unity; of the authority and orders of the ministry, with a statement and elucidation of the principles of Ecclesiastical Polity, and an explanation and defense of that of the Episcopal Church; and also, an exhibition of the authority and advantages of Liturgical service, with a history, explanation and defense of the Liturgy of the Protestant Episcopal Church, and of its rites and ceremonies"
8. "Pastoral Theology and Pulpit eloquence; explaining and enforcing the qualifications and duties of the clerical office; and including the performance of the service of the Church and the composition and delivery of sermons"[68]

There was nothing peculiar about this course of study,[69] nor was it devised without faculty involvement. The first two professors, Keith and Wilmer, were on the committee that devised it, along with Meade and Norris, the former, in time, to teach pastoral theology, and the latter to be for a brief time professor of pastoral theology. In essence the plan involved the fourfold theological curriculum: biblical languages and literature, apologetic and systematic theology, ecclesiastical history and polity, and pastoral theology, including liturgics and homiletics. But, as indicated, the four were divided into eight, according to the board rules. With the supposition that each department should have one professor, there is already the possibility of a faculty of eight and the eventual fragmentation of theology as a unitive and comprehensive discipline.

Connected with the plan for a course of theological learning was the further description of the course of theology extended over three years. Details were provided for beginning and ending the academic year and holidays along the way. Juniors (called here "the third class") were to study "Oriental and Greek literature," Scriptures, and "evidences of revealed religion and of Jewish antiquities." Middlers were to continue the study of the Scriptures and begin "study of moral science in its relation to Theology, of systematic divinity and Ecclesiastical history." Seniors were to "finish the study of Systematic Divinity, of Ecclesiastical History, and shall also complete the course of instruction in the nature, ministry and polity of the Christian Church, and in the Book of Common Prayer and Canons of the Church."[70]

The basic method of teaching was by recitation, involving the oral examination of students on the assigned readings by a professor who would make appropriate comments following the recitations. Lectures, such as those given and published by Meade on pastoral matters, were not common in the early days. The "rules of government" provided that, in addition to recitation, all students should "produce such expositions of Scripture, critical dissertations, sermons or other compositions, as the Professors shall direct." Furthermore, once each week all classes were to meet with their professors for worship, "the delivery of original sermons, and such other exercises as they may think proper."[71] Textbooks used were to conform to those texts prescribed by the House of Bishops, "or otherwise be approved by the Faculty." No mention was made of board approval, something that developed in the early years and involved the disciplining of at least one faculty member for not obtaining board approval of texts used in his courses. Finally, the three-class system was to be strictly adhered to, unless on examination by the faculty, a student "is found qualified to take his station" in a higher class.[72]

The chapter on the faculty is very brief but also significant. It states that the "Bishop and Professors shall constitute the faculty, and meet according to their own rules."[73] Thus the bishop, as president of the board, is also in the position of dean or chief executive officer and chief of the academic staff. A major element in the history of the seminary is the gradual shifting of authority from the board to the faculty and in the latter days to a dean who is also president of the institution.

The chapter concerning students is more detailed. Students were to be admitted either by virtue of being candidates for holy orders or by providing "satisfactory evidence of religious and moral character, and of classical and scientific attainments," and by their readiness for ministry. Once admitted they were required to subscribe to a declaration promising to obey the rules of the institution and to "prosecute all the studies prescribed" and furthermore to "uniformly cultivate religious and moral dispositions and habits," in every way promoting the "reputation and interests of the Seminary." The faculty, "consisting of the Bishop and Professors," had power to expel a student for sufficient reasons, informing the offender's bishop or other ecclesiastical authority if there were such. There follow further details.[74]

Finally, there is a statement that not only sets forth expectations but reveals something of the theological and ecclesial character of the nascent institution:

As mere theological learning, unaccompanied with real piety, is not a sufficient qualification for the ministry, it is declared to be the duty of every student, with an humble reliance on Divine Grace, to be assiduous in the cultivation of evangelical faith, and a sound practical piety; neither contenting himself with mere formality, nor running into fanaticism. He must be careful to maintain every day stated periods of pious reading, meditation and devotion; and occasional special seasons for the more solemn and enlarged observance of these duties, together with such abstinence as is suited to extraordinary acts of devotion, having due regard to the ways and seasons recommended for this purpose by the Church. In order to excite just views of the nature, responsibilities and obligations of the Clerical Office, he should frequently and carefully read over the services for the ordination of Deacons and Priests, with a view of making their contents the subjects of serious reflections, and of incitements to fervent prayer, that, if admitted to either of those offices, he may have the grace to be faithful in the discharge of its duties.

The statement concludes with insistence on regular attendance at the public worship of the church on Sundays and other days. To assist students, faculty were to open their class sessions with prayer and in the course of "their respective lectures or recitations" give "such advice and directions as may tend to the religious improvement of the students."[75]

This statement has the strong flavor of Evangelical piety in the Angli-can mode. An "evangelical faith" and a "practical piety" are phrases remi-niscent of William Wilberforce with his emphasis on "real Christianity" and Charles Simeon with his devotion to the Book of Common Prayer. A high priority was given to what some in this day might call "formation," the development of a personal religious discipline informed by the ordi-nation services and the examples of the faculty. It was such formation that seemed best developed in a community of teachers and students bound together, nourished, and transformed through common worship.

To accomplish more adequately all that was required, the board ap-pointed the Reverend Oliver Norris, rector of Christ Church, Alexan-dria, and one of the energetic threesome of Meade, Wilmer, and Norris, to be professor of pastoral theology. They further appointed the Reverend John Johns, who would become assistant bishop and then bishop and presi-dent of the board, as professor of systematic theology and pulpit eloquence. Should Johns refuse, Wilmer, Keith, Norris, and Meade were to corre-spond with the Reverend Edward R. Lippitt, the Reverend Benjamin Smith, and any others, with power to elect one of them to the faculty. In order to facilitate Norris' serving as a professor, the board ordered that Keith preach once a week at Christ Church and that the same service, by other professors, be afforded Wilmer at St. Paul's Church.[76]

This action was taken in May. On August 19, 1825, Norris died, and the responsibilities that were meant to be his devolved upon the other professors. In addition, Keith took full charge of Christ Church for a while. Johns declined his election, and Lippitt was elected professor of theology. The board report to the Virginia convention in 1826, prepared by Meade, speaks specifically first of the studies pursued during the academic year 1825–26 and of community life, in terms of worship and service. The account of studies pursued is worthy of extensive quotation;

. . . the class attending the Professor of Ecclesiastical History, has during this session gone through Mosheim's ecclesiastical history with reference to collat-eral authors, has commenced Potter on Church Government, and expects to complete the work together with Hooker's Ecclesiastical Polity, during the present session. This class in addition to recitations in the above mentioned text books, has also been exercised in writing original dissertations on the promi-nent points of their course of study, and the members in rotation one each day in each week have read the service and an original sermon, when their perfor-mance has been subjected to the criticism of all the students, and on the fol-lowing week the Professors by turn have analyzed and criticized the discourses. The second class has during this period been engaged under the Professor of Sacred Literature, in the critical study of the Epistles, and to the Professor of systematic divinity has recited twice in each week on such subjects as have been previously appointed, references being made to the authors who have written with most ability on the several subjects. The third class has been engaged in the critical study of the Old and New Testaments in the original languages and of Jewish antiquities. The members of this class have read sixteen chapters of Genesis and ten Psalms in Hebrew, and the four Gospels in Greek. They have also gone through the first volume of Horne's introduction to the Sacred Scriptures, have read the principal part of Prideaux's Connexions, and will complete Butler's Analogy and Paley's Evidences by the close of the session. They have also been engaged in writing essays on the most important arguments for revealed religion.[77]

Such was the demanding academic program directed by Keith as professor of sacred literature, Wilmer as professor of ecclesiastical history, and Lippitt as professor of systematic divinity. Instruction by recitation quickly revealed sloth or ignorance among the students. In addition, as Meade reports, there was worship in the classroom before recitation and each morning together at "the rising of the sun." Furthermore, students worked outside the seminary to visit "the needy and afflicted at their homes, to inquire into their spiritual condition, to establish prayer meetings at the most suitable places, to exhort all to attendance on public worship, and to beseech parents to send their children to the Sunday Schools which are established in the town" and which the students assisted in conducting. To this end Alexandria and environs was divided into districts.[78] Here was a form of field education, an exercise in evangelization, and the beginnings of the seminary's missions that were to be so important in the life of the institution. Meade could boast that twelve men who received all or a part of their theological education at the seminary had entered the ordained ministry, eight in the Diocese of Virginia, and that of the twenty students at the seminary as he reported, seven were expected to "offer themselves for ordination in the course of the present year."[79] He concluded that "surely it is within the power of the wealthy gentlemen of our Church to raise a permanent fund which shall place our school on a sure foundation."[80]

7. THE FIRST TEACHERS AND THEIR THEOLOGICAL VIEWS: KEITH, WILMER, AND LIPPITT

The first teachers at the Virginia Theological Seminary were exceptional men. They were in various ways typical "Anglican divines," scholarly, pastoral, and spiritual.[81] None has been remembered as an outstanding scholar. None had an earned doctorate. Yet all were competent theologians.

Oliver Norris, born November 17,1786, made professor of pastoral theology, was among the first but died before he could begin. He is remembered chiefly for his ardent support of the seminary as well as his tenure at Christ Church, Alexandria, succeeding Meade in 1813.

The first teacher was Reuel Keith. Born June 26, 1792, in Pittsford, Vermont, he died at the house of his brother in Sheldon, Vermont, in 1842. A graduate of Middlebury College in 1814, he went south to Virginia for his health. According to Packard, "the doctors said he had a large hole in his lungs."[82] For a time he was a tutor in a prominent family in Prince George County and while there served as a lay reader in the parish church. He was praised for the work he did in renewing the dormant congregation there.[83] He returned to Middlebury as a tutor, studied theology, and prepared for ordination under J.P.K. Henshaw, who had baptized him. He was also resident at Andover Theological Seminary, where he was influenced by Calvinist Evangelicalism and by Moses Stuart. Keith was ordained by Bishop Moore in 1817. Enticed to return to the South to join in the work of a new college to be founded in the District of Columbia, Keith became assistant to Walter D. Addison at St. John's Church, Georgetown, and then rector of the newly established Christ Church, of which Dr. Thomas Henderson and Francis Scott Key were major benefactors.

We have noted his resignation from Christ Church in 1820 and his brief career at Williamsburg. In 1823 he became the first professor at the seminary in Alexandria and spent the rest of his life in its service. In 1837, however, he was evidently thinking of a change and had to be persuaded to remain at the seminary.[84]

Keith possessed, according to Packard who knew him well, "the power of abstraction in a very high degree—the highest of all mental powers—and he would become so absorbed in his subject as to forget everything else."[85] He was a serious scholar, learned in Hebrew, Greek, Latin, and German. The most tangible and lasting evidence of his scholarship was his translation of E.W. Hengstenberg's *Christologie des Alten Testaments und messianischen Weissagungen* (1829–35). This was the *Christology of the Old Testament and a Commentary on the Predictions of the Messiah by the Prophets* (volume 1, Alexandria, 1836; volume 2, Washington, D.C., 1839). The first volume had to be printed at Andover (although published at Alexandria), where Packard, who was then studying there, saw it through the press just prior to beginning his own teaching career at Virginia Seminary.[86] Ernst Wilhelm Hengstenberg (1802–69) taught at Berlin, attacked rationalism, and was much reviled by liberal scholars for his orthodoxy. He wrote his *Christologie* to defend the Old Testament and to refute critics of prophecy and miracles. In all likelihood Keith learned of the *Christologie* from Moses Stuart. Whereas Keith had nothing but praise for Hengstenberg's work,[87] Stuart publicly criticized it, objecting to the German's theory that in the Prophets the human soul is replaced by the Spirit of God, Stuart preferring to think of a purifying and strengthening of the human mind.[88] Keith evidently viewed himself more as translator than as editor or commentator and did, in fact, do a creditable job of translation.[89]

We have some indication of Keith's teaching in notes made by the Reverend Churchill Jones Gibson (1819–92), who studied under him at the seminary. One set of notes is on "Dr. Keith's Lectures On the Internal Evidences of the Inspiration of the Bible." The easiest method of proving "that the Bible is the book of God" is the "testimony of Jesus" as found in the New Testament and the fact that Jesus received the Old Testament "as coming from God." The second method is that of evidences largely repudiated by the rationalists, such as miracles, prophecies, "antiquity, the sublime doctrines, power over the hearts of men, etc." Such evidences are not to be analyzed separately but rather as parts of "a general plan, institutions in harmony with and furthering the purpose of the plan, such plan and purposes from their nature—must have come from God. Conclusion. The Bible comes from God." Gibson notes that the argument is from design: It is like an examination of an edifice, its design known— "the relation of parts to each other and adaptation to general design is sought for—for proof of the character of the builder . . . if it appears at last that a high degree of skill and ability were necessary to such a work— then the conclusion is that a wise Master-builder was its author. Such is the Bible." Subsequent lectures will prove this to be so, the teacher asserts. Unfortunately, we have only a portion of the next lecture.

Another set of notes is on "the Will of God. The Decrees of God. The Doctrine of Election with its practical uses." Keith's teaching conforms to that of Calvin in the *Institutes* and to the Thirty-Nine Articles of Religion. Commenting on Eph. 1:4–6 and the doctrine of election, Keith is reported as saying,

> The election of which he [Paul, whom he believed to be the author of the Epistle] treats was an election for no cause in man could be assigned or imagined: it was an act of the Divine Sovereignty to be contemplated with the most profound humility, reverence and awe, as a deep and inscrutable mystery. Had Paul held the Arminian view of election he would have had no occasion to appeal to the sole good pleasure of God.

Later Keith remarked that

> if God predestinates men to faith as the means of their salvation, it by no means follows on the other hand that he also predestinates those who per-

ish to unbelief and impenitence, for they are not the effect of a Divine influence, but the natural offspring of the human heart, but "by grace are we saved through faith, and that not of ourselves; it is the gift of God."[90]

Within the seminary Keith's reputation depended not so much on his scholarship and teaching as on his piety. Tall, stooping, with a pronounced forehead and "piercing eye," Keith was renowned for his presence, his reading of the service, and his preaching. Packard gives an excerpt from a sermon preached at New Year's, 1840:

Pause, I beseech you, and reflect deeply and solemnly on the nature, the greatness, and the eternity of this salvation, that the thought of its nearness may forever dispel the slumbers of your immortal spirits. It is a salvation which interested the affections and occupied the councils of the holy, blessed and glorious Trinity before the foundations of the world were laid, and which were deemed of sufficient importance in the sight of God to be accomplished at no less expense than the incarnation, sufferings and death of His only begotten Son. It is the salvation of a rational, accountable and immortal being, of boundless capacity for enjoyment or sufferings; a salvation which rescues him from all that is evil, and confers upon him all that is good, through the whole extent of his never-ending existence: for it delivers him from the curse of God and makes him the object of His everlasting love. It is a salvation so glorious that every instance of its being secured by one of our fallen race heightens the happiness even of heaven itself: "for there is joy in the presence of God and of the holy angels over one sinner that repenteth." It is a salvation which God has accomplished for us expressly in order that He might show in the ages to come to an admiring, and adoring, and rejoicing universe what His almighty love can do, and what is the exceeding riches of His grace in his kindness toward us through Christ Jesus.[91]

Such was the preaching of a man who was remembered by his students for his presence at faculty meeting, "sitting with his eyes closed, and his meditations seemed a heavenly conversation. Sometimes with a flashing gaze, as if he were standing in the midst of heavenly visions, his speech was affluent of sacred wisdom, as though the rivers of life overflowed in our midst."[92] Goodwin commented that Keith "brought with him to the Seminary the impress of Andover and a theological system colored by the prevalent Calvinism of Protestant New England."[93] Packard called him "a moderate Calvinist."[94] He told of "a student on one occasion, after Dr. Keith had presented the Calvinistic view of a subject," saying "to him, 'When, Doctor, are we to have the other side' he answered, 'There is no other.'"[95]

Packard reports that Keith "was of a very nervous temperament, moody and subject to fits of depression. He could and did fear at times that he was lost, saying to the man he rebuked for swearing that he should accept salvation, and adding, 'You can do it now, but as for me it is too late; there is no hope for me.'" But as Packard also remarks, recovering from depression "he would be in very high spirits." He was not always dour; he had a sense of humor. Once a student, reciting Butler's Analogy, said, "Oh, Doctor, I have detected a flaw in Butler's reasoning." Commented Keith: "Then you have caught a weasel asleep." And when a student, considering the Flood and Noah's ark, asked, "Doctor, what became of the fish?" Keith remarked, "Fine time for the fish, Mr. ——."[96]

Keith was a man who could enjoy himself, and he was devoted to his wife and to the New England from which he had come. Packard tells us,

> Dr. Keith was very fond of horses and spent much of his leisure in riding or driving. He was much given to exchanging them, in which he generally got the worst of the bargain. He would spend his vacations driving over a good part of New England in a yellow carryall with two horses, one probably a large, bony, grey horse, and the other a small sorrel.[97]

Next in order came William H. Wilmer. Born in 1782 in Maryland, Wilmer was passionately committed to theological education and throughout his fourteen years as rector of St. Paul's Church, Alexandria, labored to improve the condition and the quality of education for the church's ordained ministry. He taught students in his own home, he was a founder of the Education Society and its first president, and he is rightly accounted a founder of the Virginia Theological Seminary, as has been previously mentioned. He was active in the revival of the church in Virginia and in securing Richard Channing Moore as bishop. He was active as a missionary in a large part of Virginia, itinerating to visit families isolated from the church's common worship, holding services, helping new parishes to begin and reviving old ones. He was president of the standing committee of the Diocese of Virginia from 1813 to 1826, presided over the convention that elected Bishop Moore, and was four times president of the General Convention of the Episcopal Church. In 1826 he left Alexandria to become president of the College of William and Mary, dying the next year at age forty-five.[98]

Wilmer's letters reveal something of his performance as a tutor and advisor to students prior to the establishment of Virginia Seminary. His wisdom and skill were well known. In 1816 he wrote to Benjamin Smith, whose ordination was delayed until he reached canonical age, giving advice concerning his behavior and what some would now call formation:

We ought my friend to be able to say in all things to our flock "Follow me as I follow Christ." Let us be meek and lowly in our eyes—moderate in our gestures, calm in our passions, deliberate in our conversation, circumspect in the matter of it and in all conduct. A jealous eye is always upon us and will rejoice to see us departing from the Christian spirit.[99]

In 1817 he wrote to Benjamin's brother, Thomas, about his coming to Alexandria from Dumfries, Virginia, so that Wilmer could better assist him in his studies. He argued that Thomas had much yet to do before he would be qualified for ordination, particularly since the bishop would not grant dispensation from Greek and Latin. Wilmer went on to say,

The Course of studies required by the house of Bishops embraces a large body of reading and practical digestion. Our young men ought, at least, to be as learned as the Presbyterians, and they are filling our land with very shining lights. A minister ought to be a workman who needeth not to be ashamed. It is true, that all human learning will be insufficient, and a mere sounding brass and tinkling cymbal, without that anointing of the spirit and that fervent zeal which attest the movements of a renewed heart. But it is equally true, that, now miraculous influences are superseded, a competent share of erudition is essential for the proper understanding of Holy Scriptures, for convincing the unbeliever, and for sustaining, in all departments of life that respectability of character upon which success eminently depends, under the blessing of God. The attainment of this is arduous, and requires labour and patience . . . By devoting all your time, you may succeed.[100]

And succeed they did, for in time he was addressing both brothers as ordained ministers.

In 1823 Wilmer began teaching as a member of the faculty in the new seminary, responsible, as need arose, for systematic theology, church history, and ecclesiastical polity. We have no records of his teaching, but the character of his mind and his theological orientation are revealed by the contents (especially the theological expositions) of the *Washington Theological Repertory*, which he edited, and by his book *The Episcopal Manual* (Philadelphia, 1815).[101] We have observed the Evangelical nature of theological statements in the *Theological Repertory*. Now we note the basic Anglicanism of Wilmer, whose theological position was called "Evangelical-Sacramentarian"[102] and whose *Manual* was characterized by John Coleman as "devoted to the *united* interests of the *Gospel* and the *Church*— to the defence of both *evangelical truth* and *apostolic order*."[103] Grounding his understanding in Scripture and in the formularies of the sixteenth-century English church, the Prayer Book catechism, Jewel's *Apology* (part

2), Nowell's catechism, the two Books of Homilies, the liturgy of the Prayer Book, and the Thirty-Nine Articles of Religion, Wilmer declared his intention to avoid two errors. The one was to "undervalue" the church's "order and institutions." The other was "to exhaust all our zeal in behalf of external concerns, and to permit the spirit and essence of religion to evaporate in this way."[104] He defended the episcopal government of the church, acknowledging that this government is not authentic by virtue of any "express revelation in Scripture." It is grounded in the "practice of the Apostles." What they did, they did "by divine direction, and is therefore of sacred obligation." This position he held "without intending any ill-will or disrespect to others;" he simply wished "that they could view the subject in the same light" as did Episcopalians.[105]

As to doctrine, Wilmer desired to follow the example of Anglican formularies, exercising restraint, influenced by the spirit of charity, in humility admitting that there is much which is "too mysterious for human apprehension," emphasizing "that which is essential to salvation." This he summarizes in a few words, reminiscent of statements in the first issue of the *Theological Repertory*:

> There must be a sense of our depravity; there must be faith; there must be penitence; there must be a restoration of the lost image of God; and lastly, the sanctified effect of a righteous, godly, sober life, must *follow* this restoration. These truths our Church faithfully inculcates and unceasingly enforces. Let us listen to her voice, and we shall be made wise unto salvation.[106]

In the light of this summary of fundamentals, professing that he was "not a Calvinist,"[107] Wilmer sought to go beyond the confines of Calvinism and Arminianism to the essence of faith in both, to the Articles of Religion, which are neither Arminian nor Calvinist, and thus to the basic teachings of Scripture. He pled for controversy to cease and for "a spirit of meekness, of love, of obedience."

> That God is love; that he desireth not the death of a sinner; that he wills all men to be Saved; that man's salvation is wholly of grace, and his perdition of himself, are propositions clearly laid down in scripture. If there be a doctrine which seems to contravene these principles of religion, we may conclude either that we do not understand that doctrine, or that it is false. But in carrying this rule into action, it should be kept in mind, that we have no right to deny what is plainly revealed in scripture, merely because *our conceptions* cannot reconcile it with the known attributes of God; for his ways are not our ways, nor our thoughts his thoughts.[108]

In this spirit Wilmer explored the great doctrines, from the Trinity through the sacraments. For instance, in treating the doctrine of justification he emphasized its fundamental importance, quoting widely from the formularies and from Anglican divines, giving as his own definition the statement by St. Paul: "By grace are we saved, through faith; not of works, lest any man should boast."[109] He then sought to demonstrate that Paul and the Letter of James were not diametrically opposed, that they were addressing different persons in different situations. Paul was speaking to those who looked "for salvation through obedience to the ceremonial and moral law," thus emphasizing justification by faith only. James was speaking to those who, professing faith, supposed "that they were released from the obligations of moral duty," thus arguing that faith "which did not produce good works, was a dead faith." They both, Paul and James, said Wilmer, "maintain the value and necessity of faith as the originating principle of good works, the ground of our justification, and also the necessity of good works as evidencing that faith and justifying their claim to that blessing."[110]

In a lovely passage, Wilmer argued against those who say that the doctrine of justification produces licentiousness. This doctrine "is the only one which can guarantee with certainty" that which he called "holy living."

> Implant in a child a reverence and love for his parents, and you more effectually secure his filial obedience, than by all abstract arguments you can think of, on the fitness and propriety, and utility of virtue. While his heart is disaffected towards his parents, his obedience will be contravened and partial, suited to his own convenience and policy; but when love takes possession of his heart, he will delight to honour and obey his commands. The heart of man in his unrenewed state is enmity against God. Faith is the instrument through which the Holy Spirit effects its amelioration and works by love.[111]

Subordinating all arguments, however persuasive they may be, to the inculcation of "love to Christ," founded on "faith in him," Wilmer reinforced Hooker's teaching that holy fear cannot be productive without a prevenient sense of holy love,[112] and he pointed toward William Temple's emphasis on God as love, inspiring love.[113]

In line with this, writing of the sacraments, which to Wilmer were "not only signs of grace, but 'means whereby we receive the same,'"[114] he pointed to the cross. The Lord's Supper "is not merely a memorial of the Redeemer in general, but is expressly designed as a visible representation of his death," of his sacrifice for us, and as an atonement for sin. Here he quoted liberally from the Prayer Book. In this sacrament the faithful receive the Lord Jesus Christ, by faith "partaking of his body and blood, for their spiritual sustenance."[115] It is a gracious means of repentance and salvation.

In another statement, Wilmer said,

We hereby publicly avow ourselves to be the disciples of a crucified Master, and that we will not be ashamed to confess him before men, but fight as good soldiers under his banner, to our life's end. We promise to follow his example, to be crucified to the world, to deny ourselves, and to take up our cross. We promise, like him, to do the will of God, to go about doing good, to forgive and love our enemies, to return good for evil, to weep with those who weep, as well as rejoice with those who rejoice, to bind up the brokenhearted, and relieve the distressed, to "visit the fatherless and the widow in their afflic-tion, and to keep ourselves unspotted from the world." We own him not only as a teacher sent from God, to be our instructor and guide; but we confide in him as our Almighty Friend and Saviour; rely upon his sacrifice; and commit ourselves to him, to be redeemed, sanctified and saved.[116]

This is what is professed by those who "partake of the Lord's Supper." It is intensely personal, but it has widespread social effects. He wrote, "By partaking of the Lord's Supper, in a social manner, with the members of Christ's Church, we profess our sincere love to them as brethren, and our determination to perform all the duties of this relation. . . . "[117]

In justification of C.B. Wilmer's designation of his grandfather as an "Evangelical Sacramentarian," it should be noted that by far the longest part of the *Manual* concerns the sacraments. This was partly due to contro-versies abroad in 1815, such as those concerning baptismal regeneration.[118] But it was also a matter of conviction, including his affirmation of the im-portance of the Prayer Book for maintaining uniformity in doctrine.

Wilmer was devoted to Prayer Book worship, to the sober richness of it. "It is with *solid truths*, and not with fluent words, that we are to be im-pressed," he wrote, arguing the superiority of the formal, set prayers of the Prayer Book to the supposed exhilaration of extemporaneous prayer so fan-cied by many. And yet he could and did compose extra prayers and medita-tions, some to be found in his *Manual*. For example, he wrote a prayer to be used by the faithful "at any time before the elements are consecrated."

O my soul, come now and go down to the Garden of Gethsemene, where thy Saviour is about to commence the course of his sacred sorrows. Look up to the mountain of Calvary, and behold him extended there upon the cross. The nail strikes deep through his hands and feet. The spear pierces his blessed side, and blood and water flow out." It is finished." Thy Saviour bows his head and dies. And was it for thee, O my soul, that Jesus suffered and died? O my God, may the thoughts of it awaken in me a deep and genuine repentance. . . . Renew and sanctify me by the power of thy grace; prepare me to come with advantage to thy holy altar; accept of the unworthy offering I am about to make, and let no improper thought, or unholy desire, intrude upon those sacred hours in which I come into thy presence. . . ."[119]

In such meditation and prayer, Wilmer was a part of a great tradition and proved himself to be a person of great conviction and devotion. For him theology was rooted in worship, and worship was the wellspring of theology.

Edward Russell Lippitt joined the seminary faculty in 1826. Lippitt was born in 1798 to a Rhode Island family, traced by Philip Slaughter back to Moses Lippitt, buried at Warwick, Rhode Island in 1745. A lifelong Episcopalian, Lippitt was educated at Brown University and in 1817, on graduation, became master of Brown's Latin School. He then studied for the ministry and was ordained to the diaconate by Bishop Griswold in 1819 and to the priesthood by Bishop Moore in 1822. From his first assignment at Quincy, Massachusetts, he went to be rector of Norborne Parish, Berkeley County, Virginia, and then to Germantown, Pennsylvania. Beginning in 1826, he taught at the seminary for sixteen years, resigning in 1842 to take charge of the *Southern Churchman*, which he edited for six years before retiring. His last employment was as "Master of an Institute for young ladies in Washington." He died in 1870, having spent his last days with his sons in Clarke and Jefferson counties in Virginia.[120]

From 1826 until Joseph Packard joined the faculty in 1836, the entire teaching responsibility rested upon Keith and Lippitt. According to Packard, Lippitt was initially appointed to be professor of systematic divinity.[121] By 1837, after Packard's arrival, Lippitt was described in the seminary catalogue of that year as "Professor of Pastoral Theology and Church Polity, and Instructor of Ecclesiastical History." Undoubtedly, the latter subjects were in his care long before 1837, he and Keith having to divide the entire curriculum between them. Of Lippitt we know little more. That he adhered to the Evangelical tradition with Meade, Keith, and Wilmer is evident, especially in his editorship of the *Southern Churchman*.[122] That we know so little about him is due in part to his personality. Packard, reflecting on Lippitt after his quiet death, reported, "Dr. Sparrow said that his mind was highly cultivated, but that his extreme modesty repressed the exhibition of his powers. He was the only man I ever knew overburdened with modesty."[123]

Such was the original faculty. It is noted by Goodwin that the first six full-time professors (including Keith, Norris, Lippitt, Packard, May, and Sparrow) were all trained in colleges and seminaries "under the dominance of Puritan, rather than Church influence."[124] But all adhered to the churchly tradition of the English Evangelicals, of Wilberforce and Simeon, in varying degrees, Wilmer perhaps more than Keith.

NOTES

1. Meade, *Old Churches* 1:40.
2. Henshaw, *Moore*, 167.
3. Ibid., 171.
4. Goodwin, *History* 1:103–104.
5. Meade, *Old Churches* 1:41.
6. Dawley, *General Theological Seminary*, 27–35.
7. Ibid., 35–39.
8. Ibid., 40.
9. See *Address of the Board of Trustees of the Protestant Episcopal Theological Seminary of Maryland to the Members of the Church in this Diocese* (Georgetown, D.C., 1822), 4.
10. Lawrence L. Brown, "Richard Channing Moore and the Revival of the Southern Church," *Historical Magazine of the Protestant Episcopal Church* (1966), 13.
11. In Henshaw, *Moore*, 180–188; see Brown, "Moore," 30.
12. Henshaw, *Moore*, 206–207; see Brown, "Moore," 40–41.
13. Henshaw, *Moore*, 149.
14. Henshaw, *Moore*, 210.
15. Henshaw, *Moore*, 455–456.
16. See, for instance, John Jewel, *Works*, ed. J. Ayre, (Cambridge: Parker Society, 1847), 2:1042; Lancelot Andrewes, *Ninety-Six Sermons* Library of Anglo-Catholic Theology (Oxford: Parker, 1841), 134ff.
17. Henshaw, *Moore*, 457–58.
18. Richard Hooker, *Of the Laws of Ecclesiastical Polity*, V.67.
19. Henshaw, *Moore*, 460.
20. Ibid., 121ff. Wilmer's letter to Moore, suggesting that he be Bishop of Virginia, is dated January 27, 1813.
21. The constitution and officers of the society at its inception are found in Goodwin, *History* 2:617–18. Minutes of the society follow to 1842.
22. Dawley, *General Theological Seminary*, 41.
23. *Wash. Theol. Rep.* 1 (December 1819): 157.
24. Goodwin, *History* 2:618.
25. Ibid., 619.
26. Ibid., 621.
27. Ibid. 1:130–31.
28. Ibid. 2:621.
29. Ibid.
30. *Wash. Theol. Rep.* 2 (July 1821): 381.
31. Goodwin, *History* 2:591; page 1 of the actual minutes is in the seminary archives.
32. Meade, *Old Churches* 1:40–41.
33. Board of trustees, *Maryland* (1822), 5–6. See note 9, ABOVE.

34. Ibid., 21–25, for bylaws.
35. Ibid., 7–8.
36. Ibid., 9.
37. Ibid., 19.
38. Ibid., 20. It is further significant that it was reported in the *Theological Repertory* 4 (October 1822) that "William H. Wilmer, D.D. was nominated as the professor of the [Maryland] Seminary."
39. *Wash. Theol. Rep.* 4 (June 8, 1823): 347–48.
40. Henshaw, Moore, 169.
41. Ludwell Johnson, "How Not to Run a College," in *The College of William and Mary: A History*, ed. Susan H. Godson et al., (Williamsburg: King and Queen Press, 1993) 1:213–14. See Meade, *Old Churches* 1:40.
42. Packard, *Recollections*, 94.
43. Johnson, "How Not to Run a College," 214.See Meade, *Old Churches* 1:40–41.
44. Goodwin, *History* 2:621. My emphasis.
45. Ibid., 622.
46. Ibid., 591–92.
47. *Wash. Theol. Rep.* 3 (July 1822): 370.
48. Goodwin, *History* 1:318. The board minutes from 1839 to 1866 are lost, having been taken from the rectory of Christ Church, Alexandria, during the war.
49. Ibid.; again, no certainty due to loss of board minutes.
50. Goodwin, *History* 2:593; board minutes, 1821–66, 12.
51. Goodwin, *History* 2:594; bd. min., 1821–66, 16.
52. Goodwin, *History* 2:593; bd. min., 1821–66, 10–11.
53. Goodwin, *History* 2:595–96; bd. min., 1821–66, 21–27.
54. Goodwin, *History* 2:596; bd. min., 1821–66, 27–29.
55. Goodwin, *History* 2:593, 594; bd. min., 1821–66, 14, 19.
56. Goodwin, *History* 2:596; bd. min., 1821–66, 28.
57. Goodwin, *History* 2:596.
58. Bd. min., 1821–66, 29.
59. *Wash. Theol. Rep.* 4 (January 1823): 171–77.
60. Ibid. 5 (August 1823): 19–27.
61. Packard, *Recollections*, 81.
62. Goodwin, *History* 1:149.
63. Goodwin, *History* 2:595; bd. min., 1821–66, 22.
64. Goodwin, *History* 2:595.
65. See Giltner, *Moses Stuart*, 43.
66. See John Jahn's *Introduction*, trans. Samuel Turner with William R. Whittingham (New York: Carvill, 1827).
67. Packard, *Recollections*, 79.
68. Goodwin, *History* 2:596–97; bd. min., 1821–66, 31–33.
69. See Lynn, "Notes", 123.
70. Goodwin, *History* 2:598; bd. min., 1821–1866, 37–39.

`71. Goodwin, *History* 2:598; bd. min., 1821–1866, 39–40.

72. Goodwin, *History* 2:598; bd. min., 1821–1866, 40–41

73. Goodwin, *History* 2:597; bd. min., 1821–1866, 33.

74. Goodwin, *History* 2:597; bd. min., 1821–66, 33–35.

75. Goodwin, *History* 2:597–98; bd. min., 1821–1866, 36–37.

76. Goodwin, *History* 2:599; bd. min., 1821–1866, 41–42.

77. Goodwin, *History* 2:600; bd. min., 1821–1866, 48–49.

78. Goodwin, *History* 2:600; bd. min., 1821–1866, 50.

79. Goodwin, *History* 2:601; bd. min., 1821–1866, 51.

80. Goodwin, *History* 2:602; bd. min., 1821–1866, 59.

81. See my essay, "Standard Divines," in Sykes and Booty, eds., *Study of Anglicanism*, 163–64.

82. Packard, *Recollections*, 94.

83. Ibid.

84. See *Southern Churchman* 3/52 (December 29, 1837): 207.

85. Packard, *Recollections*, 94.

86. Ibid.

87. See the translator's preface to vol. 1, v, vi.

88. See Giltner, *Moses Stuart*, 51–52 and n. 23.

89. Another translation, this by Theodor Meyer, was published at Edinburgh in 1854. And an abridgement of Keith's translation was done by Thomas K. Arnold and published in London in 1847.

90. These and other quotations from the notes of Churchill Jones Gibson are in the Gibson family papers, VTSA, no pagination.

91. Packard, *Recollections*, 95–96.

92. Goodwin, *History* 1:549.Goodwin is here summarizing the recollections of Bishop Bedell.

93. Ibid. 1:546.

94. Packard, *Recollections*, 95.

95. Ibid.

96. Ibid., 96–97.

97. Packard, *Recollections*, 96.

98. Goodwin, *History* 1:76–82.See William A. Clebsch, "The Reverend Doctor William Holland Wilmer (1782–1827): His Life, Work, and Thought"(Unpublished S.T.M. thesis, Protestant Episcopal Theological Seminary in Virginia,1951).

99. Wilmer letters, VTSA, (January 8, 1816) 6–7.

100. Ibid., 19–20, letter to Thomas G. Allen (November 18,1817).

101. See C.B. Wilmer in Goodwin, *History* 1:367.

102. Ibid. 1:373.

103. William H. Wilmer, *The Episcopal Manual* (Baltimore: E.J.Coale, 1841), iii (editor's preface).

104. Ibid. (1822), x.

105. Ibid., 45–46.

106. Ibid., 51.

107. Ibid., 49.

108. Ibid., 48.

109. Ibid., 73.

110. Ibid., 73–77.

111. Ibid., 80.

112. See Hooker, *Laws* VI.3.3.

113. See William Temple, *Personal Religion and the Life of Fellowship*, (London: Longman's, 1926) 39–40.

114. Wilmer, *Manual* (1822), 106.

115. Ibid., 138–39.

116. Ibid., 140.See John Booty, *The Godly Kingdom of Tudor England: Great Books of the English Reformation* (Wilton,Conn.: Morehouse-Barlow, 1981), chap. 1.

117. Ibid.

118. Ibid., 114ff.

119. Ibid., 151–52.

120. *Virginia Theological Seminary Semi-Centennial* (Baltimore:Virginia Seminary, 1873), 60–61, 64–65; Goodwin History1:555–58.

121. Packard, *Recollections*, 83.

122. See Goodwin, *History* 1:557.

123. Packard, *Recollections*, 84.

124. Goodwin, *History* 1:431.

—◦◦◦—

THE SEMINARY SETTLES IN THE WILDERNESS 1827–1841

1. TIMES OF OPTIMISM, TIMES OF REFORM

In 1827 the Virginia Theological Seminary moved from Alexandria into the wilderness, to a hill overlooking Alexandria, the Potomac River, and the nation's capital. In the next year Andrew Jackson was elected president, and a new era in American life began. Samuel P. Huntington has characterized the 1820s and 1830s as the Jacksonian decades.

> In politics and government these years witnessed: the introduction of universal white male suffrage and a major expansion of political participation; the fading of the congressional caucus, and the formation of national political parties and the first national political party conventions; popular election of presidential electors and the emergence of the President as the "tribune of the people." . . .[1]

Such were some of the developments that caused many to regard these decades as revolutionary. With the president the champion of "plain people" and the enemy of special interests, this was also an age of reform. There were reforms in banking, the disestablishment of the Bank of the United States and the beginning of state banking systems, as well as reforms in education and penal policies.[2] Inherent in this revolution and the accompanying reformist zeal was a philosophy called Transcendentalism, represented by clergymen such as Ralph Waldo Emerson,

Theodore Parker, and William Ellery Channing. Emerson wrote, "The power which is at once spring and regulator in all efforts of reform is the conviction that there is an infinite worthiness in man, which appears at the call of worth, and that all practical reforms are the removing of some impediment." Thus they sought to remove superstition, ignorance, poverty, and more.[3]

Reinforcing the conviction of the "worthiness of man" were the many successes involved in westward expansion and the industrial revolution, together with the growth of national identity and of the idea of progress. As John Kasson says, "From the 1820s onward, with the development of new or improved machines, modes of production, communication and transportation, and particularly after the introduction of the railroad, Americans increasingly identified the progress of the nation with the progress of technology. . . ."[4] John Adolphus Etizler wrote *The Paradise within Reach of all Men, without Labor, by Powers of Nature and Machinery* (1833). "Etizler's specific vision was certainly eccentric, but not his broader faith in the transforming power of American technology."[5] One effect of such a faith in an era of reform was the ever more complete combining of the destinies of technology and republicanism.

This spirit of optimism and reform was evident in the churches. Sidney Ahlstrom says, "The antebellum period was the great time of evangelical triumph." He goes on to explain:

> These were the days above all when the "Evangelical United Front" took up the manifold causes of moral renewal, missionary advance, and humanitarian reform—with revival preaching almost always leading the way. Its aim was to bring the gospel to all America and to heathen lands abroad, but primarily it hoped to make America the world's great example of a truly Protestant republic.[6]

Major tools for pursuing this vision were the interdenominational voluntary associations, such as societies promoting temperance and Sunday schools, missions and reformist social causes.

The Protestant Episcopal Church from 1815 to 1835 and beyond experienced the steady expansion of the church both geographically and numerically. The triennial reports to General Convention made by each diocese indicate, with a few exceptions, an almost uniform rate of progress.[7] But expansion was inhibited initially by the lack of support for new work. Recognizing a great need, the General Convention in 1820 and 1821, brought into being a voluntary society (except for the fact that all bishops and all members of the House of Deputies were automatically enrolled) called the "Domestic and Foreign Missionary Society in the United States of America." In 1835 this society was made "into an agency of *all* the Church, by declaring every baptized member of the Church to be by his baptism a member of the society."[8] Through this development the Evangelicals, both High and Low Church, were in the ascendancy. Furthermore, the Episcopal Church was in the process of gaining a stronger central power and a more thorough national identity. But as in the national political scene where parties were forming, so in the Episcopal Church, party spirit was growing during these decades. By 1837 there was a tacit agreement, never wholly accepted, that domestic missions belonged to the High Church party and foreign missions to the Evangelical Low Church party.[9]

The party spirit was fostered in America by the beginning of the Oxford movement in England in the 1830s and the importation into America of the *Tracts for the Times* with their clarion call for bishops to stand fast against the forces of political and theological liberalism; with their appeal, back beyond the deeply flawed reformation of the sixteenth century, to the examples of the medieval and early church; and with their trend toward romanticism and the adoption of post-Tridentine Roman Catholic dogma, ritual, and piety. The *Tracts* were read in America and commented on, by some positively, as by some at General Seminary; by some cautiously, as by Samuel Seabury in the *Churchman*; and by some with alarm, such as Bishops Moore and Meade, who regarded them as an assault not only on the Episcopal Church but on the Evangelical faith that they located at the heart of the gospel.

If they had any doubts, *Tract 90*, with its distortion, as they saw it, of the true doctrine of justification, ended all doubt. Early on, the *Southern Churchman* exhibited the great concern of Evangelicals concerning the *Tracts* and their influence.[10]

Less certain is the extent of influence on the Episcopal Church by the English Reform Act of 1832 and the forces involved in it, against which the Tractarians were reacting. But it is certain that reform was in the air, that liberal confidence in human worthiness and progress was widespread, even influencing such Evangelicals as seemed convinced of the depravity of man. Their confidence was not in natural man, however, but in redeemed humanity, which could aim at and accomplish great good for the physical, mental, and spiritual progress of Protestant America.

Chiefly, Virginia Seminary was committed to mission and educating men for missionary activity. It was also committed to educating young men to be faithful and orthodox Evangelicals, perpetuating the spirit of the English Reformers, withstanding arrogant liberals, Unitarians, atheists, Roman Catholics, and Tractarians. At the semicentennial celebration of the seminary in 1873, Joseph Packard, who joined the faculty in

1836, proclaimed the intention of the founders in three words. "It was to be *Protestant*," protesting against "the idolatry and superstition of the corrupt Church of Rome" and "holding in purity all the articles of the Christian faith." "It was to be an *Episcopal* Seminary," standing "firmly on the ground of Hooker and White," holding to the apostolic origin of Episcopacy, avoiding "judgement on the validity of the ministry of other Churches." "It was to be *Evangelical*," adhering to the gospel doctrine "of a complete justification by the sole merits and death of our Lord and Saviour Jesus Christ." All of these words were related to a piety and a love that "would rise as high as a Missionary temperature."[11] In this there was power to overcome obstacles and to build a school for Christians on mission, going into all the world, with expectation of ultimate triumph.

2. LIFE IN THE WILDERNESS

It was at a meeting of the board of trustees on May 17, 1827, that a committee was appointed, consisting of Wilmer, Keith, Meade, McGuire, and Col. Hugh Mercer,

> to meet in Alexandria on the third Wednesday in June at the house of Rev.
> Mr. Keith at nine o'clock A.M. to take into consideration the propriety of
> purchasing a parcel of land in the neighborhood of Alexandria and State of
> Virginia, with or without a dwelling on which to build or repair and adapt
> a house for the purpose of entertaining the Professors and pupils of the
> School, and if they shall deem it expedient to contract for the same in a
> sum not exceeding $4,500, that they also be instructed to appoint an addi-
> tional Professor, and to adopt the necessary measures for collecting funds
> for the above mentioned purposes.[12]

The reasons given for removing from the town into the wilderness were various: "Inconveniences were found to attend the residences of the students and the Professors in a town," the expense of living in town was too great, and there were too many interruptions, deflecting students from their studies. "The want of a building exclusively devoted to their use, and where they may live in the most retired manner, and in the simplest way, has been felt, and often expressed by the Professors."[13]

The committee, having reviewed a number of possibilities, chose the land which is presently the heart of the seminary campus, deeded on September 28, 1827, by Jonah Thompson and his wife.[14] It was described in these words:

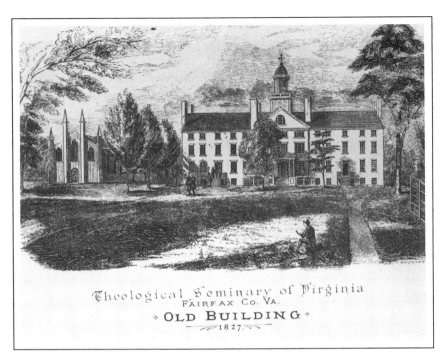

Theological Seminary of Virginia
FAIRFAX Co. VA.
OLD BUILDING
1827.

The lot of land which was purchased contained about sixty-two acres,[15] the half of which was cleared, well enclosed and covered with grass. The remainder is in young timber, which will soon yield no inconsiderable allowance of fuel. The buildings upon it consisted of a new brick dwelling house, with all necessary out buildings for the comfort of a family. A well enclosed garden and promising young orchard were also among the improvements of the place."[16]

The main house, where Keith lived, was supplemented hurriedly by the building of "a brick house, of three stories, containing 12 rooms, besides a basement story affording a dining room, kitchen, and closets."[17] This was the first major seminary building. Next there came a house built for Professor Lippitt, who until it was built was "living at an inconvenient distance." A second major building was constructed in 1832 and stood opposite the first. The two were connected in 1835 by a center building. The early campus was completed with the building of the chapel, begun in 1839 and occupied in 1840–41. A farm was maintained, and Keith and Lippitt were allotted portions of it, provided they kept "the same in good order."[18]

This remarkable achievement was made possible first by the advance of $5,000 from the board's treasurer, John Gray, to be repaid; second, by the loan of $2,000 from the Education Society; and third, by friends of the seminary who subscribed "somewhat more than eight thousand dollars," payable in annual installments over two to four years, to cover the loans and provide for further construction.[19] A third professor had been authorized, but funds for one were not available. It was estimated that it would require $30,000 to endow two professorships. The permanent funds or endowment of the seminary in 1828 amounted to $10,734.42, a sum insufficient to maintain Keith and Lippitt. The board was thus dependent upon support from the Education Society, which in 1831 informed them "that the state of their funds will not justify" continuance of an annual grant of $400 towards Keith's salary of $600.[20]

The board, convinced that the seminary had to have sufficient endowment to support its faculty, appointed a committee (consisting of Cobbs, McGuire, Ducacet, and Meade for Virginia and Henshaw, Bedell, Jackman, Mann, Tyng, Johns, and McIlvaine for outside Virginia) to raise funds.[21] By 1829 the endowment was $13,965;[22] by 1830, $17,000 "in good bonds";[23] by 1834, $20,822.80 "in good Bonds and Bank Stock";[24] and by 1840, $27,517.[25]

During this same period the student body grew from ten in 1827 to thirty-two in 1840 and forty-six in 1842. Since there was no tuition charge, the seminary, needing to expand plant and faculty, was heavily dependent upon the Education Society and other such societies around the country and upon parishes in Virginia and beyond, as well as upon other benefactors, for both day-to-day expenses and capital expansion. Student contributions toward the cost of their education, according to a report in the Southern Churchman in 1840, consisted of $80 to $90 for board "and lights," $8 to $12 for laundry (the board had authorized the building of a laundry in 1829),[26] and $8 to $12 for fuel, for a total of from $96 to $114. No charge was made for "room rent and furniture," and it was suggested that the basic expenses could be covered by grants from the Education Society.[27]

When he arrived at the seminary in 1836, Packard found its life to be austere and its buildings buried in the surrounding woods. "It was no wonder," he wrote, "that, twenty years after, Phillips Brooks lost his way in coming out to the Seminary, for the road seemed to end at no place."[28] At the time of Packard's arrival there were the central building and two wings, north and south, with thirty-six rooms, a prayer hall or chapel, and a refectory with kitchen. The library of fifteen hundred books was housed in two rooms, the wall between them removed. Chapel, refectory, and kitchen were all in the basement. He found the buildings to be a mishmash, "put up in different portions after an unrecognizable order of architecture" and destitute of ornaments. The basement was low, the halls narrow, the windows with small panes. He continued,

There were twenty-nine students in the Seminary when I came. . . . There were but two professors on "The Hill", Dr. Keith and Dr. Lippitt. The students had a common woodpile where each sawed his own wood which he carried to his room. They did not fare sumptuously every day on a board bill of $75 a year. The students took the management of the refectory pretty much into their own hands and constituted themselves an *imperium in imperio*. There would be occasionally a bread and butter rebellion when the faculty would meet the students for consultation. I remember on one occasion the difficulty was settled by resolution that the students should not be limited in their demands for fried apples.

No carpets covered the floors. The age of luxury had not yet come. It was the iron age of the Seminary. The Post Office was in Alexandria and each student in turn walked in and brought out the daily mail.[29]

From the outset life was influenced in the new location by the presence of a seminary matron, who, as Goodwin says, "was as a mother in our Seminary home" always available to the students for advice, caring for the sick. It was in the refectory "that her restraining influence was most strongly felt. The instincts of selfishness and even animalism, and the forgetfulness of the amenities and decorum of good breeding, are not totally eradicated from a man's life upon his matriculation even in a Seminary."[30] Miss Mary Dobson was the first matron. Packard notes her presence as early as 1828. She continued until 1843, when she was succeeded by Miss Mary Stuart. Packard remembers, "Miss Dobson, our first matron was once congratulated by a friend on having such a pleasant life and associating with such holy men.

She said very calmly, 'There is a great deal of mortality even among theological students.'"[31]

3. COMMITMENT TO MISSION AND MISSIONS: FOREIGN AND DOMESTIC

Dr. Goodwin writes with conviction that, "The chief glory of the Theological Seminary in Virginia has been her loyalty and devotion to the mission of the Church."[32] It is true to say, as has been observed, that the call of the gospel to "go ye into all the world and preach the gospel to every creature" was and remained a basic motive for the seminary's being and its success. It was in the period 1827 to 1841 that graduates went out to Greece, to China, and to Africa. In later years they would go to Japan, Brazil, and indeed into all the world.

John H. Hill of the class of 1830 went with his wife, Frances Maria, to

Greece immediately upon graduation and was the seminary's first missionary. He accompanied J.J. Robertson of Maryland, the first foreign missionary appointed by the church. But within two years Robertson moved to Syria, then to Constantinople, and returned to the United States in 1842. Hill, remaining in Greece for almost fifty-two years, must be accounted along with his wife the real founder of the mission. Their work was carefully designed not to offend Greek Orthodox churchmen and was chiefly known for its schools, beginning with a school started in 1831 by Frances Maria Hill. By 1841 there were a thousand students enrolled, including the daughter of the prime minister of Greece. As a part of their educational mission, the Hills founded a press that printed textbooks for the school and for other missionary schools, as well as other secular and religious books.[33]

The distinction of being the first to embark from Virginia Seminary for China belonged to Francis R. Hanson of the class of 1833. He, along with one Lockwood, was refused entrance into China and withdrew to Java, where in time he was joined in October 1837 by William J. Boone, class of 1835, and his wife.

Hanson and Lockwood returned to the United States, leaving the Boones, who studied language and arrived at Macao in 1840. With this the China mission of the Episcopal Church began, and in 1844 Boone became its first bishop. From then on there was remarkable growth.[34] From the start, Boone sought for an indigenous ordained ministry, ordaining Wang Chi a deacon in 1851, just six years after his arrival in Shanghai. As Stephen Neill says, "This concentration on the indigenous ministry was of vital importance, and proved its worth a century later in the general collapse of missions in China."[35]

The mission to Liberia in Africa was begun in 1822 when the Domestic and Foreign Mission Society appointed Mr. and Mrs. Ephraim Bacon as catechists to the newly formed colony there, the work of the American Colonization Society for the resettlement of freed slaves. But because the Colonization Society refused to support the Bacons, they did not leave the United States and the mission was at a standstill. Further attempts failed, but in time appeals from the colony prevailed, and in 1835 three men of the class of 1836 decided to devote themselves to this mission. They were Launcelot B. Minor, John Payne, who was to be the first bishop of Liberia, and Thomas S. Savage, M.D. Savage went first to work with a mission already established by laity at Cape Palmas. He also explored the country and started a school. In 1837 Minor and Payne, with his wife, joined Savage, and the work of the mission prospered, but not without difficulties.[36]

In seeking to account for the remarkable missionary spirit at the newly

founded seminary, Philip Slaughter asked Bishop Payne for an explanation. Payne reported that it was in part due to the increase of missionary
spirit generally, influenced by the memoirs of Martyn, Buchanan, Brainerd,
and others; in part by "the teachings and lives of our Professors"; and in
part by William Boone and his missionary zeal. Slaughter remembers "a
prayer-meeting, held before the break of day, in Boone's room, and conducted chiefly by Boone, Payne, Minor, and Savage. I cannot but regard
that prayer-meeting, as one of the chief motives which sent that burning
light, William Boone, on his grand mission to China."[37] Packard reports
that when he arrived at the seminary in 1836, Payne, Savage, and Minor
were preparing to go to Africa. He knew that as students they "used to
have a praying circle which met once a week at six o'clock in the morning
for prayer and converse as to the duty of going to preach the gospel to the
heathen." He then recalls that Payne in his diary for January 1835 spoke
of Boone making "a most thrilling appeal in behalf of foreign missions."
Wrote Payne,

> Never was I so deeply affected. O Lord, shall I go? He that will not leave
> father and mother, house and home, for My sake is not worthy of Me. O
> Lord, thou hast created me, Thou hast preserved me, Thou hast redeemed
> me. . . . I am thy servant and am bound by the most weighty obligations of
> duty and of love to honor and serve Thee all the days of my life. O Lord,
> here I am. If it be thy will, send me. . . . After mature deliberations and full
> survey of the risk to life and health brother Minor and myself determined
> to devote ourselves to preaching the gospel in Africa.[38]

Payne was referring to a meeting reported in the *Southern Churchman*.
It took place on the first Monday in January 1835, a day "set apart by the
students . . . as 'a day of humiliation and prayer with reference to Missions—or the state of Missions in the Church.'" There was a morning
service at which the Reverend Charles Mann preached. Mann was a member of the board of trustees, an agent of the seminary for raising funds, and
at one time was considered for a professorship in pastoral theology.[39] There
followed addresses by Keith and Lippitt. "At night the monthly concert
was observed among the students, and one of their number, Mr. Boone,
delivered an address." In his address Boone said,

> A contemplation of the missionary cause, brings us immediately in con-
> nection with all that is pure and holy. In its origins we discover the expan-
> sive benevolence, the boundless mercy and love of God; in enlisting our-
> selves as its humble friends, we associate with the holiest and best of all
> ages, who have invariably been its warmest supporters.[40]

4. THE EARLIEST SEMINARY SOCIETIES

Deeply involved in arousing concern for the church's mission was the oldest of the student organizations, founded in 1824 and called the "Society for Inquiry upon the Subject of Missions." It was designed "to inquire generally into the state of Christ's Church militant and especially into that branch of it to which the Seminary is attached."[41] The catalogue gave as the object of the society "the acquisition of missionary intelligence, and the collection of funds for missionary enterprises." The society was scheduled to meet on the first Monday evening of each month, at which time an essay on missions was to be read. There was also to be an annual sermon preached in connection with the final exercises of the seminary in July.[42] It is evident that the meeting reported in the *Southern Churchman* and referred to in Payne's diary was a meeting of this society. Boone's address was the required essay. In 1835 a circular was distributed inviting persons to join the society as life members for $10 and as patrons for $25. One of the aims expressed in this circular was that of building a library of missionary books, periodicals, and charts.[43]

There were other societies. In 1830 the Rhetorical Society was founded. According to a circular printed in 1842, "its chair is filled, ex officio, by the Professor of Pulpit Eloquence who decides each question after the debate. The association is strictly speaking a debating society, having for its object the promotion among its members of logical habits of thought, facility of expression, a manly and efficient delivery, and a general acquaintance with subjects bearing a near or remote relation to theology." There then follows a statement of considerable interest, indicating that at this early date theological students were expected to possess a general knowledge in the area now called "church and society." The circular says that the society's "main object is to enable its members . . . to keep pace with the spirit of the age, which seems to require of the clergy not only a strict acquaintance with their profession but a large share of general knowledge." The circular closed with an appeal for books to enlarge the seminary's library holdings.[44] The seminary catalogue for the following academic year states the object of the society as being "Improvement of Extemporaneous Speaking" and indicates that there were weekly meetings.[45]

Next was the Temperance Society, organized in 1834. It was dedicated to "the Promotion of the cause of Temperance," with semiannual meetings "in November and May, when addresses are delivered."[46] The Temperance Society can be understood as serving the missionary cause and as training men for evangelism. The temperance movement developed in close association with evangelism, as did other reform movements. Ahlstrom notes that "the

American Society for the Promotion of Temperance was formed in Boston in 1826 by men active in the missionary movement."[47] Which is to say that the temperance movement arose out of the piety of Evangelicals with its emphasis on proclamation and reform.

The fourth society in the earliest days was the "Society for the Moral and Religious Improvement of the neighborhood of the Seminary." Its object was "to establish Sunday schools and Bible classes; to distribute tracts, and to use such other means as prudence may dictate to exert a healthy moral influence in the surrounding neighborhood." It met monthly with the professor of pastoral theology as president, according to the 1842–43 catalogue, which notes that it was "reorganized March, 1839."[48] The president was Bishop Meade, elected Assistant Bishop of Virginia and named by the board of trustees professor of pastoral theology in 1833.[49]

It was Bishop Bedell who linked in his reminiscences the "Missionary Society of Inquiry" with "practical efforts for 'improving the religious and moral condition of the neighborhood.'"[50] "Field education" at that time was engagement in mission. As Bedell remembers, "We were taught to put the principles of the recitation room and chapel into immediate practice in neighboring Sunday schools, in alms-houses, in tract distribution, and in visiting among the poor, from house to house, with prayer and exhortations."[51] As Goodwin points out, this activity began in Alexandria and continued in the wilderness and was the beginning of the seminary missions. "When the Seminary moved out on 'The Hill', gradually Mission Stations were established in the neighborhood," he wrote, "where Sunday Schools were conducted and the Church services held by the students who were also given license to make exhortation." This work was assisted by the faculty who took the sacraments to the stations.[52] Professor Wallis stated that the church, otherwise absent in the area around the seminary, was planted and tended by students. "They generally began by going about from house to house, on Sunday afternoons, holding short religious services wherever it was possible, chiefly in the form of modified prayer meetings, if we may use that expression, as it must be remembered there was very little education amongst the people in those days."[53]

5. THE EPISCOPAL HIGH SCHOOL

The missionary work of the students in the neighborhood involved a concern for the general education of the people. At the 1835 Virginia convention, the seminary board of trustees reported that "a Bible Society has been formed in the institution, and a Charity School for the benefit of the neighboring poor."[54] In 1831 the widow of William H. Wilmer opened a school adjacent to the seminary in a house called Howard. The Howard School for Boys was limited to eighteen pupils. The teachers were Jonathan Loring Woart and John Woart, alumni of the seminary in the classes of 1831 and 1834.[55] The school closed in 1834, and in February 1835 the *Southern Churchman* announced that Mrs. Wilmer intended "to open an academy for females . . . at her residence near Virginia Theological Seminary,"[56] an enterprise endorsed by Charles Mann, Reuel Keith, and E.R. Lippitt. It evidently did not last, for by 1839 the property was in the possession of Dr. William Alexander. The proximity of the Howard School to the seminary meant that the two institutions inevitably interacted. Packard relates that there was some "friction between the boys . . . and the Seminary students, and the boys used to invent ways of teasing them. They would put ropes on the stile to trip them up on their way to see the Misses Fairfax, and played many other tricks."[57]

At the Virginia convention of 1837, J.P.B. Wilmer proposed that, the diocese having "no institution of learning" adequate to meet the needs of "sons of our Episcopal families," the existent schools being either "sectarian in their character, or totally unorganized and desultory in their operations," a school should be founded. The convention agreed.[58] The responsibility was assumed by the seminary board of trustees. They did so arguing that such a school would be useful in preparing men who should later enroll in the seminary and that being in close proximity to the seminary would provide "religious as well as literary education."[59] It was perhaps at this time that Packard went with Bishop Meade to look over the Howard property as the site for the new school.[60]

On May 15, 1839, the trustees reported to the Virginia convention that the school was in process of formation, a principal secured, funds being raised, a committee appointed to see the plans executed, and a chapel under construction for use by the seminary and the school.[61] The Reverend William N. Pendleton was chosen to be the Principal. He was a friend of the seminary, a colleague of Packard's at Bristol College, and a professor at Newark College, Delaware.[62] The plans were approved by the convention, and on May 17 the board met with Pendleton,[63] a decision was made to call it Howard High School, and enrollment was limited to thirty with none under fourteen years of age. Tuition was to be $200 and sons of clergy were to be taken at half price, while those who could not pay at all were to be taken for nothing.[64] A board committee went north to investigate schools at Andover and Flushing. The Reverend Milo Mahan, a teacher at Flushing and a student of William Augustus Muhlenberg, was hired as an assistant master, and with money provided by Meade and friends, the seventy-seven-acre Howard tract adjacent to the seminary was purchased for $5,000. Later "$12,000 was subscribed for buildings and equipment."[65]

In his report to the Virginia convention of 1840, Pendleton said that the high school began operation on October 15, 1839, with thirty-five pupils—ranging in age from eleven to twenty—and four instructors, including the principal. The main building, designed to accommodate one hundred pupils, was well under way. Most of his report concerns the instruction being given, both literary and religious. Of literary studies he wrote,

> The subjects which have been taught are Arithmetic, Algebra, Geometry and general Physics, to a class of 16 of the older boys—most of the same youths carrying at the same time the careful study of higher Latin and Greek authors, accompanied by frequent exercises in writings, translations, and occasional exercises in declamation and composition.

> A second class, less advanced, has been pursuing a similar course, though in subordinate grades; and so for several classes, some of whom are also pursuing the study of geography and History—and some also requiring to be exercised in ordinary reading and spelling: all being engaged with the necessary practice of writing.

Concerning religious instruction, Pendleton reported,

> Religious instruction has engaged my special care—and this consists of the daily household devotions, the Sunday exercises at the Seminary, with classes principally conducted by myself each Sunday—and the occasional study of short works on religious subjects. About twenty of the elder youths have since October carefully studied with me Bishop Porteus' Evidences of Christianity, and the excellent treatise of Scougal on "The life of Jesus in the soul of man." It has also been understood, and from the first punctually practised as a rule of the school, that each scholar recognize, and for himself perform, the regular duties of personal prayer, and reading of the Scriptures morning and evening.[66]

The *Southern Churchman* reported that, in addition to Porteus and Scougal, "Whately on Rhetoric and Logic, Watts, Locke, and others on the Mind, Paley's and Wayland's Moral Philosophy, Paley's Natural Theology, Butler's Analogy, and other works on the evidences of Christianity" were in use at the school.[67] With varying degrees of success, Pendleton sought to enlist the aid of the seminary professors in this work.[68] Cornelius Walker indicates that Sparrow taught at the high school for two sessions.[69]

Perhaps the most important connection between faculty and students of the seminary with faculty and students of the high school was their worship together every Sunday, along with another neighborhood school, necessitating the construction of an adequate seminary chapel.[70] The chapel, although incomplete, was consecrated at the final exercises of the seminary in 1840 in a special service. One eye witness reported the emotional impact of that service in which thirty-seven ratified "their baptismal vows, of whom four were adult males, three were white females, three were colored, and twenty-seven were members of the two schools located near the Seminary."[71] Pendleton wrote of the "gracious visitation from on high," "whereby nearly every pupil at the school; if not every one, has been within the last few weeks solemnly awakened to a deep religious concern."[72]

The school at first prospered; in the 1841–42 session there were one hundred ten boys. But it then declined, incurring serious financial debts. The principal was forced to close the school in 1844, and operations were suspended until the Reverend Edward A. Dalrymple of Maryland was named "rector" of a renewed institution, beginning over again in 1845 with nine boys.[73] With the exception of the Civil War years when it was closed, the high school continued under the seminary board of trustees until 1923, when it became independent.

6. THE SEMINARY FACULTY:
THE COMING OF PACKARD AND SPARROW

From 1827 to 1836 the full-time faculty of the seminary consisted of Keith and Lippitt. From the time of the move into the wilderness, the board had been seeking a third professor but at first was prevented by insufficient finances.[74] In 1835 William Sparrow of Kenyon College was elected but declined.[75] At a special meeting of the executive committee of the board on October 28, 1835, Joseph Packard, "a professor in Bristol College, Pennsylvania," was appointed contingent upon "further satisfactory inquiries" as to his qualifications.[76] Packard, born in Maine in 1812, was educated at Bowdoin College, where Henry Wadsworth Longfellow was professor of modern languages and librarian. Longfellow taught Packard French and made him assistant librarian. While at Bowdoin, Packard was converted to Christianity.[77] He was attracted to the Episcopal Church by its liturgy and was confirmed. He taught briefly at Brattleboro Academy in Vermont and then went to Andover Seminary, where, according to his testimony, Moses Stuart "exerted a greater influence upon my life and character than any other man I have ever known."[78]

From Andover, Packard went to Bristol College, near Philadelphia, where he was "Professor of Latin, Hebrew, and some other branches." There he came to know benefactors of the college, including Bedell, Tyng, Milnor, and Bishop Meade. Packard as an Evangelical was at home in this Evan-

Joseph Packard   William Sparrow

gelical college, but his tenure there was curtailed when the college closed its doors in 1836.[79] He was ordained a deacon by Bishop Griswold at St. Paul's Church, Boston, on July 17, 1836,[80] and, having been called to teach at the seminary, left for Alexandria in October. He was ordained to the priesthood by Bishop Meade "in the basement of the Seminary" on September 29, 1837, "a very solemn occasion for me."[81] Packard remained at the seminary until his death in 1902 and thus will emerge as a central actor in the drama of the seminary as it unfolds.

A staunch and at times quite conservative Evangelical who loved the church, its ministry, and its liturgy much as did Simeon and Meade, Packard was a teacher better known for his piety than for his scholarship. The great event of his scholarly life was his association with Schaff on a revision of the Bible, Packard serving on the Old Testament committee and being invited by Schaff to "write the commentary on Malachi in his edition of Lange's Commentary."[82] Carl Grammer, who taught on the faculty from 1887 to 1898, recalls Packard's teaching as professor of biblical literature.

His interpretations might be at times too literal, but he was always guided by a sound literary instinct. He never allowed himself to be drawn into farfetched and tenuous deductions from slender premises, and not being a systematic theologian, did not try to force a vast and complicated theology into the text. He used to pour quiet contempt on the Churchly exegetes, who are always trying to force their system into the Bible. . . . He has a great dislike of ponderous discussion on matters that could be settled by a little common sense in interpretation. He would call such argumentation "shooting a cannonball at a fly."

Of course he followed the scholars of his day in finding Messianic references everywhere in the Old Testament, even in such an epithalamium as the Forty fifth Psalm. What else could be expected of a scholar who had helped his revered leader, Dr. Keith, to get through the press his translation of Hengstenberg's Christology?[83]

Often professing that "the old is better," Packard had little interest in the changes taking place around him either in scholarship or in churchly customs. He was, as Grammer says, "moderately Calvinistic, a believer in the highest views of Inspiration . . . an Evangelical Churchman of the type of Bishop Johns,"[84] and he remained so throughout his life. According to those who knew him best, he was a kindly man who mellowed with age and was admired by students and appreciated by younger faculty.

Some time in 1840 William Sparrow was elected for a second time a professor in the seminary and, according to Packard, "came in that year to visit the Seminary" and preached at Christ Church, Alexandria.[85] Packard called him "the Seminary's greatest professor,"[86] and we shall have reason to consider him and his thought along the way. Here it must be noted that he was born in Charlestown, Massachusetts, in 1801 and was educated in Ireland, to which he returned with his parents. There he came under strong Evangelical influences. Returning to the United States, he studied briefly at Columbia University and was influenced by Dr. Milnor. In 1822 he joined his family in Ohio, became acquainted with Bishop Philander Chase, taught Latin and Greek at Miami University, and was ordained by Chase in 1826. He taught at Chase's school at Worthington, eventually in the theology department there, and in 1833 moved to Gambier, Ohio. He became vice president and chief executive of Kenyon College and taught ecclesiastical history and then systematic theology in the theological department and was professor of moral philosophy in the college.[87] Sparrow left Kenyon, no longer able to cope with a situation in which the bishop had the final say over the actual operating head of the college. There was also a question of salary and the need to support more adequately a growing family.

When first arriving at the seminary in the spring of 1841, Sparrow taught church history and "had classes in Mental and Moral Science, and Political Economy" at the high school. Keith's health then declined, and Sparrow was required to take up his teaching in "Systematic Divinity and Christian Evidences," subjects Sparrow preferred. He had come to the seminary acknowledged by one of his colleagues at Kenyon to be an accomplished scholar, especially in "the mental and moral philosophies. He had mastered every able book on these subjects" and was able to write a better book on either subject than any then existing.[88] As to Sparrow's piety, there is nothing more illuminative than his diary, composed in the tradition of the English Evangelicals, the Venns and the Thorntons. For instance:

January 28, 1834. I have entered upon the important duty of a theological class. How unequal am I to the task. How imperfect my furniture of talent, strength, knowledge, heart and spirit. Lord, pity and guide, enlighten and direct me. . . .

March 12. Another birthday has come, but there is little to cheer me in the recurrence. My whole life seems to be nothing more than a blot. Nothing has been done for Christ, or His Church, or the world. Time has been frittered away. . . . Lord pardon and help me. . . .

May 25. My religion is seated too much in my head, and too little in my heart . . . I study religion too much as a science, and having to do this in poor health, with little vigor of mind and body, it leaves me little time or ability for private religious exercises. . . .[89]

Such a piety, publicly conveyed in the pulpit and the classroom, strongly recommended Sparrow to Meade, Keith, Lippitt, and Packard. So too did his churchmanship, his devotion to the Prayer Book, and his support of episcopacy, so long as bishops did not become too powerful.[90]

Sparrow's early Evangelicalism was to be broadened, as his grandson Carl Grammer said, "by his studies in Butler and Paley, by his reading of Coleridge and Issac Taylor, by the teachings of Whately and Arnold, not to speak of the sanity and moderation of the excellent though uninspiring Knapp, whose theology he used as a textbook. His liberal tendencies were manifest in his theory of the will, in his views of the elevation of woman, and questions of that character, and in general by his reliance upon the spirit-illumined reason."[91] He never ceased to regard himself as an Evangelical. Phillips Brooks located Sparrow's genius in the singular unity or harmony of intellect and spirit in the man. "The best result of his work in influence on any student's life and ministry must have been to save him from the hardness on the one hand, or the weakness on the other, which purely intellectual or purely spiritual training would have produced."[92] It was under the influence of his Evangelical piety as modified by his broad reading in modern English theology that Sparrow trusted in spirit-illumined reason. "Seek the truth, come whence it may, cost what it will," the closing words of a classroom discussion, were chosen by Dr. Norton as a fitting inscription for his teacher's monument. "He taught us," said Bishop Brooks in an address at the seminary, "that however far thought might travel, it would still find God."[93]

7. THE COURSE OF STUDY IN THE EARLY YEARS

Students and faculty were engaged in a course of study dictated in the first place by the House of Bishops' list (1804), the rules established in 1825 by the board of trustees, and the gifts and limitations of a small faculty. In 1829 there appear to have been two classes. First year students, of whom there were seven, studied evidences and the New Testament in the fall, using Horne's *Introduction* and Ernesti's *Interpretation*. In January they began the study of Hebrew and read fifteen chapters of Genesis "and are now pursuing their studies by the aid which the Hebrew Chrestomathy of Professor Stuart affords." They were required each week to turn into the professor "original compositions on the most important proofs of Divine Revelation, and occasionally, a critical dissertation on some difficult passages of the New Testament."

The second or senior class had been examined "on nearly the whole of Mosheim's Church History, with reference to Milner, and such other ecclesiastical histories as the library afforded." In addition, "they were engaged in the critical study of the Epistles in Greek and of the Prophet Isaiah in Hebrew." They completed a "comprehensive system of Scriptural Divinity," in accordance with the rules of the seminary, with the Bible as the sole textbook, prior "to the examination of human systems, and the articles of our Church."[94]

A decade later the faculty produced their own reports attached to the board's annual report to Convention. Reuel Keith, as professor of systematic divinity and teacher of pulpit eloquence, reported in 1839 that he had held six recitations or lectures each week, had attended chapel each Wednesday to criticize sermons delivered by students, and lectured "once a week on the internal evidences of the divine origin of the Bible and the nature of its inspiration." By then there were clearly three classes, Keith indicating that he met the junior class once, the middle class and the senior class three times a week. The juniors were studying "Horne on the Evidences" and Butler's Analogy. The middlers were studying biblical theology. And the seniors were studying Burnet on the Articles and Pearson on the Creed, finishing with Whately's Logic.[95]

E.R. Lippitt, as professor of pastoral theology and church polity, reported that he had instructed the seniors using "Bridges on Christian

Ministry," in his judgment the best textbook on the subject. He supplemented Bridges with references made to "Burnet on Pastoral Care" and "Bishop White on the Ordination Services." In church polity Lippitt used "Onderdonk's Episcopacy tested by Scripture," "Potter on Church Government," "Barrow on the Pope's Supremacy," "Wheatley on the Book of Common Prayer," with reference to "Palmer's Origines Liturgicac" and "Bishop Brownell's edition of the Prayer Book." As he wrote his report, the students were studying "Hooker's Ecclesiastical Polity" and had already read "the first four books." Finally, they studied the constitution and canons of the Protestant Episcopal Church.

As the "acting Professor of Ecclesiastical History" Lippitt reported that he "instructed the middlers two days a week in church history, using Murdock's translation of Mosheim as the textbook, with reference to Milner, especially at the period of the Reformation." He concluded his report bemoaning the lack of "works of reference" on church history in the seminary library.[96]

Joseph Packard, as professor of biblical literature, reported dedicating two hours a week to recitation. The juniors had read Genesis, making use of Stuart's chrestomathy. In Greek they had read the Gospel of John, consulting a Greek harmony. In addition they worked through Moses Stuart's Hebrew and Greek grammars. "Instruction has also been given in the principles of Interpretation, Jewish Antiquities, and the Geography and Chronology of Scripture." In addition the juniors have written "critical essays on the most difficult and important subjects in the Gospels, such as the Apparent Discrepancies of the Evangelists, the Genealogies of Christ, the Demoniacs of the New Testament, and the Nature and Object of the Temptation of Christ, an Analysis of the Sermon on the Mount, and others." The middlers had started the Epistles to the Romans and Hebrews "and carefully examined in Hebrew the prophecies relating to Christ in the Old Testament, following the order set down by Hengstenberg."

As librarian, Packard reported that he had spent sixteen hundred dollars on additions to the library, including "the most valuable works, chiefly in Pastoral Theology, of the Divines of the Church of England, as well as those of the Dissenters. About six hundred volumes, chiefly of English editions, which necessarily enhanced their cost, have been added to the Library."[97]

The faculty may have been small at this time, but so were the classes. In 1839 there were six seniors, eight middlers, and five juniors.[98] The next year the entering class numbered seventeen, an amazing fact, prompting Packard to remark that "the present is the largest class which he has ever been privileged to instruct."[99]

The catalogues for this time basically confirm what we have learned from the professors, except that the catalogue list of works studied in systematic divinity, gives more details than Keith provided in his report. After a description of the subject taken from the Rules and Regulations (1825), textbooks are listed: the Bible, Pearson on the Creed, and Burnet's exposition of the Thirty-Nine Articles. Reference books include "the Homilies. Stackhouse. Dwight's Theology. Dick's Theology."[100] Here for the first time is listed George Christian Knapp's *Lectures on Christian Theology*, translated by Leonard Woods of Andover Seminary (2 volumes, 1831), a book that was to become the textbook for the study of theology in the seminary for many years.

Knapp was a member of the theology faculty at Halle, where he was a professor from 1777, and from 1785 a director of the Franke Institutes. Woods spoke of "his strictly evangelical piety" and his opposition to growing "rationalism and unbelief."[101] Knapp's theology was described as "Biblical Theology." He wrote, "The Bible is the proper source of our knowledge of those truths of religion, which Christians receive as revealed. The New Testament is the more immediate source of the *Christian* system." He did not, however, neglect reason and tradition. "Reason (Vernunft) is the power, which guides and regulates, by its spontaneous action, the other faculties of our minds in the acquisition of knowledge" and has a role to play in relation to revelation. "Without the use of reason," he says, "we cannot ascertain the truth of Christianity, the credibility of the history of the sacred books, their divine authority, or the rules by which they should be interpreted." Tradition as *paradosis*, oral or written instruction handed on, has its place, but a limited place beside Scripture; it is not, as the Reformers taught, "a sure source of knowledge respecting the doctrines of theology."[102] Knapp was far less clear concerning the proper role of tradition than he was concerning the role of reason. We note the entrance of Knapp into the curriculum here in part because of its importance for the future and the fact that it was there before Sparrow's arrival.

Finally, in this section, we must recognize the great importance put on the public examinations of students at the conclusion of each academic year. They took place at the time of the Alumni Society annual meeting and were thus assured of a considerable audience. The examinations and colloquies were held in July and usually lasted for three days. While there is no mention in reports of the examinations in the early days of anyone failing, the events must have been entered into by students with some anxiety. Bishops Moore and Meade were usually present, along with other members of the board of trustees, some of the managers of the Education Society, and sometimes other bishops such as Bishop Kemper, who attended the 1836 examinations.[103] The examinations were followed by a kind of graduation exercise, and concluded with the ordination of deacons.

It was the custom for the professors, and others, to ask questions of students. One observer remarked in 1839 that improvements could be made in the examinations; a more adequate place where the audience could better hear the students as they read essays and delivered addresses, and more carefully prepared questions that would elicit from students replies more extensive than "a brief negation or affirmation."[104] The chapel soon to be built would meet the first objection, providing the necessary space.

In 1840 essays read by juniors and middlers ranged from "The literal or figurative interpretation of 'This is my body'" by John M. Todd to "The Doctrine of Justification" by Joseph Earnest.[105] Public examinations at the high school were held following the ordination of deacons at the seminary. In 1841 there were present at the examinations two missionaries, Hill from Greece and Payne from Liberia.[106] That year the ordinations were held at Fredricksburg rather than at Alexandria, as was the custom, and Payne delivered the sermon.[107]

8. THE DEVELOPING ORGANIZATION OF THE SEMINARY

The seminary in those early years was very much a diocesan institution, although from the beginning it was meant to serve the entire church. Its board of trustees was elected by the Virginia convention. The Bishop of Virginia was its president. Its faculty was chosen by the board, and the textbooks were approved by the board. Thus in 1836 the board specified that Keith should teach systematic divinity. Pulpit eloquence (homiletics to future generations) was added to Keith's chair "till such time as further provision can be made for the same." Packard was to teach "Sacred Literature." Lippitt was to teach church polity and pastoral care, "with instruction in Church History 'till further provision is made for that branch of study."[108] The curriculum was determined by the board, in accordance with the board regulations of 1825.

In 1830 the board created "an Executive Committee of three . . . to act during the recess of this Board whose duty it shall be to carry into execution the measures of the Board, to exercise a general superintendance over the Seminary and its concerns, and to adopt such measures in relation to it (subject always to the revision of the Board) as its exigencies from time to time demand."[109] From that moment the executive committee was to be a vital force in the seminary's life. Its first three members were Bishop Meade, vice president of the board; E.C. McGuire, secretary; and John Gray, treasurer.

There was no dean. At the annual meeting of the board of trustees in May 1837, it was proposed to the faculty that one of the professors "should exercise superintendance and act as an organ of intercourse and communication with the board of trustees." This was to be "for the good order of the Seminary." The idea was that each of the professors in rotation, by seniority of age, should "act as Chairman of the Board of Professors for one year," calling and presiding at meetings of the faculty, keeping a record of proceedings, making a full report to the board of trustees at their annual meeting, including "an account of the general conduct of the students—the course of their studies, and any other matters which a majority of the Trustees may deem it proper to report—and do and perform all such other offices and duties as generally devolve on the President or Provost of a College or Theological Seminary." Furthermore, he was to address students, trustees, and others at the annual examinations in July, as he began his term of office.[110]

On July 13, 1837, a special meeting of the board of trustees was called at which the faculty reply was received, stating that the faculty already had its organization with "a Chairman and Secretary appointed by ourselves," was accustomed to fulfilling as a body the duties specified for the chairman, was ready to do whatever more was required, and objected to the idea of a rotating chairmanship.[111] The faculty had in mind the regulations of 1825, which stated that "the Bishop and Professors shall constitute a faculty, and meet according to *their own rules*." It is fair to assume that with three faculty in place, Keith as senior was chairman and Lippitt, as indicated by the letter to the board, was secretary. The board could then have insisted upon its instructions for the organization of the faculty, but it did not. It withdrew its proposal and acquiesced "in the private organization of the Faculty." As the letter from the faculty indicates, the practical function of the chairman of the faculty only applied when the president was not present.

In December 1837 the board met in an emergency meeting to consider the threatened resignation of Professor Keith. The problem would seem to have been financial, for at the special meeting, at which there was no quorum, those present adopted "measures" with "reference to the continuance of Dr. Keith's connection with the Seminary, these measures being subject to the future sanction of the Board of Trustees."[112] At the annual meeting in May 1838, Keith was granted a salary increase of "$250 per annum."[113] There is no indication that Keith had contemplated resignation as the result of the board's request for a rotating chairmanship of the faculty. He had, after all, won that battle, forcing the board to withdraw its request. But it would have been natural for him to have felt some offence. An increase in salary always is soothing to offended faculty members.

The next critical step in organization came in 1857 when the board requested the faculty to organize "with a Dean as President,"[114] and in 1868 the board appointed Sparrow as dean.[115] The records show that the organization so familiar in the twentieth century only gradually emerged in the nineteenth. Although the board provided for a dean in 1857 and appointed Sparrow dean in 1868, the 1874–75 Catalogue of the institution lists the faculty with no mention of a dean, but with the clear designation of the Bishop of Virginia as President.[116] Nevertheless, it seems clear that Sparrow was in fact the first Dean. The 1880–1881 catalogue lists Packard as dean and makes no mention of a president.[117]

9. MEADE AS PRESIDENT: THE LAW OF PROPORTION

The year of 1841 was of major significance in the life of the seminary. It was in that year that Bishop Moore died and William Sparrow began his teaching on the Hill. In 1842 the two men who held the seminary together for so long, Keith and Lippitt, were gone, the first having died,[118] and the other having resigned in January 1841 to become the third editor of the *Southern Churchman*.[119] Lippitt was no longer on the faculty, but he was close by, the offices of the paper having been moved from Richmond to Alexandria, to the corner of Fairfax Street and Printer's Alley, and the editor having continued to reside at the seminary.[120] Lippitt was editor until 1848, the paper being at that time in the care of the board of trustees, who were the chief stockholders.

With Moore's death, Meade became chairman of the board of trustees and president of the seminary. He had long before exerted a strong influence in seminary affairs and had begun to teach as professor of pastoral theology. We know much about his activities as vice president and then president from the board minutes and from reports (his own and the board's to the Virginia convention). Reference will be made to these activities as we proceed. Concerning his teaching of pastoral theology, which occurred in his yearly lectures to the senior class in the midst of his busy life as bishop, our best evidence is to be found in the lectures as published in 1849.[121]

A major portion of the Lectures (4–14) was concerned with preaching. Lectures 1–3 dealt with the ordained ministry: power, holiness, and performance. Lecture 15 was on the sacraments and, in connection with confirmation, religious instruction of the young. Lecture 16 was on pastoral duties, lectures 17–18 on weaknesses and improprieties that hinder the "minister's usefulness," and lecture 19 (the last) on ordination vows and subscription. Imbedded in the lectures on preaching is one (lecture 7) on the "law of proportion," which incorporates a major section of Meade's pastoral address to the clergy and laity of Virginia entitled *The Law of Proportion in the Church of God*, published in 1843.[122]

The *Lectures* exhibit the accumulated wisdom of an Evangelical bishop, one dedicated to the gospel, wary of Rome and Tractarianism, devoted to the doctrine of justification and to the ministry and discipline of the Protestant Episcopal Church, imbued with the spirit of Anglicanism as most profoundly demonstrated by his treatment of proportion as a law, relying for his understanding on Richard Hooker but also upon other Anglican divines. He began by saying,

> In the last lecture I maintained that Christ should be the great and constant theme of discourse. But lest you should suppose that I thereby encouraged the neglect of any part of God's word, I shall now speak of the duty of weighing well the comparative importance of every doctrine and duty in order to lay the proper emphasis thereon. It is of great importance, that ministers of religion form a right estimate of the relative value of the different parts of the great scheme of redemption, lest by forming a wrong judgment we disturb the proportion of the whole, thereby throwing into confusion what God appointed to be all order and harmony, and greatly weakening what he designed to be power and strength.[123]

Meade had in mind zealots who disturb the truth by emphasizing one part to the neglect of others. He also had in mind persons who constantly seek the middle ground, to avoid controversy. "Truth is not that which always lies just halfway between the opposing parties or opinions. That is truth which God's word teaches, that is duty which it commands, and it is our part humbly and diligently to seek it out."[124]

Meade, who was no stranger to controversy himself, believed that what was ultimately important was the attitude or demeanor of the participants. In *The Law of Proportion* he wrote,

> It would greatly help us to avoid the evils, and receive all the benefits of controversy, if we would carefully attend to the principle for which we are pleading, and let our zeal be proportioned to the certainty and importance of the things discussed. While we are bound earnestly to contend for the faith—the great principles of religion essential to salvation—so held by the great body of Christians in every age—we should maintain all other things according to the place, which a dispassionate consideration of scripture, and observation upon their effects, seem to assign them.[125]

He goes on to point to the example established by the English Reformers.

Meade's important sermon, given on February 15, 1840, before the faculty and students of the seminary, has been touched upon in chapter 1.[126] Here I would point out that that sermon is in line with the *Lectures* and *The Law of Proportion*. His text was 1 Thess. 5:21 ("Prove all things;

hold fast that which is good"). His title was "The Wisdom, Moderation, and Charity of the English Reformers and of the Fathers of the Protestant Episcopal Church in the United States."[127] *Wisdom, moderation,* and *charity* were not only words to describe the Reformers and fathers but goals expected in the education of men for ordained ministry. The sermon expects that students will "diligently . . . critically . . . candidly"—this is true of all ministers—"study the sacred Scriptures, seeking the whole truth, that they may regulate their principles and ministrations accordingly, and thus 'be perfect, thoroughly furnished unto every good work.'" Recognizing the divisions and parties in the church, "the candidate for orders has also to examine and decide, as to what division of the Church militant he must choose," and be able to give "good counsel" to the people concerning "the diversity of sentiments on various points of order, doctrine, and practice." To his mind the English Reformers provided the best example to be followed in such matters, employing that which is essential to salvation which for him was focused in the doctrine of justification, called by Luther *"articulus stantis vel cadentis ecclesiae" "bringing* forth a system which at the same time frowns indignantly upon all needless and petty disputations, or metaphysical niceties, yet boldly protests against all false doctrine, heresy, and schism." Meade himself, in a footnote to the sermon, protested "that in the writings of some of the Oxford divines [Tractarians], the consecrated language of Scripture, of the articles and homilies, is set aside and another language used" to the detriment of the fundamental doctrine of justification. There is a delicate balance here, between adhering to the essentials of faith and allowing the operation of private judgment, in a spirit of moderation, according to the rule of adiaphora.

Meade insisted upon the virtues of wisdom, moderation, and charity and located them in the church's formularies, citing in particular the Articles of Religion on Scripture and predestination. Such an attitude or demeanor requires the acceptance of diversity in the church and agreement "to differ and bring no railing accusations against each other." Bishops and seminary professors have the responsibility to defend the faith in every essential, but the bishop is not at liberty to reject candidates for the ministry who differ with him in things nonessential. Meade wrote,

The applicant for orders may be a thorough Calvinist, or decided Arminian, an ultra High-Churchman, or the very lowest who can conscientiously subscribe the appointed testimonials, and utter the ordination vows, and the ordaining Bishop may be the opposite in sentiments to the candidate; the views of the candidate may be freely declared in his examination, and as freely condemned by the Bishop; the Bishop may argue, remonstrate, and warn, appealing to the Sacred Scriptures; and yet, except the whole past history of the Church be forgotten, and its practice despised, and its spirit of moderation be gone, and a new order of things be introduced, the Bishop will proceed to ordain him, and all the brethren must receive him as a true son of the Church and minister of Heaven.[128]

Meade's treatment of the external organization of the Church exhibits the same wisdom, moderation, and charity. He believed that the English Reformers, with the Bible in their hands, did right when they held fast to episcopal government for the church, a government purged of all "superadded by the folly, pride, ambition, and superstition of man." But he argued against all efforts to unchurch others because they did not have episcopacy. Ultimately it is piety that matters. A person may be deficient in externals but adhere to "the foundation," which is Jesus Christ, the head of the Church. "We must not remove him from his place, to put any King, Pope, or other officer or form of government in his room."

Meade concluded,

I have thus, my young friends—candidates for the glorious ministry of Christ— set before you what has ever appeared to me to be the ground assumed by our forefathers, in relation to the points noticed in this address. I delight ever to tread that ground, for I believe there is peace there. To depart from it, would, I am sure, lead to unhappy contention. . . .

On the points, then, where our fathers differed, and agreed to differ, let us not be positive and dogmatic, or we shall certainly be uncharitable. Let us agree that there be some things, even in the Scriptures, hard to be understood, and about which the wise and pious of every age have certainly differed.

Let us ascertain what are the great, important and undoubted truths, and hold them fast. Let us show our zeal for religion, and love to the Church, not by extravagant devotion to opinions about which men have differed and will differ, but holding fast those things which are delivered to us in our good book of prayer, for our devotion and our observance.

It is not weakness or bigotry, my young friends, to love the forms, the ceremonies, the prayers, the government of our Church. . . . I have not much hope of usefulness from one who does not ardently love the Church; who does not enter fully into all the beauties and excellencies of her Liturgy, and all the admirable advantages of her Apostolic form of government. In order that you may love them, therefore, I pray you to study them, not in a spirit of bigotry . . . but that you may see all that is excellent in them, and point it out to the people. . . . In this, and all other studies in which you shall engage, may the Spirit of truth ever be with you, to lead you into all truth, to pre- serve you at one and the same time, from all narrow and unworthy views of

God's mercy and grace, and from that false liberality, which would allow every man to think and act as he pleases. . . .[129]

Such was the attitude and demeanor of William Meade, which he impressed upon students and faculty in the Seminary's antebellum, formative years.

NOTES

1. Samuel P. Huntington, *American Politics: The Promise of Disharmony* (Cambridge, Mass.: Harvard, 1981).
2. Ibid., 116–117.
3. Cited in Allan Nevins and Henry Steele Commager, *A Pocket History of the United States*, 7th ed. (New York: Pocket Books, 1981), 173. See Anne C. Rose, *Transcendentalism as a Social Movement, 1830–1850* (New Haven and London: Yale, 1981).
4. John F. Kasson, *Civilizing the Machine: Technology and Republican Values in America, 1776–1900* (Harmondsworth: Penguin Books, 1976), 41.
5. Ibid., 42.
6. Sidney E. Ahlstrom, *A Religious History of the American People* (New Haven and London: Yale, 1972), 387.
7. James Thayer Addison, *The Episcopal Church in the United States, 1789–1931* (New York: Scribner, 1951), 126. He illustrates this by noting that in 1817 the clergy number 261; in 1835, 763.
8. Lawrence L. Brown, "1835 and All That: Domestic and Foreign Missionary Society Membership and The Missionary Spirit," *Historical Magazine of the Protestant Episcopal Church* (1971), 399. See the rest of this article and the material to which it refers.
9. See Addison, *Episcopal Church*, 132, and Brown, "1835 And All That," 403.
10. See *Southern Churchman* 5/14 (April 5, 1839), editorial, and Bishop Moore's address to Convention, 5/21 (May 24, 1839): 82.
11. *Semi-Centennial Celebration of the Theological Seminary of the Protestant Episcopal Church in the Diocese of Virginia. Held on the 24th and 25th Days of September, 1873* (Baltimore: Virginia Seminary, 1873), 18–20
12. Goodwin, *History* 2:602–603; bd. min. 1:61–62.
13. Ibid. 2:603; bd. min. 1:64–65.
14. Ibid. 1:159.
15. Ibid. fifty-nine and one-quarter acres according to the deed cited by Goodwin.
16. Diocese of Virginia, *Journal of Proceedings* (1828), 31.
17. Ibid.
18. Goodwin, *History* 2:605; bd. min. 1:73–74.
19. Diocese of Virginia, *Journal* (1828), 31.
20. Goodwin, *History* 2:635–36, and treasurer's report, 1831, in Diocese of Vir-

ginia, *Journal* (1831), 31. It is of interest to note that the treasurer recorded receipt of $150 from Keith as "one year's rent of his house and half of the Seminary farm" in 1828; Diocese of Virginia, *Journal* (1828), 33.

21. Diocese of Virginia, *Journal* (1828), 32; Goodwin, *History* 2:604; bd. min. 1:68.
22. Treasurer's report, May 16, 1829; Diocese of Virginia, *Journal* (1830), 13.
23. Ibid. (1831), 31.
24. Ibid. (1835), 19.
25. Goodwin, *History* 2:615.
26. Ibid. 2:605.
27. *Southern Churchman* 6/12 (March 20, 1840): 47.
28. Packard, *Recollections*, 76.
29. Goodwin, *History* 1:168; Packard, *Recollections*, 90.
30. Goodwin, *History* 1:403–4.
31. Packard, *Recollections*, 237; see Goodwin, *History* 1:406.
32. Goodwin, *History* 1:171.
33. See Wallace E. Rollins' detailed account in Goodwin, *History* 2:252–70. Mary Donovan (*A Different Call* [Wilton, Conn.: Morehouse, 1986], 69) is right in reminding us of the part played by women, beginning with Frances Maria Hill, in this and other missions.
34. See Lloyd R. Craighill's detailed account in Goodwin, *History* 2:271–94.
35. Stephen Neill, *A History of Christian Missions* (Grand Rapids, Mich.: Penguin Books, 1965), 288–89.
36. See Paul Due's detailed account in Goodwin, *History* 2:295 323.
37. *Semi-Centennial Celebration*, 64–65.
38. Packard, *Recollections*, 140.
39. Diocese of Virginia, *Journal* (1834), 35; Goodwin, *History* 2:608; bd. min. 1:85.
40. *Southern Churchman* 1/6 (February 6, 1835): 21.
41. Goodwin, *History* 1:410.
42. Catalogue (1843–44), 11.
43. Goodwin, *History* 1:411.
44. *Southern Churchman* 8/13 (April 22, 1842): 51.
45. Catalogue (1842–43), 11.
46. Ibid.
47. Ahlstrom, *Religious History*, 426.
48. Catalogue (1842–43), 11.
49. Goodwin, *History* 2:607; bd. min. 1:84.
50. Ibid. 1:487.
51. Ibid. 1:487–88.
52. Ibid. 1:178.
53. Ibid. 1:417.
54. Diocese of Virginia, *Journal* (1835), 17.
55. See Packard, *Recollections*, 181–83, and Goodwin, *History* 2:411–12.
56. *Southern Churchman* 1/5:22.
57. Packard, *Recollections*, 183.
58. Goodwin, *History* 2:412.

59. Diocese of Virginia, *Journal* (1838), 21.
60. Packard, *Recollections*, 183.
61. Diocese of Virginia, *Journal* (1839), 17.
62. See Packard, *Recollections*, 185–86.
63. Goodwin, *History* 2:615; bd. min. 1:111.
64. Ibid. 2:413.
65. Ibid., 414.
66. Diocese of Virginia, *Journal* (1840), 18.
67. *Southern Churchman* 6/34 (August 21, 1840): 135.
68. Packard, *Recollections*, 184.
69. Cornelius Walker, *The Life and Correspondence of Rev. William Sparrow*, D.D. (Philadelphia: Hammond, 1876), 112. Walker was a student at the high school at the time.
70. See board report, Diocese of Virginia, *Journal* (1839), 17.
71. *Southern Churchman* 6/29 (July 17, 1840): 114.
72. Diocese of Virginia, *Journal* (1840), 19.
73. See Goodwin, *History* 2:416–18, and Diocese of Virginia, *Journal* (1845), 49–50. The number soon rose to seventeen.
74. Goodwin, *History* 2:609; bd. min. 1:62.
75. Ibid. 2:609; bd. min. 1:91.
76. Ibid. 2:609–610; bd. min. 1:93.
77. Packard, *Recollections*, 41.
78. Ibid., 55.
79. Ibid., 63–64.
80. Ibid., 68.
81. Ibid., 73.
82. Goodwin, *History* 1:569; see Packard, *Recollections*, 330–36.
83. Ibid. 1:568.
84. Ibid. 1:561.
85. Packard, *Recollections*, 168.
86. Ibid., 167.
87. See Walker, Sparrow, 17–72.
88. Ibid., 42.
89. Ibid., 82–84.
90. Ibid., 43.
91. Goodwin, *History* 1:599.
92. Ibid., 188.
93. Ibid., 589. A more detailed assessment of his thought will come when we note his death in 1874.
94. Diocese of Virginia, *Journal* (1829), 32.
95. Ibid. (1839), 18.
96. Ibid. (1839), 18–19.
97. Ibid. (1839), 19.
98. Ibid.
99. Ibid. (1840), 17.

100. Catalogue (1839), 9.
101. George Christian Knapp, *Lectures on Christian Theology*, trans. Leonard Woods 1 (New York: Carville, 1831): xxiv–xxv.
102. Ibid., 52–58.
103. *Southern Churchman* 2/31 (July 29, 1836): 123.
104. Ibid. 5/29 (July 19, 1839): 114.
105. Ibid. 6/29 (July 17, 1840): 114.
106. Ibid. 7/26 (July 23, 1841): 102.
107. Ibid. 7/27 (July 30, 1841): 106.
108. Goodwin, *History* 2:610; bd. min. 1:75–76.
109. Ibid. 2:605; bd. min. 1:75–76.
110. Ibid. 2:611; bd. min. 1:98–99.
111. Ibid. 2:612; bd. min. 1:101–102.
112. Ibid. 2:613; bd. min. 1:102–103. See Richard Channing Moore, correspondence, VTSA, in which there is evidence that Keith had been called to a parish in Pittsburgh, Pennsylvania. Moore pled with Keith not to leave, wrote a letter to the church in Pittsburgh asking that they not pursue Keith, and instructed the board to do all in its power to keep Keith. See Moore to Keith, October 19, 1837 (41.3.24); Moore to Mr. Norwood, October 23, 1837 (41.3.26); Moore to Henshaw and Johns, November 7, 1837 (41.3.32); and Moore to Jeremiah Butler, Esq., Pittsburgh (41.5.20–21).
113. Ibid.; bd. min. 1:105–106.
114. Board minutes of July 7, 1857, found loose in the minute book for 1866–1898, 2.
115. Bd. min., 1866–1898, 90.
116. Catalogue (1874–75), 5.
117. Ibid. 1880–81, n.p.
118. See *Southern Churchman* 7/43 (November 19, 1841): 170.
119. Ibid. 7/3 (January 15, 1841): 10.
120. Ibid. 7/14 (April 30, 1841): 54, and 7/19 (June 4, 1841): 73.
121. William Meade, *Lectures on the Pastoral Office, delivered to the Students of the Theological Seminary at Alexandria, Va.* (New York: Stanford and Swords, 1849).
122. William Meade, *The Law of Proportion in the Church of God: Considered in a Pastoral Address . . . to the Ministers and Members* [of the Diocese of Virginia] *in compliance with the 27th canon of the General Convention* (Alexandria: Southern Churchman Office, 1843).
123. Meade, *Lectures*, 78.
124. Ibid., 87. See John Booty, "The Law of Proportion: William Meade and Richard Hooker," in *Grace and Obedience, Papers in Honor of John Maurice Gessell*, ed. Donald S. Armentrout, *St. Luke's Journal of Theology*, 34/2 (March 1991): 19–31.
125. Meade, *Law of Proportion*, 41–42.
126. *Southern Churchman* 6/13 (April 3, 1840): 53–54.
127. Ibid.

CHAPTER FOUR

PROSPERITY
AND
GLOOM
1842–1865

1. THE TESTING OF THE NATION:
THE COMING OF THE CIVIL WAR

The more than two decades covered by this chapter were dominated by the Civil War, the War between the States. The Virginia Theological Seminary, existing as it did in northern Virginia, adjacent to the nation's capital, with a faculty from the North, with financial support from North and South, could not escape the consequences of the world's first "modern war" and did not, being very nearly obliterated.

The causes of the Civil War were complex, involving economic, political, social, and religious factors.[1] All seemed to tend toward the arrest of growing nationalism and a renewed assertion of sectionalism for which the issue of slavery emerged as a major symbol. During the colonial period, slavery as an institution was by and large accepted in all of the colonies, north and south. There were some who complained, such as the Quakers, but they were not numerous. In the eighteenth century, during the revolutionary era and beyond, antislavery views became more prominent, partly as a result of the Enlightenment and its understanding of the "rights of nature."[2] In Virginia, men including Washington, Jefferson, Madison, and Henry looked upon slavery as an evil.[3] Churches began to speak out; in 1780 the Methodists condemned slavery as "contrary to the laws of God, man, and nature." To implement antislavery sentiments, the North and the South pursued different courses. Southern states promoted private manumission, enacted measures to abolish the African slave trade before federal law became a factor in the matter in 1808, sought restrictions on domestic slave trade, and supported the American Colonization Society, which had as its aim the repatriation of slaves to Africa. Northern states sought the abolition of slavery as an institution, so that by 1846 slavery ceased to exist, officially, north of Maryland and Delaware.[4]

During the 1830s there was a distinct change of mood in the nation, an escalation of tempers and feelings. Northern denunciation of slavery increased with the advent of strident abolitionists such as William Lloyd Garrison and *The Liberator*, founded in 1830. Garrison favored immediate emancipation instead of the "popular and pernicious doctrine of gradual abolition."[5] Such a demand from the North provoked an increasingly defensive attitude in the South, with extremists such as Matthew Estes asserting in 1846 that he would not hesitate to say that the slave trade "had been the source of incalculable blessing to mankind." "The slave, it was claimed, did not suffer as the property of his master, for he was assured 'peace, plenty, and security, and the proper indulgence of his special propensities.'" William Gilmore Simmons proclaimed that "Providence has placed him [the slave] in our hands for his good, and has paid us from his labor for our guardianship."[6] The historian wonders, had there not been a Garrison, would there have been a Simmons? As H. Richard Niebuhr said,

> The abolition movement was not only a symptom of conflict but one of the causes as well. Unconcerned, frequently, with facts, but swayed by a towering passion for reform, it painted every slave in the guise of an Uncle Tom and every master in the lurid colors of a Simon Legree. In consequence it probably was less effective in influencing the social psychology of the North than in consolidating the pro-slavery feelings of the South.[7]

If the 1830s saw the advent of the abolition movement with its effects on the South, the 1840s witnessed, in addition, an effort to contain slavery, preventing its spread, drawing a line at 36 degrees 30 minutes, north of which there would be no slavery. This, the Missouri Compromise, was challenged as pro slavery forces sought to expand slaveholding into the territories, a strategem led by Calhoun and other southern extremists. As Nevin and Commager say, "Year by year the nation moved closer to war. A great drum seemed to beat out the march to conflict, stroke after stroke. In 1856 a hot-headed South Carolinian member of Congress, Preston Brooks, attacked Sumner of Massachusetts at his Senate desk and hammered him so heavily with his cane that Sumner was an invalid for years." They go on to comment, "The provocation, a grossly abusive speech by Sumner, had been great, but the act was indefensible. Early in 1857 Chief Justice Taney and a majority of the Supreme Court declared in the Dred Scott case that Congress had no power to exclude slavery from the territories. It was a bad interpretation, badly argued. At once the free-soil press and politicians attacked the court with unprecedented bitterness. . . ."[8]

The drum beat went on until at Fort Sumter the drum stopped beating and the cannons roared. Horace Bushnell saw in the bloody conflict that ensued "a nation wrought in the fires of history upon the anvil of suffering under the hammer of a providential God." For him the way marked "an historic transition from 'a compact, or a confederation, or a composition made up by the temporary surrender of arms,' to 'a national-God's own nation.'"[9] Though it was horrendous, it seemed to many to be momentous and necessary and, in an ultimate sense, "good." For Virginia Theological Seminary it was, for the time being, an unmitigated disaster.

William Meade belonged to a family owning slaves. But he and other
1816,
Meade became a charter member of the "American Society for Colonizing the Free People of Color in the United States," along with Francis Scott Key, William H. Wilmer, and Edmund J. Lee. The aim was to colonize ex-slaves in Africa and there, with the aid of missionaries, to found a Christian nation, which in time became known as Liberia. In 1819 Meade became the first general agent for the society and traveled through the eastern states raising money, securing ex-slaves for transportation to Africa, and establishing local colonization societies. In time he became discouraged, realizing that the society was incapable of solving the problem of slavery in America. After 1825, he freed all but his infirm slaves but was alarmed at how poorly freedom treated them. He did not encourage others to take the same course.

David Holmes makes clear that as opposed as Meade was to slavery and as fond as he was of the black people in Virginia ("the most amiable race of savages which I believe exists on earth"), "he remained a segregationist and a white supremacist to the end of his life." Writes Holmes,

Believing the institution of slavery to have been distinctly recognized and formally legislated about, by divine authority in the Sacred Scriptures, "he was unable to consider slave owning per se a sin." . . . Five years before his death, Meade could still speak of slavery as an act of Providence similar to the Israelite invasion of Canaan, note with some pride that slave states were free of "the Unitarian heresy," and declare that slavery—despite all its acknowledged evils called forth "some of the finest traits in the character of man."[10]

Something of Meade's complexity is revealed here. To his mind slavery was evil as practiced but could be defended in the abstract and thus to some degree in actuality.

We know something of Sparrow's attitude toward slavery. In 1844 he was invited to return to Kenyon College and wrestled with the decision. Cornelius Walker tells us that the only difficulty at Virginia Seminary that might have influenced his decision and made him return to the North "was that concerned with the use of slave labor, in the domestics of his household, to which he had not been accustomed, and to which he felt reluctance."[11] His uneasiness was not exceptional; others from the North felt the same reluctance and more. Phillips Brooks, who arrived as a student at the seminary in 1856, reported, "All the servants are slaves. Those in the seminary are let out by their masters for so much a year, paid of course to the master just as you'd pay for a horse hired."[12]

Slaughter tells of Sparrow's interest in the Colonization Society, whose meetings he attended as a delegate, and cites a letter from Sparrow in which he advocates the gradual elimination of slavery. Sparrow wrote, distinguishing between the ideal in which there would be no slavery (or war or "in a certain sense" divorce) from the actual situation he confronted at the seminary and throughout the South.

> How is Christianity to realize in the actual this beautiful and infinitely desirable ideal? It must not precipitate matters; that would prove disastrous. It would be like plucking up the tares before the proper time. As the defects and abuses of society referred to are *governmental*, to assail them directly would bring the kingdom of Christ in direct collision with the kingdoms of this world; which would be pernicious in several ways. Humanly speaking it would exterminate the Church of Christ. . . .[13]

When the war came Sparrow, no abolitionist, did not return to the North as did his colleague May, but stayed in Virginia and was an active delegate to the General Convention of the Episcopal Church in the Confederate States in 1861 and again in 1862. He was an alternate in 1865.[14]

Joseph Packard wrote favorably of the treatment of slaves before the war, saying that slaves were not "neglected generally. Being the most valuable property, they were of course well cared for, and I can bear my personal witness to the kindness and care usually shown them." He argued against Frederick Douglas who claimed that Negro children were not allowed to be baptized. "This is false in regard to the Episcopal Church . . . as our parochial records will show."[15] He seemingly advocated gradual emancipation, saying that if Henry Clay's "views and advice had been adopted a fearful war would have been saved the country."[16] Like Sparrow, Packard, whose roots were in the North, stayed in

Virginia during the war, but he did not take part in the General Convention of the Confederate Church.[17]

As has been said, the causes of the Civil War were complex. Slavery was in some ways the central issue, but W.A.R. Goodwin reminds us that for many Virginians the issue was a constitutional one: the right of a state to secede from the Union. Virginians believed in the right but did not advocate its use. However, when South Carolina seceded and was denied the right and the war necessitated the passage of Union troops through Virginia, "Virginia finally reached the conclusion that the issue having been forced, her duty called her to secede in the defense of her rights under the Constitution. She finally took the step with deep regret and yet with full conviction of duty."[18] Packard wrote from his perspective,

It is extraordinary how few persons brought on the war. The more I think of it the more unnatural it seems. The mass of people, North and South, did not desire the war, and some of the strongest Union men were Southerners, who, however, felt constrained to go with their States. Clay and Webster had with equal earnestness tried to preserve the Union in their day.[19]

2. DECLINE, REVIVAL, AND THEN WAR

The story of the seminary in the prewar years is one of recurring problems in the 1840s, of steady growth in the 1850s, reaching a high point in the academic session of 1860–61. Then there came, toward the end of that session, virtual collapse and the seizure of the seminary campus for use as a Union hospital. Student enrollment was forty-six in 1842–43,[20] fell to twenty-five in 1849,[21] and slowly rose again until in the year of the seminary's dissolution it had an enrollment of seventy-three, fifteen being in the preparatory department.[22] The drop in enrollment was of serious concern, but the board argued that a similar drop had occurred in other places. The number seeking ordination in the entire Episcopal Church had declined. The board attributed the decline to "the want of faithful, ardent, persevering prayer."[23]

By 1855 the supply of candidates for the ministry had been increasing for the "last four or five years."[24] Furthermore, students were coming from all over the country. In the 1860–61 session, according to Packard, one half of the student body came from the North.[25] In 1856 a report in the *Southern Churchman* claimed that "what the New York School is in name," the Virginia School had become in fact: "the General Seminary of our Church. It has furnished all, or nearly all, of our foreign missionaries, and a large number—between three and four hundred—of our most devoted and useful parish ministers," a notable record attributed to the "Evangelical character" of the Virginia Theological Seminary.[26] The 1860–61 catalogue indicates that the students of the seminary came from a variety of colleges: Hampden Sydney and William and Mary, among others in the South, including the University of Virginia; Kenyon, Yale, and Williams, among others in the North, including the Universities of Pennsylvania and New York. In addition there were graduates from Queen's College and Trinity College, Dublin.[27] The seminary was a diocesan institution, serving the entire Episcopal Church.

By 1856 there were 318 graduates of the seminary, of whom 277 were alive, distributed in twenty-seven dioceses and in England, Africa, China, and Greece. Virginia had the most (93), followed by Pennsylvania (43), Maryland (35), and Massachusetts and New York (18 each). Graduates were found from Florida to Maine, from Rhode Island to California, and from Texas to the "Northwest Mission."[28]

The Education Society reported a similar story. By 1842 it had aided 122 men "from nearly every state in the union," working in almost every diocese of the Church, although a disproportionate number were to be found in Virginia and Maryland.[29] Throughout this period the Education Society endured financial problems. The executive committee, with Lippitt and Packard as members, stated that in 1842 "never had it [the society] been more straitened than during the past year."[30] The spirit seemed to have departed from the society.[31] Efforts were made under the president of the society, William Meade, to remedy the situation, including a widely distributed circular. But by 1856 the "results were not encouraging," receipts during the year amounting to $1,773 of which $846 came from Virginia.[32] Nevertheless the society continued to aid needy students; fourteen in 1842 but only nine in 1856. It provided salaries for two professors in 1842, but only one in 1856.[33] In addition it did much to maintain the "boarding establishment" of the seminary and even sought the contribution of a horse for the "use of the Boarding establishment."[34]

Clearly, the trustees of the seminary had to consider ways and means of support beyond that of the Education Society. In 1847 they discussed the fact that there were still no charges for tuition nor for room rent. If such charges were to be avoided, they would need a larger permanent, interest-earning fund or endowment. They said, "The funds, now obtained and vested amount to $40,442.50. But they are still insufficient. . . . Some $20,000 or $25,000 should still be raised."[35] In the next year $2,023 was added to the fund. In addition $18,000 was subscribed, and $10,000 was being added, bringing the total to $70,000. "The interest of this sum is absolutely required in order to support the Professors comfortably."[36] In 1849 the total had been $47,479.24[37] and in 1850, $55,000.[38] In 1851 it

The Class of 1856

had been reported, "The permanent fund is now about $60,000, yielding an annual income of six per cent."[39] By 1858 Meade reported that the fund had reached $90,000 "whose interest is expended on the support of three Professors, with families, in a place where living is very costly, and on the taxes, insurances, repairs, and improvements which are annually called for in an establishment, having so many buildings to keep in order."[40] The fund had more than doubled in ten years.

Much of the credit for raising the funds belongs to Meade and, increasingly, to John Johns, who was consecrated bishop in 1842 to assist the diocesan bishop. In July 1844 the bishops sent out an urgent appeal.[41] They then went north, to Baltimore and Philadelphia, seeking endowment for two professorships.[42] Others, especially members of the board and of the Education Society, were active in raising funds. One who deserves special attention in this period was the Reverend John Cole of the class of 1828. As agent of the board of trustees and of the Alumni Association, he was successful in raising large sums (over $40,000 according to one account). This he did beginning in 1851 in return for a salary of $1,000 plus expenses.[43]

In 1855 he was busy seeking funds from northern alumni, to endow the professorships of the institution.[44] In answer to a letter from the Reverend Dr. William B. Stevens of St. Andrew's Church, Philadelphia, Cole wrote a glowing description of the seminary, pointing to the service it provided to the entire church ("it has always been more general than the General Seminary itself"), including the church's overseas missions. He pointed to the "self-denial of our Professors," two receiving but $1,200 a year (to rise to $1,500 depending on the success of the current fund drive) and one but $2,000, although the trustees were only able to provide $1,600, the rest coming from "educational or private sources." When asked to name the institution's greatest need, Cole specified endowment as primary and then "a fireproof library building and lecture room." As to whether there was any narrowness or sectionalism in the teaching of the professors, he replied that the only qualifications demanded of professors in the seminary were that "they hold and teach the great Evangelical doctrines of our articles of religion and the Reformation"—and, one assumes, that they be proficient in the theological disciplines for which they were responsible.[45]

In relation to his financial efforts, Cole sought for and acquired from the Virginia legislature in 1854 a charter for the seminary. Previous efforts had not been successful, evidently because of denominational prejudices. Meade had realized the importance of a charter if the seminary and the high school were to be fully successful in fund raising. But the bishop had become discouraged and only with reluctance gave Cole permission to make another attempt. Cole worked hard, ingratiating himself with the speaker of the house, whom he knew, and working with other legislators, exercising considerable skill as a diplomat. The result, "An Act incorporating the Protestant Episcopal Theological Seminary and High School in Virginia," was passed on February 28, 1854. Besides providing for the holding of property under certain conditions and for the conduct of the institution (the trustees having "power to appoint a President, Treasurer, Secretary, Professors, Tutors" and to establish "bylaws, rules and regulations"), the trustees—and this was of particular concern to Cole— "shall have power, either by themselves or their agents, to take and receive subscriptions for said institution. . . ."[46] On April 5, 1854, the board of trustees met, accepted the charter, and reorganized in accordance with its specifications.[47]

In addition to the growth of the endowment, the successful fund raising of the 1850s resulted in what was virtually a new campus. In 1855 the chapel was expanded and consecrated, with the expenditure of $4,000. It had formerly accommodated two hundred people and then seated five hundred.[48] Increased enrollment necessitated further dormitory space. In 1856 St. George's Hall was erected, due to the generosity of Dr. Stephen Tyng and the people of St. George's Church, New York. Designed to accommodate twelve students, it was constructed for about $5,000.[49] In the same year a "fireproof Library" was erected. Meade persuaded John Bohlen and his sister, both of Philadelphia, to contribute toward the $4,000 required and provided the rest from funds left to his disposal "by the late Mrs. Sophia Jones of Prince William."[50] The building, described by Samuel Wallis as "a gem of collegiate Gothic architecture,"[51] served as the

The "New" Aspinwall Hall, 1859

seminary's library until Packard-Laird Hall was built in 1921, when the former library became the seminary's refectory. It is now Key Hall, a practice chapel. Built to accommodate the growing library collection and to house records of the churches of the diocese, it housed eight thousand volumes in 1860–61,

Next it was determined to replace the original buildings middle, north, and south. Through the good auspices of Bishop Bedell, then rector of the Church of the Ascension, New York, in 1857 $10,000 were obtained from William H. and John L. Aspinwall of New York, a sum raised to $20,000 the next year. The plan was to use this money to build a new central building "immediately in front of the old one," which was to be used until the new one was completed.[52] The board of trustees authorized the building of Aspinwall (initially called Ascension) Hall under Mr. Bedell's direction.[53] Its dedication took place on October 4, 1859, just prior to the General Convention that met in Richmond. There were present at the dedication, in addition to Meade and Johns, Bishops Benjamin Smith of Kentucky, Leonidas Polk of Louisiana, and John H. Hopkins of Vermont. It was a festive occasion. After a collation provided by the "ladies on the Hill," the Alumni Association met in the chapel, chaired by Bishop Polk. Bedell displayed his plans for Meade Hall and strongly urged that the north and south buildings flanking Aspinwall be built at once. Alumni present pledged $2,500.[54] John Bohlen of Philadelphia, who had contributed toward the new library, was present at the meeting and informed Meade "of his wish to erect, at a cost of $10,000 one of the wings."[55] Thus, before war devastated the campus, Meade and Bohlen Halls were built and the old buildings dismantled. Finally in this period a new home was erected for Sparrow, "sometimes playfully referred to as 'Sparrow Roost,'

though generally called 'The Wilderness,'" in 1840–41. Other improvements were made to the professors' houses, including the enlargement of
"Maywood" in 1856—Professor May's house.⁵⁶

Thus was the Virginia Theological Seminary campus complete in the
eyes of its governors, accommodating a growing student body, and supported by a rapidly increasing endowment. The new campus possessed a
capacious chapel, a new library, and a magnificent set of buildings for
living and instruction. Then came the war, and all seemed lost.

3. FACULTY: MEMBERSHIP ORGANIZATION, TEACHING BEFORE THE WAR

With the death of Keith and the resignation of Lippitt in 1842, followed
by the election of James May, the faculty during these antebellum years
consisted of Meade as president and (part-time) professor of pastoral theology; William Sparrow as professor of systematic divinity and the evidences of Christianity; James May as professor of ecclesiastical history
and polity, and pulpit eloquence; and Joseph Packard as professor of sacred literature and as librarian.⁵⁷

James May was born October 1, 1805, in Chester County, Pennsylva-
nia, and graduated with high distinction from Washington and Jefferson
College in 1823. Having undergone an intense conversion experience ("I
beheld God," said he, "as a reconciled Father"), he was devoted to the
Christian life as lived through the ordinances of the Episcopal Church.
After gaining a B.A. degree, he studied law under his brother-in-law in
Maryland but in 1825 turned to theology, entering the middle class at
Virginia Seminary. After a year he returned to Pennsylvania to continue
his studies under the Reverend George Boyd and was ordained by Bishop
White in 1826. May entered the pastoral ministry, serving churches in
Wilkes-Barre and Philadelphia until he became seriously ill and on his
doctor's advice went to Europe to recuperate. On returning, May accepted
a call to teach ecclesiastical history at Virginia Seminary. That was in July
1842. He was to spend the next nineteen years teaching at the seminary.⁵⁸

May had studied history while in Europe and was reputed to be a sound
scholar and a successful teacher. A sermon preached at the Virginia diocesan convention in 1847 yields some evidence of his intellectual abilities.
Entitled "The Advantage of Church Membership with Reference to some
Errors, Historically Viewed," this erudite, lengthy sermon (based on Rom.
3:1–2) rests upon the authority of Scripture and the evidences of history
through the ages. Denouncing the theories of ecclesiastical prerogatives
and sacramental efficacy as taught by the Roman church, May empha-

sized the spiritual dimensions of Christianity and the necessity of life lived in conformity to Christ. He wrote,

> Membership in the visible Church does not, simply in itself, make us share in the life of Christ's mystical body. It brings us into possession of means of being trained and nurtured in spiritual life. The sacraments are not channels, through which life from Christ flows, without reference to any thing but the divine ordinance. They are means of grace, "moral instruments of salvation," as Hooker calls them, their efficacy being suspended on the penitence and faith of those who receive them. Apart from these conditions, that baptized man may be, to all intents, a pagan, having no more than a mere name in the Church. . . . The sacraments, when used according to their proper intent, as "moral instruments" of grace are of inestimable value. They are tokens or seals of the covenant of life made by God with men in Christ. . . . The title conveyed or assured, through the sacraments, belongs to those only who have the inward and spiritual qualifications.[59]

According to his biographer, Alexander Shiras, May was no Calvinist,[60] but he was undoubtedly an Evangelical in the tradition of Wilberforce and Simeon. Further evidence of this is available in a sermon preached at the seminary before the alumni in 1844 entitled "The Proper Office and Spirit of the Ministry." The office of the ministry is chiefly to proclaim the good news of salvation through Christ, and the spirit of that ministry is to live a life worthy of that high calling. He affirmed, unequivocally, citing 1 Tim. 1:15 ("Christ Jesus has come into the world to save sinners"),

> this is the gospel in sum. All evangelical truths spring out of this. It is the alphabet of religion, to be learned as the element of all gospel knowledge. It involves the doctrines of man's fall, of his inbred depravity and guilt, the curse of God on his soul, the way of justification and life through the propitiatory sufferings of the incarnate Son of God, the sanctification of the believer through the operation of the Holy Ghost, and his final glorification with his ascended Redeemer.[61]

May's colleague Packard remembered him chiefly for his character and piety, writing, "Dr. May was at his best at Faculty meetings. There his 'tongue dropped manna.'" Indeed, he was regarded as saintly. "There was an atmosphere of holiness about him," said Packard, "so that no one could be long in his company without seeing his calm and heavenly spirit." He was known to be an Evangelical churchman, supporting the threefold ministry of bishops, priests, and deacons as set forth in the Ordinal.[62] Philip Slaughter, reflected on the many and excruciating pains suffered by May in the deaths of those dear to him, concluding with the death of his wife in 1861, as well as his own poor health and the coming of the war. Slaughter wrote,

> He now seems to have gathered up the fragments of his shattered earthly affections, and garnered them in this Seminary; and when this tie was about to be sundered, and he roamed over these hills, taking a last lingering look at the objects of Nature and Art, which he loved so well, "the new Building, the beautifully green lawn, the trees in green leaf, and the birds filling the air with song," he exclaims, "Who knows how soon everything here may be destroyed?" "If the tears shed on this hill were gathered," he continues, "what an amount would appear! And yet is not this but the beginning of sorrows!"[63]

Such was the man who so loved the seminary and regarded its future with foreboding and sorrow.

How was this faculty organized? At a meeting of the board of trustees on July 7, 1857, where it was reported that the professors were paid $1,500 per annum, it was "resolved, That the Professors be requested to organize as a Faculty, with a Dean as President, a secretary of their own appointment—that all matters pertaining to the management and order of the Seminary be determined in regular meetings of the Faculty. And that a Record of their proceedings be kept, to be submitted to the Board of Trustees at their Meetings."[64] This recommendation, briefly noted in the last chapter, did not appear to have any dramatic effects, but it is evident that Sparrow, although not designated in the catalogue as dean, was functioning as chairman of the faculty and is listed before May and Packard but after Meade, the president. Sparrow did sign at least one letter to the board "Dean of the Faculty," this in 1861.[65]

The curriculum continued much as it had in earlier times. There were four faculty (including Meade), one for each department of the theological encyclopedia. Toward the beginning of this period of time, the faculty began to write detailed reports to the trustees. By the 1850s they were very brief. In 1853 May simply said, "The usual course of studies committed to my care has been followed." Sparrow and Packard said much the same.[66] The earlier reports were much more informative.

In 1845 Packard stated that he taught Hebrew and Greek and required students to read parts of the Old and New Testaments in the original languages. The juniors read "Jahn's *Jewish Antiquities*, Horne's *Introduction to the Old Testament*, and Ernesti on Interpretation, and had been examined on them, two or three times a week." They also studied "Sacred Chronology and Jewish History" and wrote "more than 40 Exegetical Essays." The middlers "read, in Hebrew, the principal Prophecies of Christ, with the commentary of Hengstenberg, and in Greek, the Epistles to the Romans, Hebrews," and the two Epistles to Timothy. He added that "there has been, according to the resolution of the Trustees, a weekly exercise with the senior class, alternately in Hebrew and Greek"—evidently an innovation.[67]

Sparrow reported in the same year that the juniors studied "the Evidences of Christianity with care; the middle class, after a thorough study of Butler's 'Analogy,' has been busily occupied with Biblical Theology; and the senior class has reviewed Theology in its connection with our Protestant Episcopal standards of doctrine." The "customary Text Books, have been employed" in this work.[68] Beside Butler's *Analogy*, this would have included Paley's *Evidences*, Horne's *Introduction*, and "Leslie's Short Method with the Deists" for evidences, and the Bible, "Knapp's Theology," "Burnet's Exposition," "Pearson on the Creed," "The Homilies," "Dwight's Theology," and "Stackhouse's Divinity" for systematic divinity.[69] In 1847 Sparrow reported the addition of a brief course in mental philosophy, logic, and rhetoric, "in conformity with the vote of the board at the last convention."[70] This course was discontinued in 1851 "for want of time."[71] In 1853 he reported "that the middle class has read, as an extra duty, Reid's 'Intellectual Powers,' with the notes of Sir William Hamilton."[72] Thus there were minor changes made either by Sparrow himself or at the direction of the trustees. By 1845–46 textbooks by Stackhouse and Dwight were dropped,[73] and Knapp's text on theology loomed larger, accompanied by the Bible, the homilies, Burnet, and Pearson.

In 1845 May reported that the middle class has "studied the General History of the Church, with Mosheim as a Text Book" and the seniors "have gone through the History of the Church of England with Bishop Short's work as a Text Book. . . . They have studied also Ecclesiastical Polity, using Hooker's work on the subject."[74] In the absence of the bishop, May was also responsible for pastoral theology, presenting a set of lectures on that subject to the senior class.[75] This was the basic fare. May also reported on "the composition and delivery of Sermons, in a weekly meeting of the [senior] students for this purpose."[76] Many other texts were listed in the catalogue for May's department, but his report seems to indicate those books that were most important in his teaching.[77]

This regimen was academically demanding, and the faculty was not always satisfied that the students had been adequately prepared for it. Some of the worthy students who applied for admission lacked college degrees or any higher education, either because of poverty or because of late vocations, their earlier callings not requiring a college education. Rather than lower their standards, the faculty and board founded in 1855 a "preparatory department."[78] The aim was to equip men to meet the admissions requirements as specified in the seminary Rules and Regulations of 1825 and to procure that "classical and scientific" learning requisite for the study of theology.[79] Thus those admitted were taught as needed; Latin and Greek, history, mathematics, natural philosophy, mental and moral science, and rhetoric.[80] The first teacher specifically designated for the department was Phillips Brooks, a student in the seminary. He was paid a salary of three hundred dollars.[81] Normally, one teacher was employed for the department. Most of the work was done by the three full-time professors. Like the seminarians, students in the preparatory department had tuition and room free and paid $100 per session for board. The department was abolished in 1894, partly because of increasing expenses and partly "because of the limited educational advantages offered by the department compared with the advantages of college education."[82]

The academic year concluded, as before, with examination of the students by their professors in public and with essays read by seniors. There followed ordinations and meetings of the alumni, the Missionary Association, and the Education Society.[83] Furthermore, work in the seminary missions continued (Phillips Brooks was stationed at Sharon Chapel), as did the work of the Society for the Religious Improvement of the Neighborhood of the Seminary, which in 1846 distributed twelve Bibles, twelve New Testaments, forty Books of Common Prayer, four thousand children's tracts, and fifty-one thousand pages of tracts for adults. It was said, "Here in our quiet retreat, we not only study the Pastoral work from Books as a theory, but practice it by visiting the sick and dying, the hardened sinner and the anxious inquirer, putting into practice what we learn."[84] May, as president of the society, presided over all of this work. An account in the *Southern Churchman* of an anniversary celebration of the Sunday school associated with the seminary chapel, began with "a picnic in a nearby woods" and ended with a service of song and prayer, which was led by May and involved addresses by two students and the collection of a missionary offering.[85] In another account, the work of the students in the neighborhood, in Sunday schools, "the alms-house and the prison," and in "three or four" mission stations, was lauded as sanctifying the hearts of the students and making them "practical men."[86]

In addition, faculty meetings, Friday evening prayer meetings, the monthly meetings of the Missionary Society, and the weekly meetings of the Rhetorical Society were mentioned as contributing to the same effect.

4. MEMORIES OF PHILLIPS BROOKS

Phillips Brooks graduated from Virginia Theological Seminary in 1859 and was to become one of its most illustrious and loyal alumni, as a great preacher, a leader of the Broad Church movement in this country, as Bishop of Massachusetts, and as a prominent benefactor of the seminary. Brooks entered the seminary in 1856, a Harvard graduate who had just finished a disappointing teaching experience. From his correspondence, especially with his family, from his notebooks, and from the insights of his biographer, A.V.G. Allen, we learn much of Brooks at Virginia Seminary, including his inmost thoughts, and of the seminary itself, a place he both loathed and loved.

Brooks wrote to his brother William on the day that he arrived at the seminary, November 7, 1856, expressing that mixture of emotions to which he was to give vent repeatedly. He was roomed in a sparsely furnished garret, from which he fled on first seeing it. He, as a Northerner inclined toward the abolitionists, deplored the use of slaves as servants at the seminary. But he found the students friendly and played "a game of 'base' this afternoon with my new friends."[87] In another letter he spoke of the seminary as "a lonely, desolate sort of place" and the people he encountered as "wretched, shiftless, uninteresting, lazy, deceitful," which he attributed to the degrading effects of slavery.[88] All of this Allen understood as expressions of a young man's homesickness. "The change was too great for him from the home and center of the Puritans to a country which held in no respect the Puritan traditions, where manners and customs were strange and repugnant."[89]

To his father, Brooks wrote,

It's the most shiftless, slipshod place I ever saw. The only stated expense is $100 per annum for board in commons. We all dine together in a large low room down cellar. It seems cheap, but I assure you it's quite as much as it's worth. Besides that we have expenses for fuel, some articles of furniture, lights, washing, and sundries. I have as yet got half a cord of wood for $3.00. I think I shall have to get a new stove, and if I do I shall burn coal. It's cheaper. For washing I pay $2.00 a month. I have not yet bought a lamp, but burn candles at present. Have bought no furniture excepting a pair of curtains for $1.00.

Of the teaching he said, "The instruction here is very poor. . . . All that we get in the lecture and recitation rooms I consider worth just nothing."[90] Brooks studied, however, mostly on his own, digging into Hebrew, which he enjoyed, working with Conant's edition of Gesenius' grammar, and reading Genesis. By the end of November he was writing, "I do like the place, the studies, and the profession very much, and better every day."[91] But then he encountered animosity toward northern students and felt uneasy. Thus his emotions rose and sank. Winter in the Washington, D.C. area he found depressing. But then he wrote in February, "I like my situation here quite well—work pretty hard, read considerably, and live really quite a pleasant life." He had been "reading Herodotus, partly for the Greek and partly for the story."[92] Then in March he began to speak of his doubts at having come to the seminary, wondering if there wasn't a better seminary and whether it might not be better to study at home. To William he wrote in April, "I feel a little blue; if I wasn't twenty-one years old I believe I should say homesick, tonight."[93] He then wondered if Andover might not be the place for him and warned his father that he might not—probably would not—return for a second year.

As Allen said, by the end of his first year Brooks had begun to take root in Virginia. In effect, as Brooks' friend Charles Richards said, "the primitive life and the dull teaching did not arouse enthusiasm. There were no lectures to supplement the textbooks." "The recitations were hardly calculated to impart knowledge; they were designed rather to betray how little we had acquired. There was much in fervor and piety among us, less enthusiasm for scholarship." But, as Richards argued, the life they lived was free and secluded. "Thoughtful men, whose springs were in themselves, enjoyed the judicious neglect, found time to meditate, to browse on the offshoots of their own minds, and put out roots after their own fashion. Brooks employed his opportunity."[94] His notebooks reveal the amazing scope and quantity of his reading in the Greek and Latin classics, the church fathers, English literature, and English theology, as well as the antiquated textbooks assigned by his teachers, including Knapp's *Lectures on Christian Theology*. He would and did return for a second year.

During the session of 1857–58, Brooks was still critical of the South and of the seminary; he was very sensitive to the worsening climate concerning slavery and explained his dissatisfaction with his situation at the seminary. His father did not encourage him in this, emphasizing the great advantages he had as a student.[95] The year passed; the complaints subsided. In March Brooks wrote, "I get up every morning and read theology all day, and go to bed to get up and read, and so on again the next day. It is a good place to pass time, and a pretty good place to *spend* it, getting a fair though not exorbitant amount for your money."[96] In June, as he left Alexandria for the summer, he admitted to his brother, "I have enjoyed the year here much better than the last, have seen a good many pleasant people, like Virginians and hate Virginia more than ever."[97]

One of the reasons for the change in heart was the fact that Brooks was getting to know Professor Sparrow, and Sparrow Brooks. In the first year Sparrow had been a shadowy figure, in part due to ill health. Now during the summer Sparrow was writing to Brooks about prospects for the next year, including enlargement of the preparatory department. Upon returning to the seminary in October, Brooks was invited to take charge of this department. He was deeply impressed by Sparrow's confidence in him and took the job, which involved teaching "Latin and Greek two or three hours *per diem*" at a salary of "$300 and board, equal to $400 in all. Not very large pay, but all they can afford to pay, and as much, I suppose, as I had any right to expect."[98] His time and energies were now fully and happily engaged, and the teaching, in contrast to his earlier experience in Boston, went well. He began to write sermons, finding the task pleasant and daunting. And he began preaching at Sharon Chapel "to a small congregation of from fifty to seventy-five people," feeling that he was "better for the work, more and deeper in sympathy with simple, honest men." Then in March he began to consider where he would go on leaving seminary, specifically considering a call to the Church of the Advent, Philadelphia.

As A.V.G. Allen said, during his senior year "Brooks was becoming intimate" with Sparrow. "Many were the evenings spent in his study, when the subject of conversation was theology. He knew how to understand and sympathize with the thoughts germinating in the mind of his pupil."[99] Looking back, Brooks was to remember not the unpleasantness experienced at the seminary so much as the satisfaction he took at being with Sparrow. Thus he wrote in 1886,

> It is easy to say of men who have not much accurate knowledge to impart that they are men of suggestion and inspiration. But with the doctor [Sparrow] clear thought and real learning only made the suggestion and inspiration of his teaching more vivid. I have never looked at Knapp since he taught us out of it. My impression of it is that it is a very dull and dreary book, but it served as a glass for Dr. Sparrow's spirit to shine through, and perhaps from its own insignificance I remember him more in connection with it than in connection with Butler's Analogy. His simplicity and ignorance of the world seemed always to let one get directly at his abstract thought. . . . The best result of his work in influence on any student's life and ministry must have been to save him from the hardness on the one hand, and the weakness on the other, which purely intellectual or purely spiritual training have produced. . . . He loved ideas, and did all that he could to make his students love them.[100]

5. THE CIVIL WAR: A SEMINARY IN EXILE

Hostilities began when southern forces opened fire on Fort Sumter in Charleston Harbor. This was on April 12, 1861. South Carolina had seceded from the Union on December 20, 1860, and in February 1861, delegates of seven seceding states met at Montgomery, Alabama, founded the Confederate States of America, and elected Jefferson Davis as provisional president of the new nation. While the 1860–61 session of the seminary may have opened calmly enough, as the months passed discussions among students increased, and in April 1861 approximately half of the students, all of them from the North, departed. According to a report in the *Southern Churchman*, about thirty students went north. "It was pleasing to know that the young brethren there parted from each other with true Christian feeling and brotherly kindness."[101] Sparrow denied that these students were driven out, as some reports suggested, and stated that "some three or four" from the North "were the very last" to leave the seminary. He wrote to the board,

> The Institution has from the beginning embraced students from all sections of this northern continent, and when differences of opinion began to arise in the country on sectional questions, as was of course to be expected, the sons for the most part partook of the sentiment of their fathers, and did not fail also of course occasionally to express them. Nevertheless through the moderating influence which was studiously exercised over them, and by a strict and exclusive adherence to the teachings of scripture on points involved, as well as by their own sense of Christian duty and propriety, a remarkable degree of forbearance and good feeling was preserved among them. . . .[102]

Instead of rancor, Sparrow reported a growing sadness. The parting was painful. "So strongly did the Southern students feel this painful interruption, that they held a meeting, and by a resolution unanimously passed, expressed their feeling of affection for their Northern brethren . . . and their deep regret at the separation." Cornelius Walker was careful to note that there were "disputes at times" among the students,[103] but as long as possible the routine studies and the work in the neighborhood continued.

By May 1 it was clear that the seminary could not continue. Finances were a problem, the seminary's funds being invested in Virginia and the campus lying in the path of military maneuvers. Families in the neighborhood began to panic. "The Mayor of Alexandria sent out word that there might be firing and they had better move away."[104] Final exercises were held on May 7 when two seniors were examined and ordained the same day in the chapel.[105] Packard took James May into town and sent him on his way to Philadelphia. Packard and his family went to the home of his brother-in-law, Dr. Robert E. Peyton, "near 'The Plains' in Fauquier County," Virginia, and Sparrow sent his family to the interior of Virginia, staying behind at the seminary for another three weeks.

Sparrow was not alone at the seminary. Some seven or eight students were with him. But it was almost as though he were alone in the now deserted new buildings. He wrote on May 14 to his friend Edward Syle, saying that he was alone in his house, would go to Richmond for convention, and then return "to take charge of the premises, as I have been doing since the Seminary was prematurely closed. . . . I have no heart to speak about things here. I feel really brokenhearted. Is there on record the case of a nation holding to its lips a cup so full of blessing, and so wantonly and wickedly dashing it to the ground? My own individual trials in this matter are most peculiar and painful; but oh, my country, it is for thee I feel!"[106] About June 1 Sparrow joined his family in exile at Staunton, Virginia.

For Packard the pain was focused in part on leaving his house and home and everything in it: "linen, pictures, books, china, furniture, and silver in a box in the library."[107] For Sparrow the pain was focused on a divided family, with two daughters in the North and one in China, and two sons in the Confederate army and one in the service of the Confederacy elsewhere. The pain, too, involved physical sickness, wounds, and deaths in the family. In and through all was the pain of war. Sparrow remembered the horrors of civil war while he was a youth in Ireland. As Walker said, "as a follower of the Prince of Peace, he deprecated all war"[108] and sought to avoid any discussion involved with it. Sparrow had strong ties to the North and great sympathy for the South, but as Grammer said, "He himself endeavored as much as possible to stand aloof. He was a good deal of a pacifist, and had lost some property rather than engage in a family suit. He abhorred war as a method of settling a constitutional question."[109] No such sentiments were expressed by Packard, but there is sadness in his statement that, as he looked back on his experiences in the Civil War, "they do not seem to have happened to me, but to someone else. They do not differ materially from those of many others who were refugees, like myself."[110]

During the summer, Sparrow was at Staunton and for a time stayed at Stribling Springs, Augusta County. He was restless and distressed at hearing of the depredations befalling the seminary campus which in June, along with the high school had become a military hospital. His family would not let him return to Alexandria, and he knew they were right.[111] In October Meade, Johns, some of the trustees and other clergy, and Sparrow met in Richmond to reorganize the seminary. Various possibilities for its continuance were considered, one being the "buildings and grounds of the Hugonot Springs, in Powhatan county, some sixteen miles above Richmond," which could be purchased for ten thousand dollars. A committee examined and reported back on the property, which would have accommodated the high school as well as the seminary. But such a relocation was abandoned, in part for financial reasons and in part because, having heard that the campus in Alexandria was uninjured, it was decided to keep the seminary going on a reduced scale at Staunton.[112]

By December Packard had joined Sparrow at Staunton, and four or five students took up their studies with them. Edward H. Ingle was there and reported that William H. Meade and Philip D. Thompson composed the senior class, joined later by Telfair Hodgson. In the spring of 1862, under military threat from Union troops, Sparrow with his family and some students moved to the tobacco plantation owned by the Reverend John T. Clark, rector of Roanoke Parish in Halifax County. In the summer Union troops reached Halifax, and one of the students was killed in the resulting tumult.[113] In the fall of 1862 the seminary returned to Staunton with Sparrow, where it remained for the duration of the war.

William H. Meade wrote of Sparrow at Halifax and of the deepening love and admiration the students had for the man, his joining them in their games, his strong influence on the community, his delight in holding services for the "colored folks," his scholarship and his ability as a teacher.[114] The admiration for Sparrow was no less at Staunton. "I saw a great deal of Sparrow during the War," one observer wrote, "and greatly enjoyed intercourse with him. He bore his trials . . . with Christian fortitude. Indeed, his cheerfulness was truly admired."[115]

In the fall of 1863 Randolph McKim arrived at Staunton to study with Sparrow. He had, previous to his arrival, studied "alone Horne's 'Introduction to the Bible'" and had learned Latin and Greek at the University of Virginia. He found Sparrow to be "a fine Greek and Hebrew scholar, a theologian of great learning, and a profound and original thinker."[116] Under Sparrow he read, as he states in his autobiography, "Conant's Gesenius Hebrew Grammar. Gesenius Hebrew Lexicon. Hebrew Bible. Greek Testament. Paley's Evidences. Butler's Analogy and Sermons. D'Aubigne's History of the Reformation. Mosheim's Ecclesiastical History. Schaff's Church History."[117] No mention is made of any systematic theology, such as that of Knapp, nor any Anglican divines, such as Hooker. He does say that he had the use of the Reverend Richard H. Phillips' library, Phillips being his wife's father, and had access to the "counsel and experience" of that clergyman. He also notes that "Dr. Sparrow required of us an essay on some topic assigned by him once in two weeks, and later we began the composition of sermons, of which I had a store of, I think, twelve."[118]

By February 1864 McKim was licensed by Bishop Johns to conduct services, doing so "in the hospitals and elsewhere and had practice in extempore speaking, which was a useful preparation for my work in the army." He mentions fellow students "Wm. F. Gardner, Edward H.

Ingle, and Horace Hayden." McKim was ordained in May 1864 by Bishop Johns at Staunton and began his duties as chaplain to a battalion of artillery.[119]

Sparrow continued at Staunton until the summer of 1865, teaching, ministering in the community, preaching, caring for his family, and all the time struggling against ill health. A Mrs. Sheffey at Staunton commented,

His health was not robust: he suffered much from languor. . . . He was afflicted with sleeplessness; and the noise of the streets, and the barking of dogs at night, affected his delicate temperament, so as to drive away refreshing slumber. . . . He frequently spoke of death, and expressed the desire that he might not have to endure a long and wasting sickness. . . .[120]

In January of 1865 Horace Edwin Hayden, a seasoned veteran of the war, mentioned by McKim as having been a fellow student in 1864, arrived in Staunton. "I found a seminary in name," he said, "but hardly in fact, since it consisted of only one professor, Rev. Dr. Sparrow, and one student, Mr. Thomas C. Hutchinson, of Canada, a discharged soldier."[121] By then the institution had reverted to that which prevailed before the founding of seminaries: study under the guidance of a learned pastor.

One other note concerning Sparrow during this time must be made here. He was a clerical delegate to the "General Council of the Protestant Episcopal Church in the Confederate States" in 1861 and again in 1862, and an alternate in 1865. Representing Virginia at the council meeting at St. Paul's Church, Augusta, Georgia, November 17–22, 1862, Sparrow was chairman of the committee on the state of the church[122] and a member of the committee on the Bible and the Prayer Book.[123] The report of the committee on the state of the church is a masterpiece, most likely the work of Sparrow himself, reflecting his spirit and his understanding of the nature of the church in Anglican tradition. In the report the action taken in founding another branch of the Anglican Church is defended in terms of the arising of a "new nationality." The reality of secession is recognized, but the claim is made that the church of the Confederate States is fixing its attention "on that mighty and mysterious hand by which all events are ruled and overruled, and on the paramount interests and well-being of that Kingdom which is everlasting, the Kingdom of Christ on earth. . . ." The report then says,

To Christian men the changes which take place in the "kingdoms of this world," must ever have their chief significance in their bearing on the

Church of the living God, even though the precise nature and effect of that bearing be for the present hidden from their eyes. What the God of the nations means to bring about ultimately by the events which have recently taken place, it is not for man to know; but His Church, if found in an attitude of docility, dependence and prayer, is authorized to be very hopeful, and to look for the happiest results. While, therefore, with a firm and tranquil faith, we leave future events in the hands of Him who is head over all things, to and for His Church, let present duty be our concern.[124]

The report proceeds to affirm that the church, though divided by political boundaries, "remains essentially one." Two goals are proposed, the one being the promotion of missions: "Never is the church more herself, than when she is listening to and endeavoring to observe her divine Master's last command, 'Go ye into all the world and preach the Gospel to every creature.'" The other goal was to attend to "the spiritual welfare of the colored population." Finally, the report speaks to "the spirit in which all our work should be done in the church of Christ." It points directly to "the presence and influence of the Holy Ghost" and the need to depend upon "the direct blessing of Heaven." In a statement that encapsulates the spirit of Anglicanism and reflects, to my mind, the insight of Sparrow, we read,

Is it not possible, that the great lesson needed and designed to be impressed upon us at this time, and transferred afresh from our creed to our hearts, is, that 'Paul may plant and Apollo may water, but God giveth the increase'? Surely it is not too much to believe, that blessed as we are with a Scriptural creed, an Apostolic ministry, a spiritual liturgy, a wise constitution and canons, and a general system at once orthodox and yet liberal, stable and yet comprehensive, possessing all the advantages of antiquity, without obsoleteness or a rigid applicability; if our minds were turned with more intensity to a devout consideration of the great doctrine of divine influences as a practical doctrine, and to a more distinct and habitual recognition of our need of what our Catechism calls God's 'special grace' in all our doings in the church of Christ, it might inaugurate a course of prosperity among us, more proportioned to the desires of our hearts and the wants of the world.[125]

Here is the voice of reason but also of deep piety, which in the midst of war, when many voices were loudly proclaiming what God is doing, why and how, implores openness to the influence of the Holy Spirit, openness to divine grace. It is also a voice that speaks clearly about the design of the Anglican ethos—"a Scriptural creed, an Apostolic ministry, a spiritual liturgy, a wise constitution and canons, and a general system at once orthodox, and yet liberal. . . ."

The Seminary during the Civil War

6. THE WAR-TORN CAMPUS: A PLACE OF PAIN AND DEATH

For much of the war, while Sparrow was at Staunton, Packard was at Alexandria or elsewhere in the North. His route to Alexandria was circuitous, involving weeks and months in which he crossed back and forth between Union and Confederate territories looking for his son Walter, who died of typhoid fever while serving in the Confederate army. His son William died while a prisoner of the Union forces. In the fall of 1862 Packard was ill with an "indolent tumor or carbuncle" in his right shoulder, which he suspected might be cancerous. The tumor was removed, but he did not mend and went to Washington, D.C., where surgeons worked on it, the result being that he had a permanently stiff arm, finally amputated in 1884. After three months of convalescence in Washington, he went to Alexandria and there, for a time, occupied the parsonage of Christ Church. Forced out by military orders, he and his family settled in the house of "Mrs John Lloyd (C.F. Lee's sister) corner of Queen and Washington."

While in Alexandria he conducted services where he could, Christ Church being used by Union chaplains for the army and St. Paul's being a hospital, and ministered as a pastor to many. During this time he managed to be arrested and was quickly released. He also managed to make a long trip with Dr. Addison to Lake Superior. There is no mention of any formal seminary teaching.[126] Packard wrote,

> During the two years I spent in Alexandria I recorded in my book sixty-three burials, chiefly of infants. I had a Bible-class in my house on Sunday afternoons for ladies, which was well attended, and I preached where I could in halls, and performed baptisms and burials for Methodists, Lutherans, and Presbyterians, as well as for my own people.[127]

At the end of the war he was ill again, this time with jaundice, and was transported to Fauquier for convalescence before returning to Alexandria to join Sparrow and eleven students to begin again.

In June 1862 Packard had driven with his wife from Fauquier to Washington. "We stopped at the Seminary and entered our house, which was occupied by bakers and their families. My wife went to open her wardrobe to see if any of her property was left, but was not allowed to do so."[128] The fact is that in spite of the hopeful report received in Richmond in October 1861, the seminary buildings and grounds were in process of being despoiled even before all of the students were gone. Persons breaking in to loot unguarded houses on the campus prompted a request for an army guard. An eye witness reports going out to the seminary with Cassius Lee, the board member who assumed responsibility for caring for the seminary during the war, and finding soldiers of the requested guard stacking their rifles in Prayer Hall. Lee objected but left only to be informed shortly after that the situation had deteriorated. He arrived back at the campus to find the houses of May and Sparrow broken into, seemingly to be searched, and the guard in possession of the property.[129] Within weeks the seminary had been commandeered to become a Union hospital. Some property was preserved, such as the library and its books. But damage was widespread, and personal properties, including furniture, were all lost.[130]

Temporary buildings, such as barracks, were erected. Dr. May's house was the residence of some of the surgeons; Sparrow's house was occupied by his son-in-law, the Reverend Mr. Jerome, chaplain to the hospital; Packard's house became a bakery; and Bishop John's house was occupied by Union officers. In 1862 the library was the office of Dr. H.A. Armstrong, the surgeon in command, his desk being on the "gallery overlooking the floor where his clerks worked." The rest of the buildings were the hospital proper. Private Edward P. Tobie, Company G, 1st Maine Cavalry, wrote a report of his stay at the "Fairfax Seminary" as a patient and then as a hospital clerk. As we read in Lt. Col. Thomas Atwood's account of Tobie's observation, the hospital was a grim place.

Initially deaths were few in the hospital, but when the wounded from second Bull Run and the sick from the Chickahominy arrived, they increased rapidly. . . . Patient deaths were now occurring at the rate of seven to ten a day, and this went on for some time. Unlike most hospitals in the Washington area, Fairfax Seminary conducted military funerals. Although the chaplain was not always available, the soldiers were buried under the American flag, and the customary three volleys were fired over the grave. Tobie considered it the right thing to do, but the daily occurrence of these "lonesomest of all ceremonies" for soldiers far from home, family and friends rendered the honors almost meaningless.[131]

Time would erase the memories of guns firing over graves, the screams of agony from men in pain, the sobs of relatives informed of the death of sons, fathers, husbands, brothers. But the reality would remain that the Virginia Theological Seminary was involved in that horrendous war and that its soil was stained by the blood of dying men.

At the end of the war, while the buildings stood, they were, as Cornelius Walker tells us, "a good deal injured, the furniture of the rooms entirely gone, the enclosures and out-houses had disappeared, and large portions of the grounds were covered with temporary structures for the accommodation of the sick and wounded."[132] One visitor in 1862 observed, "We find the country so much altered that we could scarcely recognize it. All the trees for miles in the rear of the Seminary have been cut down. A grove has been left around St. George's, and a few trees in front of the Seminary and those around Dr. Sparrow's and Dr. May's houses have been mostly spared." The same was true at the high school. "No fences have been left upon the grounds."[133] The contrast between the seminary as it appeared in May 1861 with its new buildings and its lush green grounds, resplendent with woods all around, and the seminary in the summer of 1865 must have been heart-rending, raising questions in the minds of many as to the future of the seminary—in this place or any place.

7. WILLIAM SPARROW: ANGLICAN THEOLOGIAN

On March 14, 1862, William Meade died. Bishop Johns, in his address at Meade's funeral in Richmond, reported that on the night before his death Meade spoke to him privately and said that he affirmed the "views of evangelical truth and order" that he had held for fifty years. He also had affirmed his initial resistance to secession but admitted that, once secession could not be avoided, he supported the South in its cause. "I trust the South will persevere in separation," he said. He also affirmed his "hope is in Christ, 'the Rock of Ages,'" and stated that he was prepared to die. "I am at peace with God through Jesus Christ, my Lord, and in charity with all men, even our bitterest enemies." But he then added, "All that has ever been said in commendation of me I loathe and abhor, as utterly inconsistent with my consciousness of sin."[134]

John Johns succeeded Meade as Bishop of Virginia and president of the Virginia Theological Seminary. He knew well the diocese and the seminary, having been made assistant bishop in 1842 and having lived at the seminary in the house called "Malvern" since 1854, while also serving as vice president of the board of trustees. Like Meade he was to serve as professor of pastoral theology, to which was added the discipline of homiletics. Educated at Princeton, he was highly regarded as a student by Charles Hodges and was chosen to teach Hebrew in Princeton Seminary. Randolph McKim, whom Johns confirmed and ordained, depicts the bishop as a staunch Evangelical. He seemed to find his motto in Paul's words: "I am determined not to know anything among you save Jesus Christ and Him crucified."[135] As such he was strongly opposed to the Tractarians and defended the views of Zwingli on the Holy Communion against the views of Canon Liddon and Bishop Browne. He was also "unwaveringly attached to the Church of his birth." His father being warden of the church in New Castle, Delaware, he "was thoroughly loyal to the Prayer Book and the Articles of Religion which he held to be of the greatest importance as interpretive of the doctrine of the Prayer Book. With the great Hooker he held Episcopacy necessary, not to the *being*, but to the *well-being* of the Church, and gladly grasped the hand of every Christian man as a brother in the faith."[136] Johns was to be a key figure in the next stage of the seminary's development, that of reconstruction.

The other key figure, and indeed the person who most embodied the institution in 1865 as the new beginning was underway, was William Sparrow. His was the vision and the dedication necessary to keep the seminary going, even if nominally during the war, and to revive the seminary in Alexandria after the war's end. On July 13, 1843, Sparrow had given an address at commencement, "The Right Conduct of Seminaries,"[137] which provides a glimpse of his vision and dedication. Sparrow began his address by affirming the interconnectedness of religion and education, while lamenting the times when Christians viewed them in opposition, some regarding education with suspicion, other's overestimating the importance of learning, substituting philosophical conclusions for the truths of revelation. He stated, "The history of all ages shows that a cold, philosophic formalism produces a wild and ignorant enthusiasm, and *vice-versa*. The true remedy is to retain learning, but in its proper place." The same is true of seminaries. "Here learning and religion are necessarily brought into the closest contact. That they may be abused is most manifest, because learning may be abused; but that on that account they should be discarded, no more follows than that learning should be discarded."

In quest of the right relationship between learning and religion, Sparrow noted three things that "should be aimed at in theological seminaries" and thus indicated the divisions of his address: "that *knowledge* be attained; that this knowledge be important *truth*; and that this truth be vivified and actuated in the mind of the student by the *right spirit*."

Concerning the first aim, the attainment of knowledge, he said,

> Let there be a prescribed course of study, let works full of well-arranged information be selected as text books; let time, full time be taken; let the officers be punctual in their duty, and see that the students are equally prompt and regular; let examinations be held at suitable periods; and let such other subsidiary means be employed as are usual in all educational institutions, for stimulating the mind and preserving its inquisitiveness and elasticity; and the general result must necessarily be success.

Sparrow was confident that with such a regimen, guided by men of scholarly aptitude, learning would occur. His worry was that in seminaries the effort expended "cultivates the head, but neglects the heart."

The second aim was that the knowledge attained "be truth—the truth of God." Such truth is in Scripture and is prior to sacraments. He had in mind here "the simple gospel, such as St. Paul prescribed . . . which has been ordained as the power of God unto salvation." The basic means for obtaining truth is the Bible, and he means "the Bible, not with the authoritative aid of tradition, but ALONE." He protested that this did not mean ignoring aid in interpreting Scripture, "come it from Christians, Jews, Turks, Infidels, or Heretics; come it from common sense, or from philosophy; come it from the church or from the world; but these helps are all of the same class . . . being destitute of authority to bind the conscience except that authority which belongs to all human testimony." He was convinced that "implicit reliance can be placed upon God only, in his word, by his Spirit, and through his Son." This he held against all who taught to the contrary, Roman Catholics and Tractarians alike.

Nevertheless, Sparrow went on to say, "It is not enough to have the Bible for our rule of faith: we must be guided by right principles, both intellectual and moral, in the study of its pages. Under the head of right intellectual principles," he said, "I include not only a correct system of hermeneutics, but right logical principles in general." He had in mind primary truths "connected with our intellectual and moral nature," which neither are nor can be proved by other truths "gathered by induction from the constitution of the human mind, and the constitution of universal nature which cannot be lost sight of, without exposing revelation to undeserved assault, and ourselves to unnecessary error." Furthermore, "there are principles deducible from a general view of the dispensation under which Heaven has cast our lot, and from the nature of Christianity as a spiritual religion." All such truths and principles must be taken into account as we search the Scriptures and "look into the details of the Christian system," for, he concluded, "without them we shall see things out of proportion, and be as incapable of understanding their true spirit and relations as inhabitants of an ant-hill of taking in the geography of a continent." Here is the "law of proportion," so important to Meade and to Anglican understanding.

In brief, Sparrow urged that "common sense" be heeded. "Plain common sense, a practical habit of mind, a habit which makes most of fundamentals, which is shy when men would lead it off into subtleties, which the first masters of language can hardly express, and which is slow to admit distant deductions from concrete premises, when they conflict with plain matters of fact; such a habit of mind is invaluable." Sparrow expanded this thought, speaking of "the *spirit* of the Baconian philosophy . . . which best accords with the right use of the Bible as the standard of all religious truth." This philosophy is humbly cautious, patient, simple, practical, and distrustful of itself. The Bible and logical principles were not sufficient, however, for the Christian "must have an honest *desire* to know that truth, and as honest a *purpose* to abide by it" [emphasis added].

It was with the Bible in hand, together with right principles and the exercise of the proper spirit, "that our Church, under God, arrived at those conclusions which constitute that system we teach—that form of sound words which we find in the Articles, Homilies, and Liturgies." He then summed up that system in a few words, much as A.T. Mollegen, a distant successor to Sparrow, was prone to do. The summary begins with the Fall and with the fundamental inclination toward evil in all people, resulting in their ruin. The way out is provided by the gospel, by the sacrifice of the Lamb, who died for all and through whom salvation is made available to all. The positive response to the salvific event is conversion and new life ("by grace they are saved through faith, and that not of themselves"). This salvation involves both a change of nature and of relationship—"of God's view of the individual sinner, and the individual sinner's disposition toward God."

Sparrow then went on at length about the doctrine of justification, arguing that in articles, homilies, and liturgy, in the doctrine, discipline, and worship of the Protestant Episcopal Church, we subscribe to this doctrine of justification "by grace through faith"—which faith *necessarily* produces the fruits of righteousness in heart and life." We note here a statement that reflects not only Sparrow's view but that of Anglicanism:

> The moment a man is justified, that moment is he (in part) sanctified: so the scriptures and the standards of our church teach: and yet these same primary and secondary rules of faith teach also, that works of righteousness are the fruits of that faith by which alone we are justified; that they follow after justification; and that works done before this gratuitous justification, however useful for this life, and however valuable in human judgment, before God partake of the nature of sin.[138]

That justification should thus precede sanctification is to be explained in terms of "the necessity of beating down the pride of the human heart, and making it look, where only it is of use to look for acceptance before God, the merits, unaided and alone, of the Lord Jesus Christ."

This, then, was Sparrow's fundamental belief. Beyond it are other, "deeper questions" that require the exercise of reserve and caution, as articles, homilies, and liturgy suggest. The English Reformers show the way with "great decision and clearness on things fundamental, and great caution, with perhaps some want of consistency, on matters lying further in the region of speculation and metaphysics." He then enunciated a most important principle:

> When we reflect that from the Reformation down to the present day, there have lived and taught in the Church of England men who have held to Calvinism, Baxterianism, Arminianism, Nationalism, and Ecclesiasticalism, filling every station, from the throne of Canterbury to the humblest curacy; we are constrained to believe ourselves bound to the utmost toleration on the profounder points of theology, and to a free allowance of the rights of these several schools to the privileges of our communion, and the work of our ministry; *provided always*, that on the plain, practical and vital points, they fail not to speak as do the Bible and the Prayer Book.[139]

He feared not only unwarranted dogmatism on obscure matters of doctrine and not only a narrowing of the church into a sect but also such latitudinarianism on doctrinal matters as disregards Scripture, violates the best philosophy, and tends to put too much emphasis on externals.

Sparrow was much concerned that students understand the proper place of externals in relation to the internal state of the church. The external arrangements of the church, including episcopacy, may rightly be based on "inspired precept where it exists, and where it does not, on apostolic precedent; on primitive and almost universal usage, and on the fitness of things, as seen in the agreement of ecclesiastical arrangements with the principles of the human mind, and the nature of our civil constitution." On this basis Sparrow defended "all the externals of our church which are of prominent importance." The former conflict over externals in the Protestant Episcopal Church he attributed to the violation of "the law of proportion as a rule of reasoning," which is to ignore the logical principles he has considered.

The third aim is that the important truth, the gospel of salvation, "be vivified and actuated in the mind of the student by the *right spirit*." Here he affirmed that "a body of divinity without the spirit of Christ, is dead . . . and . . . when being left in that condition, it decays and dissolves—a nuisance to all spiritual men and a pest to society at large." It is a mistake to assume that personal piety will grow in a theological seminary without intentional cultivation. "The professors should exhort the students to cultivate the life of God in the soul, and the students should exhort one another. Meetings among the students, under proper regulations, should be encouraged. Active benevolence, also, should be urged upon them, to prevent their piety from growing morbid and monastic. Above all, private prayer, secret communion with God through Christ, should be represented as something which ought not to be omitted by inmates of such a building as this, no more than praise can be omitted in heaven. A holy atmosphere should surround the place,—a heavenly spirit should actuate every heart."

Sparrow concluded:

This, after all is the main thing. Knowledge we should have, and mental discipline, and proper elocution, and right views of truth; but what are they all, if the good Spirit of our God abide not in the midst?[140]

These, then, were the convictions of the man who would lead the seminary in the difficult days ahead of reconstruction.

NOTES

1. See, for instance, D.M. Potter, "National and Sectional Forces in the United States," *The New Cambridge Modern History*, vol. 10, *The Zenith of European Power, 1830–1870*, ed. J.P.T. Bury (Cambridge: At the University Press, 1960), 614–15.

2. H. Shelton Smith, Robert T. Handy, Lefferts A. Loetscher, eds., *American Christianity: An Historical Interpretation with Representative Documents* (New

York: Scribners, 1960), 1:469.
3. But espoused different ways and means for ending slavery; see Addison, *Episcopal Church*, 190.
4. Potter, "National and Sectional Forces," 616.
5. Russel B. Nye, *William Lloyd Garrison* (Boston: Little Brown, 1955), 48.
6. Alice F. Tyler, *Freedom's Ferment: Phases of American Social History* (Minneapolis: Augsburg, 1944), 519.
7. H. Richard Niebuhr, *The Social Sources of Denominationalism* (New York: Meridian, 1960), 190.
8. Nevins and Commager, *History of the United States*, 206–207.
9. William A. Clebsch, "Christian Interpretations of the Civil War," *Church History* 30 (June 1961): 217.
10. David Lynn Holmes, Jr., "William Meade and the Church of Virginia, 1789–1829" (Unpublished diss. Princeton University, 1971), 206–207.
11. Walker, *Sparrow*, 129. We have very little information of slavery at VTS.
12. Alexander V.G. Allen, *Life and Letters of Phillips Brooks* (New York: Dutton, 1900), 1:149.
13. Walker, *Sparrow*, 135–36.
14. William A. Clebsch, ed., *Journals of the Protestant Episcopal Church in the Confederate States of America: Centenary Edition in Facsimile* (Austin: Church Historical Society, 1962), II-4 and elsewhere, III-12 and elsewhere, IV-6.
15. Packard, *Recollections*, 107.
16. Ibid., 111.
17. In Clebsch, *Journals*, III-209. He is simply listed as a clergyman resident in Virginia.
18. Goodwin, *History* 1:219–20.
19. Packard, *Recollections*, 264.
20. Catalogue (1842–43), 6.
21. Diocese of Virginia, *Journal* (1849), 37.
22. Catalogue (1860–61), 10, indicates fifty-seven students, which is probably the number for 1859–60. The figure of seventy-three is found in Packard's *Recollections*, 264. Most likely Packard is counting fifteen men in the preparatory department. See Goodwin, *History* 1:218 and 221.
23. See Diocese of Virginia, *Journal* (1849), 37, and (1852), 30.
24. Ibid. (1855), 47.
25. Packard, *Recollections*, 264.
26. From the New York correspondent of the *London Record* in *Southern Churchman* 22/26 (July 4, 1856): 102.
27. Catalogue (1860–61), 10.
28. *Southern Churchman* 22/34 (August 29, 1856): 135. But see list in Goodwin, *History* 2:170.
29. *Southern Churchman* 8/36 (September 30, 1842): 142.
30. Ibid. 8/13 (April 22, 1842): 51.
31. Goodwin, *History* 2:643.
32. *Southern Churchman* 22/26 (July 4, 1846): 102.

33. On this and other matters, see the "Annual Appeal," *Southern Churchman* 10/9 (March 22, 1844): 34.
34. Ibid. 10/4 (February 16, 1844): 15.
35. Diocese of Virginia, *Journal* (1847), 33–34.
36. Ibid. (1848), 45,
37. Ibid. (1849), 38.
38. Ibid. (1850), 50.
39. Ibid. (1851), 39.
40. Ibid. (1858), 31.
41. *Southern Churchman* 10/31 (August 23, 1844): 123.
42. Ibid. 10/49 (November 1, 1844): 163.
43. Goodwin, *History* 1:205.
44. *Southern Churchman* 21/17 (May 3, 1855): 67.
45. Goodwin, *History* 1:209–210. See pp. 205–210.
46. Diocese of Virginia, *Journal* (1854), 29–30.
47. Ibid., 30–31.
48. *Southern Churchman* 21/51 (December 28, 1855): 203.
49. Ibid. 22/16 (April 25, 1856): 63.
50. Diocese of Virginia, *Journal* (1856), 23.
51. Goodwin, *History* 1:354.
52. Diocese of Virginia, *Journal* (1858), 31; Bishop Meade's report.
53. Report of meeting, July 7, 1857; manuscript found loose in the trustee's minute book for 1866–98, 2.
54. *Southern Churchman* 25/40 (October 7, 1859): 2.
55. Meade to the Virginia convention, May 16, 1860, *Southern Churchman* 26/21 (May 25, 1860): 2.
56. Diocese of Virginia, *Journal* (1857), 25. See *Southern Churchman* 22/45 (November 14, 1856): 179.
57. Catalogue (1850–51), 4.
58. For the biography of May, see Alexander Shiras, *Life and Letters of the Rev. James May, D.D.* (Philadelphia: Protestant Episcopal Book Society, [1865]); John S. Stone, *A Discourse, Commemorative of the Life and Character of the Rev. James May, D.D.* (Philadelphia: J.S. McCalla, 1864); and Goodwin, *History* 1:615–17.
59. James May, *The Advantage of Church Membership with Reference to some Errors, Historically Viewed, A Sermon Delivered at the Opening of the Diocesan Convention of the Protestant Episcopal Church of Virginia, in Winchester, May 10, 1847* (Philadelphia: Stavely and McCalla, 1847), 27.
60. Shiras, May, 32.
61. James May, *The Proper Office and Spirit of the Ministry, A Sermon Preached Before the Society of the Alumni of the Theological Seminary of Virginia* (Washington: Wm. Q. Force, 1844), 5–6.
62. Packard, *Recollections*, 177.
63. *Semi-Centennial*, 70.
64. See note 53, above.

65. Goodwin, *History* 1:223.
66. Diocese of Virginia, *Journal* (1853), 33. For another detailed account of the curriculum and teaching, see *Southern Churchman* 18/29 (July 29, 1852): 114.
67. Diocese of Virginia, *Journal* (1845), 50.
68. Ibid., 51.
69. Catalogue)1843–44), n.p.
70. Diocese of Virginia, *Journal* (1847), 34–35.
71. Ibid. (1851), 40.
72. Ibid. (1853), 33.
73. Catalogue (1845–46), 10.
74. Diocese of Virginia, *Journal* (1845), 51.
75. Ibid. (1853), 33.
76. Ibid. (1848), 47.
77. See catalogue (1860–61), 14. In addition to Mosheim and Short, May listed church histories by Schaff, Guericke and Neander, "Bishop White's Memoirs of the Protestant Episcopal Church," and, under the "Nature, Ministry and Polity of the Church," in addition to Hooker, "Wheatley on Common Prayer," and, for a time, "Onderdonk's 'Episcopacy tested by Scripture,'" "Potter on Church Government," and "Barrow on the Pope's Supremacy." Under "Pastoral Theology and Pulpit Eloquence," we find "Burnet on the Pastoral Care," "Bridges on the Christian Ministry," and "Whateley's Rhetoric."
78. *Southern Churchman* 21/29 (July 26, 1855): 115, and Goodwin, *History* 1:333–34.
79. Goodwin, *History* 2:517.
80. *Southern Churchman* 25/31 (August 5, 1859).
81. Allen, *Brooks* 1:275.
82. Bd. min., 1866–98 (June 26, 1894), 291–292.
83. See *Southern Churchman* 26/27 (July 8, 1859): 3.
84. Ibid. 12/22 (June 19, 1846).
85. Ibid. 25/25 (June 24, 1859): 2.
86. Ibid. 12/22 (June 19, 1846).
87. Allen, *Brooks* 1:149–150.
88. Ibid. 1:151.
89. Ibid. 1:153.
90. Ibid. 1:154.
91. Ibid. 1:156–57.
92. Ibid. 1:162.
93. Ibid. 1:163.
94. Ibid. 1:174.
95. Ibid. 1:206.
96. Ibid. 1:216.
97. Ibid. 1:268.
98. Ibid. 1: 275.
99. Ibid. 1:279.

100. Ibid. 1:285.
101. Goodwin, *History* 1:220.
102. Ibid. 1:221–22.
103. Walker, *Sparrow*, 240.
104. Packard, *Recollections*, 264–65.
105. Walker, *Sparrow*, 242.
106. Ibid., 243–44.
107. Packard, *Recollections*, 265.
108. Walker, *Sparrow*, 257.
109. Goodwin, *History* 1:592.
110. Packard, *Recollections*, 264.
111. See letter of Sparrow to C.F. Lee, July 13, 1861, in Goodwin, *History* 1:247–48.
112. Walker, *Sparrow*, 248–49.
113. Goodwin, *History* 2:185–87.
114. Ibid., 186, where Ingle reports that Sparrow "was a great quoit pitcher." See also Walker, Sparrow, 251–52.
115. Walker, *Sparrow*, 256. See other tributes, 256–58.
116. Randolph H. McKim. A Soldier's *Recollections*: Leaves from the Diary of a Young Confederate (New York, 1911), 211.
117. Ibid., 213.
118. Ibid.
119. Ibid., 211.
120. Walker, *Sparrow*, 257–58.
121. Ibid., 259. See Goodwin, *History* 2:190, for another report from Hayden.
122. Clebsch, *Journals*, III-16, III-103.
123. Ibid., III-117, III-183.
124. Ibid., III-100.
125. Ibid., III-102.
126. Packard, *Recollections*, 276–84.
127. Ibid., 283.
128. Ibid., 276.
129. Walker, *Sparrow*, 244–45.
130. See Goodwin, *History* 1:226–229 for details.
131. Thomas W. Atwood, "Life in a U.S. Army Hospital, 1862," *Army* (January 1988): 56.
132. Walker, *Sparrow*, 261.
133. Goodwin, *History* 1:228.
134. Johns, *Meade*, 512.
135. Goodwin, *History* 2:2.
136. Ibid., 5–6.
137. *Southern Churchman* 9/31 (1843): 121–22.
138. Ibid.
139. Ibid.
140. Ibid.

━•❀❀•━

THE
RECONSTRUCTION
OF THE
SEMINARY
1865–1895

1. BEGINNING AGAIN: SPARROW AND JOHNS

The war came to an end on April 9, 1865, in the living room of Wilmer McLean at Appomatox, Virginia. James M. McPherson writes of Lee and Grant: "The vanquished commander, six feet tall and erect in bearing, arrived in full-dress uniform with sash and jeweled sword; the victor, five feet eight with stooped shoulders, appeared in his usual private's blouse with mudspattered trousers tucked into muddy boots—because his head-quarters wagon had fallen behind in the race to cut off the enemy. There in McLean's parlor the son of an Ohio tanner dictated surrender terms to the scion of a First Family of Virginia."[1] The reconstruction of the humili-ated and devastated South began, and the revolutionary expansion of northern industry and of the economy in general, stimulated by the war, continued. The plight of the South was evident: its economy shattered, proud cities such as Atlanta, Richmond, and Charleston laid waste by military bombardment and all-consuming fires, farms abandoned, and lo-cal communities in ruins.

In later years some were to conclude that the reconstruction had a positive effect, but in 1865 that was not at all apparent.[2] Furthermore, the best minds were convinced that victory by the North having been achieved and the Union preserved, there should be no rancor, no vindictive punishment levied on the South. Grant said, when after Appomatox he ordered his troops to stop their celebrations, "The war is over; the rebels are our countrymen again, and the best sign of rejoicing after victory will be to abstain from all demonstration."[3] Not all were as wise as Grant nor as forgiving. Divisions continued, notably among churches such as the Baptists and the Presbyterians, North and South. The Episcopal Church was different. The church in the North welcomed back the southern Episcopalians, never having recognized their secession, holding seats for Southern delegates to General Convention, awaiting their return. As Addison said, what was significant for the future of the Episcopal Church "was the action which was not taken."[4] The healing of the wounds was not immediate, however. The General Convention meeting in Philadelphia in October 1865 was attended by few Southerners. The General Council of the "Church in the (late) Confederate States" met in Augusta, Georgia, in November where, mindful of the "spirit of charity which prevailed in the proceedings of the General Convention" held in Philadelphia and recognizing that the "exigency" which brought about the forming of an independent church "no longer exists," supported the right of any diocese to withdraw from "union with this Council."[5] And so the deed was done.

As the war came to an end, the seminary was still a hospital and its future was in doubt. Some thought was given to the reorganization of the institution, and having decided to do so on the old campus, efforts were begun to secure the return of land and buildings to the board of trustees. Soon after the end of hostilities Sparrow and his wife left Staunton and traveled by way of Richmond to Baltimore, to the home of their daughter Frances and to a reunion with their two surviving sons. While there, Sparrow received an invitation to return to Kenyon College and declined it, saying to Cassius Lee, "I have no disposition to leave Virginia while she thinks my services worth having. Her being in distress is a reason with me, if I can live at all, to abide with her, and share her lot."[6] The declining of this invitation was of the greatest importance for the future of the seminary.

While at Baltimore Sparrow wrote a letter to a former student, Eli Canfield, in Brooklyn, revealing to him the degree of his identity with the South and his participation in a mood widely felt by Southerners reestablishing contact with northern friends. Sparrow said, "I confess I stand in doubt how such as I will be regarded, even by old friends at the North. If you can exercise no more flattering feeling toward us, I trust that, in your magnanimity, you will, at least, pity us!"[7]

By the middle of July, Bishop Johns, as president of the board of trustees, went to Alexandria, where, with the counsel of Sparrow and Cassius Lee, who had cared for the seminary's interests all through the war, he made "a formal application for the restoration of the property" by the War Department to the board. In his diary for August 13, Bishop Johns wrote,

> Understanding that our application to the Secretary of War . . . has been successful, I returned to Alexandria, to participate in arrangements for the purpose of resuming the exercises of the Seminary . . . I am happy to report that Professors Sparrow and Packard are again occupying their houses, and that the several halls will be ready for the reception of students as advertised, in October next. Funds for the salaries of our Professors have been most providentially obtained, but we shall much need aid in maintaining our beneficiaries, for which we appeal earnestly. [8]

The high school buildings, he reported, "have been so seriously damaged as to forbid any hope of being able to use them at present." [9]

Packard, now recovered from jaundice, and Sparrow, bothered by a rheumatic hand and never robust, had to contend with restoring their own houses, as well as the seminary property in general.[10] Sparrow was also concerned at this time for the reunion of the church and specifically for the return of the Diocese of Virginia to the General Convention. He attended the diocesan council at Richmond in September where he found the majority of the delegates opposed to reunion, tabling the matter until the next council meeting.[11] Sparrow rightly understood that the future of the seminary depended upon such reunion; for although an institution of the diocese, it was dependent upon raising funds and obtaining students from the North and the rapidly developing West.

The seminary was fortunate in that the main buildings were still standing. They had been damaged; their furniture was gone; fencing had disappeared, and temporary structures erected by the army were left strewn about the grounds. From mid-August until October much had to be done if the seminary was to open as advertised. Bishop Johns secured access to the only money readily available and appealed for more. That available was in the form of a bequest from the late John Johns of Baltimore, funds deeded before the war and deposited in a Baltimore bank, amounting to $8,632.[12] As Walker commented, "Things were righted up as far as possible. Some few rooms were furnished in the Seminary, furniture enough, of the simplest kind, to enable them to live, was obtained by the professors; temporary buildings connected with previous occupants were removed, a rough enclosure for the grounds was put up, and the anticipated opening anxiously awaited."[13]

The first students to arrive were veterans of the war, wearing their old Confederate uniforms and often addressing each other as major this and colonel that. When David Barr arrived, he found the place looking desolate. Walker, visiting the campus the next April, found the "appearance of things, especially of the grounds . . . peculiarly discouraging. The very grass had, in many places, in the succession of camps, been killed to the roots, leaving the fields full of bare spaces."[14] For Barr the first impression was offset by the warm greeting he received from Sparrow. On Barr's arrival there were five students.[15] Sparrow reported to John P. Hubbard in November that there were seven students, with three more expected "before New Year's Day."[16] Packard remembered the seminary opening with eleven students.[17]

Sparrow and Packard were the only teachers. According to Walker they divided the work between them, Sparrow teaching church history as well as systematic divinity and apologetics. Packard likewise taught subjects beyond those at first assigned to him. There were two classes, the middle class composed of students who had begun work at Staunton, joined by one or two others, and the junior class. In addition preparatory department students were taught by Sparrow alone until Thomas Dudley, a seminary student, provided some teaching assistance.[18]

David Barr recalls Sparrow at this time with admiration, noting that in the first winter, having no means of riding into Alexandria, they walked. Sparrow walked into town and back almost every day, sometimes nearly frozen, arriving at the seminary on one occasion with "his eyelids frozen together."[19] Sparrow's classes were held either in his "study or in one of the students' rooms." Packard's were "either in his study or in Prayer Hall." Of Sparrow, Barr said, "The preparatory classes in Greek and the sciences [were] recited to Dr. Sparrow in his study. His fondness for Greek made him a painstaking teacher in it, and he was so instructive a teacher, that things which others might consider dry were invested by him with interest and freshness."[20]

The students dined at first in a second-story room in Aspinwall Hall, the dining room under Bohlen being too large for their small numbers. In the spring of 1866 a Miss Jones arrived to be the seminary matron. The dining room in Bohlen was reopened, and living conditions were greatly improved.[21] At the beginning, according to H.E. Hayden, a student, the food "was very little better than the rations we had received in the field. We had, however, been soldiers and had learned to endure hardness."[22] The students were scattered, two or three in each building (Aspinwall, Bohlen, and Meade); they preferred Aspinwall "as affording better rooms and rendering things more cheerful and home-like."[23] The chapel was not used at first, although it, having been used for religious services during the war, was in fairly good condition. In fact it was judged to be too large for the small congregation and too expensive to heat. "Prayer Hall was furnished, to be used for morning and evening worship, as also for Sunday services during the first four or five months of the session."[24]

Faculty meetings (the traditional meetings of the student body with the faculty) were not held at first. They began again in January 1866 in Prayer Hall. Thomas Dudley reported,

> According to custom, after one of them had said some prayers, and a hymn had been sung by the little company of students present, the two Professors, Dr. Sparrow and Dr. Packard, sitting in their chairs, talked to us briefly, simply, and earnestly, about the spiritual life, and specially about the temptations and trials of a Clergyman. I remember that I went away from this first meeting disheartened and afraid. The ideal which had been set before us was so high, that I felt unequal to even attempt its attainment. And I cannot forget the sweet and comforting words of Dr. Packard, which he spoke to me on the way to his home, in response to my expression of fear that I could not go forward to the work of the Ministry.[25]

Thomas Dudley, later Bishop of Kentucky, remembered Sparrow as possessing "the greatest intellect with which I have come in contact in any department of life," teaching students to think. Of Packard he said that he was "preeminently . . . the student of the Bible" whose "presence was a benediction." The two professors, he tells us, taught their students carefully and well, inculcating "an intelligent, rational, loyal devotion to the Historic Church, her Orders, her Doctrine, her Prayer Book, her Spirit of Missions."[26]

Thus Dudley spoke of the first difficult year in the reconstruction of the seminary, concluding, "A second year I passed at the Seminary, but of that period I need not speak, for the conditions were then almost normal."[27] In time, the Missionary and Rhetorical societies began meeting again. Students began arriving from the North, some of them veterans of the war. A rumor was spread about that the Ku Klux Klan "had been organized in the neighborhood and that one of its objects was to assault and even kill the Northern students, and one of them became alarmed and left the Institution." Goodwin asserts that there was "absolutely no foundation to the rumor, and from the day when the Seminary reopened, a cordial welcome was given them at the Seminary."[28] It should be noted that the rumor had to do with the neighborhood and not the seminary itself. In 1867 the Alumni Association met again with a large representation from both North and South. Goodwin tells of an interesting occasion "when a Confederate soldier student was relating the incident which had occurred in a certain battle, a student on the other side of the table responded, 'Yes, I was there and saw what you speak of from the other side of the battle line.'"[29]

2. REBUILDING: FINANCES, STUDENTS, AND A NEW CHAPEL

On May 17, 1866, the board of trustees of the seminary and the high school met formally for the first time in the postwar period. There were but few in attendance: Johns as president, Grammer, Andrews, Woodbridge, McGuire, and Cornelius Walker, who took the minutes. Cassius F. Lee and Dr. Clagett represented the laity. The meeting opened with a minute memorializing Bishop Meade.[30] This was followed by Bishop Johns' report, principally a statement, dated October 12, 1865, of funds received and disbursed by him on behalf of the seminary. With reference to the $8,632.00 deposited at the bank in Baltimore, he said that $3,132.00 was loaned to Cassius Lee "to be used for fencing and repairs on Seminary Buildings, to be paid back from any appropriation made by Government for damages"; $1,250.00 was paid to Sparrow and $1,500.00 to Packard toward their salaries. This left a balance of $2,750.00. Cassius Lee, appointed treasurer pro tempore, reported receipts of $3,864.56 and disbursements of $3,850.10, leaving a cash balance of $14.46.[31] Such was the tenuous financial condition of the seminary.

The board at this meeting nominated eight additional members, accepted John P. McGuire's resignation as rector of the Episcopal High School, appointed a committee to reopen the high school, elected Cornelius Walker to the faculty to fill the chair vacated by May, and requested Sparrow to raise the funds needed to pay the new professor fifteen hundred dollars per year for five years. Of the eight men nominated to board membership, the Reverend Messrs. George H. Norton and Churchill J. Gibson, and Mr. E.S. Pegram were elected.[32]

Sparrow then proceeded on a circuit through Baltimore, Philadelphia, and New York seeking funds for the new professor and for the general expenses of the seminary. He admitted that up to the end of November 1865 "we have received nothing from north of Baltimore, which is fairly overrun with Southern beggars!"[33] On his first trip he raised five thousand dollars to be paid in five annual installments and on a second, briefer trip he raised more. He wrote to Cassius Lee from New York in August 1866, complaining that the people he needed to see were not there, that the Portland fire had priority in people's giving, and that the Diocese of Virginia's reluctance to rejoin General Convention was a stumbling block. Nevertheless, he felt certain that he could raise the money for Walker's salary and would try for two thousand dollars rather than the fifteen hundred dollars specified by the board. Sparrow wrote,

Yesterday I met Mr. —, and before we parted he pledged $250 per annum for five years. It may be that I shall get as much from a couple of other gentlemen of this city. Besides the necessary annual subscriptions to make up the salary, it may be that I shall get a little something for the endowment. Some may give out and out who will not pledge themselves ahead. You see I speak cautiously, because I am nervously timid. Still, I can say to you with confidence, *the salary will be made up*. It takes time, and it is very trying to the patience, but I am prepared for anything that will secure the end.

He went on in this letter to speak of other prospects in Baltimore and Philadelphia and to confess that he had to move slowly. "I was very unwell in Baltimore, from over exertion. . . . The very noise and confusion of this city break me down. It is well called 'Babel.'" He was not always successful; one man refused to give more financial assistance. This man did, however, suggest that the congregation of which he was warden might make an annual subscription of one hundred dollars.[34]

In a letter to J.A. Jerome on October 4, 1866, Sparrow pointed out that he had spent the summer raising money not only for one new professor but for two salaries, the board being capable of only one salary, plus repairs to "roofs, etc., and to support indigent young men." He then wrote, "My trips North have increased my anxiety of this and of every other Evangelical Institution. Ritualism seems to be sweeping over the Church. Not that I care so much about forms, and gestures, and garments, etc.; it is the principles out of which these things grow, and which are, under their cover, gradually introduced, that trouble me."[35] Sparrow heroically persisted in spite of poor health. He closed his letter to Lee saying, "Excuse this scrawl. I am so nervous I can hardly hold my pen, and my head is as unsteady—not with strong drink—as my hand."[36] He knew that his persistence was of the utmost importance for the continuance of the seminary.

In the period between 1865 and 1894, covering the deanships of Sparrow and Packard, the student body averaged forty to fifty persons including the preparatory department. The initial growth was rapid, from thirteen at the end of the 1865–66 session to fifty-three in 1868–69. But then in 1870–71 the number fell to thirty-eight. The total increased thereafter but fluctuated. In 1894–95, when the preparatory department had been discontinued, there were again thirty-eight students in the seminary.[37] At this distance it is difficult to explain the fluctuations, but it is clear that the preparatory department at times made a great difference. In 1886, when there were but four seniors, nine middlers, and four juniors, there were fourteen in the preparatory department.[38] This is to be compared to an enrollment of seventy-three at the beginning of the 1860–61 session (including fifteen in the preparatory department.)[39]

The finances of the seminary gradually improved, due to the continued efforts of Sparrow, the growing efforts of Packard,[40] and the efforts of the bishops of the diocese, John Johns and Francis Whittle, the latter elected assistant bishop in 1867. In the winter of 1868–69, Johns and Whittle visited potential donors in New York, seeking funds for the endowment, with some success.[41] By 1877 the endowment, which had been $90,000.00 before the war, was $196,350.00, and rose to $231,350.00 by 1884, providing an income of $12,825.50.[42] By 1891 the endowment was $344,389.78, yielding $19,209.80 annually.[43] During this period the treasurer's reports showed receipts of $17,794.99 and expenditures of $16,902.08 in 1869,[44] and in 1887 receipts of $36,486.92 and expenditures of $35,271.03.[45] We must not conclude that this represents steady growth.

A financial crisis in 1879 necessitated a reduction in expenditures, including a reduction of one professor's salary to $1,200, or so it was suggested. The board's action to increase salaries, taken at its meeting on June 25, 1878, was rescinded, and all salaries were to be limited to $2,000 per annum,[46] the amount established for professorial salaries in 1867.[47] By 1882 salaries were increased.[48] In 1887 salaries were raised to $2,500, although Carl Grammer was hired in that year at $1,500 and raised to $2,000 the next year.[49] In 1890 Grammer complained that he was not paid as much as the others on the faculty. By 1891 all were paid $2,500 with a promised increase of $250 the next year but with the warning that financial conditions might necessitate a reduction. At a special meeting of the board on October 15, 1892, there was discussion of a growing financial crisis and the possibility of selling some seminary acreage. An agent was appointed to raise funds.[50] In 1893 the professors' salaries were again $2,000, and further efforts were made to raise funds.[51] This review of salaries indicates that, while the endowment grew dramatically during these years, there was as yet little financial security. The faculty, responsible for the day-to-day operation of the institution, was required to bear the brunt of the financial drought. It should also be noted that while the number of students did not dramatically increase in these years, the faculty rose from two in 1865 to five in 1894–95, in addition to John McElhinney, semiretired and acting as librarian on a reduced salary.

Goodwin comments that if the board had been as zealous in raising funds as were certain faculty, such as Sparrow and Packard, the increased salaries could easily have been maintained. He further remarks that the board should have recognized that the faculty could not "solicit funds for the payment of their own salaries" and should have taken that responsibility upon themselves.[52] There is a sense in which Goodwin's remarks were unjustified. The board did work hard, beginning with the visit of the bishops to New York, to increase the seminary's endowment, to assure income sufficient to maintain a growing faculty. Furthermore, financial difficulties related to the fluctuations in the economic condition of the country made fund raising difficult. But having said that, it cannot be doubted that the faculty, even with additional income by way of perquisites, was not adequately paid—a situation that persisted in coming years.

During this period no capital improvements were made comparable to those in the decade preceding the war. One major building was constructed. In May 1879 during a financial crisis Packard alerted the board to the need for a new chapel.[53] The reason given was the unsafe condition of the old chapel. Cornelius Walker and Kinloch Nelson refused to hold services in it. The board, meeting on June 24 to deal with the crisis, appointed a committee composed of Kinloch Nelson, Arthur Herbert, Cassius Lee, and C.R. Hoof to see to the erection of "a new Chapel on the site of the present Chapel at a cost not to exceed $5,000."[54] At the consecration on June 23, 1881, Packard noted that building and furnishings cost $11,000, "of which the materials of the old building contributed about $1,500." The board appropriated $1,500, and the remainder was contributed by alumni and friends, "the larger portion coming from the cities north of the Potomac."

Packard described the new chapel, essentially the present building, saying that it

is in the decorated Gothic style, stands nearly on the site of the old one, fronting east, and covers about the same area. It is built of dark red brick laid in red mortar, with brown stone trimmings. In plan it is cruciform, consisting of nave and aisles, transept, choir, and choir aisles. The clerestory is supported by an arcade of columns, the clerestory windows being in the crown of the arches of the arcade. At the southeast corner is a square tower. . . . The architect was Mr. Charles E. Cassell, of Baltimore."[55]

As this suggests, the chapel was built in the Gothic revival style, represented in England by All Saints', Margaret Street, London, and in the United States by the Church of the Advent, Boston, both churches of the Oxford movement, the movement so strongly opposed by the professors of the Virginia Theological Seminary.[56] The architectural (and theological) decision made more difficult the maintenance of the plain style of worship associated with Virginia Low Churchmanship. Indeed, it may be said to have been an omen of the future when cross and candlesticks on the holy table would highlight the Sacrament of the Altar and detract from the lectern and pulpit. Nevertheless, the new chapel met a need. Its consecration was celebrated with a great congregation of clergy and laity, with plain but appropriate ceremony, and with the reading of Morning Prayer and Ante-Communion. The sermon was delivered by Packard, then

Dean, who expressed his pleasure in the knowledge "that this Seminary has not been forgotten in Africa, as this chancel rail, brought from that dark continent by Bishop Penick, attests."[57]

3. FOUNDING THE BISHOP PAYNE DIVINITY SCHOOL

The board of trustees was engaged in another venture involving financial investment and careful planning. This was the founding of the Bishop Payne Divinity School. Robert Bennett has indicated that as a result of the General Convention's policy of taking no action on the slavery issue, the Reconstruction period witnessed the flight of most black churchmen and churchwomen out of the Episcopal Church into other churches. "It has been estimated that in some southern states 90% of the Black Episcopalians left to become African Methodist Episcopalians or Colored—now Christian—Methodist Episcopalians." Those who remained struggled for recognition and representation in the legislative bodies of the church, a struggle that was to encounter failure upon failure. The limited aid provided by the Freedman Commission, begun by General Convention in 1868, did not meet the need for self-control, although it seemingly reached some 5,500 students in its schools established in the South before it was disbanded in 1906. "Though depressed and greatly diminished the Black Episcopalians who remained in the Church pressed not for independence, but for the development of their own leadership within the Church."[58]

To meet the need for black leadership, the board of trustees of the seminary in 1876 began discussing ways of providing theological education for black students.[59] It is of interest to note that in the centennial history of the seminary pains were taken by W.A.R. Goodwin and F.G. Ribble to explain that black candidates for ordination could not be educated at the seminary. They were not prepared even for admission to the preparatory department. They were black and, it was said, preferred their own institution. With honesty Ribble stated that "the social conditions and traditions of the South would not have permitted the induction of these men into the life of Virginia Seminary." Such action would not have been congenial to the white students and would have been distinctly disastrous to the Negro students.[60] Indeed, the seminary was not prepared to welcome blacks on an equal basis to its own chapel services on Sundays, and as a result the board authorized the building of a "chapel for colored people in the South East Corner of the grounds belonging to the seminary" in 1882, an action rescinded in 1883.[61] It would not be until 1951 that a black Episcopalian, John T. Walker, later the Bishop of Washington, would be accepted as a full-time student of the seminary.

At its meeting on June 25, 1878, the board authorized the collection of funds "to establish a Theological School for colored people" to be located at Petersburg, Virginia, "under the care of the Rev. Thomas Spencer."[62] A parish day school had been established at Petersburg and under the Reverend Giles B. Cooke, a Confederate veteran, developed into a "normal school" attached to St. Stephen's Church. It seemed to be a logical location for a new school, and Thomas Spencer seemed eminently suited to be its first teacher, being himself ordained, rector of St. John's Mission in Petersburg, and owner of a publishing company that for years produced the Franklin Press series of Sunday school lessons.[63] Thus the St. Stephen's Normal School became, in addition, the St. Stephen's Theological School. It was not until later that it was named the Bishop Payne Divinity School. Its beginnings were modest, and the board was not unalterably committed.

The board report to the Virginia diocesan council in 1879 stated "that the branch institution at Petersburg promises well." Thomas Spencer in his first report stated that he had begun teaching, having six students in all—three Episcopalians, two Methodists, and one Baptist—two of whom remained but for "about two months each." He wrote,

Instruction has been given in Paley's Evidences, Smith's Old and New Testament History, Butler on Common Prayer, Townsend's Elements of Theology, lectures on some of the Thirty-Nine Articles, and exercises in Homiletics, in the department of theology. Also on elementary Greek and Hebrew, and in Haven's Mental Philosophy. About three hours per day (except Saturday) has been occupied in the work of the recitation room.[64]

He expressed satisfaction with the students and their work but noted that because of their limited education they required "a very special, patient training." Finally, protesting his own limited education, Spencer begged "leave to resign my appointment at the close of the session in July."[65] His request evidently was refused. He continued teaching, making reports to the board through the 1886–87 session, and remained in the then constituted Bishop Payne Divinity School until 1894. In 1882 the board paid him a salary of $650, which was increased to $700 in 1887.[66]

In 1881 a committee of the board appointed to investigate the situation in Petersburg reported on considerations involved in organizing a theological school. It was agreed that the academic studies of the black students should be in the hands of the Reverend Giles B. Cooke, who agreed to teach without salary and to employ whomever he chose at a salary not to exceed $400.[67] This was seemingly Thomas Spencer, who bore the whole responsibility of teaching during the first years. In 1884–85 the board continued its discussions and planning, and proceeded to appoint a local committee for better oversight, including the Reverend Messrs. Gibson, Hains, and Spencer, and Messrs. F.E. David, Franklin Wright, and R.O. Egerton. The committee was empowered to find quarters for the students "without violating any existing contract with the Rev. Mr. Cooke" and to admit students to the school, with the bishops prescribing "the course of studies."[68]

A charter had been granted by the Virginia legislature on November 22, 1884. On February 18, 1885, the Board of Trustees of what was now called the Bishop Payne Divinity and Industrial School met in Richmond, chaired by Bishop Whittle. The Reverend Pike Powers was elected secretary and R.O. Egerton, treasurer. The board of the new school met the following July in Petersburg to adopt bylaws and an order of business, and to receive news of a generous gift of railroad stock from the Reverend James Saul, a gift with conditions attached that had to be negotiated. On the basis of this gift, valued at $5,800, temporary quarters were rented in Petersburg for the school.[69] In the minutes of the Virginia Seminary board, support for the Bishop Payne School was pledged; it was agreed that $900 would be given to it; and students under Thomas Spencer's care, understood to be the responsibility of the Virginia Seminary board, were transferred to the care of the Bishop Payne board. They also pledged that they would "support an instructor or instructors" for the students transferred.[70] By 1887 the merger of St. Stephen's Normal and Theological School into the Bishop Payne Divinity and Industrial School was completed and purchase of property in Petersburg was authorized, financed by gifts from Philadelphia, Richmond, and Petersburg. The Reverend A.R. Goodwin was appointed principal and general manager, and a faculty was appointed.

Thomas Spencer was to teach Hebrew, Old Testament, exegesis, systematic divinity, church history and polity—in all, five and a half hours each school day at a salary of $700. The Reverend F.G. Scott, rector of St. James' Mission, Petersburg, was appointed to teach mental and moral science, Greek, New Testament exegesis, and Latin—two hours each school day for a salary of $200. Mrs. Payne, the widow of Bishop Payne, was to be the matron of the school. Goodwin succeeded Giles Cooke as rector of St. Stephen's Church and principal of the normal school in 1884. He served as principal of the Bishop Payne School from 1887 to 1893, when he became rector of St. John's Church, Richmond.

The Bishop Payne Divinity and Industrial School soon ceased to be a normal school, and it was never actually an industrial school, although attempts to make it such were discussed in 1892. In time it was known simply as the Bishop Payne Divinity School and became "the accredited school of the General Church for the education of colored men for the ministry."[71] In the years to come it was to experience financial crises, move its campus in Petersburg, and see major changes in its faculty. But it continued, supported year after year by modest grants from the Virginia Theological Seminary, until in 1951, with its student body greatly reduced in numbers and its financial condition worsening, it ceased operations and its assets were turned over to the Virginia Seminary for the education of black students. Dean Ribble wrote in 1923,

> If an absolutely correct list of the men sent out from this school since 1878 was available, the number would not fall short of one hundred. About eighty-one alumni (more than sixty per cent of the colored clergy of the Church) are now laborers in the Lord's vineyard. One is working in Sierra Leone, Africa; two in the British West Indies; two in Cuba; and one in the Canal Zone. Two of them, the Rev. J.S. Russell, D.D., Archdeacon of Southern Virginia, and the Rev. S.W. Grice, B.D., warden of the School, have refused the Episcopate, feeling that they could better serve their people in their present positions. The Rev. George F. Bragg, D.D., of Baltimore, and the Rev. J.W. Johnson, of New York, are distinguished alumni. The Rev. E.L. Baskervill, is Archdeacon of South Carolina; the Rev. W.T. Wood, of Florida; the Rev. E.L. Braithwaite, of Atlanta. And there are others . . . in the cities of the North and the South, and especially in villages and country districts of the South, that are leading their people into a better understanding of the religion of Jesus Christ.[72]

4. BOARD AND FACULTY: STRESS AND STRAIN

During the period from 1865 to 1894 the faculty of the Virginia Theological Seminary changed and grew. Whereas in 1866 there were three full-time faculty, in 1894 there were five. One of the major concerns of the board was the selection and supervision of faculty. In 1865 Cornelius Walker was elected professor of ecclesiastical history and polity, in succession to Dr. May.[73] Walker, born on June 12, 1819, was the first Virginian to join the faculty. He entered the Episcopal High School in 1839 and the Virginia Seminary in 1842, where Sparrow became his hero. After ordination in 1845 he was married and served Virginia churches, remaining for twelve years at Christ Church, Winchester, until called to Christ Church, Alexandria in 1860. When the war came, he fled with his family to become rector of Emmanuel Church, Henrico County, where he served until called to the seminary. Between Walker's election and his arrival in 1866, Sparrow managed to find the necessary funds for his salary. As Carl Grammer attests, while in the parochial ministry Walker "studied solid books and able reviews with an eager and analytic mind. He read Latin easily, and carried on his studies in Hebrew. He also took up Syriac, and wrote articles for the reviews."[74] The results of his studies were evident in his preaching, which was greatly admired. The quality of his mind was demonstrated in his three books, the *Memorial of Sparrow*, the *Outline of Christian Theology*, and the *Lectures on Christian Ethics*.

At a board meeting on June 20, 1871, it had been agreed that there should be a fourth professor and, if possible, instruction in elocution. In 1872 John J. McElhinney was elected to the faculty, with Bishop Johns dissenting. McElhinney was born in Pittsburgh, Pennsylvania, in 1815; attended Washington and Jefferson College, Cannonsburgh, Pennsylvania; was ordained; served churches in Ohio and Pennsylvania; and for fifteen years was professor of systematic divinity at the seminary connected to Kenyon College. Packard considered McElhinney to be the most learned man "that had ever been on the faculty."[75] A scholarly Evangelical, he was author of *The Doctrine of the Church: A Historical Monograph* (1871), a careful historical study ranging from Clement of Rome to Mohler and Schleiermacher, with extensive treatment of the Anglican divines, concluding with a sixty-six page bibliography.

In his book he sets out the two opposing views, the Roman Catholic and the Protestant, as the only options—"there is no middle ground"— and indicated his preference for the ecclesiology taught by the Reformers of the sixteenth century.[76] What is significant here is the choice of subject, the doctrine of the church, which at that time was seemingly preempted by Roman and Anglo-Catholics, as well as the attention he paid to the historic evidence and accuracy in the use of that evidence. The same care for historic detail is evident in a paper, *Regeneration in Baptism*, published in 1871,[77] and in an extremely erudite lecture "read in Prayer Hall" called *Eternal Hope Reviewed*, published in 1878 and replete with Hebrew, Greek, and Latin citations.[78]

Professor Wallis tells us, however, "As a teacher Dr. McElhinney was not always interesting to the careless student." Wallis goes on to say, "Like the late Professor Sanday of Oxford University, Dr. McElhinney always gave a summary of all possible conclusions which the various writers deduced from any particular subject, without ever definitely stating his own." He adds, "Perhaps this was done to allow each student the pleasure of working one out for himself, and thereby strengthening his own mental powers."[79] McElhinney, that is, was somewhat "dry," his teaching not exciting; he was not practical but rather studious; and in not committing himself on the views he presented he would not please strong Evangelicals such as Bishop Johns.

With McElhinney's arrival, the duties of the professors were spelled out anew by the board: McElhinney was to teach apologetics, church polity, and Greek exegesis; in addition he was to give instruction in the composition and delivery of sermons. Sparrow, as professor of systematic divinity, was to continue teaching theology and Butler's *Analogy* (which might have been in McElhinney's department). Packard, as professor of biblical learning, was to give instruction in Hebrew exegesis and literature and the harmony of the Gospels. Walker, as professor of church history, was to teach biblical and ecclesiastical history, pastoral theology, and canon law.[80]

With Sparrow's death in 1874 there was need to elect a new professor. Until the election, McElhinney was to teach systematic divinity as he had done at Gambier, with others relieving him of Greek exegesis and liturgics (which seem to have been added to his department at some time).[81] At the board meeting on May 19, 1874, when this was decided, a committee was established, composed of Bishops Johns and Whittle and the secretary of the board, the Reverend George H. Norton, to further consider the distribution of subjects.[82] The committee on the distribution of subjects reported on June 23 recommending that Packard teach Hebrew and Greek exegesis and literature; Walker, in addition to biblical and ecclesiastical history, pastoral theology, canon law, homiletics and polity; McElhinney, in addition to apologetics and the history and interpretation of the Book of Common Prayer, systematic divinity and Butler's *Analogy*.[83] Evidently a concerted effort was being made to do without a new faculty appointment.

In 1876 Bishop Johns died, and Bishop Whittle was elected president of the board. At that same meeting, on May 16–17, Walker was appointed professor of systematic divinity (over McElhinney), and the board elected the Reverend A. M. Randolph professor of ecclesiastical history and canon law.[84] At the next meeting, June 20, it was reported that Randolph had declined his election. The Reverend Kinloch Nelson then was elected.[85]

Nelson, who was to stay at the seminary until his death in 1894, was born in 1839 into a distinguished Virginia family. He was educated at the Episcopal High School and was at the University of Virginia when the war began. During the war he served in the Confederate army, rising to second lieutenant before surrendering at Appomatox. After the war he attended Virginia Theological Seminary for one session and was then ordained by Bishop Johns in June 1868. Nelson then married and spent the next eight years as a parish priest in the Diocese of Virginia before joining the faculty.

As James Morris admitted, Nelson was not prepared for teaching in the "approved way," and yet he "was a successful teacher. He never pretended to profound learning or extensive reading; but as a man of practical action and decision, with definite ends of a practical kind held steadily in view, he did teach in a down right and indubitable fashion that was of tremendous value to men beginning the study of theology."[86] Walker having moved to systematic divinity, Nelson was made professor of ecclesiastical history and was also assigned in 1877 to teach pastoral theology.[87] For many years he was in charge of the seminary missions, assisted by his old comrade-in-arms, Launcelot Blackford of the Episcopal High School.[88] Nelson also participated in the work of the preparatory department.[89] He was an extrovert of great energy, in various ways very different from the learned, sometimes aloof and indecisive, McElhinney.

In 1884 Packard was unwell, and some of his duties had to be assigned to others on the faculty.[90] The board was now forced to think about the future of the faculty as Packard, dean and professor of biblical learning, approached the fiftieth anniversary of his arrival at the seminary.[91] In 1886 the board was discussing the advisability of procuring instruction in the English Bible and the Prayer Book. In June the board discussed retiring Packard on a salary set by them. They would then proceed to hire a professor of "Biblical Learning and Apologetics." No decision was made as to whether Packard would continue as dean, which in fact, he did until 1894. He was assigned to teach English Bible, including introduction, criticism, exegesis, and interpretation. The Bishop of Virginia was to give instruction in the Book of Common Prayer.[92]

There followed various, sometimes confusing, machinations. McElhinney was aging rapidly and was retired from teaching but remained as librarian. The committee appointed to search for a professor of Hebrew and Greek Languages and biblical literature nominated the Reverend Carl E. Grammer of Cincinnati. After discussion the nomination was withdrawn. Were there those who already sensed that Grammer would be troublesome? Further discussion followed, one suggestion being that the faculty not be increased, another being that an adjunct professor of Hebrew and Greek languages and biblical learning be appointed. Bishop Randolph unsuccessfully attempted to delay action. Cassius Lee nominated Grammer to be adjunct professor, Norton moved to change *adjunct* to *assistant*, and Grammer was elected by a vote of eight to seven.[93] That was in February 1887; in May the board met and behaved as though no action had been taken in February. The committee, appointed under the chairmanship of Bishop Randolph to search for a professor of Hebrew and Greek languages and biblical literature, reported names had been submitted to the committee but indicated that the committee, desirous of having the best instruction "in the critical study of the Holy Bible," was having difficulty in finding anyone qualified to do so.

The demand created by modern investigations in oriental literature, in archeology, and in historical science, as it bears upon the Old Testament, for a higher grade of scholarship in these lines in the Seminary professor, seems to forbid the selection of an ordinary general scholar for this special work.[94]

Bishop Randolph, who had sought to delay the action taken to elect Grammer in February may have been instrumental in the operations of this committee, which he chaired. He had been elected Assistant Bishop of Virginia in 1883 and came to the board as an erudite man who was to give the Paddock lectures on "reason, faith, and authority in Christianity." As rector of Emmanuel Church, Baltimore, he was known as a pastor and preacher and for "his midweek lecture on the Bible," which "drew to the Church a large congregation made up of the most cultivated people in Baltimore—university professors, lawyers, men of letters, and others."[95] He was thus, deeply involved in the study of the Bible and anxious to see someone better qualified than Grammer elected professor of Hebrew and Greek languages and biblical literature. Randolph's committee nominated and the board elected the Reverend Angus Crawford to the position by a vote of eleven to one.[96]

Born in 1850 on a farm in Ontario, Canada, Crawford studied at Queen's College, Kingston, for two years and then went to the University of Toronto. Raised a Presbyterian and determined to enter the ministry of that church, he went to Princeton but left there to enroll in the Philadelphia Divinity School after discovering that he could not accept the doctrines of predestination and election as then taught. On graduation in 1876, he chose not to return to Canada where churchmanship issues were too strong. He was ordained by the Bishop of New Jersey, sent to Trinity Church, Mount Holly, New Jersey, and was there for ten years, during which time he studied Hebrew under William R. Harper at Yale in the summers. With Harper's recommendation of Crawford, the board was convinced that here was the scholar they needed.[97]

What was to happen to Grammer? At the board meeting on June 21, 1887, he was appointed professor "with duties to be assigned" at a salary of fifteen hundred dollars, well below the salaries of the other faculty members.[98] That Grammer expected to teach Hebrew is indicated by his going to Yale to study Hebrew in a special course under Harper.[99] He then might have expected to teach Greek, but by 1887–88 he was professor of church history and canon law, and Nelson was professor of Greek, New Testament literature, church polity, and pastoral theology.[100]

Grammer was the son of Julius E. Grammer and the grandson of William Sparrow. He studied at Baltimore City College and graduated in 1879

First Row: (l to r): Cornelius Walker, Joseph Packard,
John McIlhinney, Kinlock Nelson
Second Row: Angus Crawford, Carl Grammer

with an A.B. from Johns Hopkins University. After a year in law school
he entered Virginia Seminary, graduating in 1884. Ordained that year, he
served churches in Maryland and Ohio before coming to the seminary to
teach. Of all the professors to this point, Grammer is regarded as the most
controversial. A brilliant scholar who came to the seminary as a dedicated Evangelical, Grammer's teaching was demanding, critical, argu-
mentative, and, according to one report, was developing in a "progressive" direction.[101] We shall have reason to delve more into this later. For
now it is sufficient to indicate W.A.R. Goodwin's assessment of
Grammer's critical mind and teaching.

In his teaching of church history, Grammer assisted the Greek language department by beginning with a study in Greek of the Acts of the
Apostles. In the course of this study Grammer insisted on a careful, scholarly investigation of the text during which he dealt as he thought proper
with certain aspects of polity involved in the history of Christian institutions. Goodwin reports,

> A thin partition alone separated Dr. Grammer's class room from that of Dr.
> Kinloch Nelson, the officially delegated teacher of Church Polity, but there
> were wide stretches between the views of the two teachers as to orders in
> their succession and consequent authority. There was official Greek and
> officially taught Church Polity with strong emphasis placed on "Episcopos"
> and the succession on Dr. Nelson's side of the partition, and subrosa Greek

138

and interrogatively taught Church polity with the major emphasis on "*Presbyteros*" taught on Dr. Grammer's side of the partition. The situation was stimulating to the students and we could but wonder, at times, if it did not have a certain disciplinary value in its effect upon the temper and good nature of Dr. Nelson, who strongly believed in "the Church as the seamless robe of Christ."[102]

When Grammer, an Evangelical, submitted Evangelicalism to the same criticism he would use in analyzing any system of thought and when he fearlessly pursued "biblical criticism and historical interpretation," Grammer was ahead of his time and at odds with others in addition to Dr. Nelson. He resigned his position at the seminary in 1898 to return to the parochial ministry but remained active in the affairs of the seminary.

The final change in the faculty during this period occurred in 1894 when Nelson died suddenly. Earlier, Crawford, in preparation for a year's leave of absence, procured the services of the Reverend Samuel Wallis to take his place, paying his salary out of his own income.[103] At a special meeting on November 1, called to deal with the consequences of Nelson's death, Wallis was elected to fill the vacant chair.[104] Like Crawford, Wallis was born and received his early education in Canada. When his parents moved to Virginia, he studied at the University of Virginia and entered the seminary in 1878, graduating in 1881. Wallis served churches in Virginia, including Pohick Church, until returning to the seminary to teach Greek New Testament, church polity, liturgics, religious pedagogy, and pastoral theology. Like Nelson, he supervised the seminary missions. Wallis was remembered chiefly as a pastor and served the seminary until his retirement in 1920.

As is evident, the board spent much time and energy on faculty appointments and on supervising the faculty in their work. It took seriously its responsibility to see that the requisite subjects were taught and taught well, with the approved textbooks and no others. At times this resulted in strained relations between the board and the faculty. Two examples must suffice here. On May 20, 1873, the board authorized its secretary (who was, significantly, Cornelius Walker of the faculty) "to call the attention of the Rev. Dr. Walker, to the fact that he has mentioned in his Report the use of a book which has not received the sanction of the Board."[105] We do not have a copy of that report, but according to the minutes of the board on June 24, the book could have been "the Church History of the Rev. Clement M. Butler," which Walker then was given permission to use "for larger trial." At this latter meeting a resolution was offered and adopted, that said, "That in case of any proposed change in the text books or courses of study in the Seminary the proposal for such change shall be made at the annual meeting of the Board of Trustees, to be acted upon at the next annual meeting, except there shall be an unanimous vote of a quorum of the Board, to take action at the time when the proposal is made."[106] The board then ruled "that until the Trustees appoint text books in the Department of Apologetics, the Professor be at liberty to use such books as he may think best."[107] The faculty, in all likelihood, was not happy with the board's exercise of authority in this matter and could have appealed to the Rules and Regulations of 1825, which allowed those textbooks to be in use that were recommended by the House of Bishops or "as may be approved by the Faculty," with nothing said of the trustees.[108]

At their June 23, 1874, meeting, the trustees called the attention of the professors to rule 4 of the Rules and Regulations of 1825 which requires "that each class shall attend some one of the Professors at least once a day" and requested them "to report annually the number of times during the session, the recitations in each department have been omitted."[109] This did not settle well with the faculty, who protested against such a request. The board on June 22, 1875, resolved "that complaints having come to the Board from the Professors of the resolution passed at the last June meeting calling upon them to report the number of recitations omitted during the session, we hereby disdain any intention in the Resolution of reflecting upon them in any wise and do hereby express our undiminished confidence in them."[110] That is the last that we hear of the matter, but the board had achieved its aim of warning the professors against unwarranted absenteeism.

5. THE CURRICULUM: CONTINUITY AND CHANGE

The course of study prescribed by the House of Bishops in 1804 was a basic guide to the teaching at Virginia Seminary, as it was in other theological seminaries of the Episcopal Church. But as we have observed, professors were turning to textbooks of more recent vintage, and the House of Bishops was aware of the need to revise the course of study. At the General Convention of 1868 a committee was appointed to revise the course of seminary study, making it "adequate to the needs and facilities of the present day."[111] The committee of five bishops met and discussed various possibilities until it submitted its report in 1889. A key figure in its work was William Whittingham, Bishop of Maryland, who died in 1879. In their final report the bishops reaffirmed the 1804 course of study, with the supplement provided by the Bishop of Lincoln. They provided a further list, according to an outline provided by Whittingham, and they allowed that "each Bishop will direct his candidate according to his own judgment," not doubting "that in general, an almost entire agreement will be found among us as a result."[112]

Instead of four "classes" and an abbreviated list, the 1889 report has twelve subject areas: (1) introduction to the study of Scripture, (2) the interpretation of Scripture, (3) Christian evidences, (4) church history, (5) doctrinal theology, (6) moral theology, (7) church polity, (8) canon law, (9) liturgics, (10) homiletics, (11) pastoral theology, and (12) polemics. Recent scholarship is acknowledged, such as that of Westcott and Lightfoot. Mosheim's history had been replaced by the church histories of Milner, Schaff, and others. Knapp is not mentioned, but Martensen on Christian dogmatics is. The works of numerous Anglican divines, are recommended, from Hooker to Pusey, and of the American divines White and Seabury, among others. Almost 350 titles are provided.[113] At the end, the discretion of the bishop is stressed with the suggestion that the lists of texts contained in the report be given to the candidate with annotations. The committee's overall policy was explained as follows:

This compilation has been made in favor of no narrow school, but with a designed comprehensiveness, excluding only a class of writers who, though often godly and well-learned, have been justly censured for a morbid or an immoderate turn of mind, at variance with the fresh, and wholesome spirit of the Common Prayer, and of the large freedom, within bounds, awarded to all her children by the Anglican Church.[114]

Indeed, the Evangelical churchman might very well be dissatisfied with the list, but then one imagines that those of any and all parties would be dissatisfied. There was no minimal list of subjects and books provided as there had been in 1804, which might have compromised the stated policy, even inadvertently. Rather, a very long list was added to the lists of 1804, in effect allowing very much more leeway to the faculties of seminaries. But on the other hand, the discretion allowed to bishops could work adversely, limiting the number and kinds of texts to be used.

A perusal of the seminary catalogue for 1890–91, and of the professors' reports of May 1891 does not indicate that the faculty sought to bring their assigned texts into line with the new House of Bishops' list. Walker kept on using Knapp, with Chadbourne's "Natural Theology" and Hopkins' "Outline Study of Man," none of these being on either the 1804 or the 1889 lists. But he did use Butler's *Analogy*, which was on the earlier list, and Broadus' book on homiletics, which was on the later list.[115] Walker did not replace Knapp until his own *Outline of Theology* was published in 1894, but then he listed Knapp as a book for reference.[116] For basic texts in church history, Grammer used Smith's *Ecclesiastical History*, Fisher's

History of the Christian Church, and Perry's *History of the Church of England,* none of which was on the 1889 list.[117]

The professors' reports are missing from the records during the first decade after the war. The catalogues indicate that the curriculum continued along the route established by the Rules and Regulations of 1825, although the distribution of courses over any three years might vary. For instance, in 1866–67 ecclesiastical history (including biblical history) extended over all three years of study. In that session, with Sparrow, Packard, and Walker constituting the faculty, juniors studied the Scriptures in Greek and Hebrew, along with the principles of scriptural interpretation, the evidences of revealed religion, and beginning church history. Middlers continued the critical study of Scripture and church history and began the study of systematic divinity, the latter under Sparrow being described as "methodical arrangement and explanation of Christian doctrines, with Scripture authorities sustaining them" and including "a statement and refutation of erroneous doctrines . . . and a particular view and defence of the system of faith professed by the Protestant Episcopal Church." Here middlers began their immersion in Knapp (as interpreted by Sparrow) together with the homilies of the Church of England, Burnet on the Articles of Religion, and Pearson on the Creed. The seniors continued their study of systematic divinity and church history and added polity (with Hooker's Laws), including the canons of the church, and pastoral theology. Study of the Book of Common Prayer ("an exhibition of the advantages of liturgical service; with a history and defence of the liturgy of the Protestant Episcopal Church, and of its rites and ceremonies") was included in the senior year. In addition to the obligatory recitations and attendance at lectures, juniors wrote exegetical essays, middlers theological essays, and seniors composed and delivered sermons.[118] The course of study here described continued for years to come.

In 1875 the Journal of the diocesan council began printing the professors' reports again. Cornelius Walker, who in 1875 was still professor of ecclesiastical history, indicated the pedagogical variety of his teaching as well as the breadth of his responsibilities:

The Seniors, reciting daily, have studied and reviewed Short's History of the Church of England, with written Lectures on the Early History of the British Church and the later History of the English Church, and of that in this country. As introductory to Pastoral Theology, they have read the Pastoral Epistles; have studied a course of Liturgics with questions of my own preparation, a similar course also in Homiletics, with weekly exercises and criticisms. They will be occupied for the remainder of the session with Homiletics and Pastoral Theology.

The Middle Class, reciting tri-weekly, has studied Kurtz' Sacred History, with essays at each recitation; and they are now reviewing.

The Junior class, reciting twice a week, have studied Kurtz' Sacred History: and, as introductory to Ecclesiastical History, have read, in the original, the Acts of the Apostles.[119]

Neither professors nor students could afford to relax under such a regimen, which included recitations, essays, lectures, exercises, and criticisms. In 1877, after completing all but a few weeks of his new assignment as professor of systematic divinity, Walker reported that the senior class had studied Burnet on the Articles of Religion. "They have studied, with written questions and references, a course in Liturgics." "Exercises" in homiletics had been pursued regularly through the session. The middle class had studied Knapp. "One recitation per week has been given . . . to the study of the New Testament as in the English version and with reference to the form in which its Theology is thus exhibited. . . ." Thus we have evidence of the beginning of a study of New Testament theology as a discipline in itself. Concerning the junior class, Walker indicated that then he was giving "a weekly recitation in Natural Theology" as a part of the study of Christian evidences, although the chief responsibility here was in Professor McElhinney's department. The teaching of natural theology was evidently new, for Walker sought for and obtained permission from the board to use discretion in the choice of textbooks, temporarily, as we have seen.[120] In his report Walker indicated that he was offering instruction in natural theology to juniors and seniors as an experiment, using Chadbourne's lectures, with hope that the board would approve eventual inclusion of such instruction in the curriculum.[121] The significance of this addition to the curriculum will be considered subsequently. We note here his respect for the board and its authority but also his initiative. Indeed, from here on natural theology was a separate subject, apart from Christian evidences, and remained in Walker's department with Chadbourne's lectures and Hopkins' *Outline Study of Man* as textbooks.[122]

By 1877, with four faculty, McElhinney was professor of apologetics and polity. As might be expected with a faculty member professing these subjects, they were taken more seriously and given more time in the class schedule. McElhinney's report in 1877 gives us further insight into the teaching at this time:

In the department of Church Polity the instruction of the senior class embraces: 1st, A full course of lecturing on the Church and ministry, in connection with oral and written examinations: and, 2nd, Lectures with examinations on the textbook,—Hooker's *Laws of Ecclesiastical Polity*, the third, the fifth and the seventh books;[123] concluding with a review of the entire course in written questions. The middle class continue the study of Apologetics with the use of Luthardt's *Apologetic Lectures on the Fundamental Truths of Christianity* as a textbook. In the same department the junior class pursue a course of study which begins with a series of lectures, and is continued to the close of the session in the use of Paley's *Evidences* and Butler's *Analogy* as textbooks.[124]

Biblical studies were the responsibility of Professor Packard from 1866 on. During the 1883–84 session, he was ill for a time, his teaching being covered by his colleagues. But when well he taught all three classes. The juniors studied Hebrew grammar, with written exercises and intensive study of portions of the Old Testament in Hebrew, chiefly the Book of Genesis. "In the Greek Testament they have read the Gospel of John, and have written exegetical essays on the most difficult subjects in the gospels." Clearly Packard preferred the Fourth Gospel. If time allowed, they pressed on to the Sermon on the Mount. The middle class read in Hebrew the prophecies of Christ in the Old Testament and selections from Isaiah. In the Greek testament they read the Epistles to the Romans and to the Hebrews. "They have also read exegetical essays." The seniors continued their study of Hebrews, reading more chapters from Isaiah, "and in the Greek Testament they have studied the two Epistles to the Corinthians."[125] Biblical studies were reinforced by Walker, who in 1884 had the middlers study "most of the Epistles of the New Testament as to their structure and peculiarities, with exercises in analysis of texts and plans of sermons." Nelson, as a part of his teaching of church history, had juniors read "Dr. Smith's Old and New Testament Histories, and the Acts of the Apostles in Greek." He had seniors read the Pastoral Epistles in Greek, as we have noted, as part of their study of pastoral theology.[126]

In 1888, as a result of changes made by the board in the previous year, including the hiring of Grammer and Crawford, Packard taught English Bible. Nelson taught Greek and the literature of the New Testament. Crawford taught Hebrew and oriental languages and, although his title did not specifically indicate this, the literature of the Old Testament. Grammer, as professor of church history used "Smith's Old and New Testament Histories," and had the students work through the Acts of the Apostles.[127]

One motive for teaching the English Bible, proposed to the board in 1886,[128] would seem to have concerned covering more of the Old Testament than was usual, especially books where the Hebrew was difficult. In 1891 Packard reported working through Ecclesiastes, the Minor Prophets, Daniel, and Ezekiel with the seniors and the Psalms ("with constant comparison with the Prayer Book and Revised Versions, and with reference to the original, the Septuagint and the Vulgate") with the middlers. "Both classes have paid special attention to the authorship and age of the books studied." Thus was a scientific approach to the literature encouraged. Packard ended his report saying that he felt "an increasing conviction of the importance of the study of the English Bible."[129] At this time all of the faculty were involved in one way or another with teaching the Scripture, for Walker, who was not mentioned above, was not one to ignore Scripture in teaching theology. In 1891 he had middlers read "Oehler's Old Testament Theology" and give weekly recitations on their reading.[130]

6. STUDENTS: THE LIGHTER SIDE

A glimpse into the lighter side of seminary life is provided by a crudely produced newspaper called *The Rhetorical Budget*.[131] That of February 1879 contains news bulletins from abroad and from the homefront. From abroad came the report that in South Africa "25 Zulus caught 15 British in a valley and smothered them to death with snowballs." At the seminary the chief event of note was the arrival of examining chaplains.

> Much apprehension was felt on the part of the students at the Chaplains' approach. As they hove into sight the bell was tolled, many solemn requiems were said and each animated the other to be brave and hold on to the end. The siege was long and boring especially to the Chaps. Some dangerous wounds were received, but no deaths, up to the time of our going to press.

In addition there was concern at the passage of the "Chinese Bill"— evidently because Chinese laborers were being expelled, some parents were sending for their sons to come home and work. Finally, there was an outbreak of measles: "The measles are slight," William Stevens Campbell, the editor, reported, "so far, only broken out in spots." But there was much effort expended by "some of the students, the evening before examinations, to catch them. The measles got disgusted and refused to be caught under any circumstances."

Some seminarians wrote verses to commemorate the visit of the chaplains. They tell of one student crossing the campus "mid snow and ice," bearing with him an examination paper "with the strange device, Chaplains!"

> In happy homes he saw the lights;
> He saw his Na-hosh sweet and bright;
> Above the glistering cupola shone,

And from his lips escaped a moan,
Chaplains!

"O stay," the maiden said, "and rest
Thy empty head upon this breast!"
A tear stood in his sad blue eye,
But still he answered with a sigh,
Chaplains!

The student trudged on, resisting temptation, and the next day some of the "ladies of the hill" found him:

Half-crazed and gazing blankly 'round,
Still grasping in his hands of ice,
That paper with the strange device,
Chaplains!

There in the twilight, cold and gray,
Corked, but beautiful, he lay;
From the ladies, serene and faint
A voice fell on the still night-air,
Chaplains!

Such was the trauma of canonical examinations that even day and night were confused.

As this less than noteworthy poem indicates, the students were preoccupied—some, if not much, of the time—with thoughts of ladies young and old. The paper reports on preparations for St. Valentine's Day. A certain Mr. F—of the preparatory department persuaded his friend, Mr. C—, to help him compose a valentine, which read in part,

Shall my heart within me thrill,
For other girl upon this hill.
Till the Sun fore're shall set
Behind some tall old Minaret,
Till the Moon at last shall sink
In some frozen skating rink . . .
I shall call that girl my love,
Who is so like a turtle dove.

The student who managed the post office evidently spent much time trying to decipher valentines going out and coming in. The explanation—farfetched—was that he "has been dangerously ill . . . with brain-fever, brought on by overanxiety to get the stamps canceled and counted right." One valentine, received by Mr. C—of the middle class "from his sweetheart," read,

> Work hard, my dear,
> Save your money
> And when you get rich,
> Take me for your honey!

The editor reported on a meeting of students called to decide "the most proper way for us, as a body of theological students to observe Lent." Edward Lewis Goodwin made this suggestion: "The best hand at keeping Lent he ever knew was a quarter which a classmate had borrowed last October. It had kept Lent ever since." Various other suggestions were made, including renting their clothes as a sign of mourning ("Malachi with garments rent, completes the ancient Testament."). The only problem is that students were already "wearing just such rent garments, save those who are so extravagant as to have their clothes patched." Finally, by resolution the students determined that they could best keep Lent by setting it "apart as a special season for na-hashing," adopting "a scheme of visiting [ladies] in regular succession," and providing escorts for ladies to all services day and night. The motion was adopted and signed by, among others, Arthur Selden Lloyd (a future bishop) and Samuel A. Wallis (a future member of the faculty)!

There was a report of a meeting of the Rhetorical Society at which "Shall women be allowed to vote?" was debated. There were ladies of the Hill, high school teachers and students, as well as seminarians and their teachers present. Hardly a sane word was spoken. Those on both sides of the question postured and prowled about. "Mr. F. showed very poor taste in raising his eyes to the chandelier for inspiration instead of looking on the fair faces before him. . . . Mr. Funston followed next on Aff(irmative). If we had not known that the gentleman does not indulge in cosmetics, we should have thought that he had whitened his face for effect. . ." Mr. Campbell closed the debate for the negative: "He was indignant at the idea of giving women more power since she ran everything now. He told us something about . . . women whipping their husbands and some other pretty stories from Wyoming." When the question was opened to the floor, one starry-eyed student spoke

with an air of audacity only accounted for by the fact that he has not yet put himself in the power of the ladies on the Hill. . . . [He] declared in the words of the immortal Billy [Shakespeare] "Frailty thy name is woman." (Better be careful young man.) Mr. C's curls were grand but he would stick

woman on a pinnacle and we know he never saw a lady sitting on a pinnacle. But perhaps he would like to put the fair sex at a safe distance.

So much for impartial reporting! The debate concluded with a negative vote.
There were further news items.

A paper announces that by the recent burning of an ice house, twenty-
thousand tons of ice were reduced to ashes.
    A gentleman of the Junior class was heard to express a great desire to
one of the chaplains, to have the subject of polygamy explained to him.
    Mr. W. superintendent of the S.S. "Boys, can you tell me why the chil-
dren in Israel made a golden calf and worshiped it, after they had been
forbidden such idolatry by Moses?" Precocious little boy: "Because they
hadn't got enough gold to make a cow with."

And there were fashion notes—one is enough, if not too much.

The ladies do their hair up so high now that they have to stand on something to put on their hats.

7. THEOLOGICAL DEVELOPMENT:
"ARMINIAN EVANGELICALISM"

Seminary life at the end of this period (1865–95) was dominated by academic routines—class work, reading with the assistance of a growing library, writing essays and sermons—culminating in the year-end examinations and commencement, at which no degrees were conferred but written testimonials were given on the completion of the three-year course,
signed by the president and the professors. The Thursday night faculty
meetings and chapel worship were influential. The two major societies,
that for Missionary Inquiry and the Rhetorical Society, were still in operation with the former taken most seriously, exhibiting the missionary
zeal that still inflamed students' hearts and minds. The work of students
in the missionary stations nearby provided the chief means for what a
later age would call field education.
    The changing society influenced seminary life in various ways. The
board authorized the installation of a telephone on May 25, 1883, and a
year later noted that it was in operation.[132] It has not stopped ringing
since. The board was involved in a multifaceted organization including a
preparatory department, the high school, and the Bishop Payne School,
as well as the seminary proper.

148

Students were highly regarded by their professors, as was affirmed routinely in their annual reports. Students valued their teachers, not without an occasional complaint. There were incidents reflecting student unrest and board concern. We note in the board minutes a student petition in 1879 requesting a Christmas holiday, on which no action was taken.[133] In 1880 it was decreed that the dean had "authority to determine all questions concerning occupation of rooms by the students."[134] Were the students seeking to exercise such authority themselves, with negative results? In 1891 the board set down certain rules: Students were to keep their rooms neat and preserve seminary property, stoves were not to be "moved into the halls," nails were not to "be driven into the walls," and so on in great detail.[135] In 1892 students were denied their request for an enlarged reading room in the library.[136] Far more serious was a formal complaint from the students against Professor Wallis, the board then urging Wallis to exercise greater discipline in the classroom.[137]

When we inquire as to the general tenor of the times, we do well to look to the semicentennial celebration of 1873. Held on September 24 and 25, this involved giving thanks in a service of Holy Communion with Bishops Johns, Lee, and Whittle officiating; historical reminiscences by Professor Packard, Philip Slaughter, and Stephen Tyng; and a meeting of the alumni to consider the future. The alumni, expressing great confidence in their "beloved Seminary," pledged themselves "to love her more and serve her better." In fulfillment of this pledge they made plans to raise one hundred thousand dollars for her benefit.[138] The remarkable recovery of the Seminary after the Civil War had been accomplished and a bright future lay ahead.

Toward the end of his address at the celebration, Packard catalogued the many fruits realized in the seminary's brief history. He noted the 570 alumni, including ten bishops and thirty-one foreign missionaries working in Greece, Africa, and China. Toward the end of 1895 Brazil was added when James Morris and Lucien Lee Kinsolving of the class of 1889 were sent by the American Church Missionary Society as missionaries to Brazil.[139] Furthermore, alumni were found in almost every diocese. "We have no small representation in Boston, Chicago, St. Louis, New Orleans, in Iowa, California, Texas, Oregon, Kansas; and two in Dacotah among the Ponka Indians are from our Seminary." Packard noted that "they have generally been 'Warmhearted and devoted Parish Clergy,'" and he was proud of that fact.[140] He concluded on a somber note, warning against false teaching and/or "Romish practices."[141]

Packard urged that the seminary continue as it began, in the spirit and with the theology of William Meade. The question arises as to whether or not the old theology was maintained in this period. It is certain, at least to the student of history, that there would be change. Before the war the contest with Tractarianism was bound to have its effects, strengthening the commitment among Evangelicals in their fundamental convictions. These included their strong emphasis on the doctrine of justification, their strong opposition to ecclesiastical fundamentalism and, when they came, to "Romish practices." The dramatic developments after the war would also have their effects. In writing of the development of liberalism at Andover Seminary, Daniel Day Williams summarizes the emerging challenges:

> Economic expansion developed at an unheard of pace; and the influence of modern culture became correspondingly enhanced. Scientific achievements dramatically represented by On the Origin of Species, were destroying the basic premises of the old theology in the general mind. Herbert Spencer's speculative philosophy claiming science as its support and based on the idea of development became the focal point of the modification of basic categories in the general mentality.[142]

That peculiar form of the idea of progress embodied in social Darwinism challenged the old theology's evaluation of humankind and the Fall. The postwar era was one of growing optimism and of disenchantment with the Calvinist worldview. Furthermore, the attitude of the times bred skepticism and a critical approach to formerly unquestioned propositions and truths. Here we have an indication of the nature and meaning of that difficult label "liberal" in relation to theology. Williams, writing of the emergence of liberalism at Andover, about 1879, says that the

> substitution of inquiry into the meaning of the gospel for dogmatic statement of its "eternal" truths is the most striking difference between Andover liberalism and the New England theology from which it came. It is the one certain basis on which this school can be called liberal, for liberalism is not primarily a system of doctrine, but rather an attitude toward doctrine. It is the position that truth can be attained only through a never-ending process of criticism and experiment. It is the willingness to understand many points of view.[143]

Was there a development of liberalism at Virginia Seminary during the years 1865 to 1894? Certainly there was nothing comparable to the liberal transformation of Andover Seminary, which at times inspired accusations of heresy. Carl Grammer, in his review of theological tendencies at the seminary, regarded the first teachers (Keith, Packard, and May) as Calvinist Evangelicals, maintainers of the old theology so well represented in the *Theological Repertory.* The separation from this Calvinist Evangelicalism and the beginning of an Arminian Evangelicalism with a kinder view "of human nature" and a "more generous recognition of the will's power," both contributing to "a friendly attitude toward reason"—he attributes to Sparrow.[144]

J. Barrett Miller has argued that, strong Evangelical "though he was, Sparrow was an Arminian; making the acceptance or rejection of God's gracious atoning act . . . dependent on man's will." He seems to deny irresistible grace and to side "with the Arminians in seeing God as the Lord who offers salvation to mankind and is waiting for a response."[145] Based on a reading of Sparrow's sermons, among the few substantial primary sources we have for Sparrow's theology, Miller's conclusion is correct; but what weight are we to give it? Perhaps it can be said that Arminianism opens the door a crack and thus allows the development of liberalism, but Sparrow's Arminianism does not prove very much beyond that fact.

A saying (which Grammer reports as coming at the conclusion of a classroom discussion) is engraved on Sparrow's tombstone: "Seek the truth; come whence it may, cost what it will."[146] Here is a statement that could be attributed to most liberals. But what exactly did Sparrow mean by it? In a commencement address toward the end of his life, Sparrow urged the adoption of a "true conservatism" over against a false conservatism, as we meet the age in which we live "face to face in kindliness," recognizing that the "movements of an age are to be regarded as part of that progress of things which belong to the scheme of Providence. . . . The providence of God is everywhere, and not confined to us; and everywhere it is instructive."[147] There must be study of this world, therefore, and the exercise of influence, not arbitrary authority, in the guiding of this age by the principles of the gospel. His line of argument was influenced by his purpose, which was to oppose papal infallibility and all coercive force with another authority: the Protestant principle. There was, then, for him, an external authority. He stated,

> Man was never meant to be entirely unrestrained in his opinions by external authority. And what our very constitution thus calls for, through God's goodness we have. I allude now not to conscience, by which man is chained to the throne of God; nor yet to reason, which is something indestructible, and when plunging into darkness is still a light. I allude to nothing so subjective, so unsteady, so much under man's control to shape and modify in its working. I allude to something outside of man, given to man, addressing itself to his senses; something providentially provided to the race, and made a part of the permanent moral furniture of the world: I allude to *the Bible, the inspired Word of God.*[148]

Sparrow went on to sing the praises of the Bible, in which are "the essential *truths*." It is "perfect as it came from the hands of God." It is inspired and as such commands the "obedience of the reason and the conscience, which is due to no other book, because no other is infallible."[149] He was confident that in seeking the truth anywhere, the quest would lead to the Bible. There was in this a degree of trust, a favorable view of humanity and of the providence of God working in it. He demanded that his students be seekers, intellectually rigorous, fearlessly honest. In contrasting Sparrow's views with the Tractarians, Grammer, his grandson, said,

Cornelius Walker

His opposition was not due to a conservative repugnance to new views, but to a profound opposition to their philosophical first principles, as well as to their specific dogmas. They feared the dissolving force of the intellect; he trusted that the soul was naturally Christian. They looked backward; he looked forward. They turned to the authority of the Church; he appealed to the authority of the Truth. "He taught us," said Bishop Brooks, "that however far thought might travel it would still find God."[150]

Grammer believed that Sparrow was influenced by Butler and the early Broad Churchmen, such as Arnold and Whateley. But we must remember here the strong Evangelicalism of Sparrow's sermons and the general tenor of his 1843 commencement address.

Sparrow may have begun the trend toward a more Arminian and liberal theology at Virginia Seminary, but it was Cornelius Walker, Sparrow's student, friend, biographer, and successor as professor of systematic divinity, who led the way and developed a coherent liberal—Evangelical theology, published in two books, the fruits of his teaching, *Outlines of Christian Theology* (1894) and *Lectures on Christian Ethics* (1895). Walker deserves more attention than he has been given, with a testing of Carl Grammer's thesis that Walker alone of all the faculty of the seminary of his day welcomed the fruits of the new age. The faculty all shared common Evangelical religious experience and all stood opposed to Tractarianism. But, says Grammer,

> Dr. Walker stood alone among them in his frank trust in the operations of reason. His was the only classroom where Science was looked on with a friendly eye, and his the only mind that was seriously at work coordinating, systematizing, and scrutinizing its own operations and store of facts. . . . While he was naturally opposed to the assumptions of Higher Criticism, he never fled to the arms of the Church for refuge, and was willing to see the battle of the scholars joined. He had a calm confidence that the Truth would win.[151]

Furthermore, he rejected the doctrine of eternal punishment of the wicked, asking "whether it was conceivable and credible that God could combine punishment with reformatory measures. . . ." We must exercise caution here, for just as Robert A. Gibson in his recollections of Sparrow's theology apologizes for the intrusion of his own sentiments into his account, so Grammer may have been reading into his account of Walker convictions of his own. Grammer went beyond Walker, whom he greatly admired, setting forth a progressive philosophical understanding in the course of which he extended "the rights of reason . . . into the realm of Biblical criticism and historical interpretation," incurring the wrath of some of his colleagues.[152]

A reading of Walker's *Outlines*, however, indicates that Grammer was basically right. Walker emphasized reason, or human capacity, and its ability "to ascertain and verify" revelation, "to find out its meaning; the different ways in which that meaning is exhibited."[153] In writing positively of evolution he said, "The operation of Divine law, material, chemical, vegetable, and organic forces, is not, by the Divine will, excluded. At the same time, the operation of these does not and cannot exclude the presence and agency of Him who called them into existence—originating not only the material, but its laws and forces. If this be called evolution, there is no difficulty with it, if it be recognized as the working out of the previous involution of the Divine purpose, as the accompanying Divine agency, controlling it to His designed result. His hand is in and over the evolution, as is His mind, His purpose in the involution."[154]

Walker took seriously positivism and agnosticism and affirmed the progress of the race.[155] He disliked the term *total depravity* and preferred to speak of that to which the term points in Knapp's words, who says that depravity is "that tendency to sinful passions, or unlawful propensities, which is perceived in man, whenever objects of desire are placed before him, and laws are laid upon him."[156] He affirmed that justification and

sanctification are "co-instantaneous": "The blessing of forgiveness, of re-
mission of sin, of acceptance in Christ, is the beginning of an inward
change corresponding. The faith which takes Christ's offered blessing,
and thus justifies, also and in its very nature begins to sanctification."[157]
His Arminian tendencies are evident in such a statement as this: "Salvation in every such instance is of Divine grace—in the blessing offered as
in the constraining influence of Him who offers it. And yet it is as Divine
grace yielded to and accepted that it becomes savingly operative."[158]

In his *Lectures on Christian Ethics*, Walker exhibited a breadth of understanding that causes him to assert the rightful place of "natural" ethics
and morality in Christian ethics: "In Christian ethics are all the elements
of natural morality, theology, and religion, plus the contents of inspired
revelation."[159] At the heart of all is "human brotherhood." Such brotherhood ascends from that found in humanity's "common origin and nature"
and rises to its highest perfection in Christ and his disciples" the conscious and loving brotherhood of Christ's brethren in Him and with one
another. . . . This is the highest and most sacred form of earthly sympathy
and association."[160] This brotherhood "is that of the race."[161] Here was
a sentiment with which Washington Gladden and the social gospelers
could agree.[162]

Through such a teacher as Walker, the seminary was grappling with
the new age while seeking to retain continuity with the old theology. As
Grammer said, "Evangelicalism in his hands insensibly became less emotional." One might say that in his hands it became more reasonable.

NOTES

1. James M. McPherson, *The Battle Cry of Freedom: The Civil War Era* (New
York: Ballantine Books, 1989), 849.
2. See Nevins and Commager, *History*, 238–46.
3. McPherson, *Battle Cry*, 850.
4. Addison, *History*, 198.
5. Clebsch, *Journals*, IV-32, IV-33.
6. Walker, *Sparrow*, 263–64 (June 26, 1865).
7. Ibid., 262 (July 8, 1865).
8. Diocese of Virginia, *Journal* (1865), 23.
9. Ibid., 24.
10. Walker, *Sparrow*, 262.
11. Ibid., 263.
12. Goodwin, *History* 2:616; bd. min., 1821–66, 116.
13. Walker, *Sparrow*, 263.
14. Ibid., 266.

15. Ibid., 271; Goodwin, *History* 1:231.
16. Walker, *Sparrow*, 270.
17. Packard, *Recollections*, 284.
18. Walker, *Sparrow*, 266. The Dudley speech prize is named for this teacher.
19. Ibid., 272, see the rest for anecdotes about Sparrow, revealing his sense of humor in extreme circumstances.
20. Ibid., 273.
21. Ibid., 274.
22. Goodwin, *History* 1:232.
23. Walker, *Sparrow*, 274.
24. Ibid., 265.
25. Goodwin, *History* 1:233.
26. Ibid. 1:234–35.
27. Ibid., 236.
28. Ibid., 240.
29. Ibid., 239.
30. Goodwin, *History* 2:616; bd. min., 1821–66, 114–15.
31. Goodwin, *History* 2:616; bd. min., 1821–66, 116–17.
32. Goodwin, *History* 2:616–17; bd. min., 1821–66, 117–19.
33. Walker, *Sparrow*, 270.
34. Ibid., 276. See 278–79.
35. Ibid., 279.
36. Ibid., 277.
37. These figures were derived from *Journals* of the Diocese of Virginia; catalogues of the seminary; board minutes; Packard, *Recollections*; and Walker, *Sparrow*.
38. Diocese of Virginia, *Journal* (1886), 64.
39. Goodwin, *History* 1:221.
40. Ibid. 1:243.
41. Diocese of Virginia, *Journal* (1869), 67.
42. Goodwin, *History* 1:254, for the 1877 figure; bd. min., 1866–98, 145, for the 1884 figure.
43. Ibid., 227–28.
44. Ibid., 14.
45. Ibid., 176.
46. Ibid., 108.
47. Ibid., 5.
48. Ibid., 133.
49. Ibid., 175, 179, 192.
50. Ibid., 236, 253, 255, 256.
51. Ibid., 277, 278.
52. Goodwin, *History* 1:255–56.
53. Bd. min., 1866–98, 104.
54. Ibid., 111.
55. Goodwin, *History* 1:340–41.
56. See Charles Eastlake, A *History of the Gothic Revival* (1872; reprint, New

York: Humanities Press, 1970); Wallace Goodrich et al., *The Parish of the Advent in the City of Boston 1844–1944* (Boston: n.p., 1944); and James F. White, *The Cambridge Movement: The Ecclesiologists and the Gothic Revival* (Cambridge: University Press, 1962).

57. Goodwin, *History* 1:343. The rail was made of rosewood.
58. Robert A. Bennett, "Black Episcopalians: A History from the Colonial Period to the Present," *Historical Magazine of the Protestant Episcopal Church* 43/3 (September 1974): 239–40.
59. Bd. min., 1866–98, 85.
60. Goodwin, *History* 2:491. See also 1:255.
61. Bd. min., 1866–98, 134, 138.
62. Ibid., 101–102; Goodwin, *History* 2:492.
63. Goodwin, History 2:493.
64. Diocese of Virginia, *Journal* (1879), 58.
65. Ibid., 59.
66. Bd. min., 1866–97, 133; Goodwin, *History* 2:498.
67. Goodwin, *History* 2:493.
68. Bd. min., 1866–98, 153–54; Goodwin, *History* 2:494.
69. Goodwin, *History* 2:495–96.
70. Bd. min., 1866–98, 157–58; Goodwin, *History* 2:496.
71. Goodwin, *History* 2:504.
72. Ibid. 2:515.
73. Bd. min., 1866–98, 3–4; meeting of October 12, 1865.
74. Goodwin, *History* 1:621.
75. Ibid. 1:643–44.
76. John J. McElhinney, *The Doctrine of the Church: A Historical Monograph, with a full bibliography of the subject* (Philadelphia: Claxton, 1871), see 383–84.
77. John J. McElhinney, *Regeneration in Baptism: A Paper Read at a Conference Held at Columbus, O., September 13, 1871* (Columbus: Nevins and Myers, 1871).
78. John J. McElhinney, *"Eternal Hope" Reviewed. A Lecture Read in Prayer Hall, Theological Seminary of Virginia, May 1st, 1878* (Philadelphia: James Moore, 1878).
79. Goodwin, *History* 1:644, 645.
80. Bd. min., 1866–98, 41. In 1868 Johns had been made professor of pastoral theology, to lecture as Meade had before him. There was some overlapping here.
81. Ibid., 53.
82. Ibid., 56, 58–59.
83. Ibid., 62–63.
84. Ibid., 78.
85. Ibid., 85.
86. Goodwin, *History* 1:649.
87. Bd. min., 1866–98, 87.
88. Goodwin, *History* 1:652–53.
89. Bd. min., 1866–98, 87. Nelson was to teach the Ionian Greek class. See also Diocese of Virginia, *Journal* (1877), 54.
90. Bd. min., 1866–98, 150–151 (June 5, 1884).

91. Ibid., 159–60 (May 19, 1886).
92. Ibid., 161–66 (June 22, 1886).
93. Ibid., 171 (February 17,1887).
94. Ibid., 174–75 (May 18, 1887); Goodwin, History 1:262–63.
95. Goodwin, History 2:17.
96. Bd. min., 1866–98, 174.
97. Angus Crawford, "Life of Dr. Angus Crawford for His Children" (Unfinished typescript, VTSA). This is the source of much of the information about Crawford. The biographical sketch in Goodwin's History is inadequate. See next chapter concerning Crawford's autobiography. See also Southern Churchman (October 11, 1924): 15; (November 1, 1924): 8; (June 24, 1926): 11.
98. Bd. min., 1866–98, 179.
99. Goodwin, History 1:661.
100. Diocese of Virginia, Journal (1888), 47.
101. Goodwin, History 1:663.
102. Ibid. 1:263–64.
103. Bd. min., 1866–98, 287.
104. Ibid., 295.
105. Ibid., 46.
106. Ibid., 48.
107. Ibid., 50–56.
108. Ibid., 1821–66, 40; Goodwin, History 2:598.
109. Bd. min., 1866–98, 60; see 1821–66, 40.
110. Bd. min., 69–70.
111. General Convention, Journal (1868), 232, 265. The need to revise the list was recognized as early as 1856, see General Convention, Journal (1856), 206.
112. General Convention, Journal (1889), 748.
113. Ibid., 754–61.
114. Ibid., 761–62.
115. Diocese of Virginia, Journal (1891), 58; catalogue (1890 91), 16.
116. Diocese of Virginia, Journal (1895), 212; Walker's Outlines was in use, in manuscript, before this. See catalogue (1891–92), 17.
117. Diocese of Virginia, Journal (1891), 60; catalogue (1890 91), 16.
118. Catalogue (1866–67), 12–14.
119. Diocese of Virginia, Journal (1875), 190.
120. Bd. min., 1866–98, 88.
121. Diocese of Virginia, Journal (1877), 52.
122. See, for instance, catalogue (1880–81), 12; (1894–95), 13, 17, where it is indicated that juniors studied Chadbourne; seniors, Hopkins.
123. Nelson assigned Book I of Hooker's Laws; see Diocese of Virginia, Journal (1879), 56, and subsequent Journal reports.
124. Diocese of Virginia, Journal (1877), 53. The reports of Packard as professor of biblical learning and Nelson, just beginning as professor of church history and canon law, are perfunctory, the latter indicating total reliance on recitations in all his teaching. Diocese of Virginia, Journal (1877), 54.

125. Diocese of Virginia, *Journal* (1884), 41.
126. Ibid., 42–43.
127. Ibid. (1888), 46–48.
128. Bd. min., 1866–98, 159.
129. Diocese of Virginia, *Journal* (1891), 58.
130. Ibid.
131. *The Rhetorical Budget* 3/9 (February 21, 1879), VTSA.
132. Bd. min., 1866–98, 143, 146.
133. Ibid., 107.
134. Ibid., 118.
135. Ibid., 242.
136. Ibid., 252.
137. Ibid., 310, 317.
138. Goodwin, *History* 1:248.
139. Ibid. 2:362–64.
140. *Semi-Centennial* (1873), 31–32.
141. Ibid., 35.
142. Williams, *The Andover Liberals*, 26.
143. Ibid., 64.
144. Goodwin, *History* 1:630.
145. J. Barrett Miller, "The Theology of William Sparrow," *Historical Magazine of the Protestant Episcopal Church* 46/4 (December, 1977): 450. See Sparrow, *Sermons*, 329, 331, 342.
146. Goodwin, *History* 1:589.
147. William Sparrow, *Our Times and Our Duties. An Address Delivered at the Annual Commencement of the Theological Seminary of the Protestant Episcopal Church of the Diocese of Virginia, June 27, 1872* (Philadelphia: Leighton Publications, [1872]), 4–5.
148. Ibid., 12.
149. Ibid., 13–14.
150. Goodwin, *History* 1:631.
151. Ibid. 1:634.
152. Ibid. 1:663. For Robert Gibson, see Goodwin, *History* 1:603.
153. Cornelius Walker, *Outlines of Christian Theology* (New York: Whitaker, 1894), 17.
154. Ibid., 126–27.
155. Ibid., 85.
156. Ibid., 159, referring to Romans 7.
157. Ibid., 206.
158. Ibid., 217.
159. Cornelius Walker, *Lectures on Christian Ethics* (New York: Whitaker, 1895), 2.
160. Ibid., 114–15.
161. Ibid., 67.
162. Charles Hopkins, *The Rise of the Social Gospel in American Protestantism 1865–1915* (New Haven: Yale, 1940), 125, and elsewhere.

—◦〰◦—

INTO THE TWENTIETH CENTURY: A MODERN SEMINARY 1895–1923

1. THE CHALLENGES OF THE PROGRESSIVE ERA IN THE UNITED STATES

This chapter involves the years often identified as the Progressive Era in American history. In Professor Samuel P. Huntington's view it is one of the periods of "creedal passion," along with the Revolutionary and Jacksonian eras and the 1960s and 1970s. Near the beginning of the Progressive Era was the election of 1896 and the Spanish-American War of 1898. In the election of 1896 populism and its champion William Jennings Bryan emerged as forceful influences in national politics. It was observed by many that in Bryan there was an intimate relationship between Presbyterian Evangelicalism and moral outrage against vested power interests reaping benefits at the expense of working people. James Q. Wilson said, "In 1895–1910, there was . . . an outburst of new gospels, many of them this time secular in nature though still evangelical in tone: free silver, prohibition, nativism, suffragism, the social gospel, Marxism, Taylorism, the settlement-house movement, and countless others."[1] As Huntington said, that was an era of reform, whose principal targets "were the trusts and the machines." To correct the evils "associated with" big corporations and massive economic power more and more concentrated in the hands of a few, "the first antitrust laws, regulatory commissions, consumer legislation," and other such laws were enacted to control the ways in which businesses conducted their activities. Popular control was strengthened by the introduction of direct primaries and other measures. Institutions such as civic commissions and church leagues were founded to alleviate the sufferings of the poor, no longer blamed for their condition as in the past.[2]

Nevins and Commager comment that a whole range of issues drew critical attention, including the impact of urban centers, inequalities in wealth, class structures, and the vexing problems connected with immigration. Virtually all of the notable persons of the time, "Weaver, Bryan, La Follette, Debs, Roosevelt, and Wilson in the political arena; William James, Josiah Royce, and John Dewey in philosophy; Thorstein Veblen, Richard Ely, and Lester Ward in scholarship; William Dean Howells, Frank Norris, Hamlin Garland, and Theodore Dreiser in literature . . . were all reformers."[3] It is true, of course, that there would have been no reform movement, no Progressive Era, without the trusts and monopolies, the corporations such as United States Steel and entrepreneurs such as Andrew Carnegie. America was a burgeoning giant, flexing its corporate muscles. The Spanish-American War brought confidence and glory to the United States. "It was a little war," said Teddy Roosevelt, "but it was the only one we had." To many Protestants it was a crusade, with imperialism rationalized as a missionary adventure. It was seen by many as a "holy war" designed to "destroy 'Romish superstition' in the Spanish West Indies."[4] And it whetted the national appetite for more such glorious adventures. There was a mounting nationalism, patriotism, and Protestantism in the belief that under God America was fulfilling its national destiny.

In some ways, as has been implied, the Progressive Era was a time of triumph for Liberalism. But as Richard Hofstadter said, it had a deep strain of conservatism, men such as Bryan, La Follette, and Wilson looking back to a near ideal past now besmirched by self-interest. Such men sought "to undo the mischief of the past forty years and recreate the old nation of limited and decentralized power, genuine competition, democratic opportunity, and enterprise."[5] Nevertheless, in trying to effect reform persons such as Bryan were radicals, attacking and seeking to revolutionize the status quo, seeking, in Huntington's terms, "to realize the ideals of the American Revolution," which though backward-looking and thus conservative will always be radical and influence the future. In many ways this is similar to the reform of the commonwealth men in sixteenth-century England, whose leaders sought to restore the commonwealth of the Middle Ages, subverted as it had been by greedy gentry and nobility, working great hardship on yeoman farmers. Persons such as Hales and Latimer were "conservative radicals."

Just as in the sixteenth century in England when the church was involved in reform, so in the United States at the end of the nineteenth century and the beginning of the twentieth, the churches in America were involved in progressive reformism. The social gospel movement in-volved a small number of the members of the Protestant churches in America, but it was immensely influential, inculcating a social awareness and social concern informing almost every aspect of church life. It in-volved a vision of Christian economic order distinct from that capitalism which set private gain above public welfare. For Walter Rauschenbusch, the prophet and theologian of the movement, it involved the realization of the "Kingdom ideal" that is "a social order that will best guarantee the highest development of personality, in accordance with Christ's revela-tion of the divine worth of human life. It likewise implies the progressive reign of his law of love in human affairs."[6] F.D. Maurice in England con-trasted the Christian ideal of cooperation with the secular and capitalist dedication to competition. The social gospel movement also greatly as-sisted the rise of the new social science of sociology. It is significant that at Virginia Seminary in 1902 Berryman Green was named a full professor of English Bible and of *sociology*.[7]

The Episcopal Church in the United States was first influenced by the Christian socialism of F.D. Maurice and others and then by the social gospel movement in America. Hopkins notes that during the 1870s "the Protestant Episcopal Church began to show the deep concern in social problems that has characterized its significant contribution to the growth of American so-cial Christianity."[8] In 1884 the Church Congress had Henry George speak on "Is our civilization just to working men?" Bishop Henry C. Potter of New York, one of Virginia Seminary's most avid benefactors, issued a pastoral let-ter in 1886 opposing the doctrine that labor and the laborer were commodi-ties "to be bought and sold as the market shall decree." In 1887 the Church Association for the Advancement of the Interests of Labor was founded and in 1889 the Society of Christian Socialists.[9] This did not mean that the church as a whole was embracing socialism. In fact such organizations as those men-tioned increased the stress and strain within the church between the social gospel and the gospel of wealth, between those who stressed social concerns and those who emphasized individual concerns.

Here we must note that as this period began with the "little war" against Spain, it ended with the "Great War," World War I, the war to end wars, and its aftermath in the first years of the 1920s. While Americans by and large agreed with President Wilson in 1916 that they should keep out of the war in Europe, once it had seemingly reached out to involve them, it became another great crusade. Virginia Seminary alumnus Randolph H. McKim declared from his pulpit in Washington, D.C.,

It is God who has summoned us to this war. . . . This conflict is indeed a cru-sade. The greatest in history—the holiest. It is in the profoundest and surest sense a Holy War. . . . Yes, it is Christ, the King of Righteousness, who calls us to grapple in deadly strife with this unholy and blasphemous power . . . .[10]

The postwar years saw a reaction against international commitments and an affirmation of *laissez faire* economics (howbeit with government subsidies to private enterprise). It was the Jazz Age, the age of optimism, and the beginnings of modern technocratic America. Virginia Theological Seminary's centennial celebration reflected the optimism of the age. It looked back, with Dr. Goodwin, to the history of the seminary, concluding that "no other Seminary has been closer to the best and truest in the life of the nation."[11] It looked forward with Dean Berryman Green to a future of greater and greater achievements.[12] It listened to the challenge presented by George Bartlett, dean of the Philadelphia Divinity School, to recognize the perplexity and drifting of many Christians in the postwar era and to enter with courage, along with others, into the necessary task of thinking out the Christian message anew. Bartlett said, "the Gospel of Christ must become incarnate once again, must, that is, restate itself in language understanded of the people, in thought terms that are theirs and not their fathers',—must adapt itself in its applications and interpretations to the actual problems, perplexities, and conditions of the world it seeks to save."[13]

As we shall discover, the curriculum and the faculty both provide evidence that the challenge was accepted and taken seriously. But it was accepted not without hesitation and not without misgivings implicit in the necessity of remaining faithful to the Scripture and the teachings of the English Reformers while striving to speak clearly to a world where more and more people knew less and less about the Scripture and the Reformation, where many Christians were themselves perplexed and drifting.

2. A TIME OF STABILITY: THE CONTINUING GROWTH OF THE INSTITUTION

The period from 1896 to 1923 was one of relative stability for the Virginia Theological Seminary. It had recovered from the dark days of the Civil War and entered the twentieth century as a viable educational institution. Goodwin comments that its endowment rose from $330,000 in 1900 to $500,000 in 1912,[14] and significant funds were raised for capital improvements, such as the expansion of the chapel, the completion of a new library, and enhancement of the seminary's roads and grounds. The raising of money was the chief responsibility of an agent of the board employed to do the work of a modern development department. He was assisted in major ways

The Seminary, c. 1900

by board members and faculty, most importantly by Dean Crawford. Alumni support was developed beginning in 1889 with a direct appeal to leading alumni for $100.00 each, the goal being $100,000.00. In fact $17,451.75 was raised (in addition to $800.00 for the Education Society).[15] In 1908 the class plan was inaugurated, "the object of which was to secure a permanent and corporate interest on the part of the Alumni, and through them, of friends of the Seminary in the development of the institution."[16] The results of the plan were not spectacular but did enable the seminary to install electric lights, a water plant, and a heating plant.

At the suggestion of the faculty, the first major capital funds drive was inaugurated in 1923 by the board of trustees and the Alumni Association. The "Centennial Endowment Fund" was designed to raise $500,000, after the example of a $1,000,000 drive at the Episcopal Theological School in Cambridge. Half of the total was to be raised through major gifts and half through contributions from the alumni themselves. The alumni were asked to set aside 5 percent of their parish budget for five years, as a contribution to the seminary.[17] The resulting monies were to be used both for immediate needs and for permanent endowments. Those needs included an enlarged chapel, a new dormitory to be named Sparrow Hall, a professor's house, and improvements in the seminary grove, for a total of $110,000. The endowment was to include the founding of the Phillips Brooks Professorship of the Theory and Practice of Preaching and Pastoral Care ($85,000), an increase in salaries ($175,000), a library book fund ($20,000), an increase in the yearly grant to the Payne Divinity School ($50,000), and an endowment for the upkeep of the physical plant ($60,000).[18] The drive was a success and signaled a major change in the way funds were to be raised through systematic development programs organized around periodic capital funds drives.

One measure of the fairly stable financial condition of the seminary before 1923 concerns faculty salaries, which in 1897 were $2,000. Due in large part to Mr. John Black of Baltimore and his yearly gifts, salaries were raised in 1904 to $3,000 with housing provided. In 1916 Mr. Black died, leaving $60,000 outright to supplement faculty salaries and one-fifth of the residue of his estate,[19] amounting to $175,000. There were other major contributors to the seminary, including Henry Codman Potter, Bishop of New York, who gave the funds necessary to add a chancel to the chapel in 1906–1907; Mr. George Reinicker of Baltimore, who gave $6,000 in 1894 to fund the Reinicker lectures; and the Houston family of Philadelphia, whose contributions during this period amounted to more than $21,000.

Throughout the period students were provided "tuition, room, light and heat, and all principal articles of furniture gratuitously," paying only for board and laundry, which in 1919–20 amounted to $215.[20] The Education Society continued to help those students who were unable to pay for board and laundry. In 1910 the society granted $220 per annum to those students who satisfied the board of the society as to "health, religious character, competent ability and need circumstances," a sum that the faculty deemed to be too low by $30.[21] Such grants made by the society could be withdrawn by the faculty for cause, as in the case of the student who transferred from General Theological Seminary whose grades were too low.[22]

The number of the students enrolled in the seminary remained fairly constant through the period, around forty in all. In 1915 some fifty students were enrolled, but as a result of the Great War the number fell at one time to twenty-five, with students coming and going all through the year. After the war there was a steady increase from twenty-eight in June of 1919 to sixty-six in 1922–23, at which time students were having to share rooms in Aspinwall and Bohlen halls.[23] The number of dioceses represented rose from nine in 1898 to twenty-five in 1921. An increasingly smaller proportion of the student body came from the Virginia dioceses, a matter of great concern to Dean Berryman Green, as he reported in 1920.[24] In fact the seminary was gradually becoming less a diocesan and more a national school. In 1916 Dean Crawford reported students from Virginia, Maryland, North Carolina, Alabama, Tennessee, and Kentucky in the South; New York and Pennsylvania in the North; and Idaho, South Dakota, Texas, and Kansas in the West; and one student from Kyoto, Japan.[25]

"Key Hall" as Library

3. FACULTY MEETING TO CONDUCT THE BUSINESS OF THE SEMINARY

The minutes of faculty meetings, extant from 1896 to the present,[26] now begin to provide another important perspective on the seminary. In the period under review, the faculty met regularly in term time on Thursday evenings following faculty meeting at which the entire student body and faculty met. The business meeting thus began at 8:00 P.M. or later. The secretary of the faculty normally noted who spoke at the community gatherings and on what subject.

We learn that a bell was rung for faculty meeting, in Prayer Hall, where the faculty sat together facing the students. A hymn was sung and informal prayers were said.[27] Two of the faculty addressed the students on a single subject, until in 1919 it was decided that one professor should speak for three-quarters of an hour on a subject either devotional or practical.[28] In 1909, Professors Kennedy and Crawford spoke on "the relation of the Minister to Politics," and Professors Crawford and Wallis spoke on "be not weary in well-doing."[29] In 1915 Professors Wallis and Kennedy spoke on the "keeping of Lent," and Professors Green and Kennedy spoke on the "pastoral life of the clergy as reflected in English literature."[30] In 1919, when one of the faculty spoke, Dean Berryman Green addressed "the importance of the pastoral side of the ministry."[31]

As time passed, more and more visiting dignitaries spoke at faculty meeting, including Bishop-elect Capers of West Texas, Bishop Lucien Lee

Kinsolving of Brazil, and Professor Dabney of the University of Virginia, who spoke on "the spirit of Treitschke as a lecturer and leader of German political thought."[32] Such speakers did not necessarily observe the customs of faculty meeting, and the growing numbers of them caused great concern among the faculty, until in 1923 it was ordered that there be no more than one a month.[33]

After faculty meeting, the faculty was convened by a chairman or by the dean when there was a dean, with one of their number being elected secretary. When the faculty first met at the beginning of a session, the first order of business was the reception of new students. There was no staff member for admissions and no formal admissions committee. A prospective student almost certainly would be in correspondence with the dean or some other member of the faculty, but formal admission depended upon action taken by the faculty as a whole, dealing with each student personally.

In September 1900 Francis Van Rensselaer Moore presented himself for admission. A resident of Nyack in the Diocese of New York, he stated that he had taken a special course at St. Stephen's College, Annandale, New York, to study those subjects needed for admission but did not have the requisite certificate nor the necessary letter from his bishop concerning his admission as a postulant. The young man was made to squirm, was instructed to obtain the necessary documents, and was then admitted conditionally to the junior class.[34] At the next meeting of the faculty, Mr. Moore presented his certificate from St. Stephen's College "in all academics except Psychology. For this he was remanded to Dr. Micou the examiner on this subject."[35] In addition to judging the suitability of a student for admission and placing him in the appropriate class, the faculty dealt with dispensation from Hebrew, if such was indicated as necessary, and increasingly in years to come—with placement regarding knowledge of Greek and ability to take the regular course (including Hebrew and Greek) or the English Bible course.

In the background were the "Qualifications for Admission," based on the relevant section of the seminary Rules and Regulations (chap. III, sec. 1).[36] In 1900 this section began, "Every person producing to the Faculty satisfactory evidence that he has been admitted as a Candidate for Priest's Orders, according to the Canons of the Protestant Episcopal Church in the United States, may be received and entered as a student in this seminary." This included all relevant portions of the canons having to do with moral and religious character and with literary, classical, and scientific studies such as those normally associated with the attainment of a B.A. degree. Without a B.A. and without a certificate verifying that the candidate had the necessary academic preparation, the faculty would examine the student on the following (indicating that which constituted the necessary academic preparation):

The English Language and Literature, Logic, Rhetoric, Mental and Moral Philosophy, Physics and History, and the Latin and Greek Languages. In Latin and Greek a translation from some standard author, as Caesar, Cicero, Virgil, Xenophon, Plato or Demosthenes will be required of the candidate, together with a satisfactory knowledge of the grammatical forms and general principles of these languages. In History: Swinton's or Myer's General History; Physics: Brigg's "Elementary Science," Peck's Ganot; Moral Philosophy: Calderwood's; N.K. David, "Ethics"; Mental Philosophy: McCosh's or N.K. David, "Psychology"; Rhetoric: Genung's "Practical Elements of Rhetoric"; Logic: Jevon's "Elementary Lessons."[37]

It was explained that these requirements were the same as those appointed by the canons of the church (title I, canon 3, sec. vii, [2]), that substitutes might be made for the books listed, and that the examinations would be held on the Wednesday, Thursday, and Friday of the opening week of the academic year. By such means, the faculty sought to maintain fairly high academic standards. Furthermore, admission was not necessarily the end of the process. A student demonstrating a lack of preparation in any of the specified subjects could be required to drop out for further preparation after admission.[38]

Next in order came student discipline. The application of relevant Rules and Regulations required much of the faculty's attention in weekly faculty meetings. For instance, absence from class was not permitted without permission of the professor, who was required to keep a classbook and call the roll of class members at each lecture or recitation. No student was allowed to be absent from chapel without faculty consent. No student was allowed to engage in any permanent occupation necessitating absence from chapel without the consent of the faculty and the president of the board of Trustees. Finally, no student was to be absent from the seminary for more than a day without permission. As a consequence virtually every meeting of the faculty was concerned with requests for permission to be absent. Especially after holidays such as Thanksgiving and Christmas, those late in returning were expected to explain their tardiness, giving satisfactory reasons.

There was a particular problem involving bishops who expected their students to do Sunday work at nearby and not so nearby churches and missions, in violation of the rule ordering attendance at all seminary chapel services, including the Sunday morning community service. The faculty took the rule seriously, stopping short of enforcing attendance as they believed was the custom at the General Theological Seminary.[39]

In 1910 the faculty sent a letter to the bishops bemoaning the increased number of students absent from the chapel on Sundays. The seminary suffered and the students suffered as a result of the trend. The faculty argued that the seminary missions provided sufficient practical experience on Sunday afternoons and evenings. Furthermore, every effort was being made by the Education Society to make certain that students did not need to do Sunday work for financial reasons.[40] Bishop Harding of the Diocese of Washington replied, supporting the faculty in this matter but explaining that he still needed two students on Sundays.[41] Bishop Randolph of southern Virginia asked that one of his students be allowed to work in his diocese on Sundays. The faculty refused his request. The bishop rejected their refusal, forcing a confrontation. The bishop then gave his reasons and the faculty "agreed to interpose no objection" in this one case.[42] The issue was to be raised again and again.[43]

The faculty also spent considerable time scheduling courses, examinations, chapel services, and special lectures. Often one member of the faculty was asked to prepare a schedule for consideration by the faculty. Of major concern were the Reinicker lectures, founded through the gift of Mr. George Reinicker of Baltimore. Further sums were raised, with the assistance of the Reverend Julius E. Grammer, Dr. Sparrow's son-in-law and Mr. Reinicker's rector.[44] The gift was recorded in 1895, and from 1896 on the securing of lecturers was a major concern. The plan was to have two courses of lectures, with three lectures each, in each academic year. Quite often those invited had to decline and the faculty had to invite others. Hugh M. Thompson, Bishop of Mississippi, was an early choice, scheduled to give his lectures in the spring of 1897.

Bishops were often chosen, but as time passed the choice fell more frequently upon scholars such as R.D. Wilson of Princeton, whose subject was "Latest Critical Results, with reference to the Book of Daniel," and Dr. Foakes Jackson on "the Development of Christian Institutions in the Early Christian Period." In 1912 an effort was made to obtain a set of lectures on sociology, with Mr. Jacob Riis of New York and the Reverend E.W. Ward of Pittsburgh being elected. In the same year Professor William Porcher DuBose of Sewanee was invited to give the lectures. Sometimes a lecturer was asked to give all six lectures in a year; sometimes a person was chosen to give one or two. In 1901 the faculty decided that the lectures should be in publishable form; in 1910 it was decided that typescripts of the lectures should be deposited in the library.

The faculty was also responsible for managing the Sparrow postgraduate fellowships. The Sparrow Fellowship Foundation was established in 1902 largely through the efforts of Dean Crawford and the Reverend Charles J. Holt (class of 1874) of Fordham, New York. A fellow was to be chosen by the faculty from the senior class on the basis of scholarly excellence to study at any university at home or abroad—when there were sufficient funds.[45] Paca Kennedy was the first Sparrow fellow and studied at Oxford University with Professors Micou and Wallis as his Virginia Seminary supervisors.[46] Churchill Gibson Chamberlayne was chosen in 1904, in succession to Kennedy, whose two-year term had expired, to study at the University of Halle in Germany for the Ph.D. degree in history and philosophy, which he received (magna cum laude) in 1906.[47] In 1907 E.P. Dandridge was Sparrow fellow at Oxford, but the fund was low, and he would not have survived without assistance from the Reverend Peter Mayo of Richmond.[48] In 1908 it was decided to cease appointing fellows until sufficient funds were available to finance them.[49]

The chapel was a constant concern during this period. Pressures were brought to bear for the elaboration of the simple worship customary in the seminary. Informal daily family prayer in Prayer Hall was gradually supplanted by morning and evening prayer in the chapel. In 1905 a committee of students, including Walter Russell Bowie, appeared before the faculty to ask for daily morning prayer in addition to family prayer before breakfast. The matter was referred to the board.[50] In 1910 a request was made for evening prayer in the chapel, in place of the missionary prayer service in Prayer Hall.[51] In 1920 the faculty determined that in the next academic year there would be "three corporate services of the Seminary: Morning Prayer, daily except Sunday and Monday, at 9:00; Faculty Meeting; and Senior Preaching." The 9:00 A.M. service was clearly the chief one, with the faculty sitting in their stalls, wearing academic gowns. It was further decided that except on Thursdays, when there was faculty meeting, and Sundays, when students were generally at the seminary missions, there was to "be an informal student prayer service immediately after Supper, embodying the 12:00 o'clock missionary prayers and replacing Evening Prayer."[52]

As to Holy Communion, off and on students petitioned for Holy Communion at 7:30 A.M. on Sundays and at other times as well. In 1903 *The Living Church* carried a news story reporting that the seminary refused to allow a weekly celebration of the Holy Communion, although thirty-two out of forty-six students had requested it. The students disclaimed any connection with this report, signing memorials—with two students refusing—testifying to this. On behalf of the faculty, Professors Micou and Massie drafted a letter that was sent to bishops and others admitting that the student request was refused.

The reason for this refusal was that there is a celebration on the first Sunday at the 11 o'clock service, and on the third Sunday at half past seven, and also on all high festivals of the Church, averaging three celebrations each month throughout the session. In view of the fact that this congregation is small enough for all to communicate at every celebration, and remembering the strong conservatism of a large part of the constituency of this Seminary, both clerical and lay, it was not in our judgement expedient to make the change requested at this time.[53]

The Virginia Low Church tradition with its emphasis on simplicity was behind this letter, as was the anti-Roman Catholic, anti-Anglo Catholic tradition of the board and faculty. Some students were always pushing against the tradition: some requested permission to wear surplices when conducting services; one student was required to resign from the Confraternity of the Blessed Sacrament; and another was admonished for making the sign of the cross in the chapel. In 1919 it was agreed that "Black and White be the colours used for stoles in the Chapel Services, the White stoles to be used for high festivals." Emphasis was placed on preaching, but Professor Kennedy, as chaplain of the Episcopal High School, requested that Sunday services be made more acceptable to the boys, restricting sermons on communion Sundays to fifteen minutes in length.

Chapel matters revealed tensions not only between faculty and students but also between faculty and board, and faculty and dean. In 1899 the board ruled against evening prayer, insisting on the maintenance of the family prayer service in Prayer Hall. This action drew a response from the faculty, drafted by Crawford and unfortunately not preserved. The faculty evidently defended the use of evening prayer, instead of the family prayer service.[54] The student admonished for making the sign of the cross appealed to the faculty, which refused to take any action. The dean at a subsequent meeting stated that according to the rules of the board this was not a faculty matter but was for the dean alone to act upon.[55] In 1920 the board ruled that the dean was the rector of the chapel.[56]

From time to time the faculty was forced to deal with serious disciplinary problems. In 1899 Crawford reported that some students were refusing to take an examination he had required of them. They were ordered to take the examination.[57] There were cases of cheating on examinations, often resulting in dismissals. There were students dismissed for moral delinquencies, for sexual aberrations, for drunkenness, and for irascibility unsuited in those studying for the ministry. In time an honors committee composed of three students chosen by the faculty was established. In 1920 a report from the honors committee was submitted to the faculty stating that a student had been found guilty of "immoral relations with a woman before he came to Seminary" and "that he has had such relations with that woman since." He was dismissed from the seminary by action of the faculty.[58]

At the end of the academic year there were prize contests, principally the Wallace prize for extemporaneous speaking and the Reinicker reading prize. In 1908 Walter Russell Bowie, speaking on "The Twentieth-Century Minister, His Task and Outlook," a topic assigned by the faculty, won the Wallace prize. The faculty also assigned the readings for the Reinicker prize.[59] Final examinations were no longer delivered orally in public but written for each subject. After final examinations the faculty met to average grades, to determine who would advance to the middler and senior classes, who would graduate, and, of those who graduated, which would receive certificates, which diplomas, and which would be recommended to the board for the bachelor of divinity degree. At commencement graduating students were chosen by the faculty to read their senior essays, ranging in 1897 from "The Lessons of the Book of Job" to "The Influence of John Locke."

The B.D. degree was first authorized in 1898. In that first year the board determined that the degree should be awarded only to those who were graduates of some "respectable college or seminary such as this"; had completed the full course with average marks of 85 percent or higher (with no grades lower than 75 percent in any department during the senior year); had an acquaintance with Latin, Greek and Hebrew; had written a thesis on some subject specified by the faculty; "give evidence of capacity for original theological work, and be ordained a priest."[60] This meant that for years not all graduates with B.A. or B.S. degrees were awarded B.D. degrees. Dispensation from Greek or Hebrew would exclude many, as would an insufficiently high grade average. And there were those who did not complete a satisfactory thesis after graduation. Gradually the demands were relaxed. Students could be reexamined (indeed must be reexamined) in any subject they failed. In the Rules and Regulations of 1916 the statement concerning the awarding of the B.D. did not mention languages, and in 1922 the board was requested to authorize the conferring of the B.D. on non-Greek students "on the completion of adequate substitute courses."[61] The board did so.[62]

The faculty spent time in its meetings dealing with the results of the final examinations, including probation or dismissal for students who fell below the passing average. They also prepared the details of the commencement, including the transportation and housing of guests, the ceremony, and the subsequent ordination service, preceded by what the students called a retreat but what the faculty called a quiet day. They were also concerned for the missionary service, a traditional part of commencement. The Student Missionary Society proposed names of those they preferred to have as preachers at the service, the faculty chose two-thirds from the list, screening out those they thought to be unsuitable.

Around commencement the faculty also was involved in various ways in meetings of the alumni and the board. After commencement the faculty met to make reports to the bishops concerning their students—a process originally designed to be quarterly but then twice yearly, emphasis falling on the reports sent out in June. Such was the work of the faculty as it conducted business through the year. The overwhelming impression is that of hours spent discussing students, especially those who made demands on the faculty and those in some sort of difficulty, personal or academic.

4. THE BOARD OF TRUSTEES
AND ITS MANAGEMENT OF THE SEMINARY

The board of trustees minutes reveal some important matters not alluded to in the faculty minutes or, if alluded to, only in veiled ways. In 1895 the board, reacting to student complaints, ordered Professor Wallis to exercise more discipline in the classroom.[63] In 1896 the board's agent, Charles Gauss, was in Philadelphia seeking funds when he was seized by the police, diagnosed as "insane," and sent to an asylum.[64] In the same year Dr. Packard resigned from the deanship, and the board created a committee to search for a new dean and chaplain (and as was subsequently added, teacher of English Bible). The committee nominated the Reverend Beverly D. Tucker, who was elected and granted a salary of $2,000. In the minutes Cornelius Walker was made dean pro tem.[65] By May 1897 Tucker had declined his election. At the same time the board was displeased with Professor Crawford, who insisted on living off campus in Washington, D.C., because of his wife's poor health. The board insisted that professors must live on campus but allowed for temporary residence elsewhere with consent of the president of the board.[66]

A special meeting was called for November 3, 1897, at Holy Trinity Church, Richmond, where the Reverend Randolph H. McKim, rector of the Church of the Epiphany, Washington, D.C.,[67] was elected dean and chaplain. Again Professor Crawford came into the discussion with a query as to whether his residence would be available for the new dean.[68] McKim declined his election, and the board, meeting on December 15, 1897, discussed several other possible candidates and appointed Bishops Peterkin and Randolph to work on a description of the duties of the Dean.[69]

In January 1898 the board met at the bishop's residence in Richmond. The Peterkin-Randolph committee called attention to the bylaws, which specified that the dean was to be "the organ of communication between the students and the faculty." It was proposed that this be changed to "an organ of communication between the Faculty and the practical work of the institution, with the Board of Trustees." They discussed the need for more power in the deanship. After this, full of implications for the future, the board proceeded to nominate as dean and chaplain the Reverend J.

Houston Eccleston, rector of Emmanuel Church, Baltimore, and for a second time, the Reverend Beverly D. Tucker. Eccleston was elected. The board now felt under additional pressure, Cornelius Walker, dean pro tem, having announced that he would retire at the end of the session.[70] When the board met a month later in the vestry of St. James' Church, Richmond, it was announced that Eccleston had refused his election.

The object of the February meeting was the election of a dean, but it was first necessary to fill vacancies in the faculty. Professor Grammer had resigned, and the board proceeded to elect the Reverend William Meade Clarke as professor of church history, ethics, and apologetics. Professor Walker was retiring, and the board elected the Reverend R.W. Micou as professor of systematic divinity, English Bible, and homiletics. Clarke refused his election, and at the next board meeting a further search was begun, resulting in the election of Arthur Selden Lloyd, who also declined his election. At a meeting in July, the Reverend Robert K. Massie was elected and accepted his election. Micou accepted his election at once. With a faculty of no more than four this matter was of critical importance and delayed the search for a new dean.

At the February 1898 meeting it was proposed that the description of the dean in the Rules and Regulations be changed in specific ways. The changes were not made then but point toward future developments and indicate something of the problem the board was having in finding someone to accept the deanship. The proposal read,

> The Dean shall be elected by the Board of Trustees.
>
> He shall be the organ of communication between the Board, the Faculty, and the Students, and of information and suggestions to the Board upon all questions concerning the administration and the officers of the institution. It shall be his duty to preside at all meetings of the Faculty—to answer communications addressed to "the Seminary" in relation to the business of the institution—to open each term in conjunction with the other professors in some formal manner, matriculating the students, and taking such other missions as may have a tendency to make the members of the institution feel that they are attaching themselves to an organized body and coming under law.
>
> He shall be Chaplain of the Seminary and shall have control of, and be responsible for, the Pulpit and all services in the Chapel.
>
> It shall be the duty of the Dean to attend all meetings of the Board of Trustees, and he shall have the right of participation in its deliberations, and to present propositions for its consideration.
>
> He shall preside at Commencements in the absence of the President or Vice-President, unless the Trustees shall appoint one of their own number for the purpose.

He shall take a general oversight of the Seminary, and as Dean make an
annual report of its work and general condition to the Trustees.[71]

Once more the board was after Professor Crawford, requesting him, in
the light of Carl Grammer's resignation, to resume residence at the seminary. In July 1898 Crawford was considered for the position of dean pro
tem, but he was still refusing to resume residence at the seminary and
reacted strongly to any suggestion that he resign. The board expressed its
sympathy with Crawford but refused to allow that any faculty could live
outside the seminary.[72] The executive committee of the board was then
empowered to appoint a dean and seemingly did so, informing the new
professor, R.K. Massie, that he was to be dean. Massie accepted, but
Crawford, on being informed, became very angry, saying that he thought
he was dean. In the interests of harmony, the executive committee asked
the faculty to choose a chairman. They chose Crawford, and Massie was
forgotten, except insofar as he remained a professor on a small faculty
now dominated by Crawford.[73]

At its meeting on June 19, 1900, the board finally elected Crawford as
dean, once more explaining the necessity for him to be resident at the
seminary.[74] The struggle was over, and from this point on until the election of Felix Kloman after World War II, the dean would be chosen from
among the professors as the Rules and Regulations provided.[75]

Almost immediately Crawford, together with the proctor of the seminary, had to deal with a student complaining "the food is poor."[76] Subsequently, two of the students who protested were allowed to board out, and
the Rules and Regulations were revised concerning many details of seminary life, including the terms under which students were allowed to board
elsewhere than at the seminary dining room.[77]

The board was concerned with further faculty appointments. In 1899
instruction in "the literary and spiritual interpretation of the English Bible
and its uses in the work of the Christian ministry and in Liturgics" was
assured by the hiring of Arthur M. Hilliker, a member of the staff at
Epiphany, Washington. He was hired as an instructor at $750 for two days
each week through the academic year. In 1901 Hilliker resigned, and
Berryman Green of Christ Church, Alexandria, was hired as adjunct professor at $750 and invited to attend faculty meetings with voice but no
vote, except in matters pertaining to the English Bible chair. The next
year Berryman Green resigned, but the board then elected him to a full
professorship, the chair now including "English Bible, Homiletics, Christian Ethics and Sociology," and he accepted.[78] Dr. Packard having died,
his house was made ready for Professor Green.

In 1903 Bishop Whittle having died and Bishop Randolph having declined, Bishop Gibson was elected president and chairman of the board. In the same year provision was made to have alumni trustees. The Reverend R.H. McKim was the first, elected in 1905. Also in 1903 the board decided to apply to the Virginia legislature for authority to grant S.T.D. and D.D. degrees. The authority to award the D.D. degree was granted in 1911, and the first recipients, chosen by the board, were the Reverend John S. Gibson, the Reverend Landon Mason, and the Right Reverend Henry St. George Tucker.[79]

The board continued its oversight of the curriculum, adjusting the distribution of subjects with each change in faculty, suggesting new subjects, not always approved, and in 1906 seeking to have reference books, such as those of Wellhausen, Briggs, Gould, and Cheyne removed from the catalogue, their presence giving the impression that the faculty and the board approved of them and their views. The reference is to Wellhausen's *History of Israel and Judah*, listed by the ecclesiastical history department; Cheyne's *Job and Solomon* in the English Bible department; and Brigg's *Messianic Prophecies* in the Hebrew and Old Testament department—books representing the historical—biblical critical approach to the Bible. The board also objected to listing McConnell's *History of the American Episcopal Church* "by reason of its inadequacy and conspicuous absence of historical accuracy."[80]

In 1907 the board attempted to persuade Professor Wallis to resign his chair and retain a position at the seminary as chaplain. The aim was to elect a new professor of Greek language and New Testament literature in the light of a declining interest in Greek at the seminary. At the time it was decided to ascertain whether the Reverend W. Cosby Bell could teach Greek New Testament and exegesis. Wallis was then informed that he could no longer teach Greek New Testament and literature but could be chaplain and professor of pastoral theology and liturgics. Wallis agreed. Thus, what the board wished was accomplished, and the Reverend Paca Kennedy was selected for the New Testament chair with responsibility for teaching Greek. When the matter was settled, Wallis was not given liturgics but rather church polity.[81]

In 1909 another crisis arose concerning Dean Crawford. This time the faculty, including Wallis, Micou, and Green (Kennedy withheld his name, pleading lack of acquaintance with the issues due to his recent arrival), protested that Crawford construed Rules and Regulations, chapter 30 to mean that he had "sole authority to act without consultation with his faculty." They requested the board to instruct the dean that he must consult with his faculty "in all matters of importance concerning the Seminary, thus placing us in the position of associates rather than assistants." The board agreed and so instructed Dean Crawford.[82] The cause of this protest is not altogether clear, but it could have been related to Crawford's insistence upon his control of the chapel. We note that in 1910 the class of 1908 offered for a second time to give a brass cross for the communion table in the chapel. Again the board refused the offer and suggested that the class think of some other gift. A scholarship instead of a cross was suggested and accepted.[83]

The board at times clashed with the students. The trustees supported the faculty when they ordered that students stay at the seminary on Sunday mornings, at a time when more and more members of the student body felt called to be elsewhere. The board admonished the students to use the facilities of the seminary more carefully and in particular not leave the newly installed electric lights on unnecessarily. In June 1911 the dean reluctantly transmitted a message from the students in reaction to an admonishment: "We the students . . . do most respectfully and emphatically deny the charges of extravagant use of water and careless use of property," having borne with patience the lack of water. They pointed to the natural processes of deterioration of the buildings and expressed their expectation that in the future they would be afforded a hearing before the board before such accusations were made public. The board then gave evidence of political astuteness, voicing pleasure "at this evidence of loyalty and grateful appreciation on the part of the student body."[84] We are aware that there was at this time a student body organization with a constitution approved by the faculty. We are also aware that at the next meeting of the board, in November, a decision was made to drill a new well for more and better water.[85]

On December 21, 1911, a special meeting of the board was called due to Professor Micou's deteriorating health. It was decided to give him an eighteen-month leave of absence with full pay. It was also decided to elect W. Cosby Bell as professor of systematic divinity at $2,400 a year with housing. Before the eighteen months had expired, Micou was dead. The board provided financial support to the publication of a book on which Micou had been working at the time of his death.[86] In January 1913 another special meeting was called, this time because Professor Massie, who had been granted a leave of absence, indicated that he would not return. The board then proceeded to elect the Reverend Wallace E. Rollins of Sweet Briar, Virginia, as professor of ecclesiastical history, Christian missions, and canon law.[87] In 1915 a major curriculum revision was adopted, which will be described later in this chapter.

In 1914 Dean Crawford requested permission to take the leave of absence he had been unable to take two years earlier. This was granted, and Berryman Green was appointed acting dean. At the end of the leave of absence, Crawford tendered his resignation as dean and at the same meeting, June 6, 1916, the board apparently without hesitation elected Berryman Green to be the dean.[88] Also at this meeting of the board, the class of 1908 once more offered to give the seminary a brass cross for the chapel. The gift was accepted, leaving the style and the manner of placing the cross to the approval of the president of the board. The success of the offer this time could have been related to the passing of the deanship from Crawford to Green.[89]

In the period leading up to American entrance into World War I, the board was much occupied by improvements in the seminary plant, including plans for a new library in Packard's honor, Mr. W.W. Laird and his brothers having provided $10,000 of the $20,000 needed.[90] By 1917 the estimated cost of the library, the present Packard-Laird building, was $30,000, and plans were made to borrow the additional funds needed.[91] In 1918 the board was dealing with the consequences of the war, hiring Dr. H. Van Kirk as a temporary replacement for Cosby Bell, then a chaplain in the army. It was noted that Bell, who served in France, was invalided home and discharged as physically unfit.[92]

The war ended. The board proceeded to a major change in the faculty, directing Professors Crawford and Wallis to retire, hiring the Reverend T.K. Nelson and the Reverend B.D. Tucker as professors at $3,000 a year plus housing. Bishop Gibson having died, William C. Brown, Bishop of Virginia (1919–27), was elected president of the board. Work proceeded on the new library and on other improvements to the plant, including the relocation of the seminary stables and the provision of "bathrooms and waterclosets" in the dorms, in place of the old, much derided bath house. By 1921 the cost of the new library was in excess of $60,000, of which sum $47,922 were borrowed.[93] In 1921–22 the board was struggling with a deficit budget, making up the deficit from the corpus of the institution while facing the rising cost of the new library and a long list of needed physical improvements.

A major task of the board at this time was the separation of the high school from the seminary. Dean Crawford had urged that this be done in 1912, complaining that the confusion of the two financially inhibited his ability to raise funds, especially endowment funds. From 1870 to 1913 Launcelot Blackford was the principal of the Episcopal High School, controlling the school by lease from the board of trustees of the seminary and the high school.[94] Through those years the seminary board spent a major portion of each meeting on high school matters. In 1913 Archibald Robinson Hoxton applied for and was appointed principal (at which time the board determined to cease leasing the school), assumed direct responsibility for the operation of the school, and fixed the salaries of all those employed by the school.[95] The board then began spending more and more time on the school, especially on building programs. By 1921 the high school had 186 students and was growing. For the better management of both the high school and the seminary, the separation of the two was begun in 1922 and completed at a special meeting of the board on February 5, 1923. The separation was confirmed at the June 5, 1923, board meeting, arrangements for the transfer of properties and funds having been effected.[96]

From then on the board was able to apply itself to solving the problem of the seminary's deficit budget (in 1923 income was $41,905.66; expenses, $48,813.64) and to planning and carrying out the centennial celebration. This included a drive to raise $500,000 for the endowment, a major part of the plan to deal with the deficit budget.[97] Viewed from the perspective of the board, the problem was serious but the promise was great. The centennial celebration was a success, accompanied by a highly laudatory history (W.A.R. Goodwin, *History of the Theological Seminary in Virginia and its Historical Background*, 2 vols.) and the enthusiastic acceptance of the major funds drive. The faculty was strong, the dean was cooperative, and the student body was growing, with thirty-one new students for the 1922–23 session.

5. A FACULTY OF PROMINENCE: FROM WALKER TO MICOU AND BELL

The catalogue for the 1897–98 session of the seminary indicates that, in addition to Joseph Packard, professor emeritus, there were four full-time members of the faculty: Cornelius Walker, dean and professor of systematic divinity, homiletics, and liturgics; Carl Grammer, professor of ecclesiastical history and canon law; Angus Crawford, professor of oriental languages and literature, Hebrew, and apologetics; and Samuel Wallis, professor of Greek language, New Testament literature, church polity, and pastoral theology. This was a faculty well qualified to teach the canonically required subjects, with Walker as the most distinguished, Grammer the most innovative and exciting, Crawford the most learned but sometimes difficult, and Wallis seemingly the weak member of the team although dependable and competent.

Cornelius Walker, the first Virginian to be elected to the full-time faculty, was educated at the Episcopal High School and at the seminary and was rector of Christ Church, Alexandria, at the time of his election in 1866. Grammer came from Maryland, grandson of William Sparrow and graduate of Johns Hopkins University with a B.A. A graduate of the seminary, he did some postgraduate work at Yale. Crawford, a Canadian by birth, earned an M.A. from Yale and was rector of Trinity Church, Mount Holly, New Jersey, at the time of his election in 1887. Wallis was also

The Faculty with Classes of 1910–1912
Faculty Seated in Front Row: (*l to r*): Paca Kennedy; Richard Micou;
Angus Crawford, Dean; Samuel Wallis; Robert Massie

born in Canada but grew up in Virginia, studied for a time at the University of Virginia, graduated from the seminary, and served Pohick and Olivet churches, Fairfax County, until 1894 when he was elected to the faculty. Only Grammer had a B.A. degree; none had an earned doctorate; all had pastoral experience. In addition, there were the long-suffering Mr. Willoughby Reade, instructor in elocution and music; Miss Maria B. Worthington, librarian through the entire period covered by this chapter; and Mr. Joseph Wilmer, proctor or superintendent of buildings and grounds. There was also a matron who supervised numerous servants, but there was no secretarial staff. In 1918 the board authorized the purchase of a typewriter for the dean and in 1923 instructed the executive committee to see that the dean was provided with adequate secretarial support.[98]

In 1898 Robert K. Massie succeeded Grammer. Born in Charlottesville, Virginia, Massie graduated from the University of Virginia, received an M.A. from George Washington University, was ordained, and spent four years as a missionary in China. He returned to be rector of Meade Parish in Virginia, where he was when elected professor of church history and canon law at the seminary. In the same year Richard W. Micou was chosen to succeed

Cornelius Walker in systematic divinity. Born in New Orleans, he served the Army of the Confederacy after study at the University of Virginia and was awarded an honorary B.A. by that university after the war. He studied at the University of Erlangen in Bavaria and at the University of Edinburgh. Returning to America he taught Greek for a short time at the University of the South and then studied for a year at the General Theological Seminary. Ordained in 1870, Micou served churches in Louisiana, Pennsylvania, and Connecticut before joining the faculty of the Philadelphia Divinity School. From thence he came to the seminary.

Berryman Green came to the faculty to teach English Bible and homiletics. Born in Virginia in 1865 he graduated from the seminary and served various churches in Virginia before becoming rector of Christ Church, Alexandria, in 1895. In 1902, having taught briefly at the seminary as an adjunct, he was made a full professor and subsequently was elected dean in succession to Angus Crawford. It is of interest to note that Green was twice elected Bishop Coadjutor of Virginia and twice refused.

Paca Kennedy began work as professor of New Testament language and literature in 1908. Born in West Virginia in 1878, he received his B.A. and M.A. degrees from Roanoke College and the B.D. from Virginia Seminary. After ordination he studied at Oxford University on a Sparrow fellowship and served in the mission field in West Virginia until called to the seminary.

W. Cosby Bell succeeded Micou in systematic divinity in 1911. Born in Virginia in 1881, a graduate of Hampden-Sydney College and of Virginia Seminary, Bell was ordained and served churches in Virginia, including the Robert E. Lee Memorial Church, Lexington, from 1906 to 1911.

Wallace E. Rollins succeeded Robert Massie as professor of ecclesiastical history in 1913. Born in North Carolina in 1870 he graduated from the University of North Carolina with a B.A. and from Yale Divinity School with a B.D. Ordained, he served churches in Virginia until becoming chaplain of Sweet Briar College in 1908, from whence he was called to the seminary faculty.

In 1920 Angus Crawford and Samuel Wallis retired and were succeeded respectively by Thomas Kinloch Nelson and Beverly Dandridge Tucker, Jr. Nelson was the son of Professor Kinloch Nelson. He was born in 1879 and was educated at the Episcopal High School, McGuire's University School (Richmond, Virginia), and the University of Virginia, from which he graduated with B.A. and M.A. degrees. He received the B.D. degree from Virginia Seminary in 1911, was ordained, and went as a missionary to China, where he was a professor at St. John's University, Shanghai, until 1913. Returning to Virginia because of poor health, he was a parish priest until going to the Virginia Episcopal School at Lynchburg, from whence he was called to the seminary as professor of Old Testament language and literature.

Tucker was the son of the Bishop of Southern Virginia and the brother of Henry St. George Tucker. Educated at Norfolk Academy and the University of Virginia, from which he received a B.A. degree, he then studied at Virginia Theological Seminary, from which he received a B.D. degree in 1915. Tucker was also a Rhodes scholar and as such studied at Christ Church, Oxford, earning B.A. and M.A. degrees. He was parish priest in Virginia prior to joining the seminary faculty. During World War I, he was a chaplain first with the Red Cross and then with the army. In 1923 he resigned his professorship in practical theology to become rector of St. Paul's Church, Richmond. He was succeeded by his brother, Henry St. George Tucker, who had distinguished himself as a missionary bishop and was given the title of professor of systematic divinity and applied Christianity (or, professor of pastoral theology).

The most distinguished scholars on the faculty during these years were Richard Micou and Cosby Bell. Bell, who achieved maturity as a theologian after 1923, will be the subject of major attention in the next chapter. In this, Micou requires our serious attention as of major importance in the history of the seminary in the first decade of the twentieth century. His approach to theology was largely apologetic, as was necessary in an age of growing skepticism when scientism was challenging the credibility of Christian beliefs. He studied modern philosophy and the sciences extensively in order to deal with their various objections to Christian belief. As was said, he was prescient "with the wisdom of a true seer," seeing "the triumph of Idealism of the next generation, while most philosophical teachers were becoming resigned to the fact that materialism was final and that the conflict must be waged along that line to the end."[99]

Paul Micou, the theologian's son and a graduate of the seminary, who carefully prepared his father's major work for publication, indicated the nature of his father's teaching in relation to the book:

> To the Junior class he gave an introductory course on the Creeds, to the Middle class he lectured on the philosophy of theism or, as he preferred to call it, "fundamental theology," and on Christian Apologetics, and with the Seniors he took up Systematic or Christian Theology. Therefore this volume represents about two thirds of the work of the Middle year.[100]

The middle year contained the heart of Micou's teaching in relation to an introductory study on the Creeds—an encounter with the "theological given" presented to juniors—and a systematic presentation of Christian theology, based on the Creeds, and apologetics, for the seniors. That

the book *Basic Ideas in Religion, or Apologetic Theism* represents the heart
of Micou's concern is further emphasized by a *Syllabus* of sixty-four pages
and lecture notes by students, revised by Micou, published in 1907 as a
Manual of Fundamental Theology and Christian Apologetics.

In *Basic Ideas* Micou faces the reality that, for the ensuing years of the
twentieth century, *the* question is not whether the Bible is genuine, miracles
possible, and "supernatural Christianity true" but whether there is any
supernatural at all. This situation demands that attention be paid to the
great issue: "The very possibility of faith . . . depends on our world view,
on a philosophy which shall find place in the cosmos for God as Lord and
for man as spirit."[101] In pursuit of such a philosophy, Micou appealed to
"internal evidence" much as did Luther and Calvin— "the gospel's witness to itself and the affinity of the soul to the message. . . ."[102] He marked
the transition from awareness of this—Richard Hooker being "the last of
the spiritual theologians" of the Reformation Era—to the materialism of
Hobbes and Locke, denouncing Paley and Pearson, noting that Butler
was a closet spiritual thinker, and hailing the recovery of the spiritual
understanding of reality with the Evangelical revival, with the Lake poets
in England, with Herder, Goethe, and Schiller in Germany. But Coleridge
was for him "a main factor" in this return to spiritual Christianity, pointing the way to the new apologetic, writing in the *Biographia Literaria* of
"the sense, the inward feeling, in the soul of each believer of its [religion's]
desirableness—the experience that he needs something, joined with the
strong foretokening, that the redemption and the graces propounded to
us in Christ are what he needs."[103]

Kant is acknowledged as of crucial importance by Micou. The reality
and importance of doubt in relation to faith is insisted upon: "An un-
ruffled, placid faith may be the result of lazy indolence of mind and a
selfish, narrow heart, or the result of ignorant conceit."[104] Indeed, Micou
protested that the theology he proposed was not without demands for
intellectual rigor, logical, consistent, discriminating thought: "Even when
we are trying to reach the consciences and hearts of men, our approach
has to be made through their intelligence."[105] Micou ended the introduction of *Basic Ideas* saying,

Theology assumes as its postulates the personality of God and the personality of man, and further holds that God and man are in relation with one
another. Postulates are as necessary to theology as to any other science,
for they are the basis of all argument. . . . Let it suffice here to say that
fundamental theology or theism, which is the subject of this book, is the
study of these postulates themselves from the philosophical and scientific
standpoint, apart from the revelation of God in Christ. . . . The general

plan is simple. We will examine first the Idea of God, and the efforts made to deny it, and then the Spiritual Idea of Man, with the denials of it that have been attempted.[106]

Micou proceeds, along the way considering organic evolution from the perspective of Darwin and the neo-Darwinians and contemporaries such as Mendel, including aesthetics—the "Witness of the Beautiful and the Sublime"—and he makes much of the poets, at times sounding like Hans-Georg Gadamer. His emphasis on wholeness and thinking "in wholes, so that ultimate bearings of the facts will become evident,"[107] is reminiscent of the idealistic philosophy of F.H. Bradley that so influenced T.S. Eliot. Micou's apologetic theology deserves more serious attention than can be given to it here. One limited but significant indication of it is provided by a paper that he read before the alumni of the seminary on June 18, 1907. He said in part,

> We live in two worlds—one, a world of Observation composed of sensations and perceptions from without, common to all and capable of clear description and exact classification; the other, a world of Appreciation composed of conceptions and reflections and judgments of worth, intensely personal, capable of only partial revelation. This last, the inner world of consciousness, of feelings and thoughts, of motives and desires, of affections and hopes and faiths is the real world of humanity in which men live and act and will.[108]

This was Micou's sincere conviction, bred of a life lived steeped in the Scriptures and the Book of Common Prayer and informed by his Evangelical faith. He knew that it was not shared with most people in the twentieth century, but he saw signs of a revolt growing "against the sacred idol of the academic cave," bloodless rationality that "grinds out good and brings out ill, and has no purpose, heart or will."[109] Among the leaders of the revolt he acknowledged William James in psychology, Karl Pearson and others in the physical sciences, and Diewart, Brentano, and Erdman in logic. He concluded,

> The battle between Faith and Unfaith is not yet won, but we may confidently hope that the twentieth century will witness the reconciliation of the realms of Feeling and Will with that of knowledge through the inspiration of a science that is humanized and a Christianity which is spiritualized, both reverencing that inner world of nature and character, of deep convictions and noble affections, of faith and hope and love, to which the outer world of things is subordinate and wholly instrumental.[110]

6. ANGUS CRAWFORD: HIS STORY

Angus Crawford left an account of his life for the benefit of his children. In it we glimpse a farm boy in his native Canada becoming impatient with schooling, learning to plow "in straight furrows," playing pranks, and in and out of trouble. He tells of one incident involving a teacher who wrongly suspected Angus of misbehaving and rapped his knuckles. When Angus threatened to throw an ink bottle at him, he jumped at the boy who dashed away from him. The teacher chased the student around the school to the great glee of the other students. He was to suffer for this, but in the eyes of his peers he was something of a hero.[111]

Crawford was not a dedicated student, that is, not until an injury dashed his hopes of becoming a farmer. During his illness he experienced a conversion and a call to ministry. He wrote that he came "to understand, as never before, what the Divine Grace of God's forgiveness of sin meant,— God's mercy in affliction the . . . peace of fellowship with Him in Christ." He commented, "No after study of science or criticism of the Bible could shake my convictions. I concluded to enter the Christian Ministry and do my part in carrying to others, as I was able, the good tidings."[112] Supported by his family, Angus began preparation to enter the ministry of the Presbyterian Church.

Crawford entered Queen's College, Kingston, Ontario. There his feistiness was aroused again. In chapel one morning before service began, another student taunted Crawford, who flew at his tormentor "and caught him by the throat and ran him into a corner. I was choking him badly when the Principal and Faculty suddenly burst in upon us" and put an end to the fracas. The students respected him after that.[113] It was at Queen's that Crawford began a lifetime study of the natural sciences. Evolution was of particular interest. One teacher, after speaking on evolution, said to Crawford, "I hope this has not upset your theology." The student answered, "No, Sir. Not at all. It only magnifies to me the wonder of Creation."[114] This was to be his conviction through all of his life, although, as he comments, many around him were losing their faith because of Darwin's teaching.

At the University of Toronto, to which Crawford went next, he majored in natural science, graduating in 1874. While there he "made a chart on a large piece of Bristol Board of the stratas of the earth and their fossiliferous remains from the lowest infusoria to the highest mammal, man. . . . It has hung on my wall ever since and I have never lost the vision of it."[115] Speaking of a series of lectures by William Dawson of Princeton, Crawford concluded, "It has always seemed to me it made no difference whether [creation] covered twenty thousand or twenty million years; that much of the language of the Bible must be understood figuratively. . . . The long process of Evolution only gave dignity, almost infinite to his [man's] existence."[116]

While doing summer field work in 1872 at the direction of the Presbytery of Toronto, Crawford studied botany with a local physician and "made a large Herbarium of plants."[117] He was not altogether distracted from his ministerial duties. He had earlier been an evangelist in trying circumstances and during his "botanical" summer drew large crowds by his preaching. "What attracted them, I think, was the simple story of the Gospel as I told it and the enthusiasm of my youth." His work in somewhat remote country places during subsequent summers was not always regarded as successful. But he persevered and knew moments of great success—for instance, in beginning a new mission at Washago where there were many saloons but no church of any denomination. It was during this time that he learned to draw on the Book of Common Prayer as a resource for his supposedly extemporaneous services. The idea was to commit Prayer Book services to memory and provide clues for use during the services, writing down on slips of paper "leading words" from collects.[118] He was to develop a lifelong devotion to the Book of Common Prayer but questioned too strict an adherence to it.

Crawford left Canada to study at Princeton under some remarkable scholars but principally Charles Hodge. One day Crawford asked Hodge a question. This took courage since Hodge did not like to be questioned. The professor had been lecturing on predestination and election. Crawford said, "I have a bag of beans and I want a handful to plant in my garden. The beans are all of the same quality and I put my hand into the bag, take out a handful and throw the rest to the hogs. Is that an adequate illustration of your teaching . . . ?" Hodge answered, "Yes, sir, that will do." Other students seemed to object and Hodge said ("most solemnly"), "Oh, I hope there is no young man in this class who thinks anything to the contrary."[119] Realizing that he could not subscribe to such a doctrine, Crawford "abandoned my purpose to enter the Presbyterian Ministry and resolved from that time to return to the Church of England and complete my course at the Divinity School, Philadelphia, where my brother was then studying."

A further crisis occurred. Crawford was accepted as a candidate for Holy Orders in the Diocese of Toronto. But then a member of the Low Church party in that diocese wrote to say that, if Crawford and his brother were of the same churchmanship as Meade of Virginia, McIlvaine of Ohio, and Lee of Delaware, they would be welcomed. But if they were of another party— he had in mind the High Church party—they would not be well received. Crawford objected to this treatment and transferred to the Diocese of Pennsylvania. It was not that Crawford and his brother were High Church; they wanted no part of the party strife then raging in Toronto.

Thus Crawford began his ministry in the Episcopal Church and in 1876 was called to Trinity Church, Mount Holly, New Jersey. There he was appreciated as a conscientious and able pastor. He married. He continued his study of the natural sciences, and he pursued his study of the Bible and Hebrew in summer courses taken at Yale under William Rainey Harper. Crawford's work with Harper was challenging and rewarding. They became lifelong friends, maintaining contact after Harper left Yale to found, at the request of the Rockefeller Institute, the University of Chicago. Harper became convinced that Crawford was a naturally talented teacher and expert in Hebrew grammar and literature. So convinced was he that on being consulted he recommended Crawford for the Hebrew chair at the Virginia Theological Seminary.

With Harper, Crawford considered higher criticism of the Old Testament and the disputes arising from it. Crawford said,

> I went through it all with the closest attention. It was based on German scholarship much discredited today and much of it then proved to be unfounded. I myself always accepted the historical principle, but refused to subscribe to the alleged results. That Deuteronomy, for example, was not written by Moses was on the hypothesis that writing was unknown in his day. This I felt an unfounded supposition.[120]

Harper was emphatic: "Moses could not have written the Pent." But later, after the Tel el Amarna tablets were found in 1887, Crawford met Harper, who granted that he had been wrong.

Crawford noted that the influence of German higher criticism waned but argued that much was accomplished as a result of its stimulus.

> It brushed aside superstitious views of inspiration and the composition of the Scriptures and made it a reasonable book to be interpreted in a rational way and it mattered little who wrote this or that so long as we have vital truths, fundamental principles supported by the experience and enforced by the testimony of the wisest men of the ages and endorsed by the Master Himself. Capital letters designating documents and distributing words among supposed authors may appear scholarly but who really knows anything about it and who today would venture to support himself on the historic accuracy or critical judgment of German scholarship? I am thankful to have survived the storm and the Bible as the Word of God is more precious to me today than ever. Out of the extremes there was a golden mean and the bedrock of Divine Truth has become more firmly established. Un-

fortunately the faith of many was shaken while the chaff was being sifted from the wheat.[121]

Crawford arrived at the seminary in 1887 and stayed for the rest of his life, at first as professor of Hebrew and semitic languages and subsequently as both professor and dean. He arrived to find the campus badly in need of repair. Assigned to live with his family in "The Wilderness" he was greeted by its most recent occupant, Dr. McIlhenny, sitting in the parlor. "In a thin wavering voice he said, 'I have lived here twenty years but you can't live here, it's too damp.'"[122] Crawford agreed and so informed the trustees. They expressed surprise, and it was only with an exercise of the feistiness that had distinguished him in his youth that Crawford succeeded in having the trustees repair the house, making it liveable. In his time at the seminary he saw to it that other buildings were repaired, the campus provided with lighting, an adequate water supply secured, and the grounds improved. Furthermore, he raised most of the funds needed to accomplish all of this. The grounds were plowed and seeded. Dead trees were removed and new trees planted; screens were installed to keep flies out of the houses. To accomplish this Crawford, working in opposition to Bishop Whittle, president of the board, sought to have persons outside the two Virginias appointed to the board to broaden its representation, make financial appeals more plausible, and secure the support he needed. This was not to be until Whittle's death; alumni outside the Virginias were then nominated to serve on the board of trustees.[123]

Much of the remainder of Crawford's autobiography is occupied with accounts of his accomplishments as dean: raising money, increasing the size of the student body, opposing the closing of the preparatory department, and travels abroad—to Ireland in 1880 with a visit to England, to Ireland and London in 1885, to Oxford in 1894 with a visit to Berlin and the East, and to Florence and other points in 1904. Of considerable interest for this history is his account of what he called "My Department." He wrote,

The study of Hebrew and Semitic Languages was in great favor when I entered the Seminary and took charge of the Hebrew Department. Recent discoveries in Bible Lands, and the study of Assyriology had aroused the interest of scholars in the Church, and the Summer Schools under the direction of Professor Harper had increased the enthusiasm wonderfully. The High Criticism of the Old Testament was a companion study and an essential equipment for Theological learning. Every student wanted to study Hebrew in those days. Exceptions were allowed and, reluctantly by the student himself, only on account of incapacity or physical disability. I had charge of the subject of Archeology and the High Criticism and enjoyed the work thoroughly. For a time I was made responsible for Apologetics and again Homiletics, but Hebrew was my specialty and my interest in it never waned until changed conditions throughout the church made it an optional course. We had it for five hours a week at first, afterwards reduced to four on account of the addition of other Professors and new subjects. At one time we taught more Hebrew in the Virginia Seminary, according to Professor Harper, than any other Institution in the land. We arranged to cover the entire Hebrew Bible in the three years course.[124]

Crawford took pride in the ability of his students to know Hebrew and to understand not only the language but the historical context of ancient Hebrew. They were able to read commentaries critically and avoid the errors of persons such as the clergyman who believed that the statement "except a man hate his father . . ." must be taken literally. Crawford's students were familiar with "the common idiom of the language, viz. expressing in absolute terms what we and others express relatively."[125] And he was proud of Bishop Brown of Virginia, who when in Brazil was solely "responsible for the translation of the Old Testament" into Portuguese. "His knowledge of Hebrew, received at the Virginia Seminary, enabled him to do this splendid work."[126] Crawford could only regret the diminishing importance of Hebrew and Greek in the seminary curriculum.

Crawford took a special interest in the "colored people," as he called them, employed at the seminary. He reported, "The condition of the colored people on the Hill was most discouraging when I went there. They had hardly recovered from the effects of slavery and were in some respects worse. Marriage was a negligible quantity and their morals were bad and the principle of meum et tuum, especially in the matter of chickens, was not understood."[127] Crawford brought chickens with him from New Jersey, but between the "colored" folk and the high school boys, they were soon gone. His innate feistiness was aroused, and he devised strategies to catch and punish those who stole his replenished flock. He devised ways by which seminary servants, who lived in their own enclave off the Hill, were encouraged "to acquire property and possess their own homes. . . . Hitherto they were living in rented houses with few exceptions. To have one's own home meant to have a chicken yard, pigs, and perhaps eventually a cow, and the process of education would go along with the children to produce a happy and prosperous people."[128] At one time Crawford had a small house, for which he was responsible, moved to a lot on Fort Hill for a man who, incidentally, had at one time stolen some of his chickens. The house was paid for eventually, and the man's son-in-law, who was in Crawford's employ, was assisted by loans in getting his own house as well. Thus there was built "a respectable community."

Crawford also took an active interest in the chapel established to minister to the "colored people." He writes of its being repaired, in large part through the generosity of seminary benefactors such as Mr. and Mrs. S.F. Houston. "The attendance increased wonderfully, and great interest was manifested generally. The students of the Seminary had charge of the services and the effect on the community was manifest."[129] The worship at the chapel was a simplification of the Prayer Book liturgy, with much singing and "a more elaborate ritual. It is foolish to expect any material growth of our church among colored people until we consult and accommodate ourselves to the childlike stage of their civilization. They must also be taught to respect themselves, their honor and place in the body politic as against the temptations of the whites."[130] Thus did this sometimes patronizing but always concerned and well-intended seminary professor and dean write of the seminary servants.

Finally, note must be made of Crawford as a devoted family man. He married Susan Brown on May 18, 1880. The daughter of a prominent member of the church at Mount Holly, Crawford's bride was a highly educated and seemingly wise woman. The two were much in love through all of their years together and devised ways of settling quarrels without great harm to one another. They loved to travel and had the means to do so. In time their children accompanied them. During a yearlong leave of absence in 1894–95 they went first to Oxford for the summer and then to Germany where they all studied German. Their two boys were put into a school run by an Englishman, and the girls were put in the charge of a German governess. "In a few days the children were talking German so rapidly that I could not understand them," Crawford wrote. "The little one, Beatrice, began to feel she was losing her English. . . . " Crawford admitted that the language did not come as easily to him. Susan learned German readily, "but I struggled in vain."[131] The final picture is that of a benevolent father and husband who much enjoyed family life and would not allow anything to stand in the way of his fulfilling his duty to his wife and children, something which, as we have seen, vexed the board of trustees.

7. THE OBSERVATIONS OF HENRY ST. GEORGE TUCKER

A view of the seminary from the perspective of a highly intelligent, well-prepared student is provided by the manuscript autobiography of Henry St. George Tucker, a man destined to be an outstanding bishop, presiding bishop, and, for a brief time, a member of the seminary faculty. A graduate of the University of Virginia, he entered the seminary in 1897. A bishop's son, he was a candidate for ordination from the Diocese of Southern Virginia. Because of his scholastic attainments, he was admitted as a middler but was required to take all junior examinations. This was no great burden, he wrote, for although "the spiritual atmosphere of the Seminary was very stimulating, its scholastic standards were at a low ebb." The seminary was "strong on religion but weak on theology and pastoral technique." He admitted that the institution gave him that "conception of the spiritual character of the ministry . . . with its evangelical purpose" which he valued above all learning. But for him spirituality and learning were not incompatible, and the time would come (he later believed that it had come at the time he joined the faculty in 1923) when both emphases (Martha and Mary) would thrive together.[132]

In evaluating the faculty under whom he studied, he singled out Carl Grammer, whom he described as

a liberal evangelical. He was also a real teacher with the gift of arousing in his students' minds an interest which made them seekers after truth. The subject that I studied under him was the first four centuries of Church History, the formative period of Christian Theology. His liberalism was somewhat in advance of the prevailing theological attitude of that period in Virginia. This combined with a rather provocative way of presenting his arguments tended sometimes to drive his hearers to the opposite side. Whether you agreed or not, you understood and were interested. As a matter of fact Dr. Grammer's modernism was mainly manifested in the field of Biblical criticism and had no particular relevance to the doctrines of the Trinity and Incarnation with which we were mainly concerned in our history class. Here he was fundamentally "sound" though the razor edge nature of some of the problems gave small room for differences of opinion.[133]

Tucker lamented that, toward the end of his first session at the seminary, Grammer left to accept a call to Christ Church, Norfolk. He did not suggest that Grammer's departure was related to his modernism.

Of Crawford, Tucker stated that he "was an excellent business man and made a real contribution to the material development of the Seminary" and that he was "a good teacher as far as the Hebrew language was concerned, but in the exegesis and interpretation of the Old Testament he was not very helpful."[134] Tucker was severely critical of Cornelius Walker, who to the young student seemed very old. Walker's "text book for the Middle class was Butler's Analogy, a classic in its way, but lacking in relevancy to some of the main problems of modern apologetics. His method of teaching was to dictate a number of questions, after which he would dictate the answers. As most of us had inherited a copy of these from some members of the preceding class, there was little to do except to sit and meditate."[135] It would seem that Tucker had heard neither Walker's lectures on theology nor those on ethics. Both were published before Tucker's arrival, but he makes no reference to the books.

Tucker recognized that Dr. Wallis, who taught New Testament, had a great store of facts. But the professor placed them all before the students in such a manner that "his lectures were lamentably dull." Tucker suffered through classes in which students knew little if any Greek, and Wallis labored with them, almost to the exclusion of a student such as Tucker who knew Greek well. Tucker told this story:

> I was in charge of the seminary post office and was on duty there during the hour preceding Dr. Wallis's lecture. Frequently I would extend my operations there long enough to enable me to miss the language portion of the Greek class. As a result of this I was summoned to appear before the faculty and be reprimanded. The Dean, who took a practical view of things said, "Tucker, some time a large and wealthy parish might write to me about you and I would hate to have to report to them that you had been irregular in your attendance upon classes." Dr. Walker's admonition was, "Mr. Tucker, there is a little verse in the Apocalypse which is just as true as though it were in the Bible, 'He who is careless in little things, by little shall fall.'" This was a maxim worth remembering, though I was somewhat skeptical as to its applicability to the particular situation. However, I bowed to the authority of the faculty.[136]

He knew Wallis to be a forgiving man, especially when on an examination he had translated Romans 8 rather than the passage assigned from 1 Corinthians 8. Recognizing the excellence of what Tucker had done, Wallis had given him a grade of 99 ¾.

This often disgruntled student found much to admire in the seminary. The hospitality of the faculty was high on his list. There was also the highly valued companionship of his peers. Tucker lived in St. George's Hall. The building was somewhat removed from the other residences, and the men housed there "formed a kind of family" regarding themselves as an "elite body." For this reason they were frowned upon by other students and looked upon as lacking in "the serious mindedness proper to life in a theological seminary." He recognized that he and his fellows of St. George's tended to be exuberant, but he protested that "they were diligent students who found in the intimate companionship made possible by the smallness of our group, a helpful opportunity for thinking out problems that were involved in the pursuance of our life purpose."[137] His closest friend was Henry Covington, a lawyer before entering seminary who became a preacher and died "a comparatively early death." "I owe a great deal to my association with a man whose deep logical mind and worldly wisdom made his contribution to any discussion of real value."

Tucker also benefited from his experience in the seminary missions. He was assigned to Sharon Chapel, where Phillips Brooks was stationed before him. Three men were assigned to each mission, one from each class. Tucker was assigned to preach on the second Sunday after the seminary opened. He was told that his "sermon must be extempore." Never having spoken in public, he was terrified and labored hard in preparation, writing out three sermons, which he committed to memory. "When I finally stood up in the pulpit within five minutes I had exhausted all three and couldn't have said another word had my life depended upon it." He was comforted, somewhat, when the junior member of the team got up the next Sunday and "got no further than his text." He sympathized with the long-suffering congregation and wished that the seminary had done more to prepare them for the ordeal.[138]

It was while he was at the seminary that Tucker decided to offer himself for service in foreign missions. He recalls that in his first year at the seminary he "escaped any involvement in" the seminary's "traditional missionary enthusiasm." He admired the men who led the Missionary Society, but he was not especially connected to the students in the society and was thus an outsider where Missionary Society activities were concerned. But in the winter of 1899 some of his friends campaigned to have him elected as one of two representatives of the seminary to an interseminary missionary convention held at the Episcopal Theological School in Cambridge, Massachusetts. He went without enthusiasm and returned with considerable "interest in the missionary work of the Church." He did not consider volunteering, having heard "that the Board of Missions did not want any more Virginia Seminary men." Then one evening in the heat of discussion he rashly stated that any one of the students would be willing to volunteer but not if their services were not wanted. "The Dean, who happened to be at the table, smilingly extended a letter from his pocket and handed it to me." It was from Bishop McKim in Japan expressing his hope that some members of the senior class would offer themselves for service under him in Japan. "That same night," wrote Tucker, "I went to the Dean and told him that I had decided to offer to go to Japan."[139] He went to Japan and in time became president of St. John's University and Bishop of Kyoto. He admitted that his decision was made without fanfare and with almost total ignorance of the place to which he was going. But, as he tells it, he was confronted by a need and call and could not disregard either.

Such were some of the recollections of one student at the seminary from 1897 to 1899.

8. MODERNIZING THE CURRICULUM: DIVERSIFICATION

In his autobiography, Walter Russell Bowie, who was a student at the seminary from 1908 to 1911, expressed disappointment in the curriculum, as did Phillips Brooks and Henry St. George Tucker. Coming from Harvard, Bowie observed, "Of the academic side of the Seminary not so much that would be enthusiastic could be said. It was warmhearted, like the general spirit of the place. . . . But it did not show that much intellectual ferment had been working. There were no electives. . . . With the exception of one or two older men, everybody had Hebrew, New Testament Greek, the English Bible, Church History, Theology, Homiletics, and some 'Elocution.'" The hope was that such "content courses" together with chapel and experience on Sundays in missions or parishes would prepare the students "to feed the people in their congregations." He noted in particular that "the more exacting questions of Biblical criticism, creedal reinterpretation, the challenge to traditional forms of worship which a new generation was presenting, and a concern lest the church might be judged irrelevant to the social and industrial problems emerging in the modern world these seemed like sounds heard in the distance, which did not yet disturb to any degree the serene assumptions of the Seminary."[140] For the first part of his senior year, Bowie, with the permission of his bishop and the seminary faculty, went to Union Seminary, New York, where he came under the influence of A.C. McGiffert, J.A. Brewer, William Adams Brown, James E. Frame, and Henry Sloan Coffin, scholars of note.[141] In his recounting of his seminary days, Bowie mentioned Berryman Green and Samuel Wallis, the first for his kindness, the second for his naiveté—his great difficulty in maintaining order in the classroom.[142] He did not refer to Richard Micou. Perhaps he could not understand Micou; if he could have done so he would have been at least mildly excited observing a careful scholar dealing with the issues of the age.

Admittedly, by comparison with Union (and with Andover, where liberalism seemed triumphant), Virginia Seminary must have seemed very conservative. But this had already begun to change, as we have observed. Dean Crawford in his report to the board in 1912 spoke of changes.

The curriculum of the Seminary has been greatly enlarged. Compare the Catalogue of 1888 with the present one, and you will see the improvement in the course of instruction and in other ways.

In 1899 a course in the English Bible was founded, the first of the kind in the Seminaries of our Church. . . . This was followed by courses in Christian Missions, Church Music, Christian ethics and Sociology, Sunday School

Pedagogics, and Supplementary Work for Special Students.

In the courses provided for the equipment of men for the Ministry we are well up to the most exacting modern requirements.[143]

The addition of sociology to Christian ethics came with the election of Berryman Green to a full professorship in 1902 and first appeared in the catalogue in 1903–1904.[144] A senior course on Christian ethics and sociology involved lectures on the latter with the study of Peabody's *Jesus Christ and the Social Question* and Strong's *The New Era*, with reference to works by Westcott, Ely, and Riis.[145] This course was being taught while Bowie was a student, but he may have missed it, being in New York at the time. Sociology was specified, along with Christian ethics, in the Rules and Regulations beginning in 1915.[146]

In part the changing curriculum was influenced by changing expectations. In his report to the board in 1912 Crawford said that the faculty wished to start a new program of postulants "for men 25 years of age and older." The course would enable such men to study Greek and thus be able to take "the full course at the Seminary." He complained that the classics, especially Greek classics, were "being discredited in our Schools and Colleges," being "limited to about an average of 5 per cent." At Harvard fewer than 2 percent of the students study Latin, and in institutions "like Blacksburg and the Virginia Military Institute" no provision is made for the classics, for Latin or Greek, at all. This means that many able men are "barred from taking the regular course" at the seminary.[147]

The solution was not to be found in the creation of a special class of instruction in Latin and Greek classics but rather in the removal of the Latin requirement, the provision for teaching koine Greek to those without knowledge of Greek, the increase in supplemental courses for those dispensed, first from Hebrew and then from Greek as well, and the awarding of the B.D. degree to those not taking "the regular course." The process was gradual and at times agonizing. We may begin with Crawford's report, then note Professor Kennedy's statement on the "Greek problem." The junior class in 1912–13 had only four men able to do regular work in Greek New Testament.[148] In June 1915 when out of fifty men enrolled, thirty-one were dispensed from Hebrew; the faculty recommended to the board that alternatives be offered and the B.D. awarded apart from Hebrew. The dean, on behalf of the faculty stated,

The curriculum of the Seminary has become very much diversified and enlarged in comparison with former years—a condition that would seem to call for more flexibility in regard to the degree. We feel too, that it is desirable that still further additions should be made, both by way of ex-

Faculty in 1916
Seated: (*l to r*) Samuel Wallis, Angus Crawford, Berryman Green
Back Row: Wallace Rollins, Cosby Bell, Paca Kennedy

tending the scope of the curriculum and of providing opportunity for a type of intensive work such as is not possible at present. It is desirable to lay additional stress upon the English Old Testament, to introduce work in the contemporary history of the Old Testament, to provide for more intensive study of portions of the Greek New Testament, to provide a special course in ecclesiastical history during the last hundred years, to provide a course in historical and comparative religion as an introduction alike to the study of Christian Theology and Christian Missions.[149]

The requirements of eighteen seminaries were examined in the United States and in England. Theological schools such as Philadelphia, Cambridge, Seabury Western, Andover, Yale, and Harvard, and those at Oxford, Cambridge, and Lichfield in England did not require Hebrew for a degree; some gave a diploma instead of a degree (General, Auburn, Union); and some required Hebrew (Sewanee, Nashotah, Hartford, and Princeton, although the latter was about to change). The faculty at Virginia therefore proposed as an alternative to Hebrew the study of the English Old Testament under Green or Crawford, two courses in Greek New Testament, including intensive study of selected New Testament books under Kennedy, contemporary history of the Old Testament under Rollins, a course in recent ecclesiastical history, culminating in a study of religious conditions today under Rollins, and a course in the history and comparison of religions introductory to the study of theology and mission under Bell.[150] This supplementary work was provided for in the Rules and Regulations of 1916 where the section headed "Course for Special Students" specified work for those dispensed from Hebrew and/or Greek. The course in comparative religions was listed under the explanation of the required course.[151] In this way elective courses were introduced into the curriculum. In 1919–20 the electives for the junior class were contemporary history of the Old Testament (Rollins), historical and comparative religions (Bell), the wisdom literature of the Old Testament (Green). For the middle class they were New Testament theology (Kennedy) and New Testament Greek (Kennedy). And for the senior class they were Christian movements in the nineteenth century (Rollins), the church as a social organism, the practical application of Christian forces and principles in the parish and community (Green).[152]

The dean was aware of the dangers involved in the enlargement of the curriculum, the proliferation of courses, and the possible neglect of fundamentals. He asserted that it "will be a great mistake if we get away from primary sources and encourage superficial and secondhand scholarship." He believed that some things are better mastered in the ministry, after graduation, rather than in the seminary.[153] This was to be an abiding concern as the faculty grew and the number of course offerings in more and more areas multiplied. In 1923 Dean Berryman Green expressed satisfaction. "The curriculum has now nearly reached its fixed form, and the scholarship standardized, bringing the work up to as high a level as that of any other Seminary of our Church. With the improvement in scholarship we have tried to keep the spiritual life up to the same tone as in years past, though we hardly hope to raise it higher, as it was always the ideal for all seminaries in this respect."[154]

9. THE GREAT WAR AND THE
SEMINARY CENTENNIAL CELEBRATION

Two major events greatly affected the seminary in the years from 1895 to 1923. The first was the entry of the United States into the First World War. The seminary's life was disrupted. Students already enrolled departed, many of them for service in France. Professor Bell went to France as a chaplain. Many who might have enrolled did not come. Enrollment not only dropped, it was constantly changing as many left and a very few arrived. Many of the seminary's servants left, forcing students to take care of their own rooms and the hallways in their buildings. They offered to wait on tables in the dining room, but there was apparently no need for this, and the matron declined their offer.[155] A vegetable garden was started.[156] Class work was maintained to the best of the ability of those present. On November 2, 1918, it was learned that a young alumnus, Edward Howard Prince, had been killed in action and "was buried the next day in one of the little valleys along the Meuse." A service was held at the seminary in his memory.[157] The faculty considered a plan for a summer school to make it possible to do the three-year course in two. The plan, devised by deans of other Episcopal seminaries, was rejected.[158] Classes were suspended for ten days in October 1918 to allow students to participate in relief efforts associated with the influenza epidemic, just prior to the end of the war. Stories of the escapades of the Tucker brothers, Henry St. George and Beverly D., in Siberia were avidly digested.[159] On February 27, 1919, faculty meeting was cancelled to allow students and others to attend the parade in Washington, D.C., led by President Wilson, welcoming soldiers home.[160]

The second event was the centennial celebration in 1923. Reference has been made earlier in the chapter to this occasion, including challenges from prominent speakers and the launching of a great fund drive. Here we take note of the euphoria of the moment, the self-congratulations that were not without some justification in fact. Indeed, the seminary had produced church leaders of note, from Leonidas Polk to Henry St. George Tucker. There were bishops and pastors, preachers such as Phillips Brooks and Walter Russell Bowie. In addition to Polk, the first domestic missionary bishop and frontline general in the Confederate army, there was William Kip, Bishop of California, a formidable missionary figure. There were missionaries overseas including William Boone, John Payne, Channing Moore Williams, Lucien Lee Kinsolving, and many, many others who preached the gospel in Greece, China, Japan, Liberia, and Brazil. The place was illustrious, made more so still by the dedication of its sons to Christ the Savior. Bishop Beverly Tucker of Southern Virginia, speaking to the alumni at the centennial celebration, referred to the seminary's graduates and their loyalty to the school. He spoke of the "feeling of 'at homeness,' this love for the old Seminary, this loyalty to its teachings and its tradition." In a peroration suited to the occasion he said,

There may be varieties of Churchmanship, for the Seminary is not narrow, differences of interpretations, varieties of costumes, some may wear hoods of gorgeous colors, others like Phillips Brooks and Alfred Randolph may prefer not to wear the little learning they have on their backs, but, with it all, there is a unity which is the Unity of the Spirit, and a loyalty which is bound up with the recognition of the Christ, our God, our Lord, our Master, and yet our Friend. The truth for which the Seminary stands, and which its sons guard as the very citadel of their faith, is the truth as it is in Jesus. "Jesus Christ, the same yesterday, today, and forever," unchanged and unchangeable, Very God of Very God, divine and yet human. This is the truth for which The Seminary stands and which binds us together by a bond which cannot be broken.[161]

Picture the chapel full to overflowing, people singing "O God Our Help in Ages Past" and after prayers hearing for the first time the "Centennial Hymn," composed for the occasion and dedicated to the alumni by Helen C. Rollins, the spouse of the seminary's professor of ecclesiastical history.

> Cantors (unaccompanied)
> Hail! Holy Hill! Thy sons their homage bring,
> Whom thou hast taught to follow Christ the King.
> Chorus (voices and organ)
> Hail! Holy Hill! Thy sons their homage bring,
> Whom thou hast taught to follow Christ the King.
> Cantors (with organ)
> A Century God's hand hath framed our way,
> We ask His Guiding Presence here today.
> Chorus (Hail, etc.)
> Upon this ground have saints and martyrs trod,
> May we like them our lives pour out to God.
> Chorus (Hail, etc.)
> From here they dared the far Liberian shore,
> The jungle's heat, and home returned no more.
> Chorus (Hail, etc.)
> They sought the East and carried thence to them
> The Light that first did shine from Bethlehem.
> Chorus (Hail, etc.)
> Far South they bore across the estranging sea
> To fettered souls, the Truth that maketh free.
> Chorus (Hail, etc.)
> The waste and lonely places in our land
> These did they seek, to bring Christ's healing hand.

Chorus (Hail, etc.)
Teachers and shepherds of the flock of God,
These went from here, nor sought the world's reward.
Chorus (Hail, etc.)
Christ, lead us in the way of love that we
May follow them as they have followed Thee.
Chorus (Hail, etc.)
To God be all the praise the glory be,
From now and ever through eternity.
Chorus (Hail, etc.)[162]

NOTES

1. Cited by Huntington, *American Politics*, 99.
2. Ibid., 117.
3. Nevins and Commager, *History*, 336.
4. Ahlstrom, *Religious History*, 879.
5. Huntington, *American Politics*, 226.
6. Hopkins, *Rise of Social Gospel*, 230.
7. Goodwin, *History* 1:292.
8. Hopkins, *Rise of Social Gospel*, 38.
9. Addison, *History of the Episcopal Church*, 280–81.
10. Cited in Ahlstrom, *Religious History*, 884.
11. Goodwin, *History* 2:574.
12. Ibid., 576–77.
13. Ibid., 561.
14. Bd. min., 1898–1914 (January 18, 1912), 325.
15. Goodwin, *History* 2:237–238.
16. Ibid. 2:242.
17. Ibid. 2:548.
18. Ibid. 2:550.
19. Bd. min., 1914–27, 68–69. See faculty minutes, 1904–1909, 1. And see bd. min. year by year acknowledging Black's gifts. Crawford was credited with securing this largesse.
20. Catalogue (1919–1920), 12
21. Fac. min., 1910–16, 28.
22. Fac. min., 1910–16 (December 22, 1913), 175–76.
23. Ibid., 1916–25 (May 25, 1922), 212.
24. Diocese of Virginia, *Journal* (1920), 105.
25. Ibid., (1916), 104.
26. The minutes from 1896 to 1947 were rescued from almost certain total disintegration by mildew. J.H. Goodwin, librarian, discovered them in the basement of Sparrow Hall and restored them, so far as possible.

27. Goodwin, *History* 1:442–43.
28. Fac. min., 1916–25 (April 3, 1919), 114–15.
29. Ibid., 1904–1910 (February 25, 1909), 227; (March 25, 1909), 230; (April 29, 1909), 233.
30. Ibid., 1910–16, (February 11, 1915), 227; (February 25, 1915), 229; (March 11, 1915), 231.
31. Ibid., 1916–25 (May 1, 1919), 117; (October 30, 1919), 132; (January 15, 1920), 138.
32. Ibid., 1910–16 (May 8, 1913), 153; (March 26, 1914), 189; (October 29, 1914), 213; (November 19, 1914), 217.
33. Ibid., 1916–25 (September 27, 1923), 246.
34. Ibid., 1896–1904 (September 19, 1900), 117–18.
35. Ibid. (September 27, 1900), 119.
36. See the earliest form in the bd. min., 1821–66, 33–34, and later, *Charter, By-Laws, Rules and Regulations* (1916), 12.
37. *Catalogue* (1900–1901), 12.
38. See fac. min., 1904–1909, 112, where faculty complain that poor spelling in examinations and illiteracy in general would debar a man from receiving the diploma. See fac. min., 1916–25, 286–87.
39. Fac. min., 1896–1904, 103–104.
40. Ibid., 1910–1916 (September 30, 1910), 37–40.
41. Ibid. (October 6, 1910), 42.
42. Ibid. (February 6, 1911), 52–53; (March 9, 1911), 57–58; (March 16, 1911), 59.
43. For instance, in 1913 another bishop asked that students be allowed to do Sunday work. The faculty this time referred the matter to Bishop Gibson, as president, for decision (fac. min., 1910–16, 146). The faculty was gradually yielding to the demands. In 1914 they stated that no weekday work be done at seminary missions, but in 1917 it was agreed that students might work at the missions on Saturdays after lectures (fac. min., 1910–16, 182; fac. min., 1916–25, 26).
44. Goodwin, *History* 1:240, 2:280.
45. Ibid. 2:81. See 1:283, 504, and 2:117.
46. Fac. min., 1896–1904 (September 22, 1902), 207; (September 25, 1902), 208–209.
47. Ibid. (February 25, 1904), 283; 1904–1909 (November 10, 1904), 20; (January 26, 1905), 27–28; (March 16, 1905), 32; (December 7, 1905), 75–76; (March 1, 1905), 87.
48. Ibid., 1904–1909 (April 25, 1907), 153–54.
49. Ibid. (March 11, 1908), 193.
50. Ibid. (October 12, 1905), 62.
51. Ibid., 1910–16, (October 13, 1912), 44.
52. Ibid., 1916–25 (June 13, 1920), 153.
53. Ibid., 1896–1904 (December 3, 1903), 270–73; (March 17, 1904), 286–87; the letter, dated March 28, 1904, is inserted into the minute book.
54. Ibid., 1896–1904 (May 4, 1899), 59–60; (May 11, 1899), 61.
55. Ibid., 1910–16 (April 6, 1911), 67; (April 20, 1911), 68.

56. Ibid., 1916–25 (October 21, 1920), 163.
57. Ibid., 1896–1904 (June 21, 1899), 69–70.
58. Ibid., 1916–25 (November 17, 1920), 166.
59. Ibid., 1904–1909 (May 7, 1908), 199–200; (May 14, 1908), 201.
60. Bd. min., 1898–1914, 13–14.
61. Fac. min., 1916–25 (June 1, 1922), 215.
62. Bd. min., 1914–27, 178,
63. Ibid., 1866–98, 310, 317.
64. Ibid., 342.
65. Ibid., 356, 358–59, 363.
66. Ibid., 365–66; see 373.
67. See Goodwin, *History* 1:241 and elsewhere.
68. Bd. min., 1866–98, 382, 383.
69. Ibid., 384–85.
70. Ibid., 387, 390.
71. Ibid., 393–94.
72. Ibid., 1898–1914, 28–30.
73. Ibid., 33–34.
74. Ibid., 54–55.
75. See *Charter, By-Laws, Rules and Regulations* (1916) chap. 2, 11.
76. Bd. min., 1898–1914, 63–64.
77. Ibid., 68–70.
78. Ibid. (June 20, 1899), 40; (June 18, 1901), 71.
79. Ibid. (June 16, 1903), 96; (June 13, 1911), 294. See Goodwin, *History* 2:183–84 for a list of D.D. recipients from 1911 through 1923.
80. Bd. min. (June 19, 1906), 153–54.
81. Ibid. (November 14, 1906), 164; (October 14, 1907), 184–85; (November 13, 1907), 187–90.
82. Ibid. (November 11, 1909), 257.
83. Ibid. (June 14, 1910), 271–72, 282.
84. Ibid. (June 13, 1910), 295–96.
85. Ibid. (November 15, 1910), 301.
86. Ibid. (December 21, 1911), 310–14.
87. Ibid., 341, 348.
88. Ibid., 392, 395; 1914–27, 39–40.
89. Ibid., 1914–27, 45.
90. Ibid., 33–38, 49–54, 55–56.
91. Ibid. (November 14, 1917), 82–83.
92. Ibid. (June 5, 1918), 88–91.
93. Ibid. (June 11, 1919), 120–21; (November 13, 1919), 130, 133, 138; (June 1, 1921), 150.
94. On Blackford and his long tenure see Goodwin, *History* 2:437–73.
95. Bd. min., 1898–1914 (June 8, 1913), 349; (January 28, 1913), 354–55.
96. Ibid., 1914–27, 181–82, 198–201.
97. Ibid., 196, 203.

98. Ibid., 102.
99. Richard W. Micou, *Basic Ideas in Religion, or Apologetic Theism*, ed. Paul Micou (New York and London: Association Press, 1916), xx.
100. Ibid., xxi.
101. Ibid., 3.
102. Ibid., 5.
103. Ibid., 8.
104. Ibid., 11.
105. Ibid., 12.
106. Ibid., 13.
107. Ibid., 12.
108. Richard W. Micou, "The Rediscovery of Faith," *Alumni Bulletin of the Protestant Episcopal Theological Seminary in Virginia, for the year 1903* (Alexandria, Va., 1903), 9–10.
109. Ibid., 12.
110. Ibid., 20.
111. Crawford, "Crawford for his Children," 8–9.
112. Ibid., 12.
113. Ibid., 14–15.
114. Ibid., 16.
115. Ibid., 20.
116. Ibid., 21–22.
117. Ibid., 24.
118. Ibid., 25.
119. Ibid., 32.
120. Ibid., 39.
121. Ibid., 40–41.
122. Ibid., 44.
123. Ibid., 52.
124. Ibid., 61.
125. Ibid., 62.
126. Ibid., 63.
127. Ibid., 66.
128. Ibid., 69.
129. Ibid.
130. Ibid., 70.
131. Ibid., 85.
132. Henry St. George Tucker (Autobiography, unpublished manuscript, VTSA) 1:63–64.
133. Ibid., 64–65.
134. Ibid., 65.
135. Ibid., 66.
136. Ibid., 66–67.
137. Ibid., 69.
138. Ibid., 70.

139. Ibid., 73–74.
140. Walter Russell Bowie, *Learning to Live* (Nashville, 1969), 62–63.
141. Ibid., 69.
142. Ibid., 61–62.
143. Bd. min., 1898–1914 (June 18, 1912), 324.
144. Ibid. (June 17, 1902), 81.
145. Catalogue (1904–1905), 22. The same textbooks were in use in 1919–20, see catalogue for that academic year, 19.
146. Bd. min., 1914–27, 28.
147. Ibid., 1898–1914, 327.
148. Ibid., 323.
149. Ibid.
150. Ibid., 20–23.
151. Ibid., 27–30; *Charter, By-Laws, Rules and Regulations* (1916), 10.
152. Catalogue (1919–20), 16.
153. Bd. min., 1914–1927 (June 6, 1916), 43.
154. Ibid., 202.
155. Fac. min., 1916–25, 76.
156. Bd. min., 1914–27, 103.
157. Fac. min., 1916–25, 92. See also Goodwin, *History* 2:206 208.
158. Fac. min., 1916–25, 95, 96, 108.
159. Goodwin, *History* 2:205–206.
160. Fac. min., 1914–27, 110.
161. Goodwin, *History* 2:588.
162. Ibid., 542.

CHAPTER SEVEN

FROM NORMALCY TO DEPRESSION AND WAR 1923–1945

I. THE AMERICAN SCENE: ON A ROLLER COASTER

Between 1923 and 1945 the United States experienced the whiplash of sudden and violent change, not once but twice. The years before 1929 were on the whole quiescent, with the nation withdrawing from world politics into splendid isolation. Confidence in inevitable progress buttressed by economic success extended into every stratum of society. This was the heyday of laissez faire capitalism and private enterprise, Herbert Hoover declaring as late as 1931, "I am firmly opposed to the government entering into any business the major purpose of which is deliberate competition with our citizens."[1] "Rugged individualism" characterized the prevailing popular philosophies. This was a period of continuing urbanization, the emergence of the mass mind and a communications revolution. The national census of 1920 indicated for the first time that most Americans lived in cities and towns, some very large. "A dozen had more than 600,000 inhabitants; three had more than a million; and New York City, with a population of over 5,620,000, was a world metropolis."[2] Furthermore, this urbanization extended into the rural areas. For example, as Mowry and Brownell report,

> Taken together, the automobile, the movie, and the radio obliterated the village and the farm as islands of isolation from the mass luxury economy, for the entire world of fancy goods had been moved as close to the onetime provincial as the nearest movie screen or loudspeaker.[3]

The stock market crash, beginning on October 24, 1929, had a devastating effect on this nation and the world at large, challenging confidence in progress (it then became regress or worse) and exacerbating urban dependence on a money economy. The Depression brought severe hardship to millions, resulting in despair and death for many. Nevins and Commager write of the spiral of depression:

> Business houses closed their doors, factories shut down, banks crashed, and millions of unemployed walked the streets in a vain search for work. Hundreds of thousands of families lost their homes; tax collections dropped to the point where cities and counties were unable to pay their schoolteachers; construction work all but ceased; foreign trade, already badly hit, declined to an unprecedented low.[4]

The course of what was to be called the Great Depression was complex; the solutions, involving massive government interference in the system of laissez faire capitalism, ran counter to the doctrine and spirit of the 1920s, so well exemplified by Presidents Coolidge and Hoover. Franklin Delano Roosevelt inaugurated a new era with his New Deal. On coming into the presidency in March 1933, he acted immediately. He closed all the nation's banks and then presented to Congress a bill to preserve the banks and restore public confidence in them and in the nation. There followed in rapid succession the creation of agencies for relief of those in distress, including specific means of putting the unemployed to work. Private enterprise and rugged individualism were being modified, sometimes radically.

> In the four years after 1933, the President proposed at one time or another what amounted to a new bill of rights, which if enacted into law would have ensured the creation of a semi-socialist economy. He referred to the right to work, the right to adequate food, to housing, a decent education, clothing and recreation.[5]

The drift leftwards, as many saw it, was arrested by war. Preoccupied with domestic crises, the people of the United States only gradually became conscious of the totalitarian challenge abroad. In his first two inaugural addresses Roosevelt barely mentioned foreign policy, but ten months after his second inauguration the president sounded the alarm. Munich and "peace at any price" deeply disturbed many. But isolationism was still widespread. When the European conflict began in 1939, Roosevelt responded, insofar as he could, to support Britain and France. The Lend-Lease program was inaugurated, and American armed forces were strengthened. With this stimulus the economy revived so that by the time of Pearl

Harbor (December 7, 1941) almost all Americans who wanted to work were employed. From that point on a herculean effort developed to defeat the enemies in Europe and the Far East. The country became preoccupied with the war effort. When victory came in 1945, American self-confidence had been restored. Many placed great hope in the newly developed United Nations organization, but many withdrew into themselves and into the enjoyment of prosperity largely brought about by war. Warning clouds were generally ignored in the euphoria of the moment. Most importantly, most people were still unaware of the Holocaust in Europe and the probability of future genocide. Few understood the extent of influence on the nation of the detonation over Japan of the first atom bomb. The Cold War, which was to dominate much of our understanding of the world, had begun. But in 1945 and for a time after, few seemed to be aware of it. The "hot war" ended as the Cold War began, with the threat of nuclear annihilation.

To Sidney Ahlstrom, one of the major effects of this course of events was the crumbling of the Protestant establishment, culminating, beyond the time allotted to this chapter, in the election in 1960 of the first Roman Catholic as president. During the 1920s the Protestant churches had been made aware "that their ancient sway over the nation's moral life was threatened. Even as modern religious ideas steadily advanced or as concern for social issues increased, the churches tended to lose their capacity to shape and form American opinion."[6] The efforts made to impose Prohibition and maintain Sabbath sanctity were failures. And indeed there was emerging in American society a combination of religious pluralism and ever-spreading secularism, resulting on the one hand in the rejection of absolutist claims by particular religious bodies and on the other in the growth of Fundamentalism—the sect concept that separates the elect from the immoral civil society.

Among those who took theology seriously, we note the crumbling of the liberal social gospel under the barrage of events in the Depression and the war, but also under the criticism of Barthian and post-Barthian neoorthodoxy. In American religious circles this criticism was fine-tuned by Reinhold Niebuhr and his assertion of political, social, and theological realism.

The social gospel had sought for a "conjunction of righteousness and power, a fusion of the Word and politics." In this effort it failed. Along the way it had inspired optimism (the Kingdom of God was coming here and now) but had sponsored impossible causes such as prohibition and idealistic socialism. Henry Ward idealized the Soviet experiment. Kirby Page dogmatized the ideal of pacifism. Harry Elmer Barnes espoused a perfectionist credo based upon his own interpretation of the teachings of

Jesus. The Great Depression and the war exposed the weaknesses of the social gospel.

The rejection of absolutism was symbolized by Reinhold Niebuhr's resignation from the Fellowship of Reconciliation in 1934. In the face of capitalism's economic injustices, Niebuhr revolted against the Fellowship's pacifism and proclaimed the necessity for violence. H. Richard Niebuhr made a devastating attack on the Fellowship, claiming that the organization and its nonviolence "did not represent true Christian pacifism, but rather humane, humanistic moral idealism."

Reinhold Niebuhr in his 1932 book *Moral Man and Immoral Society* viewed the crisis in terms of civilization flirting with disaster. With a pessimistic view of human groups (they were all essentially predatory) he emphasized that religion and politics must not be identified one with the other (they exist in tension) but rather Christianity must realize its social function as critic. While he claimed not to be a Barthian, but emphasizing the necessity to act, Niebuhr's realism was considered by some to be pessimistic. Humanity is sinful at core, he taught. The necessary action involves dialectic—the interaction of Renaissance pretension with Reformation humility—and no expectation of an end to the tension in the world. He called for a prophetic Christianity.

Paul Tillich drove criticism beyond the economic and political levels to the foundations of culture, into the individual self. The chief threat was the disintegration of the consciousness-centered personality. Thus Tillich wrote, "The Christian interpretation of life and history is rooted in a faith prompted by repentance. It will not be convincing except to the soul which has found the profoundest enigma of existence not in the evil surrounding it but in the self."[7]

The Virginia Theological Seminary knew no strident defenders of the liberal social gospel (with the possible exception of the young Clifford Stanley), but the introduction of sociology into the curriculum was an important indication of the influence of the social gospel. Along with Walter Rauschenbusch it sought social reconstruction through the agency of sociology. In Albert Mollegen and the mature Stanley the seminary felt the impact of Niebuhrian/Tillichian (if not neoorthodox) criticism. These two men came first on the faculty in the early 1930s and studied in the middle 1930s at Union Seminary, New York, under such theological giants as Frame, Niebuhr, Tillich, and Lehmann.

There is another important factor in the culture to be taken into account, and that is the revolution in education. Robert Lynn, speaking of the theological curriculum, mentions the growth of the elective system accompanied by an increasing number of course offerings, by the development of specialized ministries necessitating "vocational tracks," each with a special curriculum, and by the increased number of faculty members with Ph.D.'s, their greater specializations and research concerns.[8]

While little was done to promote specialized ministries per se, the period from 1923 to 1945 witnessed a growth in course offerings and an increase in faculty size and in graduate school preparation. This brought a greater sense of professionalism—which at Virginia Seminary meant more specialized preparation for parish ministry. It is significant to note the increase in the number of hours allotted to pastoral theology, especially with the advent in 1943 of Reuel Howe. It is also noteworthy that with Howe the seminary made clinical pastoral training mandatory. The importance of this is clear to the historian, for with this major requirement the seminary was committed to linking psychology and psychotherapy with theology and was actively developing and promoting the idea of the minister as therapist. In this respect the seminary was most certainly promoting a professional understanding of ordained ministry.

In 1945 the report of theological education in the Northern Baptist Convention prepared by Hugh Hartshorne, professor of psychology of religion at Yale, and Milton C. Froyd "pled for theological schools to become serious about professional education." They wrote,

We believe that professional education, as distinct, on the one side from what a traditional liberal arts school does, and, on the other side, from what a trade school does, is concerned with the development of a body of graduates competent to engage in a profession, i.e., who possess a broad grasp of the basic sciences underlying the work and thought of the practitioner, a detailed knowledge of the facts related to some particular field of practice, an understanding of the principles which must be followed in successful practice, and at least so much of skill in practice as to guarantee that they are likely to grow into competent members of the profession.[9]

The Virginia Theological Seminary was on its way toward such professionalism. As neoorthodoxy waned, increasing attention was given to the minister as therapist. The full story will not be told until the next chapter, but the beginning is in this one.

For now it is enough to observe that between 1923 and 1945 the world faced crises of immense scope and importance, crises that helped inform and even form Virginia Seminary for the twentieth century. The result was to be seen in greater political, social, and theological realism; in biblical emphasis responsive to the changing times; and in a concern for people in crisis by men trained to deal with the most desperate human conditions.

2. THE INSTITUTION:
FINANCES AND ADMINISTRATION

From 1923 until the United States entered the Second World War, the number of students enrolled in the seminary varied only slightly. In 1923 there were seventy students, requiring some doubling up in the fifty-nine available dormitory rooms. This situation was alleviated by the completion of Sparrow Hall, made possible by the Centennial Endowment Fund. But even then a limit of seventy-five students was established.[10] A peak was reached in 1927 when there were eighty-two students from twenty-nine dioceses. That was in June; in November of that year there were seventy-seven students with every dormitory room occupied. In 1937 there were seventy-three students, two of whom were married, living off campus. During the war, specifically from 1941 to 1945, the number of students fluctuated and over all declined, with men coming and going at various times of the year, some being called into the armed services while others were released. In November 1945 there were forty-five students, including eleven former servicemen.

At the beginning of the period, marriage in course was forbidden by the board, and the admission of married men was discouraged but not forbidden. The faculty had to contend with petitions for marriage in course and found means of making occasional exceptions to the rule. In 1935 the dean considered requesting the board to rescind its rule.[11] In 1941 the question of admitting married men was referred by the board to the faculty for study.[12] An increasing number of married men were applying for admission after 1941, and more and more single students were requesting permission to marry in course.

By 1927 it was agreed that the dean, rather than the faculty as a whole, would (in consultation with the faculty) admit new students.[13] By 1939 the dean had appointed an admissions committee, of which he was a member.[14] In part the appointments were due to an increase in the number of applications. The dean and the committee were guided by a simple catalogue statement: "To be received as a student in the Seminary, a man must hold a degree from some reputable college and have been admitted a candidate for Holy Orders. Also he must present satisfactory credentials as to his character and fitness for the ministry."[15]

In 1938 the faculty adopted a list of recommendations for preseminary studies, a list meant to guide those seeking admission. Here the study of Greek and Latin were encouraged, along with four years of English, emphasizing grammar and rhetoric, two years of philosophy, two years of history, two years of natural science, and at least one course in general psychology.[16] Thus attempts were made to maintain the highest standards for admission. In 1939, to bring it into line with the standards of the American Association of Theological Schools (AATS), its accrediting agency, the seminary made the B.A. a requisite for the B.D. degree,[17] something not heretofore considered essential.

In 1943 the faculty noted a growing number of men applying without a college degree and considered the difficulties the seminary faced in trying to run counter to a growing trend.[18] Various ways of coping were considered, one being the hiring of an additional teacher, another being the extending of the seminary requirement from three to four years. Clearly, there were those without college degrees who should be admitted, such as William Clebsch, who in time would join the faculty, and Hugh White, one of the leaders of the Industrial Missions Movement in this country.[19] However, with the AATS in mind, the admission of noncollege graduates could not be considered normal.

The board of trustees affirmed that academic accomplishments would not be the sole criterion used in admissions. Among other considerations, they insisted upon quotas for the Virginia and North Carolina dioceses,[20] and of necessity they were determined, during the war to abide by selective service rules.[21] Restrictions limiting admission to members of the Protestant Episcopal Church were gradually relaxed, with a Methodist being admitted in 1933 to take courses for credit. A Disciples of Christ member was admitted in 1939, and in the same year neighboring Lutheran and Disciples members and a Jewish rabbi were admitted to audit courses.[22]

The finances of the seminary were unsettled during these years, with deficits being reported every year from 1923 to 1927, in 1934, and sporadically thereafter. Such deficits were sometimes covered by drawing on invested funds. But during most of this period there were budget surpluses. With budgets ranging between $40,000 and $60,000 a year, expenditures in the good years, ran from $572 to $14,500 below income. Two major means of stabilizing seminary finances were capital funds drives aimed at increasing endowment income and the reluctant introduction of a tuition fee. Major capital funds drives came at the beginning and the end of this period—the centennial fund drive of 1923 and the postwar expansion drive begun in 1944. In 1934 the board proposed to "wrap up" the centennial fund drive. In 1941 the board began plans for the next drive, which by 1945 had a goal of $1,000,000 to $1,500,000.[23]

From the beginning of the seminary, the students attended tuition-free. In 1940 the board considered whether to charge tuition as other schools were doing. In 1941 it was decided to charge $50 (which included a $10 library fee). In 1945 tuition was $30, room and board $150, and hospitalization insurance $4 per semester, for a total of $368 yearly.[24] In time the seminary budget would be established on the basis of one-third endowment income, one-third alumni giving (including Theological Education Offering), and one-third tuition and other charges. In 1940 the Theological Education Offering (TEO) had been promoted and became a major source of income, and in 1945 the Friends of the Seminary organization was founded with financial benefits to the seminary.[25] All the while the Education Society was independently (with very strong seminary involvement) providing financial assistance. In 1944 the budgets of the seminary and the society were combined, and the budget for 1944–45 was established at $88,919, with $21,000 coming from society funds.[26]

The board, now no longer responsible for the high school, was concerned to improve the administration of the seminary. For some time the executive committee of the board had been supervising day-to-day operations, but this was becoming increasingly less satisfactory. Thus we note in the years from 1923 to 1945 a major change in the way the school was administered. When Berryman Green retired in 1931, Wallace Rollins was elected dean but not before the board considered the possibility of electing Oliver J. Hart, rector of St. Paul's Church, Chattanooga, a nonacademic person successful in administering a large parish.[27] Rollins was provided with a full-time secretary who would also be the keeper of the alumni files and the registrar. The person selected was Miss Helen Tighe, the dean's niece, who was also hostess in the deanery. The board promoted A.C. Zabriskie to full professor of medieval and modern church history to relieve the dean of some of his teaching duties. Rollins continued to teach his life of Christ course and church history to A.D. 600.[28] In 1935 Rollins indicated his desire to retire but was persuaded to remain as dean until a new dean was elected.

As it happened this took five more years. In the meantime Bishop R.E.L. Strider, a member of the board, was elected dean in 1937 and declined.[29] There were then nominated the Reverend. R.A. Magill, the Right Reverend F.D. Goodwin, the Reverend Drs. John Gass, John J. Gravatt, Arthur Lee Kinsolving, W. Russell Bowie, A.C. Zabriskie, Churchill J. Gibson, and Oliver J. Hart, once more.[30] No action was taken. It seems that the board was once more concerned to choose a nonacademic who would be a full-time dean-administrator. It is significant that A.C. Zabriskie's name was included in the list of nominees, for he was elected in June 1940 over several nonacademic nominees, including Bowie, Noble Powell, and Bland Tucker.[31] Robert F. Gibson was then brought onto the faculty as a teaching fellow in church history to provide some relief to the new dean. A special advisory committee of Bishop Strider (chairman), Dr. Powell, and Bishop Goodwin was named to assist the dean.[32] In 1944, anticipating an increased administrative load with the end of the war, the dean decreased his teaching load (Gibson was made assistant professor), relinquished his duties as chaplain to the high school, and, although he was named rector of the developing parish of Immanuel-on-the-Hill, was not given pastoral or administrative responsibilities.

In 1943 the board had agreed to the need for a business manager and then actively sought for the right person.[33] In 1944, the faculty secretary, A.T. Mollegen, was made, among other things, keeper of all academic records.[34] In 1945 Mr. A.D. Clifford was named bursar with responsibility for the business management of the seminary.[35]

Faculty members continued to be involved in various administrative duties, some within their normal sphere (such as admissions and the library), some of only partial concern to them (such as the bookstore and other concessions run by students). Faculty continued to have specific assignments in relation to the seminary missions, but in 1935 it was determined to have a priest not of the faculty to run the missions.[36] Thus did the administrative staff grow, largely around the dean and then, with the inauguration of a major capital funds drive at war's end, around a development office with the Reverend Charles Sheerin as chairman of the fund drive.[37]

More and more power and responsibility were transferred from the board and the faculty to an administrative office or offices, a development not peculiar to Virginia Seminary. Simultaneously, the board grew in size. In 1937 the charter of the seminary was changed, increasing the number of trustees to no more than twenty-five and at the same time, the bylaws were changed. The number of alumni trustees was increased from two to six, with none but alumni trustees coming from outside the boundaries of Virginia and West Virginia.[38] In 1938 the Right Reverend Thomas Darst, the Very Reverend Noble Powell, the Right Reverend Charles Clingman, the Right Reverend Clinton Quin, and the Reverend F. Bland Tucker were elected to the board as alumni trustees.[39] The presidency of the board belonged by custom to the Bishop of Virginia, who nevertheless had to be elected. In 1927 Henry St. George Tucker had been elected to succeed Bishop Brown. In 1944 Tucker became presiding bishop and Bishop Frederick D. Goodwin was elected board president. In that same year a new bylaw was approved concerning the election of board members.[40]

3. THE FACULTY: THE QUEST FOR A PASTORAL THEOLOGIAN

The faculty continued to change and grow with increasing concern to provide an effective, professional head for the omnibus pastoral theology department. In a seminary that made pastoral ministry its special concern, the quest was particularly important.

We begin in 1923 with the resignation of Beverly D. Tucker as professor of pastoral theology and the election of Henry St. George Tucker to succeed him. The new professor had been Bishop of Kyoto and president of St. Paul's University, Tokyo. Recognizing his special talents and achievements, the seminary created a new chair in systematic divinity and applied Christianity. Cosby Bell, who had been elected in 1911 to fill the chair in systematic divinity, had his position redefined.[41] The details concerning the new chair in the history of religion, psychology of religion, and philosophy of the Christian religion will be considered when we inspect the evolution of the curriculum. Here it is necessary to note that Tucker's assignment involved concluding the work begun by Bell in the philosophy of Christian religion with attention to the content of Christian doctrine, as well as to teach a course on New Testament theology and ethics, another on Christian missions, and a third on applied Christianity, the latter meant to fulfill the expectations for practical or pastoral theology.

Henry St. George Tucker

In his autobiography Bishop Tucker tells of his election to the faculty and of his particular assignments. As he recalls, he was elected to the chair of "practical theology."

> I found that Practical Theology was the collective name given to a variety of subjects which did not fit into any of what might be called the basic departments such as Old and New Testament. . . . My recollection is that I was given a good deal of leeway in determining what these subjects should be. In looking through the manuscripts of my lectures, I find that I taught missions, liturgics, ethics, canon law, the sacraments, Christian institutions, New Testament Theology and Pastoral Theology.[42]

He then adds, "There is one course of lectures on Systematic Theology, which looks like an intrusion into Dr. Bell's department." Such a statement may reflect something of the man's innate humility; it also expresses a feeling of inadequacy. "For the most part they were not subjects for which my missionary experience furnished any particular qualifications, so that I had to work hard to enable me to keep far enough ahead of the students to look wise and make dogmatic pronouncements."⁴³ He persisted, knowing that his colleagues were capable of compensating "for the deficiencies of the teacher of practical theology."⁴⁴

Indeed, he found his colleagues to be an improvement over the teachers of his student days and the students better prepared. He enjoyed life on the Hill and especially theological discussions with Drs. Bell and Rollins, but he was restless, eager to move on.⁴⁵ He received inquiries and calls to go elsewhere, to be headmaster of St. George's School, Newport, to be Bishop of Pennsylvania and then of Florida. He became Bishop Coadjutor of Virginia, leaving the seminary after a brief stay.

Two instructors, both part-time, were employed in 1924. The first employed was the Reverend Henry H. Covington of Norfolk, Virginia, to teach liturgics, and the second was the Reverend Romilly P. Humphries of Baltimore, to teach reading and pulpit eloquence (or delivery).⁴⁶ In 1925, at the request of the faculty, the Reverend Alexander Clinton Zabriskie was hired as a full-time instructor at a salary of $2,500 plus housing.⁴⁷ Zabriskie was hired to teach a variety of subjects, including church history, New Testament, and religious education. His appointment was of great importance for he was to become a full professor of church history and dean of the seminary at a vital turning point in its history, during and after World War II. A staunch upholder of the Virginia Tradition of Low Churchmanship, Zabriskie was deeply involved in the ecumenical movement, especially the proposed union of the Episcopalians and some Presbyterians. And he was the biographer of Arthur Selden Lloyd and of Charles Henry Brent. Born in 1898, Zabriskie was a New Yorker, educated at Groton School, Princeton University, Cambridge University, and the Virginia Seminary, from which he graduated in 1924. During World War I he had been a naval air pilot and thereafter treasured his memories of that experience.⁴⁸

In 1926 Bishop Tucker left the faculty, and systematic divinity was returned to Cosby Bell. The board began considering the election of someone for the practical theology chair.⁴⁹ It was decided to use part-time, adjunct, nonresident instructors for awhile. In 1926 Bishop Tucker had given three lectures a week, and the Reverend Canon Lubeck and the Reverend Frederick Goodwin gave some lectures.⁵⁰ Subsequently, others were enlisted, including W.T. Thompson of the Presbyterian Seminary in Richmond, to teach religious education; Arthur B. Kinsolving, W.R. Bowie, and George T. Toop for pastoral theology; and Bishop Brown for the Book of Common Prayer.⁵¹

In the meantime the board continued its search for a "pastoral theologian." In 1929 they elected the Reverend E.P. Dandridge. He declined. They then elected the Reverend C. Leslie Glenn, and he declined.[52] Finally, they called the Reverend James F. Mitchell, then rector of the Church of the Messiah, Baltimore. He accepted, but from the outset it was recognized that a mistake had been made. Elected in April 1931, in November Mitchell submitted his resignation to accept a call to a parish in Florida. The board indicated its willingness to accept his resignation, but the plan did not work out, and the resignation was withdrawn. In 1933 the board again accepted Mitchell's resignation but agreed to continue his salary until he found an "acceptable call," no later than December 1933. Shortly thereafter he was gone.[53]

In 1929 the faculty wrote to the board explaining the need to provide better preparation for oncoming faculty members. They suggested that the example of General Theological Seminary with its tutors be considered, that Virginia Seminary hire tutors or instructors, young men who could support the present faculty and be prepared to succeed them. The further suggestion was that an instructor in pastoral theology be hired.[54] In 1930 the Reverend Clifford L. Stanley was elected instructor in the department of the "Philosophy and Theology of Christian Religion" at a salary of $2,000 plus board and lodging. He was thus to assist Dr. Bell. A Pennsylvanian born in 1902 and baptized in the Methodist Church, Stanley subsequently joined the Episcopal Church and was educated at the University of Virginia (B.A., 1924, and M.A., 1925). He was graduated from the Virginia Seminary in 1928, where he had felt the strong influence of Cosby Bell, and then served as rector of Trinity Church, Tyrone, Pennsylvania. Stanley remained at the seminary until 1935, at which time he was associate professor of the history of religion and the philosophy of Christian religion. He departed to do graduate work at Union Seminary, New York, and obtained a Th.D. degree in 1938. After another period of time in the parish ministry, this time in Missouri under Bishop Scarlett, he returned to the seminary in 1946 as professor of systematic theology, remaining in that position until his retirement in 1970.[55]

Clifford Stanley's influence—especially as a man of intellectual stature and personal piety, an Anglican interpreter of the theologies of Søren Kierkegaard and of Paul Tillich, and a devoted supporter of his seminary— was to have a significant impact on the institution and its people in the 1950s and 1960s. In his first tour on the faculty he was regarded by some as a troublesome "young Turk." When he left in 1935 it was for a leave of absence, but in succeeding months the "problem" of Professor Stanley was much discussed by the board. In November 1935 it was determined at a special meeting of the board to recommend action at a special meeting. That meeting was held on March 11, 1936. At that time the board accepted Stanley's resignation.[56] The reasons were given by the dean in his report to the board of June 5, 1935.

Professor Stanley. The Dean at some length called attention to certain problems in the Seminary connected with Associate Professor Stanley:

Mr. Stanley is very gifted as a lecturer and teacher, and has great promise of usefulness, if he can develop normally. At present he is very intense and emotional and visionary in some of his views regarding the social implications of the gospel. He spends most of his time in teaching his point of view, rather than the subject. This tends to cause divisions and antagonisms in the student body.[57]

In 1931 Paca Kennedy died, and Rollins was made dean; A.C. Zabriskie was made full professor of church history. The Reverend Stanley Brown-Serman of Nyack, New York, was elected professor of New Testament language and literature.[58] Possessing at the time an M.A. and a B.D., he distinguished himself in the eyes of board members by publishing a book, written jointly with Harold Prichard, called *What did Jesus Think? Studies in the Mind of Christ*. For this he was given an honorary D.D. by the board in 1935.[59] Brown-Serman was to spend the rest of his life at the seminary, serving as dean for the academic year 1950–51. A competent New Testament scholar, he had a keen interest in liturgics which, he taught for some time.

In 1933 Berryman Green died, as did Cosby Bell. As Dean Rollins reported, Bell's death in April "created a serious problem." Emergency plans had to be set in operation. Bishop Tucker taught the middler course in theology and Clifford Stanley the junior course. The work of the seniors was distributed among the other professors. Rollins admitted that Bell had wanted Stanley to be his successor but remarked that Stanley was too young.[60] It was then as a compensation that Stanley was made associate professor with a salary increase. The faculty, having discussed the possibility of the Reverend Charles W. Lowry as successor to Bell, made inquiries and received a letter from Dean Powell of the Church Divinity School of the Pacific about Lowry.[61] In November 1933 Lowry was elected associate professor of systematic theology and began teaching in September 1934.[62]

Charles Wesley Lowry was born in Checotah Indian Territory in 1905 and was educated at Washington and Lee (B.A.), Harvard (M.A.), the Episcopal Theological School (B.D.), and Oxford University (D.Phil.). He was Episcopal chaplain at the University of California and lecturer in theology at the Church Divinity School of the Pacific from 1933 to 1934. William Temple was Professor Lowry's theologian, and the great trilogy of *Mens Creatrix, Christus Veritas, and Nature, Man and God* was the theological mine from which he derived inspiration. But he was a widely read scholar steeped in German theology and in modern Anglican thought. Among Anglican theologians, in addition to Temple, he taught Butler, Law, Maurice, Gore, and Tennant. Among the German-speaking, he taught Schleiermacher, Dorner, Ritschl, Barth, and Brunner.

At the time of Lowry's election, the Reverend C. Sturges Ball of Bexley Hall was elected professor of pastoral theology at $4,000 plus house.[63] In addition to pastoral theology, he was responsible at the beginning for homiletics, liturgics, and religious education. Pastoral theology per se consisted of a course in pastoral care and one in parish administration, a very limited offering by comparison with what was to come. Pastoral care involved "the cure of souls" and "pastoral psychiatry"—the latter of growing importance in theological education. On the whole Professor Ball was not successful. The board discussed his effectiveness in 1936. In 1937 a committee of three was named with Bishop Strider expressing his dissatisfaction with Ball, especially his teaching of homiletics.[64] In 1938 Ball inquired about retirement but in 1941 accepted a call to be rector of a parish in Reisterstown, Maryland.[65] The board then considered Everett H. Jones, Charles Sheerin, J.W. Suter, and Moultrie Guerry for the pastoral theology chair, electing the latter, who subsequently declined his election. In the meantime Professors Kevin and Brown-Serman, Drs. Suter, Glenn, and Wedel filled in: Wedel in homiletics, Suter in liturgics, and Brown-Serman and Glenn in pastoral theology with Kevin, the latter being in charge of the "team." Thus the seminary continued to struggle with the teaching of pastoral theology.

In 1933 the Reverend A.T. Mollegen came to the seminary as instructor and left a year later to study at Union Seminary, New York, where Stanley was to join him. There Mollegen attended lectures by Paul Tillich and Reinhold Niebuhr and earned an S.T.M. degree. In 1936, with Stanley's resignation, Mollegen was asked to return to the seminary, being elected "Instructor in New Testament, Ethics, and History of Religion."[66] Thus began the distinguished career of a scholar and teacher. Born in 1906 in Macomb, Mississippi, he attended Mississippi State University. It is noteworthy, as John Krumm remarks, that there is no record "of his having received a college degree. His high school education in a small Mississippi Delta town was, by his own confession, somewhat narrow and restricted, reflecting the Fundamentalist Baptist's outlook of his environment."[67] But there could be no doubt that this innately brilliant man could have had any degrees he aspired to hold and that, in fact, no degrees could sufficiently identify his capabilities and achievements. Krumm describes Mollegen's appearance on campus in 1936 as causing "an almost immediate stir of excitement." He cites Mollegen's course in Christian ethics at that time.

Without much apology or explanatory introduction he plunged the student at once into the issues of biblical eschatology and prophetic religion. It was electrifying to look seriously at the apocalyptic material in Mark 13, for example, with which Molle began the course, and to see the outlines of the drama of the 1930s emerging from the biblical mythology. There was nothing contrived or superficial about this close relationship between his political and social views and his biblical work. The connection was never paraded before his students; it emerged naturally because of his own deep involvement at the one and the same time in the world of biblical and theological scholarship and in the world of national, international, and personal human problems.[68]

Mollegen's gift from the beginning thus was seen in the relating of biblical and contemporary history. In the process he exhibited the influences of Tillich and Reinhold Niebuhr but also the best in Catholic and Anglican tradition. He was capable of teaching New Testament, Christian ethics, and theology, systematic, dogmatic, and practical. As a traveling lecturer he made his influence felt on campuses across the land and was a mentor in the corridors of power in the nation's capital. In 1939 he was made associate professor and by 1944 was professor of New Testament language and literature, and of Christian ethics.

We have noted that when Zabriskie became dean in 1940, the Reverend Robert F. Gibson was made a teaching fellow in church history. In 1942 he was made instructor and in 1943 assistant professor in the church history department. In 1947 he left the seminary to become dean of the School of Theology in Sewanee, Tennessee, but the next year was elected Suffragan Bishop of the Diocese of Virginia. In 1961 he succeeded Bishop Goodwin as Bishop of Virginia and president of the seminary board of trustees. While on the faculty of the seminary, Gibson had been minister-in-charge of Immanuel-on-the-Hill (1941–43 and 1946–47).[69]

In 1940 Dr. Nelson died, and the Reverend Robert O. Kevin was elected by the board to be professor of Old Testament language and literature at a salary of $4,000.[70] Kevin came to the faculty with an earned doctorate from Johns Hopkins University and a profound dedication to the Evangelical tradition of the Episcopal Church, expressed in part by his concern to guard the seminary's Low Church tradition and in part by his efforts over the years in the Evangelical Education Society. His approach to the Old Testament was rooted in archeology and the Old Testament text, and his courses made rigorous demands on the students, who were required to memorize details of what they read in the text. He was not concerned much in his teaching with the theology of the Old Testament, yet he had his own understanding of that theology that became apparent to those who paid attention to his teaching.

During the war, there was a succession of visiting lecturers. We have mentioned Theodore Wedel and John Suter, who assisted with pastoral theology. There were also Howard A. Johnson, a Kierkegaard scholar and graduate of Virginia Seminary, who was at the time an assistant at St. John's, Lafayette Square, Washington, D.C., and John Krumm, also a seminary graduate and subsequently chaplain at Columbia University and Bishop of Southern Ohio.[71] In 1942 Vernon McMaster was visiting lecturer in religious education. In 1944 Mrs. A.E. Barton succeeded Mrs. A.B. Rudd as instructor in public reading and speaking.

In 1943 there were two very significant occurrences in the faculty. One was the election of the Reverend Reuel Howe to the chair of pastoral theology, and the other was the resignation of Charles Lowry, who accepted the call to be rector of All Saints Church, Chevy Chase, Maryland.[72] Reuel Howe was born in Vashon, Washington, in 1907. A graduate of Whittier College in 1927, he was granted an S.T.B. (1930), a M.Th. (1931), and an S.T.D. (1940) by Philadelphia Divinity School, where he was professor and director of pastoral and clinical studies from 1937 to 1944. He was professor of pastoral theology at Virginia Seminary from 1944 until 1957, when

Reuel Howe

he left to be director of the Institute of Advanced Pastoral Studies, Bloomfield Hills, Michigan. As we shall have cause to note, Howe was responsible for clinical pastoral education in the Virginia Seminary curriculum. He also served as a resource in the development of the Seabury series for Christian education in the Episcopal Church. A mild mannered, firm, demanding teacher, Howe was controversial both in the seminary and beyond. His impact on the seminary was considerable, contributing to the development of a generation of students who were dedicated to the therapeutic understanding of the ordained ministry, to psychotherapy, and to group dynamics.

Once more the seminary struggled to find an accomplished theologian.

Theodore Wedel of the College of Preachers and Theodore Green of Princeton were nominated in 1943.[73] In April 1944 F.W. Dillistone, a rising English Evangelical theologian who had lectured at the seminary, was elected professor of systematic theology. Aware that he might decline, the board decided that, if he did so, Mr. Victor Stanley, a senior student, should be hired as a teaching fellow in theology.[74] Dillistone declined, Victor Stanley became a fellow, and the board continued its search, eventuating in the election of Clifford Stanley in 1946. In 1944 the Reverend Robert Cox was elected tutor in New Testament. In June 1945 Miss Lucy Robb Winston was made seminary librarian, succeeding Mrs. W. Cosby Bell.[75]

4. THE CURRICULUM: ESPECIALLY APOLOGETICS AND PASTORAL THEOLOGY

The curriculum continued to emphasize Scripture, church history, theology, and pastoral theology. Provisions were made for four "courses" or tracks: "I. The English Course: In which the student takes neither Greek nor Hebrew. II. The Hebrew Course: In which the student takes Hebrew but not Greek. III. The Greek Course: In which the student takes Greek but not Hebrew. IV. The Greek and Hebrew Course: In which the student takes both Greek and Hebrew."[76] This necessitated a department of English Bible (subsumed under the Old and New Testament departments), the provision of courses in biblical languages, and elective alternatives for those not taking language courses. Bible study (including languages) dominated the junior year and continued during the middler and senior years (depending in part on elective choices). In 1925–26, while Rollins was dean and Zabriskie assisting, under the three-term scheme church history occupied ten hours in the junior year, nine in the middler, and five in the senior. The emphasis was on the church in the West through the continental Reformation. Modern European history was allotted two hours and American Christianity five hours in all. In 1942, when the seminary had changed from a three-term to a two-semester curriculum, church history, taught by Zabriskie and Gibson, was somewhat reduced in hours. Early and medieval Church history were taught in one three-hour course (in one semester), the Church of England through the Reformation in another three-hour course, and American Christianity in a third three-hour course — all required. In addition there was a required course on the mission of the church, and there were three electives, one on Christianity A.D. 313 to 500. It could be said that, at this seminary as at others, history dominated the curriculum since both Bible studies and theology were taught from the historical perspective.

Theology as a separate discipline evolved over the years with the changes in faculty teaching the discipline. The first major change in the period under review came when Henry St. George Tucker joined the faculty.[77] Tucker taught New Testament theology and ethics during the junior year, Christian missions and applied Christianity during the middler, and systematic divinity during the senior year. The latter was meant to build on Professor Bell's work in the philosophy of Christian religion. It dealt with the Creeds, the doctrines of faith, authority, God, the person of Jesus Christ, and the world as a field of progressive realization of the Kingdom of God, as well as with man, sin, salvation, eschatology, the Church, the ministry, and the sacraments.[78] Bell then headed the department of the philosophy of religion. He wrote of his aim in these words:

> This department aims to present in outline a reasoned view of Christianity in relation with the history and psychology of religion, general philosophy, and science. The effort is made to work out to positions which correlate the data drawn from these various fields with that derived from Christian experience as recorded in the Bible and in Christian history. The constructive and defensive interests are maintained throughout as correlative points of view.[79]

This was achieved in three courses: (1) the history of religion (phenomenology) in the junior year, (2) the nature of religion (psychology) in the middler year, and (3) the validity of the Christian religion (ontology) in the middler and senior years. The course in ontology extended over three terms and was described by Bell in this way:

> In this course the question of the reality and objective validity of Christian experience is formally raised, and the work is towards a Christian and Theistic philosophy of life. The main divisions are: Part I, Non-Theistic Philosophy, including a discussion of the problem of knowledge; Part II, The reasonableness of Faith in God; Part III, The Philosophy of Christian Theism. The last division aims to present in outline a Christian view of the chief realities that enter into or are implied in human experience—God, God incarnate in Jesus Christ, the world as the creation of God, man, sin, salvation, and the future life.[80]

The rest of the task was left to the department of systematic divinity. Clearly, in keeping with Bell's interests, the emphasis was on (1) the prolegomena to systematic divinity and (2) the apologetic/correlative method and task.

Tucker left the faculty in 1926, and Bell resumed teaching systematic divinity. In order to do this, he reduced the scope of his course on ontology. When Clifford Stanley arrived to assist Bell, the department began a transition completed when Charles Lowry succeeded Bell. Stanley then headed the department of the philosophy of the Christian religion, teaching the history of religion the junior year, the philosophy of religion the middler year, and eschatology and Christian ethics the senior year. Lowry had the department of systematic divinity, teaching the history of Christian thought to middlers and a system of Christian doctrine to seniors. The history of Christian thought, then begun, remained in the curriculum, placed in the church history department in 1946 but taught by the systematic theologian. It was considered by Lowry and Stanley a necessary introduction to the study of systematics. The separation of this history from the general history of the church was, however, artificial and not always accepted by the church historians on the faculty.

When Stanley left, Mollegen took over the history of religion and Christian ethics, and Lowry taught the history of Christian thought, religion, philosophy, and theology, and the system of Christian doctrine. A new course was added, taught by Zabriskie and called theology and personal religion. It was described as concerning "the nature of personal religion and its significance for the study of Theology. The Christian Life. Prayer, its philosophy and practice. The sacraments, devotionally and philosophically considered. The Christian witness. The goal of the Christian life."[81] Thus, a subject that was central to the faculty meetings, where it was considered by all faculty, was formalized and brought into the curriculum, marking the beginnings of that particular emphasis on "spirituality" and "personal religion" that was to be of major concern in the 1980s.

By 1942, with Lowry then fully in charge but soon to leave, the department of systematic theology involved Zabriskie teaching personal religion to juniors and Mollegen teaching moral theology and social ethics to seniors, as well as the history of religion to juniors. Lowry taught the rest. In place of the old course in religion, philosophy, and theology, there was now a course called apologetics, taught to juniors and described in these words:

In this course an attempt is made to deal constructively with some of the fundamental rational and philosophical problems raised by the affirmations of the Christian Faith. The characteristic ideas of Christianity are expounded with a particular view to exhibiting clearly the Christian view of God and the world alongside other possible world-views.[82]

For Lowry the most threatening other worldview was that of Soviet communism, which, in his popular postwar book called *Communism and*

Christ, he viewed as a religion. In addition, Lowry taught a course in systematic theology that extended over two semesters. This course was "intended to give a systematic and reasoned exposition of Christian teaching in the light of history and modern knowledge" and included "I. Sources of Christian doctrine, the doctrine of God, God and the world. II. Man, Christ, salvation, Church and sacraments, eschatology."[83]

Between Lowry's departure in 1943 and Stanley's return in 1946, systematic theology was dealt with in a makeshift way, utilizing the talents of Howard Johnson, who had assisted Lowry, and then Victor Stanley. With the return of Clifford Stanley a new day began.

Pastoral theology through these years was to undergo a considerable evolution. With Henry St. George Tucker there was a department of systematic divinity and applied Christianity, with the possibility of a very close relation between theology and praxis (and with separate departments of homiletics, religious education, and elocution).[84] Later a separate department of applied Christianity covered courses in religious education, missions, liturgics, Christian institutions, and pastoral theology (described as a course in "parish administration"). This involved Messrs. Kinsolving, Goodwin, Bowie, and Toop, with separate departments of Homiletics, and public reading and speaking. The first was taught by Berryman Green and the latter by Romilly Humphries.[85] With the arrival of Sturges Ball there was a department of practical theology, then including courses in homiletics, liturgics, religious education, pastoral care, and parish administration (with canon law). Pastoral care was described by Ball in the catalogue of 1935 as "the Minister's character and personal life. Parish visiting with special reference to the sick, the shut-ins, and the dying. Special cases of moral trouble—Baptisms, Confirmation, Marriages, Burials and Holy Communion. Brief study of Psychology in the cure of souls."[86] All of this was covered in one semester in the senior year without any overt connection to the rest of the curriculum and with no stated relationship to the field work students were doing in seminary missions and elsewhere.

In the meantime the field of pastoral theology was undergoing a revolution. Clinical pastoral education, pioneered by Anton Boisen and Russell Dicks, loomed ever more prominently during and after World War II. It "was designed to assist the clergy of all denominations to discover their own identities as persons, to better understand their pastoral vocations, to integrate theology and the life sciences, to build and maintain healthy interpersonal relationships, and to learn not by reading books but by studying people."[87]

As early as 1941, long before Reuel Howe's arrival, the board of trustees appropriated fifty dollars per year "for the next three years" to the Council of Clinical Training.[88] Howe made clinical pastoral education (CPE) basic to his teaching and to pastoral theology in general, as well as the seminary curriculum. In 1944 Professor Howe presented to the board a "summer program in the field of social and pastoral responsibilities" that necessitated the cessation of all other summer programs for students, a matter discussed at length. The summer session, instituted because of the war, was ended, and the board authorized "supervised clinical training under the direction of the Professor of Pastoral Theology" in the summer preceding the junior year, with field training prior to the middler year, and prior to the senior year under the supervision of the students' bishops.[89] There were once more three terms, the first term being the summer at the beginning of each year in seminary. In the 1946 catalogue clinical pastoral training (in general) was described.

> Pastoral Theology courses will assume previous supervised training in work with people. This training will be given in accredited training centers (general and mental hospitals, correctional institutions, community agencies and parishes and missions). Much of the training during the summer term of the first two years will be done in cooperation with the Council for Clinical Training in its training centers and by its supervisors under the direction of the Professor of Pastoral Theology; the third summer term will normally be spent in parishes and missions to which men will be assigned in consultation with their bishops.
>
> The purpose of clinical pastoral training is to help the student understand the causes and nature of human problems, and to recognize the opportunities for ministry to human beings. Traditional theological education seeks to illumine, interpret and change the situations in which people live. The training experience provides the material and opportunity for making every course in the seminary more concrete and relevant to the pastoral ministry.[90]

Thus began a new era in which CPE became increasingly influential in the seminary curriculum. For many students in the next phase of the seminary's history, CPE, Reuel Howe, and pastoral theology were the most challenging elements of their seminary experience.

5. THE EMERGENCE OF STUDENT GOVERNMENT

Between the years 1923 and 1945 a student government developed under the supervision of the faculty. A student council evolved in part out of the old honors committee, with members elected by students and faculty. This council met on a monthly basis with the faculty as a whole. This continued for some time, involving discussion of student issues ranging from sandwiches and milk in the evening to rules of conduct and matters concerning the curriculum and outside employment. In 1939 students and faculty meeting together agreed that the student council existed

(a) To act as Executive Committee of the Student Body;
(b) To act as liaison between the Faculty and the Students;
(c) To assume responsible leadership in matters pertaining to the moral and spiritual welfare of the Seminary;
(d) To act as a court of first instance in specified matters.[91]

Student concerns included the pinkeye epidemic of 1934 (which shut down the seminary), warfare (chiefly water fights) between students living in St. George's and Aspinwall halls in 1936, the "colored problem," special garb for seminarians, and women on campus. There were special disciplinary problems, such as an instance of homosexual activity in 1925, a student who in 1927 rudely revolted against the requirements of a professor, a student in 1931 whose check written to pay a bill in a New York speakeasy bounced, and rowdyism in the seminary dining hall in 1938.

The student government, or student association, as it was called in 1942, involved nine standing committees with membership appointed by the student council. These included the following:

1. an academic committee to assess the curriculum and recommend improvements;
2. a worship committee to assess the effectiveness of worship at the seminary and make recommendations regarding chapel attendance;
3. a student aid committee to study the financial needs of students and to assist those in need to find paying work on the campus or off;
4. a house committee to "supervise the care" of residential halls, recommend improvements in the refectory, host guests, and more;
5. a field work committee to study the problems of seminary missions and recommend improvements and to apportion students to the missions and in other field work, including the high school, parishes, and social agencies "with the approval of the faculty";
6. a work squad committee to plan with the superintendent of grounds student work on the grounds and to supervise such work;
7. a civilian defense and fire committee;
8. a recreation committee to organize seminary athletics and oversee health conditions; and
9. a missionary society executive committee.[92] There were faculty advisors for many of the committees.

"Key Hall" as Refectory, 1940

It is evident that student concerns were forcefully expressed and that the dean and faculty paid heed to the students. There were, of course, those who felt that too much time was spent on relatively trivial matters and not enough on theological studies. In 1943 a student-faculty committee appointed to study the activities of students off the Hill, in parochial and secular employment, concluded, "It is argued . . . that secular employment is only one of many pressures that intrude on good [academic] work. Others include the time spent in student government activities, the greater amount of personal housekeeping that has fallen to the lot of each student, practice air raid drills, bull sessions after hall prayers, need of some recreation, etc."[93] The reaction was to recommend closer personal supervision of students by student leaders and faculty advisers, a trend being established to protect the students, if possible, from failure. Thus was a degree of passive dependence inculcated by men who were by most measures considered to be adults.

6. THE IMPACT OF WORLD WAR II

World War II had a serious impact on the seminary. Students came and went, many being called into active service; proposals for mergers with other Episcopal seminaries were considered; an accelerated course was initiated; and faculty were persuaded to assist nearby parishes devoid of clergy.

In 1943 Dean Angus Dun proposed a merger between the Episcopal Theological School and the Virginia Theological Seminary, a proposal that came to nothing.[94] A merger between Bexley Hall in Gambier, Ohio, and the Virginia Seminary did occur, beginning in February 1943. Decreasing enrollment, along with the need to use Bexley buildings for military purposes, necessitated this move, which brought Dean Corwin Roach and seven students to Virginia. The original agreement was for 1943–44, but it was extended to cover 1944–45. Roach "acted on all Bexley admissions, and scholarship aid came from Bexley funds in Gambier. Otherwise the Bexley students followed the Virginia curriculum and grading (which was reported only in Bexley records) and entered completely in the life and worship of the Alexandria seminary."[95] By the second year there were only five Bexley students, along with Dean Roach, who did some teaching, including homiletics. On the whole Virginia Seminary was pleased with this arrangement,[96] and in 1944 it sought for a merger with the Philadelphia Divinity School. But that effort was rebuffed.[97]

In 1942 the seminary shifted into an accelerated course, making it possible to complete the three-year curriculum in two. This necessitated a summer session, divided into two halves, one half of the faculty teaching in the first half and one half in the second. Students were admitted in June, February, and September, with graduation exercises in January and May. All of this was done in relation to selective service rules. One result of those rules was a strengthening of the summer field programs, the faculty designating summer work as essential preparation for ordination and requiring supervision, reports, and grades that counted toward graduation.[98] Another result was a lowering of academic standards with the admission of greater numbers of students without college degrees but with "war certificates."[99]

The war left some parishes without clergy and placed demands on the faculty to supply assistance. In one instance of concern to the board, St. Paul's Church, Alexandria, hired A.T. Mollegen as acting rector with a monthly salary of $125. The board was displeased and withheld a proposed increase in his seminary salary. It was noted that "there are those who think it advisable to withhold his appointment as a full professor until he has completed the work for his doctorate."[100] As the record indicates, Mollegen did not complete work for a doctorate, and he was made a full professor in 1944. Furthermore, he continued at St. Paul's Church while teaching a full load, acting as faculty secretary, and administering the dean's office when the dean was absent during the summer. He did all this with good humor, noting in the faculty minutes for August 12, 1943, that the faculty met "and discussed various matters connected with the Seminary, the cosmos, and Søren Kierkegaard."[101]

By the war's end the dean and the board were addressing postwar problems.[102] A special advisory committee had been formed and reported in 1942 and again in 1944 on needed improvements in buildings and grounds. It also made recommendations for the development of the dean's office.[103] By the time the war ended, a capital funds drive was launched under the direction of Charles Sheerin. In 1945 the plans included a new administration building.[104] Although that was not to be, the concern expressed was a harbinger of things to come.

7. THEOLOGY FROM BELL TO MOLLEGEN: THE COMING OF NEOORTHODOXY

Between 1923 and 1945 a major shift took place in theological understanding in Western Christianity and in the seminary. The shift is apparent when comparing W. Cosby Bell, who looms large in the first decade after the centennial, with the corporate work *Anglican Evangelicalism*, edited by A.C. Zabriskie and published in 1943, and in particular with A.T. Mollegen's essay in that book, "Evangelicalism and Christian Social Ethics."

Cosby Bell represented the forward-looking, hopeful, optimistic Christians who abounded in the 1920s in America. He loved the earth he explored in Virginia and the Rocky Mountains. W. Russell Bowie wrote of him,

> Wilbur Cosby Bell grew up as a boy on a Virginia farm. He liked the books which he found on the shelves of the house he lived in. He liked the larger book of the out-of-doors, with fields and trees, and birds, and flowers, and rivers, and hills. After he had finished college and graduated from the Theological Seminary, he went as minister to a country parish. He loved people, and the simple, everyday interests that made up their lives. He became an accomplished scholar; but he was never sophisticated. For the earth he loved, and for the heaven he hoped for, he had the happy and humorous belief that still the simple things were best. "It is not necessary," he wrote . . . , "for those who prefer the country to be duly depressed by the apocalyptic pictures of the New Jerusalem. It is written that God once planted a garden, and it is unlikely that this was the beginning and end of his plantings. If there is a river that flows through the celestial city, it must have its headquarters somewhere in the Delectable Mountains."[105]

The man's thought was in accord with his life. In the two major lecture series he gave, which eventuated in the two books he published in his lifetime, he demonstrated a preoccupation with nature in relation to human life and Christianity. He reveled, as a Christian and a theologian, in the theory of evolution and its indication that creation is a process in which God is always involved. Thus he wrote in the Bohlen lectures (1925),

Looked at from the scientific side the world is all process; looked at from the side of interpretative philosophy, it is all God. And it has come to be neither by creation at a stroke, nor by "natural" process alone, nor yet by alternating creation and process, but by creation through process. For the course of evolution, to the eye trained to read off the spiritual meanings of events, is itself quick with Mind, and definite with Purpose. And the false antithesis between creation and evolution disappears in the insight that evolution has within it God creatively at work.[106]

This led to a belief in progress, identified with Le Conte's law of cyclical movement, a movement which sometimes is backward but ultimately and centrally "steadily upwards." In his lectures Bell said (probably with great enthusiasm),

It is like a stream running uphill, from less organization to greater, from simpler to more complex, from inorganic to organic, from body to brain, from instinct to reason that interprets what has gone before. We have the effect of a disciplined and purposeful attack and advance, a steady upward thrust sustained through the long ages, that carries the world process up a difficult and toilsome road. We have not yet reached the goal of the process, but some messages have come through to us from those regions in which we believe the process to have originated. We have been told that man has still before him the task of becoming a Christman, a man conformed to the type revealed in Jesus Christ. We have been told that Life has still to win that high perfection and balance of power which is called Eternal life. But while we cannot see the end we have already seen much; enough, indeed, to justify us in saying with St. Augustine, that nature looks like an ascending scale of Divine ideas.[107]

Although Bell found "man" to be the culmination of the evolutionary process, both physically and spiritually, in the Paddock lectures (1930) he wrote at length about sin, faith, repentance, and forgiveness, emphasizing the sacrifice of Christ. Evolution, progress toward realization of that full humanity revealed in Jesus Christ, is not automatic. It can be and is frustrated. There is no question that Bell took sin seriously as "an abuse of whatever freedom man possesses. It comes into being when a man seeing and approving the better follows the worse."[108] It requires repentance, "a radical reorientation of the entire personality, a change from unconcern about sin into serious concern, from responsiveness to its semi-fascina-

tion to actual fear of it and disgust at it, from casual admiration of good-
ness to an energetic and productive desire for it."[109] And the way of repentance, which is the way of faith and "loyal adherence to God," is
through pain, the pain which is the cross of Christ.[110] But even here, in
considering sin and repentance, Bell sounds a positive note:

> Reaction against sin is not, in and by itself, a necessarily fruitful thing.
> Remorse is one such reaction, and its natural children are not hope and life
> but despair and death; its growth to an acute stage may issue in surrender
> and suicide, the effort to escape responsibility by escaping life. The gospel
> of Christ is a gospel because it comes to us not sin foremost but God fore-
> most, because it would have us become aware of sin in becoming aware of
> God. Jesus' first call to any man met on any road of life is "Come, follow
> me." "In the pre-Christian systems," says Edersheim, "there is no welcome
> to the sinner until by some means he has ceased to be a sinner and become
> a penitent. . . . Christ first welcomes him to God and so makes him a peni-
> tent. The one demands, the other imparts life."[111]

Bell saw Christianity as the combination of a process beginning with
primitive religions, involving prophetic and philosophic traditions (the
flowing together of Hebrew-Christian religion and Greek philosophy into
Christian theology being his great concern). He noted the addition of a
"cosmic system of administration"—the gift of the Roman West. Both
Greek and Roman contributions were capable of distorting the simple
gospel of Christ. Bell took aim especially at the Western concept of God
as sovereign, "a sort of Super Emperor"—the feudal God of the Middle
Ages, the Calvinistic God— "deity as Absolute, Sovereign Will whose
say-so makes the law, whose decrees no human conscience or reason can
presume to judge."[112] He regarded Barthianism and Calvinism as forms of
"theological fascism."

In the light of historical developments Bell rejoiced that "the modern
restudy of the Jesus of History has made him the most vivid religious figure of our times"—restoring, that is, the simplicity and effectiveness of
the gospel. He rejoiced, too, in modern science:

> For Christians the heavens declare the glory of God in a more august fash-
> ion since Kepler and Eddington, and the idea of the creativeness of God
> has a vaster range since Lyell and Darwin. . . . If . . . we have always believed
> that God creates, we know better than our forefathers how God creates.
> And if we have always known that "Thou coverest Thyself with light as
> with a garment," we know better how that garment is woven in the track-
> less ether of space."[113]

Bell identified the greatest threat to Christianity not with science but rather with an inwardness of religion that is disconnected from history and natural fact—isolated and independent of all. Such dependence upon self-authenticating religious experience, which Bell does not deny, diminishes God and our understanding of God. It is necessary to take into consideration the outer world of nature and history. He concluded,

> The practice of the interior life can easily become a luxury which lets the world go hang instead of seeking to transform the world, unless it be completed by the vigorous practice of the outer life of creative service in the world. The attempt to separate the God of Religion from the God of Nature will result in religion without content and with little meaning for life. And however difficult it may be, just now, to discover God in nature, the attempt cannot be abandoned without grave loss to the value of God to human life.[114]

Bell's theology was based upon a grand vision that included no less than the entire cosmos, a vision of God informed by all we know of the universe focused in and through Jesus Christ. Thus he wrote, at the end of one of his most highly regarded lectures,

> In the Christian view, these two are one—the God of the universe is Christlike; the Christlike God is the God of the universe. Because he is the God of the universe, we have to think of Him as the Father not only of Christians but of the race of man; the creator not only of our world but of that vaster universal process whose rolling thunder fills the ages, leading the stars on their appointed pathways; the architect not only of the Church but of the family and the state; a lover of animals—mechanist, vitalist, artist and physicist. And because He is Christlike, we find Him also living as a Friend in small cottages and suburban villas—we are sure—listening patiently while small children say their prayers. He is, indeed, the High and Lofty One who inhabiteth eternity and He dwells with those that are of an humble and contrite heart. The
>
> > "Ancient of Days who sitteth throned in glory,
> > To whom all knees shall bow, all voices pray,
> > Whose love has blessed the wide world's wondrous story
> > With light and life since Eden's dawning day."[115]

Cosby Bell died in 1933. In 1943 a book of essays, *Anglican Evangelicalism*, edited by A.C. Zabriskie, was published to honor Wallace Rollins, the retired dean. The book was meant to be a contribution toward a fresh

understanding of the Evangelical tradition at a time when "the form in
which Evangelical convictions have been held are no longer satisfactory
in some respects due to recent biblical and ethical studies and the renewed appreciation of the Church."[116] The contributors were all related
to Virginia Seminary. Along with Zabriskie there were Lowry, Brown-
Serman, Mollegen, Robert E. Strider (Bishop of West Virginia and member of the board of trustees), Everett H. Jones (Bishop of West Texas),
W.R. Bowie (then at Union Seminary, New York), C.W.F. Smith of Washington Cathedral, and Henry St. George Tucker (Bishop of Virginia and
presiding bishop). The essays acknowledge that Anglican Evangelicals
are divided between conservatives and liberals.[117] They take note of the
impact of modern biblical studies on Evangelicals.[118] They indicate a keen
awareness of the "estrangement" of their generation from "the saving assumptions of the Christian religion."[119] And they assume the renewed
importance of the church linked to the ecumenical movement and related to Anglicanism's unique understanding of ecclesiology.[120] Then, too,
in the essays, there are reverberations from the events of the 1930s and
early 1940s, the worldwide depression, the rise of fascism in Europe, and
the coming of the Second World War (with its mass destruction, genocide, and holocaust). The world situation was vastly different in 1943
from that known by Cosby Bell. And theology reflected the historical
changes. The Neoorthodox and their companions were less optimistic,
more realistic, and at times seemed pessimistic.

One essay best represents the new theological climate and points a way
into the future. That is Mollegen's terse, concise "Evangelicalism and
Christian Social Ethics." It begins with a frank admission that the liberal
theology and social ethics of many Evangelicals has undergone serious,
destructive criticism emanating "from history itself as well as from a series
of brilliant and profound theologians." This calls for Evangelicals to "re-
think, deepen, and clarify" their "understanding of human society, world
history, and Christian ends for mankind."[121] He proceeds to do just that,
beginning with a "theological point of view" based on the Kingdom of
God motif and presented in a series of propositions.

"1. *The Kingdom of God is God's way, not man's. It is embodied in history,
therefore, with least distortions where God is truly worshipped.*" It is this worship
that "opens society to the transforming power of God's spirit." The chief
aim is that God be worshiped, not that we should produce a healthy culture.[122] "2. *The Kingdom of God invades history, claiming it as a totality.*" As
invading history, "it is the Kingdom of Christ and is received by faith and
most clearly expressed in 'the blessed company of all faithful people' which
is the true Church." But, Mollegen noted, while the Kingdom of Christ is
received by faith in Christ, it is also received "by covert, distorting religious

faith," a fact that "forbids any religious trust in human progress." He did not deny the realities of progress in human affairs, but such progress is devoid of ultimate purpose, it has "no end, no goal, no fulfillment." There is, therefore, of necessity a deep distrust of progress among Christians.[123] "3. *The Kingdom of Christ encounters opposition in society from human historical forces and in human personality from the indwelling principle of sin.*" Mollegen spoke of a New Testament (and Tillichian) understanding of the *daemonic* here and emphasized as truth "that every level of social achievement becomes the battlefield for the continuing war between Christ and the daemonic powers." Here he focused on the enemies of Christ, without and within, whose power is "finally broken only by the life, death and resurrection of Christ." In this conviction Evangelicalism makes the atonement central but with the realization that the death of Christ is one with the life of Christ, the Atonement one with the Incarnation.

Mollegen expressed appreciation for Evangelicalism's insistence on the Kingdom of Christ as transcendent, judging "every expression of itself in Church and society." He affirmed that "Evangelicalism is better guarded than Catholicism from the temptation to identify the institutional Church with the Kingdom of Christ. Only to the degree that Liberal Evangelicalism abandoned its classical heritage did utopianism and moral perfectionism arise in it." Sin is taken seriously, leading to the conclusion that

> Christ comes to all men as to sinners to be redeemed. He does not come to any man as to one who is merely in danger of sin and to be safeguarded from sin. Nor does he come as to one whose human nature has been deranged by sin and is to be restored. Likewise, Christ's Kingdom does not come to a history which had not crucified Him in order to restore it to an original perfection or to bring it to the actualization of its original possibilities. Every historical period, culture, race, nation, and class receives the Kingdom as being, or having been, opposed to it to the point of seeking to destroy it. Every human situation is invaded by the Kingdom, therefore, not only as a situation in which sin is present but as one which is the product of sin. The consummation of the Kingdom of God is not to be understood as the Garden of Eden, the trans-historical end is not the realization of the pre-historical potentiality.[124]

"4. *The Kingdom of Christ destroys, affirms and transforms all human achievements. A particular period of History is always experiencing this threefold action of the Kingdom, yet any one or two of the divine activities may predominate.* Where there is human rejection of the Kingdom, the rejecting individual or group is being destroyed. There is some divine affirmation of all that exists, else it would not exist."[125]

"5. In a specific historical period, the Kingdom is destroying, affirming, and trans-forming specific aspects of human existence." It is the Christian's task to discern what God is doing now and to act in consort with the divine action.[126] This is faith, and faith is centered for the Evangelical, as for the New Testament, in Christ, whose ethic of love, to God and to neighbor, is the basis of the Christian's decisions: "The good is setting oneself within God's activity, the essential quality of which is love towards men."[127] This love issues in commu-nity and in Jesus' teaching the Kingdom of God. In it there is equality ("not mathematical and not rational equality"). "Equality in community means the equal value of each person acknowledged by all; the equal opportunity for personal development provided by all; the responsibility for all assumed by each in the way he can best contribute to all."[128]

Mollegen resisted the temptation to further define love abstractly, as Jesus also resisted such temptation. "Love is finally understood by receiv-ing it as a gift from God which evokes from us a response of love. . . . Love is the result of personal relations with God, and right action personally received in love is the result of divine guidance. This is the essence of Evangelical ethics. No abuses of it—and there are many—can mitigate its absoluteness. No qualifications offered in explanation of it—and there are many—can change its essential truth. It is Evangelicalism's strong-hold against legalism, perversion of authority, and individual responsibil-ity."[129] And, one might add, here are the roots of the Evangelical doctrine of justification by faith alone.[130]

Such, in part, was the teaching of one of the seminary's younger teach-ers, a man who was to have profound influence on the school and the church at large. It reflected a wind-change in theology, emphasized by Niebuhr and Tillich and others at Union Seminary, New York, prophets at whose feet Mollegen sat and learned. What Mollegen wrote also re-flected a deep probing of Anglican Evangelicalism, and it assuredly re-flected a searching mind immersed in Scripture, in particular in the New Testament and its eschatology. It was in the synoptic Gospels that Mollegen rooted his understanding of the Kingdom of God as the Kingdom of Christ.

8. A C. ZABRISKIE, THE SEMINARY, AND VIRGINIA TRADITION

A.C. Zabriskie devoted his life to the seminary, as professor of church history and as dean. He spent much of his time and energy to provide for its well-being and pondered its history, its fundamental purpose, and its prospects time and time again, in faculty meeting talks, in articles printed in The Living Church and elsewhere, and in talks to alumni groups and gatherings of friends across the nation. In one article he stressed the seminary as providing professional competence, training men to "proclaim the Christian faith cogently and persuasively," leading men to be "deep Churchmen . . . rooted in such profound religion and theology," with their devotion "strong and realistic and humble" and doing "away with the narrowness and bitterness and the secondary causes of division." Most of all he stressed spiritual formation. The seminary, he said, is mainly concerned that its "graduates be deeply Christian men—men who have been vividly apprehended by Jesus Christ."[131]

Such a statement was very much dependent upon Zabriskie's own way of viewing things, but it was also dependent upon what he understood to be the seminary's tradition, something in and of itself. Toward the end of his life he was piecing together his own historical reflections, first given in a series of faculty meeting talks and then revised sometime after 1954 in preparation for publication with the title *No Mean Inheritance: Some Thoughts on the Tradition Handed on to the Contemporary Members of the Protestant Episcopal Theological Seminary in Virginia*. The book was never published, but the manuscript deserves attention in terms of what it tells us about A.C. Zabriskie and the seminary. It consists of an introduction and four chapters, one each on the theological, the missionary, the pastoral, and the liturgical traditions of the seminary. The last is best known, having been cited in the midst of discussions concerning liturgical change in the seminary chapel from time to time since the 1950s.

In his introduction Zabriskie described Anglicanism as the "attempt to hold together within one Communion the positive affirmations of Catholicism and Protestantism in the spirit of Christian humanism."[132] Virginia Theological Seminary takes seriously all three, but its primary emphasis has been on "the Protestant aspect of Anglicanism" with Scripture as the final test in matters of faith and justification by faith alone. Its "second chief emphasis" has been on Christian humanism. This latter was of consummate concern to Zabriskie, who carefully defined what he understood as Christian humanism. Its constitutive features

are a devotion to truth "come whence it may, cost what it will" which gives it great veneration for what has been believed by the wise and good men of the past, unwillingness to assume that there are not mistakes and inadequate knowledge in the received tradition, a desire to incorporate the new knowledge into the fabric of its theology; a desire for meaningfulness in forms of worship, public and private, and in statements of doctrine, which makes it ready to experiment with new forms and adopt them if they prove satisfactory; a "functional" rather than a "dogmatic" view of the Church,

that is to say, a concern about the task committed to the Church by its
Master and the effective discharge thereof rather than about its metaphysical nature or its "marks."[133]

He cited leaders of the seminary, Sparrow and others, who contended
against the efforts of some in the church to limit the freedom of devout
scholars "to investigate and question the text and meaning of all documents, even the Bible and to accept what the evidence showed to be
true."[134] Furthermore, they fought for the right "to experiment with forms
of worship and prayer to supplement the Prayer Book, and to incorporate
new ethical understandings."

In his chapter on the theological heritage, Zabriskie dwelt upon the
Catholic, Protestant, and Christian humanist emphases in the seminary's
theological teaching. With considerable sophistication he defined the
mainstream (the proclamation of the gospel) and its three divisions. The
one is "marked by emphasis on the objectivity, the givenness and hence
the continuity of Christian understanding of God and man," the church
and the sacraments. The second is marked by insistence "on the necessity
of the subjective, the human response to the Gospel" (justification and
the importance of the individual). And the third is marked by maintenance "without qualifications" of "the necessity of seeking fuller truth
and accepting each new increment regardless of the result thereof upon
what had been believed and cherished."[135]

He found these three emphases in the New Testament and in the history of the church. He found them present and interacting in the seminary from the time of its founding, "though on the whole the Protestant
emphasis has been the strongest and the Christian Humanist the second." He wrote of W.H. Wilmer, "one of the pioneer theologians of the
Episcopal Church," with his love of the Prayer Book, his belief in the
episcopate and episcopal orders, and his sacramentality, as an Anglican of
the Protestant Catholic type. William Meade he regarded as an intense,
even austere ("grim-visaged") Protestant. He did not observe, as we have
observed, that Anglicanism which led Meade to emphasize with Hooker
"the law of proportion." Yet he admits that no one loved the Prayer Book
more than Meade. But he "was a Puritan"; he denied the doctrine of Apostolic succession and found the doctrine of transubstantiation and the
"idea of sacrifice of the mass . . . unscriptual, untrue and (I think) morally
dangerous." Positively, Meade contributed to Virginia Seminary's theological inheritance the "combination of intense evangelical conviction
and ethical seriousness."[136] The third emphasis, Christian humanism,
Zabriskie associated, first of all, with Sparrow. He quite obviously admired
Sparrow, writing,

Dr. Sparrow was primarily a Christian philosopher and a great teacher. He loved truth: he sought it wherever it could be found; he longed "to bring reason to its rightful predominance over custom and circumstance", and placed his reliance on "Spirit-illumined reason". He it was who gave this seminary its motto "Seek the truth, come whence it may, cost what it will". He opposed anything which he thought put blinders on men. He trusted truth and wanted no truck with narrow dogmatism of any sort.

Furthermore, Dr. Sparrow believed with all his heart in tolerance in a very intolerant period—the period that saw political intolerance reach its climax in the Civil War, and ecclesiastical intolerance reach its climax in the ritualist controversy and the Reformed Episcopal Church schism. This mode of thought may have been influenced by his early life in Ireland with its perpetual fighting, and also by Coleridge's teaching that to grasp truth requires charity as much as intellect; and what is tolerance but charity in action.[137]

That Zabriskie emphasized Christian humanism, not denying the importance of Catholicism and especially Protestantism, may have been due to the influence of Cosby Bell, his teacher, colleague, and companion whom he "came to love and respect." Said Zabriskie, "During his later years, he [Bell] liked best of all to call himself a Christian humanist. Nothing human was outside his interest."[138] Zabriskie thus preferred to be known as a Christian humanist rather than a liberal or broadchurchman. Zabriskie recognized that in some ways Bell's teaching was outmoded, but he opined that "some of the things he stood for are coming back into fashion (haven't you heard people say, 'we must hold onto the values of Liberalism'?) and I venture to think that more of his insights will be vindicated in calmer days."[139] At least he hoped that they would.

How did Zabriskie view the theological situation in the midfifties? He wrote,

I should venture the remark that today our emphases are the same as they have been but are held differently. We still have the strong Protestant stress, but those who most conspicuously champion it have more appreciation of the Catholic and the Christian Humanist values than did their earlier prototypes (Mollegen and Kevin vs. Meade). We still have teachers deeply coloured by Christian Humanism, but they have a deeper grasp on the values of both Protestantism and Catholicism than did their forerunners (Howe and ACZ than Bell). Our spokesmen for the Caroline Divines-Catholic strain have drunk more deeply at the wells of Protestantism than our previous exponents thereof (cp. B-S [Brown-Serman] and especially Clebsch with Wilmer).[140]

Deans Rollins, Zabriskie, and Brown-Serman

It is significant that Zabriskie placed himself with the Christian humanist tradition. It is also to be noted that as a Christian humanist he recognized the necessity for the seminary, as Anglican, to comprehend all three emphases as elements within the mainstream of its theology (the proclamation of the gospel).

The proclamation of the gospel is central in the second chapter of *No Mean Inheritance* on the missionary heritage of the seminary. This chapter tells the story of the seminary's great investment in overseas missions, beginning with the Mission of the Hills to Greece; passing on to the Orient; to China, first with William Boone and others; then to Liberia, with Payne and others; then to Japan, with Channing Moore Williams and his companions; and finally to Brazil. He ends recognizing the service of alumni in all of these places and in Alaska, Nicaragua, Mexico, Costa Rica, Columbia, the Dominican Republic, Haiti, Cuba, Okinawa, the Philippine Islands, India, Pakistan, and elsewhere. "Two hundred and eleven Virginia Seminary men have served overseas, to the best of my knowledge. This is over 10% of all the alumni in our entire history, who total 2,238."[141]

Some were motivated in ways now incomprehensible, "such as the idea that the poor ignorant heathen would burn forever in a fiery hell if they were not converted and baptized." More valid were three other motives: loyalty to extend Christ's dominion everywhere, desire to share the benefits of Christian discipleship with others, and "the conviction that a stable and constructive world civilization could be reared only on the basis of Christian faith and moral principles. . . ."[142] One wonders to what degree, if any, Zabriskie was aware of the change of attitude at Virginia Seminary toward missions, change already occurring generally.

The third chapter concerns the seminary's pastoral tradition and concentrates on Meade's *Lectures on the Pastoral Office*, the seminary missions, and "a quite new method of pastoral training," that structured by Reuel Howe and influenced by clinical pastoral education. Zabriskie was impressed by the strong theological grounding that Meade gave to the practical skills of preaching, education, and pastoral care. Here he found what we must regard as an important clue.

> Deep pastoral concern and effective pastoral care are the outgrowth of a conviction about God, His attitude toward human beings, His purpose for them, His will for their dealings with each other. That is to say, *pastoral care is the outgrowth of faith and theology.* Our strong theological tradition from Sparrow to Bell and onwards has consistently held that systematic theology comes to its climax in what our forebears called *experimental* (or "experiential") theology: the theory must be vindicated by experience. The most correct theology is condemned as sterile unless it finds expression in love for the brethren. In the case of the clergyman this love of the brethren is manifested in pastoral concern.[143]

Second, the network of seminary missions contributed to the strong pastoral tradition of the seminary. "From the earliest days till World War II the most important pastoral training VTS men received was their work in these missions. Every student was attached to one and spent every Sunday, and often Monday too, calling, teaching classes, conducting services, preaching, doing service . . . under the oversight of the Professor of P.T. and one or two others."[144]

Third, Zabriskie acknowledged that with the arrival of Reuel Howe "a new type of training" began, making "available for pastoral care the most recently developed knowledge and skills."[145] The "new" thing "is clinical training and psychoanalysis." In his brief discussion, Zabriskie tried to be positive but was obviously preoccupied with the dangers inherent in the "new type of training"—the production of "amateur psychiatrists" and the proclamation of "another Gospel." He questioned "whether our contemporary program is as well adapted to train competent pastors in this day as Meade's was in his."

> Perhaps one can say that Meade's "thesis" was too dogmatic and systematic; the liberal "antithesis" swung too far in reaction from arid verbalizing in its stress on vitalist forces. Today in most seminaries this latter movement is past its peak, I think, and the psychological emphasis will be modified and regulated by the theological.[146]

The fourth chapter deals with the seminary's liturgical heritage, which Zabriskie argued was misunderstood and thus too often violated. He wrote

of "four underlying principles of the VTS use . . . theological, disciplinary, liturgical, and historical." That use was grounded upon the Evangelical doctrine of justification by faith alone. Thus rooted "our forebears
would not tolerate any form of service, any verbal teaching, any dramatic
action which conveyed the idea that in any way men could earn the favor
of God . . . or that their deeds or words could persuade or deceive an ignorant or unwilling God to do something He otherwise would not do."[147]
The seminary's forebears took seriously discipline and insisted that in any
regularly scheduled weekly service of any parish, the Prayer Book service
of Morning Prayer, Evening Prayer, or Holy Communion, or some authorized combination of Prayer Book offices, must be followed *without devia-
tion.*" They did, however, insist that for those to whom the Prayer Book
was new, supplementary forms of worship, consisting "chiefly of reading
and expounding the Word of God, and of 'free' prayers," should be employed.[148] In addressing the liturgical principle Zabriskie wrote of the liturgy, "the sacrament of the Holy Communion": "The rite we have in chapel
every Thursday morning . . . is the outward and visible sign of the fellowship of the Holy Ghost, a pledge to assure us of the reality of that fellowship and of our participation therein."[149] Under the heading of the historical principle, Zabriskie wrote of "simplicity and lack of ornamenta-
tion" emphasized by the founders in tune with "a sense of the fitness of
things" and "a shrewd suspicion that psychologically an elaborate service
subtly encouraged an elaboration of the lives of the worshippers and de-
tracted from their living in the simplicity of Christ."[150]

On the basis of these principles Zabriskie drew deductions, the first
being that a Holy Table and not an altar was most appropriate for use in
the service of Holy Communion or fellowship. He lamented Berryman
Green's substitution of a hybrid table-altar for the old, honest table.[151]
The second deduction was that those who participate in the Holy Communion should be marked by reverence, friendliness, and good manners
and not be preoccupied with appearances, correctness, and the like. The
third deduction was that, "when you attend the Eucharist, stay to the
end of the service, if you can."[152] Fourth, "the celebrant should kneel
when ministering to himself . . . in order to make it plain that in respect
of being in need of the divine help he is on exactly the same footing as
any layman." Fifth, "the conduct of a Christian worshipper should be
marked by a son's freedom from restraint, he should feel at home, feel
that he had been accepted."[153] Sixth, "simplicity." This involved simplicity of actions and of vestments. Clearly, Zabriskie lamented the introduction of colored stoles. He went on to say, in a kind of lament,
"The faculty began to wear academic gowns to chapel service not earlier
than 1922. I suspect that Dean Crawford, like Bishop Meade, would

have thought that to wear such gear was to indulge in pride and vanity! The special gown for the Dean was designed as late as 1951."[154] Simplicity, it would seem, was the great, overarching principle. "It is because the symbols of service can become the bonds of self-glorification that we have stood so stiffly for the irreducible minimum of glorious habiliaments and splendid vestments."

Such was the inheritance as viewed by one deeply involved in the history and life of the seminary.

NOTES

1. Nevins and Commager, History of the United States, 407.
2. George E. Mowry and Blaine A. Brownell, The Urban Nation, 1920–1980, rev. ed., American Century Series (New York: Hill and Wang, 1981), 3.
3. Ibid., 18.
4. Nevins and Commager, History of the United States, 414–15.
5. Mowry and Brownell, Urban Nation, 90.
6. Ahlstrom, Religious History, 915.
7. Much of the above analysis of the social gospel, Niebuhr, and Tillich is based on Donald Meyer's The Protestant Search for Political Realism: 1919–1941 (Berkeley and Los Angeles: University of California Press, 1960).
8. Robert Woods Lynn, "Notes Toward a History," Theological Education 17/2 (Spring 1981): 131.
9. Ibid., 134.
10. Bd. min., 1914–27, 217. The figures here are largely from the dean's reports to the board.
11. Fac. min., 1934–47, 11.
12. Bd. min., 1939–53, 55.
13. Fac. min., 1925–34, 83.
14. Ibid., 1934–47, 86.
15. Catalogue (1925–26), 12.
16. Ibid., 64, and added sheet.
17. Fac. min., 1934–47, 81.
18. Ibid., 191.
19. Ibid., 216–17.
20. Bd. min., 1939–53, 35.
21. See fac. min., 1934–47, 187.
22. Ibid., 91, 94.
23. See bd. min., 1928–38, 8; bd. min., 1939–53, 29, 80.
24. Bd. min., 1939–53, 12, 29, 92.
25. Ibid., 19, 36, 92.
26. Ibid., 59.
27. Ibid., 1928–38, 61, 62.

28. Ibid., 64–66. There had been a secretary prior to this. See catalogue (1925–26), Miss Clara Guthrie.
29. Ibid., 38.
30. Ibid., 41.
31. Ibid., 1939–53, 13–14.
32. Ibid., 27, see 20.
33. Ibid., 58, see 55.
34. Fac. min., 1934–47, 212–13.
35. Bd. min., 1939–53, 85.
36. Fac. min., 1934–47, 13, 39.
37. See bd. min., 1939–53, 85.
38. Ibid., 1928–38, 32, 36.
39. Ibid., 42–43.
40. Ibid., 1939–53, 66, 67.
41. Fac. min., 1916–25 (May 14, 1924), 258; bd. min., 1914–27, 223.
42. Henry St. George Tucker, autobiography, vol. 2, chap. 1, 3.
43. Ibid., 3–4.
44. Ibid., 4.
45. Ibid., 5.
46. Fac. min., 1916–25, 283.
47. Ibid., 1925–34 (June 7, 1925), 5; bd. min., 1914–27, 249–250.
48. Seminary Journal 3/2 (December 1956), a commemorative issue entitled Alexander Clinton Zabriskie, 1898–1956.
49. Bd. min., 1914–27, 267, 273.
50. Ibid., 279.
51. Ibid., 285; catalogue (1930), 7. Bishop Tucker concentrated on the doctrine of the church, sacraments and ministry, as well as missions. Canon Lubeck and Fred Goodwin emphasized urban and rural ministries, respectively.
52. Bd. min., 1928–38, 34, 38.
53. Ibid., 63, 79, 89, 90.
54. Ibid., 37–38.
55. See Charles P. Price, "C.L. Stanley," *Anglican Theological Review* Supplementary Series, No. 7 (November 1976): 19ff.
56. Bd. min., 1928–38, 17, 19.
57. Ibid., 12.
58. Ibid. (November 12, 1931), 80.
59. Ibid. (November 13, 1935), 17. Also see page 14. The book was published by Macmillan in 1935.
60. Bd. min., 1928–53 (June 7, 1933), box 1933, no pagination.
61. Fac. min., 1925–34 (May 25, 1933), 274.
62. Bd. min., 1928–38, 11.
63. Ibid., 3.
64. Ibid., 28, 33.
65. Ibid., 46, and 1939–53, 5, 32–33.
66. Ibid., 1928–38, 20.

67. John Krumm, "A.T. Mollegen," *Anglican Theological Review* Supplementary Series, No. 7 (November 1976): 15.
68. Ibid., 10.
69. Donald Smith Armentrout, *The Quest for the Informed Priest: A History of the School of Theology* (Sewanee, Tenn., 1979), 249–50. See bd. min., 1939–53, 19, 36, 54.
70. Bd. min., 1939–53, 11–12.
71. See fac. min. (February 26, 1942), 150.
72. Bd. min., 1939–53, 52, 54.
73. Ibid., 54.
74. Ibid., 57–58.
75. Fac. min. (January 18, 1945), 229.
76. See catalogue (1925–26), 13, and (1946), 13.
77. See bd. min., 1916–27, 223; fac. min., 1916–24, 258, 264, and appended sheets, plus fac. min., 1925–34, 12, 14.
78. Catalogue, 1925–26, 17–18.
79. Ibid., 15–16.
80. Ibid., 16.
81. Catalogue (1939), 15.
82. Ibid. (1942), 17.
83. Ibid.
84. Ibid. (1925–26), 18.
85. Ibid. (1930), 20–21.
86. Ibid. (1935), 17.
87. John Booty, *The Episcopal Church in Crisis* (Cambridge, Mass., 1988), 25. See Seward Hiltner, "A Descriptive Appraisal, 1935–1980," *Pastoral Psychology* (Winter 1980): 86–98, and Richard Dayninger, "Goals in Clinical Pastoral Education," Pastoral Psychology (April 1971): 5–10.
88. Bd. min., 1939–53, 36.
89. Ibid., 58, 60, 72.
90. Catalogue (1946), 17.
91. Fac. min., 1934–47, 82.
92. Ibid., 155–56 and appended materials.
93. Ibid., 202 and appended materials.
94. Bd. min., 1939–53, 45; fac. min., 1934–47, 89. Also see 203 and 206.
95. Spielmann, Bexley Hall, 75.
96. See fac. min., 1934–47, 194, 209, and bd. min., 1939–53, 52, 56.
97. Bd. min., 1939–53, 65, 73.
98. Bd. min., 1939–53, 206. See fac. min., 1934–47, 187.
99. Bd. min., 1939–53, 45.
100. Ibid., 48.
101. Fac. min., 1934–47, 194.
102. Bd. min., 1939–53, 48.
103. Ibid., 53, 57.
104. Ibid., 85.

105. Bowie's foreword to W. Cosby Bell, *If a Man Die* (New York and London: Scribners, 1934), vi–vii.
106. W. Cosby Bell, *Sharing in Creation: Studies in the Christian View of the World*, Bohlen lectures, 1925 (New York: Macmillan, 1925), 64.
107. W. Cosby Bell, *The Reasonableness of Faith in God* (Alexandria, Va.: Virginia Theological Seminary, 1937), 58.
108. W. Cosby Bell, *The Making of Man*, Bishop Paddock lectures, 1929–30 (New York: Macmillan, 1931), 127.
109. Ibid., 211.
110. Ibid., 222.
111. Ibid., 210.
112. Bell, *Reasonableness*, 137.
113. Ibid., 138.
114. Ibid., 140–41.
115. Ibid., 143.
116. Zabriskie, *Anglican Evangelicalism*, ix.
117. Ibid., 36.
118. Ibid., 98–101.
119. Ibid., 137.
120. Ibid., 184.
121. Ibid., 231.
122. Ibid., 231–32.
123. Ibid., 231–32.
124. Ibid., 234–37.
125. Ibid., 237–38.
126. Ibid., 238.
127. Ibid., 243.
128. Ibid., 244
129. Ibid., 245–46.
130. Ibid., see 247–48.
131. A.C. Zabriskie, "The Seminary's Aim," *The Living Church*, January 22, 1941, 12–14.
132. A.C. Zabriskie, *No Mean Inheritance* (MS, VTSA), introduction, 1.
133. Ibid., 2.
134. Ibid., 4.
135. Ibid., chap. 1, 1.
136. Ibid., 4.
137. Ibid., 5.
138. Ibid., 6.
139. Ibid., 7.
140. Ibid., 2.
141. Ibid., chap. 2, 23. He surely means "Just under."
142. Ibid., 2.
143. Ibid., chap. 3, back of page 2.
144. Ibid., 5–6.

145. Ibid., 7.
146. Ibid., 11.
147. Ibid., chap. 4, 3.
148. Ibid., 4.
149. Ibid.
150. Ibid., 5.
151. Ibid., 6.
152. Ibid., 7.
153. Ibid., 8.
154. Ibid., 9, front and back.

CHAPTER EIGHT

FROM
POSTWAR BOOM
TO THE CHALLENGE
OF THE 1960s

1. THE HISTORICAL SETTING: A TIME OF CRISIS

Between 1945 and 1969 the nation and the churches went from confidence, complacency, and optimism to uncertainty, anxiety, and a growing sense of pessimism. This was the time ranging from victory in a world war, accompanied by economic prosperity and exponential growth, to the quagmire of a war in Southeast Asia, accompanied by civil disobedience, a diminution of national purpose, and the uprising of oppressed black Americans—illuminated by burning cities and assaulted by the raucous sounds of anger and distress. Through all these years there was the Cold War with its psychological terrors and cultivation of lies and deceits at the highest levels of government.[1] The true winner of the Cold War, it is said, was neither the Soviet Union nor the United States but Japan—and I would add West Germany—the growing economic powers of the 1980s and 90s.

The specter of communism hung over the 1950s, with Joseph McCarthy seizing the opportunity to exercise vast, destructive power. And in the 1960s (one recalls particularly the Cuban missile crisis, building of fallout shelters, planning to relocate vital institutions to safer places) the "evil empire" galvanized our economics and our politics as well as our churches, enforcing our determination to stop the spread of communism in Asia and elsewhere, whatever the cost.

In this atmosphere Christianity seemed enhanced, pitted against "godless communism." Charles Lowry's *Communism and Christ* (1952) was en-

247

dorsed by Billy Graham and became a best-seller among religious books. The churches grew and the demand for clergy burgeoned, not only because of opposition to "godless communism" but also in relation to population growth and the suburban sprawl, drawing millions from the inner cities into new settlements dominated by shopping malls and pseudocolonial church buildings. In addition, and in relation to all of this, there was a "popular resurgence of piety," much discussed "in newspapers, popular magazines and learned journals."[2]

Church membership grew from 43 percent of the population in 1910 to 69 percent in 1960 (the high point), and money spent in church construction rose from $26 million in 1945 to more than a billion dollars in 1960.[3] Baptized membership in the Protestant Episcopal Church peaked in 1966 at 3,647,297 and from there declined, with a slight increase in 1983.[4] It also experienced a "building boom." In the 1950s Bishop Emrich of Michigan had set a goal of one new congregation every month.

In some respects this age of growth was an age of complacency and had its critics. Gibson Winters, in his book *The Suburban Captivity of the Churches* (1960), wrote, "In place of sacraments we have community meetings. In place of confession, the bazaar; . . . in place of community, a collection of functions; . . . every church activity seems to lead further into a maze of superficiality which is stultifying the middle class community."[5] It would seem that the churches had succumbed to the spirit of the age and that spirit was largely dominated by social Darwinism and individualistic pietism. Norman Vincent Peale was the representative churchman with his books *Guide to Confident Living* (1948) and *The Power of Positive Thinking* (1952).

If Samuel P. Huntington is correct, as the gap between ideals and institutions was recognized and hypocrisy identified, the complacency and hypocrisy of the mid to late 1950s gave way to the moralism and commitment of the 1960s. Between 1968 and 1971 the reassertion of the American creed—including equality, natural rights, liberty, and the social contract—achieved its highest degree of intensity, followed by the growth of cynicism and despair within the body politic. The church as an institution suffered as a result of this dramatic revolution in society.

Confidence in its leaders, according to one study, fell from 41 percent to 24 percent, according to Louis Harris polls of the general public,[6] and as it sought to engage the criticism of those who proclaimed its hypocrisy, it lost many of those who depended upon it to be a source of nurture for personal living but not an agent of social change.

The church can be said to have benefited by being recalled to the radical universalism of the gospel, to the advocacy of outcasts, and to the nurturing of the revolutionary community. The Episcopal Church responded to the urban and racial crisis at its Convention in Seattle in 1967 and at a special convention in 1969. It was directly confronted with the Black Manifesto at the Episcopal Church Center in that latter year. Add to this the rising women's movement (the National Organization for Women was founded in 1967), the growing opposition to the Vietnam War, and turmoil on university campuses and in the nation's cities. The age is justly called an age of crisis.[7]

Ahlstrom, admitting that this nation has experienced many crises, argued that the crisis of the 1960s was "uniquely critical." The events of the time "led to a loss of that kind of corporate commitment that a nation of unusually heterogeneous minorities desperately needed." This loss was accompanied by "the declining incidence of dedication to the moral and doctrinal message of the churches and to the religious institutions that had sustained these traditions."[8] The erosion was partly from within, as some theologians proclaimed the "death of God" and "man come of age" with no need for the moral and doctrinal traditions of Christianity. It came in part, too, from the challenge to traditional ethics as applied to sex and drugs. James Pike's A Time for Christian Candor (1964) was a tract for the times.

The seminaries were involved in the changing times. They were criticized for their racism, their sexism, and their general irrelevance. They were stung when Charles Feilding, in a study sponsored by the American Association of Theological Schools, wrote, "The greater part of the whole theological enterprise seems to be off on a vast archeological dig, preoccupied with the long ago and largely oblivious to the purpose of the exploration."[9] When some sought to respond in positive ways, they were accused by others of being hot-headed radicals.

1930s to the end of the 1960s were involved in the proliferation of goals and courses, the fragmentation of the theological discipline, and in a growing gap between theory and practice, with more and more attention being paid to practica to the neglect of the traditional disciplines. The report of a special committee in the Episcopal Church, submitted to the Seattle General Convention in 1967 and appearing under the names of Nathan Pusey and Charles Taylor, was highly critical of the church's eleven accredited seminaries. On behalf of "the professional preparation for ministry," it urged that more attention be given to the church's mission in contemporary society; stated that theological education was too expensive, largely because of its inefficiency; suggested a reduction in the number of seminaries; and urged that those that survived be placed, if not already there, in ecumenical, urban, university settings, where the bifurcation of theory and practice could be overcome by continuous interaction with society.[10]

From this report came concrete developments including the founding of the Board for Theological Education and of a national testing instrument, the General Ordination Examination. As we shall see, the faculty and board of Virginia Seminary spent considerable time and energy looking inward in response to external and internal pressures, probing for answers to questions concerning the goals of theological education and the appropriate means for reaching those goals. As it interacted with the changing society, it experienced significant changes itself while maintaining a fundamentally conservative stance in the midst of the furor. Its ability both to respond and to conserve was a factor in its growing success as an institution.

2. STUDENTS, BUILDINGS, FINANCES: POSTWAR GROWTH

With the end of the Second World War all seminaries experienced some degree of growth. In the Episcopal Church the seminaries were confronted with an influx of aspirants for the ordained ministry as dioceses sought to provide clergy for vacant parishes and for missions sprouting up in new communities, particularly in the suburbs.[11] We have noted that in 1945 there were 45 students enrolled at the seminary, including 11 former servicemen. This was compared to 70 to 80 students in the prewar years. By 1947 there were 114 students, 62 of whom were married. In 1949 there were 152 students, and in 1951, 186—100 more than the prewar high. In 1952 one-third of the students were married, many with children. By 1959, when there were 184 overall, 118 were married, with a total community of 425 persons.

Concerned about their ability to provide for so large a student body (plus families), the board sought to set limits, at first suggesting 150 students with 50 in each class.[12] However, it was difficult to maintain such a limit, and by the early 1960s the number approached 200, with 199 reported in 1963. In 1952 Dean Felix Kloman had reported to the board that the seminary opened with 170 students, 70 of whom were married, coming from three foreign countries and fifty-six dioceses. Of these, 29 were from the Virginia dioceses, well under the quota of 20 percent. In 1951–52 some 88 students were supported by the G.I. Bill, a figure that dropped dramatically in 1952–53 to 16, including a veteran of the Korean War. Kloman then asked the board to approve, as an ideal, the enrollment of 162 undergraduates and 10 graduate (S.T.M.) students.[13] A decline in registration occurred in 1966, but the total average of 170 persisted for some time.

The larger enrollment required expansion of plant facilities and an increase in the faculty and administration. The most immediate needs were for more dormitory space and for enlarged dining facilities. To this end a

The "New" Buildings, 1950s

capital funds drive was started, with a long-term goal of $1,000,000 to $1,150,000. The immediate goal was for $250,000 for the repair and re-modeling of existing buildings.[14] The Reverend Charles Sheerin was named campaign chairman, and discussion began concerning the razing of old St. George's Hall and the erection of new buildings. The firm of Leon Block and Associates was hired to assist with the campaign and the short-term goal was raised to $500,000.[15] As a stopgap measure the board authorized the purchase of government surplus buildings and furniture.[16] In November 1946 Mr. Waldron Faulkner, consulting architect, presented a plan that involved construction of a number of small buildings (rather than the one large building envisioned by the board) located across the campus from the older buildings.[17] In 1947 the Reverend William H. Kirk, a graduate of the class of 1935, was hired as general manager of the campaign fund.[18] By 1947 Sheerin and Kirk were seeking a total of $746,500, having received $116,177.

By 1952 the fund was well over $1,000,000. In addition to repairs to the old buildings, there were five new dormitories, with Wilmer and Johns

Lunch in Refectory, 1950

completed in 1949, Madison and Moore in 1950, and a new St. George's in 1952. Also by 1950 there was a large new refectory with a commodious lounge. Although there were seventy-five new dormitory rooms, forty-one students were still accommodated in the old buildings. With the increase in the number of students and faculty, a new library was required, and it opened in 1957, having cost over $350,000. With the addition of faculty housing, the building program was completed, marking one of the great achievements of Dean Zabriskie, the board and the alumni. The results were pleasing to the eye; the colonial style recommended by the architect complemented the buildings already in existence. And a greatly enlarged community was housed in ways that deemphasized size and enhanced a sense of community. No provision was made for married students other than granting of housing allowances, for the board came to the conclusion that it would be best for families to live in existing apartment complexes such as Parkfairfax and Fairlington. Subsidizing rental cost was viewed as more economical than constructing buildings to house married students and their families on campus.

Increased numbers of students and an enlarged faculty called for a larger annual budget. In 1946–47 the budget was about $110,000, by 1949–50 it was over $200,000, and by 1953–54 it was over $300,000. It continued to grow until it passed $500,000 in 1962 and was well over $1,000,000 in 1971. The seminary depended on three major sources of income to meet the budget: (1) invested funds (endowment and trusts), (2) annual giving, and (3) students fees. Invested funds increased steadily during this period, rising from $1,448,534 in 1944–45 to nearly $4,000,000 by 1962. In this latter year the total of invested funds plus plant value was $7,570,647. This growth, however, was not altogether satisfactory. Dean Trotter pointed out in May 1960 that in 1945 endowment income provided 82 percent of costs and in 1950 only 15 percent. By 1971, at the conclusion of the Second Century Fund campaign, endowment was providing 60 percent.

Annual giving included more than the Theological Education Offering (TEO) and the gifts of the Friends of Virginia Seminary (FOVS). But they were the major sources and exhibited dramatic growth, from $14,332 in 1945 to about $70,000 in 1950, $150,000 in 1962, and more than $200,000 in 1968. In 1950 some 622 parishes and missions gave to TEO for Virginia Seminary, and in 1964 the figure was 929. The success of this appeal to parishes in which Virginia graduates served was one of the great strengths of the seminary. While annual giving was rising, appeals for special funds, such as the Africa Seminary Project (in excess of $300,000 by 1964) and the dean's annual year-end gift letter, were producing significant results. The latter brought in $122,000 in 1961 and $163,000 in 1963, providing the necessary funds for a new heating plant (with a fall-out shelter). The year-end letter was to continue to be a profitable venture. Dean Trotter's greatest financial accomplishment was the Second Century Fund, to which we shall turn later in this chapter.

The third source of income was student fees. We have already noted that tuition was being charged in 1945. It was then $30 a semester. In addition room and board cost $150 and health insurance $4, for a yearly total of $368 in tuition and fees. By 1968, tuition was $800, the clinical pastoral training fee was $150, the library fee $50, registration $35, room $150, and board $450 for single students and $120 for married students. In 1971 student charges met 20 percent of the budget, as compared to 60 percent from endowment and the rest from annual giving.

Finances were never very far from the minds of deans, bursars, and trustees. But after 1945 Virginia Seminary was never in dire financial straits as it had been on more than one occasion in the past.

3. AN ENLARGED, PROFESSIONALLY TRAINED FACULTY

From 1945 the faculty grew dramatically. As it grew, expectations changed, so that by the middle of this period all except those teaching in the "practical" fields were expected to have earned doctorates in their special subjects. Furthermore, whereas under Dean Zabriskie faculty were expected to have some years of experience in the parish ministry, later deans would encourage and employ young men with but limited parish experience. With the passing of time there would be two to three members in each department, salaries would increase, sabbatical leaves and leaves of absence for further academic study and research would be instituted, and the publication of learned monographs would be encouraged and rewarded. All of this compared well with what was happening in academic institutions elsewhere.

In 1947, after a troublesome interim during which the faculty and board struggled to find a prominent theologian to succeed Charles Lowry, the seminary welcomed back the Reverend Clifford L. Stanley as professor of systematic theology.[19] To fill out the theology department, the Reverend Jesse M. Trotter was elected associate professor of apologetics and homiletics, having been rector of Grace Church, Amherst, Massachusetts, and director of religious activities at Amherst College. Trotter was born in Chattanooga, Tennessee, in 1909. After his father died in 1925, the family moved to Boston, and Trotter went to study at Amherst College, where he earned a B.A. degree in 1931. After teaching at Doshisha University, Kyoto, Japan, he entered Virginia Seminary and graduated in 1936. Ordained to the diaconate, he went to Trinity Church, Copley Square, Boston, to serve under the Reverend Arthur Lee "Tui" Kinsolving and was ordained a priest. In 1939 he returned to Amherst. Trotter's field was apologetics. In 1947 he defined apologetics as "the affirmative and constructive attempt to vindicate the truth and to establish the relevance of the Christian faith in a given age."[20] For his age the great challenge was secularism with its false dogmas. Students over many years grew to appreciate the ability with which Professor Trotter analyzed the modern world and demonstrated the relevance of true Christianity (not mere sentimental religion) to the world's questions.

With the departure of Robert Gibson in 1946, the seminary sought an associate for Dean Zabriskie in the church history department. Joe Brown taught briefly; it was suggested that Victor Stanley, no longer needed in theology, become an instructor in church history; and the faculty sought to obtain John Krumm as an assistant professor in the department. Instead, in 1946 the Reverend Kenneth E. Heim, then a chaplain in the navy, was elected assistant professor of church history and director of music for the seminary. A native of Baltimore, where he was born in 1907, Heim was a graduate of Lehigh University (B.A.), the University of Pennsylvania (M.A.), the Philadelphia Divinity School (Th.B., 1931), and the General Theological Seminary (S.T.M., 1932). Deeply interested in history and especially cultural history (students remember his lectures on Dante), Heim subsequently was drawn to a vocation in overseas missions, spending some of the best years of his life in Mexico and Japan.[21]

Faculty 1951; Stanley Brown-Serman, Dean
First Row: (*l to r*) Kenneth Heim, Reuel Howe, Stanley Brown-Serman, Robert
Goodwin, Walter Russell Bowie
Second Row: Robert Cox, William Clebsch, Robert Kevin, A.T. Mollegen, Clifford
Stanley, Jesse Trotter

The history department was expanded in 1949 with the election of the Reverend William A. Clebsch as an instructor. He had been invited as a senior in 1946 to remain at the seminary as a tutor in New Testament. In the church history department he had particular responsibility for American church history and for that purpose earned an S.T.M. from Virginia Seminary with a thesis on Wilmer and a Th.D. from Union Theological Seminary in New York with a dissertation on the Civil War. He left the seminary in 1955 to teach at the new seminary in Austin, Texas, and from there went on to teach at Stanford University. An accomplished scholar, Clebsch concentrated on the American scene but also wrote a serious monograph on the beginnings of the Reformation in England.[22]

In 1949 the Reverend Robert A. Goodwin came to the seminary from the Bishop Payne Divinity School to teach Bible and remained as professor of biblical literature until his retirement in 1956, much beloved as a caring pastor. In 1950 the Reverend Robert E. Cox was elected assistant professor of New Testament[23] and served in that capacity until 1955 when he left to be rector of the Episcopal Church in Upperville, Virginia. The board was much concerned to hire an accomplished New Testament scholar as an associate to A.T. Mollegen. Various possibilities were considered, and in 1953 the Reverend Franklin Young, then at Yale, was elected.[24]

When he declined, serious thought was given to the Reverend Lansing Hicks, who taught Old Testament at the University of the South, left there at the time of the great exodus, and taught at Virginia Seminary for a year before going to Berkeley Seminary in 1954.[25] In that same year the Reverend Holt Graham was elected and accepted the position of professor of New Testament.[26] Graham, born in Tacoma, Washington, in 1914, was a graduate of the University of Washington (B.A.), Columbia University (M.A.), and Union Theological Seminary, New York (B.D., S.T.M., Th.D, S.T.D.). He taught at Seabury-Western Theological Seminary before coming to Virginia, where he stayed until 1971. A careful, exacting scholar, Graham was also a man with a deep understanding of theological education and provided much calmly delivered wisdom to the seminary in a period of change.

The teaching of Old Testament was greatly enhanced by the election in 1955 of the Reverend Murray Lee Newman to be assistant professor of Old Testament.[27] He was advanced to full professor in 1963. Newman, born in 1924 in Oklahoma, was a graduate of Phillips University (B.A., M.A.), Union Theological Seminary, New York (B.D., Th.D.), and did postgraduate work in Europe at Basel, Heidelberg, and Fribourg. He brought to this position a strong interest in and knowledge of the Old Testament, literature, theology, and archeology, and in his book *People of the Covenant* (1962) made a distinguished contribution to the field. He has also been influential in his interpretation of current affairs through his course on the Bible and the New York Times.

Additions were made in the practical field. In 1949 the board elected the Reverend E. Felix Kloman "for the chair of assistant in the field of Pastoral Theology," having already considered him for homiletics and for the position of "coordinator."[28] Failing in this, the Reverend Barton M. Lloyd of the class of 1948 was appointed instructor in pastoral theology.[29] Lloyd, born in 1919 in Toyko, Japan, to missionary parents, was a graduate of the University of Virginia (B.A.) and the seminary (B.D.). He was on the faculty from 1950 to 1968, with an intermission from 1956 to 1960 to gain parish experience at St. Stephen's Church, Birmingham, Michigan. In 1955 the Reverend John Soleau of the class of 1952 was elected an instructor in the department of pastoral theology, becoming an associate professor in 1960. Born in Upper Montclair, New Jersey, in 1924, Soleau graduated from Amherst College (B.A.), Virginia Seminary (B.D.), and studied at Harvard in 1963. He left the seminary in 1964. In 1956 the Reverend William George Frank, Jr., was added to the pastoral theology department. Born in Chicago in 1926, Frank graduated from the University of Louisville and Virginia Seminary. After ordination he served parishes in Kentucky and Virginia. In 1960, he left the seminary to study medicine and practice psychiatry. In time he became the seminary's consulting psychiatrist. These young men were to guide the department in the years following Reuel Howe's departure.

The quest for a professor of homiletics began with the election of the Reverend C.W.F. Smith, rector of St. Andrew's Church, Wellesley, Massachusetts, to that position.[30] He had been, while canon chancellor of the National Cathedral in Washington, an adjunct instructor in homiletics at the seminary. While at St. Andrew's Church he had been an adjunct instructor in homiletics at the Episcopal Theological School. But he was to decline his election, becoming instead a distinguished professor of New Testament at the Cambridge seminary from 1951 until his retirement in 1972. Incidentally, the Virginia faculty tried to obtain Smith as professor of New Testament in 1952, to no avail.[31]

The Reverend Walter Russell Bowie, whom we have encountered as a student at the seminary, was then elected professor of homiletics and accepted.[32] This was a distinguished appointment and marked the beginning of a new and greatly enhanced emphasis at the seminary on preaching. Bowie had been rector of Grace Church, New York, where he was acknowledged to be one of the most distinguished preachers in the country. He came to the seminary, which he had served for years as an active alumnus and member of the board of trustees, upon retirement from a professorship at Union Theological Seminary, New York, during its most exciting days. Bowie continued on a year-by-year basis until 1955, when he retired at seventy-two years of age. He was succeeded by the Reverend John Q. Beckwith, who was brought onto the faculty as associate professor to develop and lead a separate department of homiletics.[33]

In addition there were numerous short-term and adjunct appointments. With the mass resignation of the Sewanee theological faculty, Dean Craighill Brown and Professor Lansing Hicks came to the seminary as sabbatical replacements in 1953–54. The faculty sought unsuccessfully to obtain Howard Johnson for a permanent appointment. Allen Reddick and then Allen Green assisted with church history, and Ernest Trice Thompson of Union Seminary, Richmond, taught early church history. Knox Kreutzer and Ernest Bruder taught counseling, and others, including Felix Kloman, assisted with pastoral theology. Leon Wright of Howard University taught New Testament Greek. Others thus employed in adjunct positions were John Turnbull and Jake Hamel.

With the growing concern in the Episcopal Church for Christian education, in 1949 Dean Zabriskie brought Marian Kelleran onto the faculty as a part-time lecturer. Mrs. Kelleran received a B.A. from the University of Buffalo; was married to the Reverend Harold C. Kelleran, who died in 1945; and at the time of her coming onto the faculty was director of Christian education for the diocese of Washington. In 1962 she was to resign that position to teach full-time at the seminary, the first full-time woman teacher on the faculty. In time she was made a full professor of Christian education and pastoral theology, and chairman of the pastoral theology department. After her retirement in 1973, she became chairman of the Anglican Consultative Council, a post of national and international importance.[34]

Toward the end of the period 1945 to 1955 another significant appointment was made. The library had experienced strong growth while being served by a series of short-term librarians: in 1946, Lucy Robb Winston, who became the wife of David Works, a student; in 1950, Carolyn Taylor, who married a student and left in 1952; and in 1953, Andrew Neal, who died shortly after assuming the position. In 1954 Mr. J.H. Goodwin, a professional librarian with considerable knowledge of theology, became librarian and held that position until his retirement in 1991.

The faculty had been intent upon taking seriously the library and the librarian and in October 1953 had invited Andrew Neal to attend faculty meetings.[35] In 1956 Goodwin was given faculty rank as an assistant professor and librarian at a salary of $4,200.[36] In time he was to rise to full professorship, taking on various responsibilities as a faculty member. He arrived just in time to oversee the transfer of the library from Packard-Laird into a new building. He then engineered the growth of a first-class theological collection with computerized accessing and was also a mentor to many students and to junior faculty as well.

By 1956 the postwar Virginia Seminary faculty was in place. Its further development was the work of Jesse M. Trotter as dean.

4. RESTRUCTURING THE ADMINISTRATION

The years from 1945 to 1969 were remarkable for the development of the seminary administration, in which the dean became increasingly the center of power. In 1946 the board of trustees determined that there should be a business manager (also designated in the minutes as comptroller and bursar). While a search was conducted for such a person, the dean was authorized to secure additional secretarial and bookkeeping assistance.[37] The executive committee of the Board drafted a job description for the business manager, which indicated that he should "be responsible to the board, though under the general direction of and working in cooperation with the dean."[38] After considering various possibilities, Mr. Harrison Fiddesof of Washington, D.C., was chosen.[39] Called bursar in the minutes at the time of his first report in November 1946, Fiddesof indicated the immense amount of detailed work he had undertaken during the first

months of his tenure.[40] Most importantly, he was responsible for the seminary budget, for buildings and grounds, and for the refectory.

In June 1948 Benton T. Boogher was elected to be the next bursar, at
which time the board added this to the job description: "In event of difference of opinion between the Dean and the Bursar in matters of importance, it shall be referred to the Executive Committee for decision."[41] In
1949 a special planning committee of the board recommended the creation of an office of "coordinator" to oversee the Theological Education
Offering, the Friends of the Virginia Seminary, "parish aid," publicity, and
fund raising, thus in effect to be the development officer of the institution.[42] Felix Kloman was nominated for the position,[43] but he declined.
Carleton Barnwell, a trustee from southwestern Virginia and secretary of
the board, was elected and accepted.[44] He resigned as trustee but remained
as secretary at the board's request.

Upon Alexander Zabriskie's resignation as dean due to poor health in
1950, Stanley Brown-Serman, professor of New Testament, was first made
acting dean and then dean, with the understanding that he would retire
in 1952. In 1951 Mr. Boogher, the bursar, was made treasurer of the board
of trustees.[45] As a result, the coordinator was secretary and the bursar was
treasurer of the board with direct access to the board, something neither
the dean nor the faculty possessed. It must be noted that at this time there
was in existence a faculty committee on administration, including the
dean, the bursar, and two faculty members[46]

Meanwhile the board was searching for a dean to succeed Brown-
Serman. In 1951 they elected Robert F. Gibson, Suffragan Bishop of Vir-
ginia, former member of the faculty, and former dean of the School of
Theology, Sewanee. His name was withdrawn, and in a few months Felix
Kloman was chosen and accepted his election.[47] Born in Virginia in 1901,
Kloman was educated at the Episcopal High School, the University of
Virginia (B.A.), and the Virginia Theological Seminary (B.D.). He served
as a missionary in Liberia, as rector of Christ Church, Philadelphia, and
was rector of St. Alban's Church, Washington, D.C., at the time of his
election. At the request of the board of trustees, Kloman came into office
as an administrator rather than an academician and set about reforming
the seminary's administration, in the process aggravating some members
of the faculty as well as others. He did much to strengthen the administration and regularize its business affairs. But various crises, already present
on his election, centered upon clinical pastoral education and Reuel Howe.
These crises were intensified by protests from some alumni and trustees,
and they proved difficult for this pastor-administrator.

When Kloman resigned in 1956, he spoke frankly and in the course of
his remarks urged further reform. After he had resigned to return to St.

Alban's Church, the faculty met, without his being either informed or present, and did two things. First, they expressed their desire "to have the deanship freed to be an academic dean and chief pastor. He should have such assistance as will promote this purpose." The faculty then submitted a design that had an academic dean responsible to the board and a "dean of administration" responsible to the academic dean and through him to the board. The design also had a bursar responsible to the academic dean but with a separate relation to the board, indicated by a broken line. It was indicated that while subordinate to the academic dean, the dean of administration "should have a title that to the 'outside world' would suggest no 'subordination' or 'difference of inequality.'" In time it was expected that the administrative dean would take over the coordinator's job, be registrar, and preside over staff meetings. The faculty then proceeded to nominate to the board Jesse M. Trotter as dean.[48]

On March 8, 1956, Dean Kloman wrote to the faculty, affirming the necessity of rethinking the administrative structure, chastising them for proceeding to nominate a dean (it seemed better to do the restructuring before considering a specific person), and giving his own suggestions. He did this having admitted that, although he had had a long association with the seminary, he had much to learn about it. He made his suggestions, too, with the assumption that the seminary would continue to grow and would need to think in terms of greater complexity (the possibility had been discussed of three units or colleges of seventy-two students each within a larger framework). His chief suggestion was that there should be a full-time, resident president with full administrative authority.

From the beginning, the chairman of the board had been the president. Kloman argued,

> It is my judgment that this Faculty is capable of working out the curriculum, the basic principles and the major details for such a school [the school envisioned in the current discussions]. I'm also convinced that this will not be done until the administrative authority rests here on the Hill in a full-time resident President. When the control is outside it tends to create the factions on the Hill that would otherwise be faced, lived with and worked out within the Faculty.

He suggested that, under the president as chief executive officer responsible to the board, there could be a dean of faculty ("one of their own members"), a dean of students, a bursar, and a director of promotion. With the exception of the president and the bursar, they would be chosen for five-year terms. In closing he expressed his frustration "not as much because of persons as because of systems and things manipulated by persons."[49]

Jesse M. Trotter was elected dean by the board and began his term of office July 1, 1956.[50] Kloman's concerns were not acted upon, but neither were they forgotten. Carleton Barnwell retired, and the Reverend John M. McCormick was elected, not as coordinator but as director of promotions and assistant to the dean. In 1960 McCormick, resigned and Trotter suggested replacing him with two assistant deans, one for promotion and another for student affairs.[51] His choices were the Reverend T. Hudnall Harvey for promotions and the Reverend A. Grant Noble, to be called assistant dean and chaplain. In November 1961 Dean Trotter arranged with Charles Taylor, then executive director of the American Association of Theological Schools, to have Hermann N. Morse visit the seminary, study its operation, and make recommendations. Morse was asked to do a general study but to concentrate on "administrative questions."

The Morse report was submitted to the board on December 5, 1961. A gold mine of detailed information, its author recommended that there be a dean as chief administrator (called president in other seminaries), an assistant dean for administration ("to assist the Dean in general executive responsibilities"), an assistant dean of the faculty with "direct oversight of academic affairs," a director of public relations and development, a chaplain and director of enlistment, a director of student field education and placement, and a bursar and business manager. With the exception of the field education officer, the persons under the dean would serve as an administrative council. Morse was critical of the lack of a formal field education program. He was intent upon distinguishing between administration and academic programs. He sought to provide the dean with adequate assistance, regarding him in effect as president, although Morse understood that that title would remain with the chairman of the board. Morse would significantly increase the administration and grant it more power.[52]

The immediate result was a recommendation by Dean Trotter that there be appointed a secretary of the faculty who would assume direct oversight and supervision of the academic affairs of the seminary.[53] In effect this happened in 1962 when Frank Pisani was hired to be director of development and Hud Harvey as assistant dean became increasingly involved in academic affairs.

In 1963 in a report to the board Pisani suggested the need, in relation to the capitol funds drive then underway, for a thorough management study. The firm of Cresap, McCormick, and Paget was hired for $10,000 and produced in September 1964 "An Alternative Plan of Organization."[54] This report followed the primary study, results of which were submitted in April 1964, concerning the "seminary's present and future requirement for physical facilities."

The "Alternative Plan of Organization" retained the presidency in the chairman of the board. The dean came immediately under the board. Under the dean, immediately responsible to him alone, came the chaplain, the director of development, business manager, faculty, assistant dean for academic affairs, and the assistant dean for student services. All came under the dean and were responsible to the board through him alone. One clear aim of this plan was to remove the bursar from his position as treasurer of the board. A second aim was to make the dean the chief executive officer in fact and not only in prestige. The plan gave detailed job descriptions and covered every phase of the seminary's operations. The third result was to make the associate dean for academic affairs second only to the dean, "serving for the Dean in his absence or at his request."[55]

The board met on September 10, 1964, discussed the plan, and adopted it, affirming that all administrative officers, including the bursar, must report to the dean. In effect the dean from this point on was "president" (although the title remained for a time with the board chairman). Dean Trotter had achieved what Felix Kloman could not. On September 17 some amendments were made to the plan that had the effect of strengthening the dean's position. Hudnall Harvey was elected associate dean for academic affairs and Philip Smith, who had succeeded Grant Noble as chaplain in 1962, was elected assistant dean for student affairs. John O'Hear was elected secretary of the board, and Millard West treasurer. It is significant that at this meeting the board agreed "to review the Charter reference to the chairman of the Board as 'President.'"[56] This reorganization, the Second Century Fund, the development of a field education program, and the continuing education program constitute the major achievements of Jesse Trotter as dean.

5. CPE, REUEL HOWE, AND THE "GOSPEL OF PSYCHOLOGY"

In the summer of 1957 Reuel Howe began a year's leave of absence to "explore and test the project of a post-ordination school in Michigan."[57] He did not return but became director of the Institute of Advanced Pastoral Studies at Bloomfield Hills, Michigan. His resignation brought to an end a major phase of the "theory vs. practica" struggle that had exercised board, faculty, students, and alumni for years, and it marks a turning point in the history of the institution.

In 1953 a series of conferences had occurred involving board and faculty, and faculty and clinical pastoral training (CPT; sometimes called clinical pastoral education) supervisors. In a meeting with supervisors the major criticisms emerged. The first was that "students frequently come back from CPT with what seemed to be anti-Christian biases. For example, some students seem to express the attitude that they no longer needed the Bible, that the only thing that was real came of their relationships. Some students came back with what seemed to be a new 'Gospel of Psychology.'" The question was raised, "Are there two gospels?" with the additional question "Is CPT set in the great historic tradition of the biblical revelation?" Professor Stanley spoke, he believed, for the faculty when he said that "the faculty looked to Clinical Training to provide students: (1) to see human need from the standpoint of the Gospel, and to see how resources of the Gospel were being brought to bear on the situation of human need from a Christian point of view, and (2) to see their own strengths and weaknesses from the point of view of being a minister of the gospel."[58] In this self-assessment many students were led to seek therapeutic help, often in the form of psychoanalysis. This was the basis of a further criticism: CPT involved too much therapy and not enough training. Board members and alumni were alarmed to hear that most students were in therapy. One board member, according to Mollegen's terse notes, stated, "Psychiatric treatment gives a man a bad reputation. Vestries would not call a man who had had psychiatric treatment."[59] The day after this meeting, Dean Kloman reported that the rumors exaggerated the truth. In fact, he found, twenty-five students had been in psychotherapy, which the faculty regarded "as a tool in the training of men for the ministry."[60]

In his report Dean Kloman referred to two significant documents. The first was "A Description of Clinical Pastoral Training" by Jervis S. Zimmerman, chaplain and supervisor of CPT at Norwich State Hospital in Connecticut. Zimmerman discussed the student's experience in relation to patients in terms of "spiritual ministry," the student being asked "to minister to the sickest members of our society: those who feel most deeply their estrangement from God, from neighbor, and from all else that is of most abiding value in life." He discussed the student's relationship to the chaplain-supervisor as pastoral, the hope being that the student would come to view his supervisor as a "father in God." "Like the community clergyman, the chaplain-supervisor strives, with the help of the Holy Spirit, to offer to those for whom he is responsible creative and redemptive experiences of God's grace." Zimmerman discussed the student's relationship to other students as, potentially, a "new and vital experience of the Christian fellowship, where it is possible to speak and be heard in a spirit of truth, forbearance and love. When this occurs men discover the creative and redemptive grace of God mediated to them by the group, no less than in their pastoral relationship with the supervisor."[61] Zimmerman and others who shared his understanding had no doubt concerning the

Christian character of CPT, but they had to acknowledge that not all shared this conviction. Much of what Zimmerman had to say is reflected in a formal statement from the faculty regarding not only CPT but the various training programs for use in the summer after the middler year.[62]

The second document to which Dean Kloman referred was a faculty statement concerning its policy with regard to psychotherapy. Here it is revealed that the faculty not only condoned the use of psychotherapy as a means of achieving "emotional maturity" in order to deal with "feelings of hostility, anxiety, and self-distrust, that impair [the students in] their ability to live happily and helpfully with themselves and others" but actually "recommend" such therapy for those they discern to be in need, referring them to psychotherapists approved by the seminary.[63] Indeed, the faculty minutes indicate that students were encouraged to undergo such treatment and that CPT reports were used by the faculty in making recommendations for candidacy and ordination.

As stated in a "minority report," some unnamed faculty were concerned that CPT and psychotherapy, which occupied so large a portion of time in the three years of seminary and had such strong negative as well as positive influence, were insufficiently integrated into the curriculum. They cited the middler pastoral theology course as inadequate "to correct misconceptions and misunderstandings from the summer's experience." Cognizant of the use made by CPT of group dynamics (the work of Kurt Lewin and the National Training Laboratories), they cited the following as examples of theological confusion: "a too easy identification of the Holy Spirit of God with human vitalities and group dynamics; the notion that our deepest human need is met when our existence is confirmed by an accepting human fellowship rather than by God in Christ, to whom the fellowship is a witness; the idea that theological ideas are relatively unimportant. . . ."[64]

Some students found, however, that CPT could be integrated with the curriculum, as, for instance, in relation to Tillich's method of correlation as taught by Professor Stanley. Human need was illuminated by CPT and psychotherapy, for which the gospel provided what was needed. For those exposed to the relational psychology of Arthur Stack Sullivan and the teachings of Friede Fromm Reichmann, psychology was not another gospel but a means of understanding more deeply the Christian gospel, the church, and the ordained ministry. Some did not make the fairly obvious connections, did not fully appreciate Reuel Howe's efforts at correlating his teaching with that of systematic theology and liturgics. His methods were sharply different from those of most of his colleagues. They relied on lectures; he preferred a teaching method that brought students to discover the activity of the gospel in contemporary life situations and in relation to the Bible and the Prayer Book.

By the time Jesse Trotter became dean in 1957, Reuel Howe was gone and pastoral theology was no longer in a position to command the attention it had under Howe. John Soleau provided continuity in a changing scene. Barton M. Lloyd left in 1956, and the Reverend William Frank succeeded him. Frank left in 1960 to study medicine and become a practicing psychiatrist. Philip Smith joined the department in 1959 and remained in it after becoming chaplain of the seminary in 1962. Bart Lloyd returned in 1960 and remained until 1968, when he left to prepare for a ministry as a career development counselor for clergy. John Soleau served as chairman of the department from 1958 until he left in 1964 to work with the Church Society for College Work. The departure of Soleau opened the way for a major appointment in pastoral theology and another change in direction.

The annual end-of-the-year faculty conference at Millwood, Virginia, on May 1 and 2, 1964, brought discussion of a pastoral theology department memo that indicated that the department was not as psychologically oriented as it had been, that the new teacher need not have an articulated theology but rather be sensitive to theological issues, and that the dean expected the new man to be brought in as head of the department. In the discussion some voiced the opinion that the pastoral theology department had altogether too many teaching hours in the curriculum. It was suggested that some hours be taken from that department to be used for an enlarged teaching of social ethics. Names were mentioned for the major appointment, including Henry Rightor, a parish priest trained as a lawyer, and Thom Blair, another parish priest. But no decision was made.[65] On May 20 the pastoral theology department asked that Henry Rightor be chosen, but Dean Trotter urged patience.[66]

By February 1965 the faculty was ready for an appointment to be made. Three persons were considered: Thom Blair, John Burt, and Henry Rightor, none of them "professional" pastoral theologians, all of them successful parish priests. The pastoral theology department made known that it preferred Rightor, but by a slim margin the faculty nominated Blair to the board.[67] The board approved in March, but Blair declined, citing his wife's poor health. On May 14–15, at another annual year-end meeting of the faculty, after many considerations, Charles P. Price was nominated to be James Maxwell Professor of Pastoral Theology.[68] Price had been a member of the theology department before leaving for Harvard, where he was Preacher to the University and Plummer Professor of Morals. He was a theologian of great strength.

Price declined, and on September 15, 1965, the faculty discussed other possibilities, including Charles Jaekle, Richard Baker, Loren Mead, and Reid Isaac. Rightor was mentioned, but the dean expressed misgivings. It was reported that the board would not elect him. In time the opposition was worn down, and Rightor was nominated and elected to be an associate professor of pastoral theology but not head of the department.[69] When the dust settled, the department was seen to be composed of Barton Lloyd, Marion Kelleran, Henry Rightor, and Philip Smith, the chaplain.

In this exhausting process issues were raised about the relations between dean and faculty and among dean and board and faculty. Proposed new bylaws were drawn up to clarify such relationships. Following Henry Rightor's election, the board determined that the dean, after consultation with the faculty, should recommend new faculty to the board committee on faculty and theological education. This committee would then make nominations to the board. Some faculty members were known to disagree with this new procedure. The bylaws, agreed to in the faculty meeting of March 31, 1965, indicated that the process should begin with and be controlled by a faculty committee on nominations, which should confer with the dean, and that the faculty as a whole, hearing the committee's report, should nominate to the board committee on faculty and theological education (i.e., curriculum). The board's action was intended to further strengthen the dean's position in relation to faculty and board.

6. THE TROTTER FACULTY, 1956–1969

During Jesse Trotter's term as dean (1956–69) both faculty and curriculum were enlarged and strengthened. At the board meeting at which Trotter was elected dean, Charles Price was elected assistant professor of theology.[70] Price, born in Pennsylvania in 1920, was educated at Harvard and Virginia Seminary, from which he graduated in 1949. He earned a Th.D. degree from Union Theological Seminary, New York, in 1962, writing a distinguished thesis, "Remembering and Forgetting in the Old Testament and its Bearing on the Early Christian Eucharist," indicating his serious interest in biblical studies, liturgics, and theology. He came to the seminary to teach after five years of parish experience and two years of graduate study and soon proved to be an invaluable assistant to Professor Stanley, whom he admired and understood. As we have noted, he left the seminary in 1963 for Harvard, having won a reputation as an excellent preacher. There at his old university he labored as a mediator and peacemaker in a time of great trial. He returned to the seminary in 1972 as William Meade Professor of Systematic Theology and taught theology and liturgics until his retirement in 1989. His arrival on the faculty in 1956 was a major event.

With the death of Zabriskie in 1956 and the departure of Heim and of Clebsch, the church history department was in need of restaffing. The

"Packard Laird" Library

The New Library, now "Bishop Payne Library"

faculty and then the board chose the Reverend Cyril Richardson, then teaching at Union Theological Seminary, New York, to be a full professor and the head of the department. Richardson declined, and two young men, who were not under consideration for the department, were given temporary charge of teaching church history. The first was Allen Green, who was made instructor for a two-year period and went to Mexico in 1958. The second was Frank E. Sugeno, a graduate student at the University of Chicago who was to become the professor of church history at the Episcopal Theological Seminary of the Southwest.[71]

In October 1957 the faculty curriculum committee recommended hiring the Reverend John E. Booty and the Reverend John F. Woolverton as assistant professors in the church history department, Booty to teach the history survey and English church history and Woolverton to teach American church history.[72] Both Booty and Woolverton were graduates of the seminary in the class of 1953 and were engaged in graduate study. They had limited parish experience, Booty in Michigan and Woolverton in Texas. They were elected by the board, and both accepted to begin teaching the fall semester of 1958. Booty, born in 1925, had graduated from Wayne University (B.A.), studied at Princeton University (Ph.D. 1960), and at the University of London, producing a dissertation on John Jewel, which was published in 1963. In that year, when Price left for Harvard, Booty began to teach liturgics also, doing so until he left in 1967 to become professor of church history at the Episcopal Theological School in Cambridge, Massachusetts.

Woolverton, born in 1926, studied at Harvard (B.A.) and at Union Theological Seminary, New York, and was awarded a Ph.D. by Columbia University in 1963. He was to teach church history at Virginia Seminary until 1983 when he returned to the parish ministry. Distinguished editor of the Historical Magazine of the Episcopal Church (now Anglican and Episcopal History) from 1978, he is the author of the definitive history Colonial Anglicanism, (1984), a model for future histories of the church.

When Booty left in 1967, the Reverend C. FitzSimons Allison of the class of 1952 came from Sewanee to succeed him. Born in 1927, Allison graduated from the University of the South (B.A.) and earned his doctorate at Oxford University in 1956. In the same year he returned to the University of the South as associate professor of church history in the School of Theology. While at Sewanee his book The Rise of Moralism: The Proclamation of the Gospel from Hooker to Baxter (1966) was published, in which he revealed his strong conviction of the importance of the Reformation doctrine of justification by faith alone. That doctrine was to be central in all of his teaching at Virginia and subsequently at Grace Church, New York, as rector and in the Diocese of South Carolina, where he was bishop from 1980 to 1990.

"The Trotter Faculty"
First Row: (*l to r*) Lowell Beveridge; Holt Graham; Clifford Stanley; J.Q. Beckwith;
Jesse Trotter, Dean; A.T. Mollegen; Robert Kevin; Murray Newman
Second Row: Hudnall Harvey, Frank Pisani, Bart Lloyd, Marian Kelleran,
Philip Smith, John Booty, W. Russell Bowie
Third Row: John Woolverton, John Rodgers, J.H. Goodwin, Dick Reid,
Tom Heath, Benton T. Boogher

It was expected, at first, that Booty and Woolverton, in addition to church history, would teach "baby Greek." But before this could be effected, the Reverend Richard Reid was elected assistant professor of New Testament with responsibility to teach introductory Greek. Reid joined a strong New Testament department including A.T. Mollegen and Holt Graham. Born in 1928, a native of Rhode Island, Reid was educated at Harvard (B.A., M.A.) and the Episcopal Theological School (B.D.). He gained his Th.D. from Union Theological Seminary, New York, in 1964, writing a thesis on the Epistle to the Hebrews. A meticulous student, scholar, and teacher, who was trained in the classics, Reid became a full professor of New Testament in 1968 and early demonstrated an interest in and talent for academic administration. He served as secretary of the faculty and, from 1969 to 1982, as associate dean for academic affairs. In 1982 he was elected dean and president of the Virginia Theological Seminary, a position he held until his retirement in 1994.

As previously noted, the Reverend Philip A. Smith joined the faculty as assistant professor of pastoral theology in 1959. Born in 1920, a native of Massachusetts, Smith was educated at Harvard (B.A.) and Virginia Seminary (B.D.). Formerly assistant to the Reverend Matthew Warren at All Saints' Church, Atlanta (1949–51), and rector of Christ Church, Exeter, New Hampshire (1952–59), Smith was chaplain of the seminary and associate dean for student affairs until he was elected Suffragan Bishop of Virginia in 1970. In 1973 he became the Bishop of New Hampshire, from which position he retired in 1986. A skilled pastor and friend to faculty and students alike, Smith was a consistent and valuable aid to Dean Trotter and has been to fellow bishops and others since his retirement.

At their meeting on June 1, 1955, the trustees decided to separate homiletics from pastoral theology, making it a department under the Reverend John Q. Beckwith, Jr.[73] In 1963, during Trotter's tenure as dean, the department was expanded with the hiring of W. Thomas Heath, who had been rector of Immanuel-on-the-Hill. He was brought in as visiting professor of homiletics and remained until the Reverend Milton Crum, chaplain at Clemson University, was elected assistant professor of homiletics and began teaching in 1966.[74] There were then two full-time members of the department, making it one of the strongest such departments in any of the church's seminaries. Beckwith was especially valued for the ways in which he examined the students' preaching for theological understanding and thus provided an important means for integration of their theological learning with the practice of preaching.

When Charles Price left for Harvard in 1963, the Reverend John Hewitt Rodgers, Jr., was elected assistant professor of theology.[75] Born in 1930, Rodgers was educated at the Naval Academy (B.S.) and Virginia Seminary (B.D.). He earned a Th.D. from the University of Basel, writing a thesis on P.T. Forsyth, subsequently published. A theologian who drew inspiration from the Reformed tradition in theology, Rodgers brought a distinct Evangelical emphasis to his teaching, including a biblically oriented piety. He continued at the seminary until 1976, teaching theology and serving as chaplain and associate dean of student affairs along the way. He left to join the newly founded Trinity Episcopal School for Ministry, of which he was dean and president from 1978 to 1990. Rodgers brought a perspective different from that of Tillich and Stanley, a harbinger of things to come.

Lastly, Dean Trotter, who was constantly looking for fresh talent to enrich the faculty, early on determined that the Reverend John Caldwell Fletcher, born in 1931, of the class of 1956, was someone worth cultivating. He encouraged Fletcher to pursue graduate studies and succeeded in having the board of trustees establish "trustee fellowships," awarding the first to Fletcher.[76] Fletcher enrolled in Union Theological Seminary, New York, and was granted a Ph.D. in 1969. He was considered as a possible member of the pastoral theology department and possible director of postordination training, but both suggestions were rejected. In 1965 he was elected assistant professor of Christian sociology, to establish a department of church and society.[77] Fletcher left the seminary in 1971, having already been instrumental in establishing in Washington, D.C., a new, practice-based institution for theological education, Inter-Met, of which he was the president. Fletcher was, as we shall see, a controversial figure not readily assimilated into the seminary faculty. That he was a challenging academician is evident from his translation of Dietrich Bonhoeffer's *Creation and Fall* and from his subsequent published works, especially in the field of bioethics.

7. WRESTLING WITH THEOLOGICAL EDUCATION: THE CURRICULUM

The changing and expanding faculty and the increasing expectations of the church toward its seminaries necessitated curricular revisions. At the same time serious questions were being raised throughout the church concerning the purpose of theological education and the adequacy of the seminaries in providing such education. At Virginia Seminary there was a constant concern over hours—the course hours required for graduation and the numbers of course hours allotted to each department. In 1956–57 an attempt was made to increase the number and hours of courses each student was to take in each semester while increasing the number of electives offered and taken. All departments were meant to surrender hours in order to make the changes possible. In the midst of this discussion the departments were asked to estimate the minimum number of hours required and the distribution of courses for a seminary of 216 men (arranged in three "colleges"). The result was a determination to maintain the basic curriculum, adjusting hours as needed, arriving at a basic 15 hours per semester. The most dramatic change came with the provision of several elective courses. The seniors now had two electives, with special courses designated as such. These ranged from advanced Hebrew to cultural and religious problems in the South.

In 1960–61 a further revision was sought. Several younger members of the faculty began meeting on Saturday mornings to discuss the curriculum. These discussions, conducted apart from the whole faculty, aroused the op-

Murray Newman in the Classroom

position of the dean and spurred further discussion in the faculty as a whole.[78] The revised curriculum proposed by the junior faculty provided for an average of fifteen course hours per semester and an increase in the number of electives. Specifically, they suggested two electives each semester of the middle year, one the first semester of the senior year, and three in the second. In the revised curriculum adopted there were to be one elective each semester of the middle year, one the first semester of the senior year, and two the second. In time students able to do so were permitted an additional elective each semester, with an increase in the number of course hours. This provided for more elective offerings over all. In theology, for example, courses were made available on advanced problems in systematic theology, on the doctrine of scripture and sacrament, on the thought of St. Augustine, and on the thought of Søren Kierkegaard. After John Rodgers arrived, electives were offered on the theology of Martin Luther and on the word of God in the theology of Karl Barth.[79]

Most innovative was the introduction of a five-week intensive term, chiefly in January, which first appeared in the junior faculty proposal and then in the curriculum recommended by the dean. The intensive term was designed to allow students to concentrate on one subject for a significant period of time. It was meant to be integrative. All faculty were to be participating, assisting in teaching subjects not in their own departments, except for the leader, or primary teacher of the course. Thus juniors would study a theologian, for instance P.T. Forsyth (with Rodgers as primary teacher), or in other years would study O.C. Quick or Emil Brunner. The theologian studied was meant to be one who in several books touched in one way or another on all of the theological disciplines. Middlers would study biblical theology, concentrating on biblical scholars such as Gerhard von Rad and Rudolf Bultmann and their theologies. Seniors would study parish administration with the help of experienced clergy as visiting lecturers. This was not exactly the sort of course that the junior faculty had in mind; but with sufficient room for reflection, it could have been. This was the ideal, but as finally put into effect, the juniors continued their study of Greek, the middlers had a course on missions (taught by Ken Heim), and the seniors had a course on the conduct of public worship, in addition to the basic courses.

In the midst of all this the board committee on faculty and curriculum affirmed "the traditional stand of the Board, that the primary function of this Seminary is to prepare men for the Parochial ministry. Since this is the primary aim of the curriculum, and since it must be assumed that the men coming have had little or no previous theological training, therefore, the basic disciplines must be stressed. It is the definite conviction of this committee, therefore, as a matter of basic policy, that the curriculum should allow for a minimum number of electives, so that in the time available the fundamental and basic courses may better be taught."[80] Thus did board members seek to restrain the enthusiasm of young, highly educated, professional teachers of theology, forcing them to face reality as the board members perceived reality.

One way in which the faculty sought to deal with reality was by instituting, at the dean's suggestion, an "old men's program" designed for those over forty years of age to spend one year on basic studies, exclusive of pastoral theology.[81] Proposed in 1961, the program began that year with five men and was abandoned the next year when only one man applied.[82] The experiment highlighted a problem. With more specialized academics teaching, the demands upon the students tended to grow; while at the same time the average age of seminarians increased, bringing to the seminary men who were ill prepared for the kind of teaching they would receive.

The next revision began in the midst of a general ferment of ideas; criticisms of the middle term, a discussion by the seminary deans of the "crisis in the parish ministry," awareness of a study underway evaluating seminary education and eventuating in the Pusey-Taylor report and in the founding of the national Board for Theological Education. In addition there was turmoil in American society—the civil rights movement and much else. There was serious concern that students were graduating with knowledge of critical problems in theology but insufficient integration of that knowledge with knowledge of contemporary society, bringing to the parishes unusable resources.[83]

The challenge was recognized by Holt Graham in an explanation of the curriculum printed for several years in the catalogue. Citing two approaches, one focused on content with little freedom and the other focused on personal appropriation "in proportion to what the individual is capable of receiving," Graham said,

> At Virginia, the emphasis tends to fall in the direction of the second alternative. It is a good school for the fully committed and the relatively mature; it is a dangerous school for the relatively immature. The emphasis falls heavily upon the personal appropriation of the Christian faith, and this means inside of class and out the struggle of incessant challenge, questioning, testing. . . . And so, while maximizing freedom to the end of personal appropriation, the seminary has designed a particular course of study that provides a structure that encourages movement toward that end.[84]

That was one viewpoint, reflecting in part the thesis that for the student the first year was purgative (clearing away the clutter of false ideas), the second nurturing (supplying basic information), and the third integrative (appropriating knowledge in an integrative way). This was, of course, debatable both as policy and in terms of what was actually happening. There were those on the faculty who wanted instead greater freedom, reduction in hours allotted to core courses, and an increase in hours for electives.

The discussion proceeded, prompted by proposals for a national study that asked basic questions such as "Who is the ordained man; what is his nature and function in our society?" "What sort of education is required?" "What is the optimum organization for achieving the desired ends?" The faculty curriculum committee began lengthy and serious discussions concerning the number and size and location of seminaries needed by the church.[85] In a meeting held on April 9, 1965, at the dean's vacation house in Annapolis, the committee questioned the idea that personal appropriation was involved in the curriculum as then constructed, questioned the traditional divisions of the theological curriculum, and discussed the best method (lecture or seminar) of teaching. The committee met with Professor William Wolf to discuss the Episcopal Theological School curriculum; talked about the experiment well underway at the Episcopal Theological Seminary of the Southwest; hired Philip Phenix of the Teacher's College, Columbia University, as consultant; and met with the rest of the faculty to confer with Dr. Randall Robertson of the National Science Foundation and with Charles Taylor of the American Association of Theological Schools. With the encouragement of Dean Trotter the committee produced for consideration of the faculty at their annual conference, May 13–14, 1966, a document called "Premises of Theological Education" with three curriculum proposals; one the current curriculum; another with two semesters and a middle term; and the third, submitted by John Booty of the committee, a tri-semester or three quarters curriculum.[86]

The document, "Premises of Theological Education," began with a theological statement concerning the church and its mission on the basis of the conviction that "the goal of theological education in the seminary is to raise up leader-servants for the ministry of the Church in the world." The focus was on the "Lord who gives . . . life" to the people of God in all of the areas of their existence. The focus also was on the people of God "gathered locally—in parishes and elsewhere." The seminary "seeks to educate men to serve this people in their mission [which is God's mission centered on the meaning and power of the cross] to the world." As such it conceives of the graduate of the seminary as serving . . . in various ways. . . . His is an inclusive ministry—that is, to lead in worship, teaching, and common life" enabling people "to be worshipers, teachers, and pastors." In part this reflected Philip Phenix's emphasis on the minister as the one remaining generalist in the community divided by special interests, training, and education. As a generalist, the graduate needs to be a person who knows "how to relate the content of the faith to contemporary thought-forms and concerns."[87] These, in part, were the concerns of those working on the curriculum. In addition and more specifically, they were concerned for integration in the faculty as well as in students and in a greater sense of theology as an unified discipline. They wanted to see a field education program rooted in theology, helping to bridge the theory/practice gap. And they wanted more flexibility, more concentrated core courses, and more elective possibilities.

The resulting curriculum emphasized maximum flexibility and freedom for experimentation and exploration of new ideas over a curriculum with a fixed structure based upon a high degree of unanimity concerning theological education. There were three quarters per year with four courses each for a total of twelve hours per quarter and thirty-six hours per year. The junior year was heavily biblical; the middle year was dominated by church history but had some pastoral theology and included liturgics and ethics. The senior year was dominated by systematic theology and pastoral theology, with homiletics. Supervised field education was required throughout the middle and senior years and was graded as other courses, with credit hours necessary for successful completion of the theology course. There were electives: five in the junior year, six in the middle year, and eight in the senior year.

The original design also called for comprehensive examinations in the final quarter of the senior year.[88] The curriculum was adopted by the faculty on January 25, 1967, and the board formally approved it on May 24.[89] With the beginning of the new curriculum in September 1967, the criticism of it also began, aiming inevitably toward further revision.

A major concern of the faculty was the added amount of work required of them. The students varied widely in their opinions. A major complaint of the senior students was that the new curriculum seemed not to meet their expectations for community. One student spoke of "fragmentation under the new Curriculum with what he considered no discernible structure" and a consequent loss of a sense of belonging. That is to say, a class was no longer as much an identifiable entity as it had been when all members of one class were taking the same courses together, with some exceptions.[90] The faculty later discussed this at length. They were critical of the desire for community in terms of security and intellectual certainty on a superficial level. "Dr. Mollegen felt that students wanted certainty in terms of a closed system but we can only give them living symbols."[91] On the other hand, some students were excited about the new curriculum. One senior "expressed gratitude for the New Curriculum because he felt that it made the students more responsible for their education. He hoped that the Faculty would not allow willy-nilly selection of electives but would require the students to plan their whole three-year programs when they enter."[92]

8. THE SECOND CENTURY FUND: NEW VENTURES

While the curriculum change was happening, the Second Century Fund was growing. The driving force behind this was Dean Trotter, with the full support of the board. The campaign for $5,000,000—later reduced to $2,500,000 and then gradually increased to $7,600,000—was discussed in 1961.[93] It was quietly begun in 1962 with the choice of the Reverend Frank Pisani, rector of the Church of the Holy Comforter, Tallahassee, Florida, to direct it.[94] The study (by the firm of Cresap, McCormick, and Paget) of the seminary and its needs was summarized in a report to the board in May 1964 indicating the immediate need of improved classroom facilities and improved, as well as additional, faculty offices. The possibility of razing Aspinwall, Meade, Bohlen, and Key halls was discussed, replacing them with new buildings. In addition a new postordination training program and a physical fitness program for students and faculty were considered. Ketchum, Incorporated, was employed to assist in fund raising.[95] As a result, a goal of $4,750,000 was established: $2,000,000 in capital funds, $1,200,000 to endow scholarship aid, $1,000,000 to endow faculty and library staff salaries,

Worship in the Chapel

$500,000 for postordination training, and $50,000 for a physical fitness program.[96] By September 10, 1964, the first million was in, and Faulkner, Kingsbury, and Stenhouse were hired to develop plans and supervise building.[97] Construction of a new classroom building was discussed, but finally the board decided to renovate the old buildings. This was begun in 1964, and in 1965 construction of six new faculty houses was authorized.[98] All of this was done before the campaign officially began.

The campaign was officially launched at a luncheon at the seminary on December 13, 1965. It was provided with outstanding leadership, including the presiding bishop, John Hines, Stuart Saunders of the Pennsylvania Railroad, Keith Funsten of the New York Stock Exchange, and many others.[99] At the same time the Reverend Bennett Sims, rector of Christ Church, Corning, New York, was creating a center for continuing education, meeting with experts,[100] developing policy and curriculum, and planning a continuing education building to be built with funds from the Booth-Ferris Foundation. His program was underwritten by a gift of $500,000 in Gulf Oil stock from the Mellon family.[101] This then became a major focus of the campaign. By February 2, 1966, $2,250,000 had been received, and Sims was made associate dean for continuing education.[102]

The Morse report had noted the lack in the seminary of a fully developed field education program, and the faculty began to plan for such a program as a part of the curriculum. There was serious talk of a Master of Arts in Religion program for the education of the laity, as well as a school for lay education. In December 1966 the end of the campaign was in sight, and a decision was made to raise an additional $2,000,000.[103] The physical fitness program was now focused on the building of a recreation center named for A.T. Mollegen, in whose honor the needed money had been given. The board authorized the gift of $100,000 out of the campaign funds for St. George's College, Jerusalem. When an estate at The Plains, Virginia—Friendship Farm—was given to the seminary, a center for lay education using that property was seriously considered. In the spring of 1967, $6,000,000 was in, the cost of raising that sum being a modest 2.5 percent.[104] The distribution of the expanded funds was made then, with $500,000 for Friendship Farm, $500,000 for the program there, and $200,000 to prepare the farm for use. The board designated $300,000 to endow a chair in field education and $500,000 for the field education program; $200,000 was apportioned to the new M.A.R. degree program and $291,000 for the expansion of the library.[105]

On October 9, 1968, a closing dinner celebrated the end of the campaign. By then about $7,800,000 had been raised.[106] The campaign over, Dean Trotter submitted his resignation on November 13, 1968, and was elected to a full professorship in the faculty. On March 10, 1969, Frank Pisani resigned to become president of St. Mary's College, Raleigh, North Carolina.[107] The Second Century Fund campaign and all that it did to increase endowment, renovate old buildings, construct new ones, and enrich the capabilities of the seminary for service to the church and the world constitutes a major historical event in the life of the seminary.

The stimulus provided would help to see the institution through difficult times ahead. Of great significance was the founding of the Center for Continuing Education. As early as 1965 it was envisioned as an "auxiliary enterprise,"[108] and in 1967 it was seen as separate from the B.D., S.T.M., and M.A.R. degree programs—"a parallel enterprise."[109] Bennett Sims viewed it as related to the board through his position as associate dean, responsible to the dean, and through the dean to the board. The seminary faculty per se would have no control over it. Furthermore, as originally planned the center would run a flexible, ecumenical, action/reflection program with a six-week conference on campus, a project in the parish from which the participant came, and a final session at the seminary. The center became a model for similar institutions elsewhere. It constitutes one of the major achievements of Dean Trotter's deanship and owes much to the skill and dedication of Bennett Sims.

Bishop Payne Divinity School
Class of 1925

9. THE ADVENT OF AFRO-AMERICAN
AND OF WOMEN STUDENTS

The 1950s and 1960s presented challenges to the seminary and to the culture at large. As late as 1945 the seminary board of trustees was not committed to the realization of racial equality in the institution for which they were responsible. In that year the question of Bishop Payne students attending Reinicker lectures was put before the board, which, realizing that the students would have to stay overnight, put off making a decision.[110] By 1947 the Bishop Payne School board was considering merger or dissolution. In 1949 the Virginia board considered admission of "Negro students" as a result of pressure from its own planning committee, alumni, and some seminary faculty. Care was taken to have the Bishop Payne School agree and possibly to send its one remaining student to Virginia Seminary.[111] By then Dean Zabriskie was actively seeking a black student well qualified for admission. Dr. Robert O. Kevin was in touch with the dean of the divinity school at Howard University in Washington, who had a student desirous of attending Old Testament lectures. The board agreed to this. But in another case a student about to be awarded a B.A. degree at Howard wanted to enroll as a full-time, nonresident student at

Bishop John T. Walker with past-Chairman of the Board, David Rose

the seminary. It was argued that there was uncertainty as to the number of future applications from the Episcopal Church; since the student in question was not an Episcopalian, his application was refused.[112]

At its meeting on November 8, 1950, the dean and the admissions committee having located the ideal candidate in John Thomas Walker of Detroit, Michigan, a postulant in the Diocese of Michigan about to be awarded a B.A. degree by Wayne University, the board formally agreed to admit a resident Negro student.[113] The faith placed in Walker was justified by subsequent events, as he went into the parish ministry, then secondary school education, to a canonry at the cathedral in Washington, and to suffragan bishop and then revered Diocesan Bishop of Washington. He was one of the outstanding graduates of the seminary, served on its board, and in 1969 was elected associate dean for student affairs, an election he declined. With the admission of John Walker the color barrier was broken, other Afro-American students followed, including outstanding churchmen such as Warner Traynham and Lloyd Casson. Relations with Howard University were strengthened with Dr. Kevin's active encouragement. In 1951 Dr. Leon Wright of the Howard Divinity School faculty was hired as a part-time lecturer in Greek.[114] Other part-time black faculty were Henry Mitchell and Carleton Hayden. The first full-time

Afro-American member of the faculty was Lloyd Alexander Lewis, who was named assistant professor of New Testament in 1978. It was one thing to break the color barrier; it was another to recruit black students. In 1958 the Reverend Isaiah Bell was hired to assist in recruitment. In 1959 he was followed by the Reverend Dr. John C. Davis, former faculty member of the Bishop Payne School, rector of Meade Memorial Church, Alexandria.[115] Single students were housed in seminary dormitories. However, in an area where segregation was still a reality, married black students, if they brought their families, had to find housing in the Alexandria area where Afro-Americans were allowed to live. There were still many obstacles to be faced, but the cause was furthered as the Bishop Payne Divinity School merged with the Virginia Seminary, bringing with it the funds to support black students and to help prepare them for admission when that was needed. The fund for this purpose amounted to approximately $280,000.[116]

In 1949 when the Bishop Payne School had closed, the Reverend Robert Gibson of that faculty had been brought to Virginia Seminary to teach Bible, as noted earlier. To signify the merger with the Bishop Payne School, the Virginia Seminary library eventually was named the Bishop Payne Library. The desegregation of the Virginia Theological Seminary had proceeded with some difficulties but without the upheaval experienced by the School of Theology of the University of the South.

Not that the issue of racism in the seminary then was laid to rest. It wasn't. The institution had to respond to the criticisms of some and to deal with its own still apparent racism. The drama of the 1963 March on Washington and the march from Selma to Montgomery had reverberations on the seminary campus. The faculty shared the grief experienced by the Episcopal Theological School at the death in Alabama of seminarian Jonathan Daniels.[117] In August 1963 John Booty, representing Dean Trotter and the faculty, led a small seminary contingent in the March on Washington. John Morris of the class of 1954 led the Episcopal Society for the Creation of Racial Unity (ESCRU) from 1960 to 1967. A workshop on racial conflict and justice was led by Cornelius Tarplee at the seminary in 1968.[118] John Walker urged the seminary board to support the Southern Christian Leadership Conference (SCLC).[119] During the Poor People's Campaign of the summer of 1968, two of the seminary dormitories were used to house a few of those coming to the nation's capitol.[120]

Not all at the seminary were supportive of the civil rights movement. There were those critical of the church's endorsement of Martin Luther King, Jr. There were those critical of Presiding Bishop John Hines and of the Virginia alumni who sought to empower the powerless black people of the decaying American inner cities. One staff member wanted to have a white supremacist at the workshop on racial conflict and justice but was denied his request by a vote of six to seven. The tension over this, inspired by the civil rights movement, the Black Manifesto, the special program of General Convention, and much else was to reach a critical point in 1970 during Dean Woods' tenure.

Regarding the advent of women on campus, as late as 1951 the faculty was only considering whether to admit student wives to Thursday evening community faculty meetings. They voted to allow them to attend for the rest of the year.[121] By 1960 the faculty was providing informal courses for wives.[122] Also by then women students were receiving instruction.

In 1956, after announcing his resignation, Dean Kloman had asked if the seminary should be open to women students. The response had been that the place would be more pleasant if they were admitted but that the matter was too much to decide at that time.[123] Marian Smollegen was the first full-time woman student at the seminary but was not seeking a degree nor ordination and was treated as a special case.[124] Such exceptions were encouraged, while board and faculty continued to consider formal admission of women to the B.D. degree program. Indeed, Phyllis Ingram began studying as an exception to the rule.

In the process, Marian Kelleran, as an adjunct and then full-time member of the faculty, was influential in admitting women to the seminary. She was active in the Women's Caucus, working for the ordination of women to the priesthood and to the episcopate. Although not seeking ordination for herself, she wrote, "I ache for the women seeking ordination when I see what they have to go through. I am willing to take a strong stand with them in this right—and I believe it is a right—to be ordained."

The problem as perceived by many was that the B.D. program was for those on their way to ordination and at that time women could not be ordained. In 1965 the faculty recommended and the board agreed to admit women students. The rule was to be that as many as five could be admitted in

Marian Kelleran

any given year, not detracting from the sixty-five men then admitted yearly.[125] In 1966 Phyllis Ingram graduated cum laude.[126] She then requested the faculty's recommendation for ordination. On March 16, 1966, the faculty, by a split vote, moved to certify her suitability for ordination if in the future she were to be accepted as a postulant. In October of that year the faculty passed a motion saying, "We declare that we see no theological objection to women in the ordained ministry of the church and that we look to a time in the near future when women shall be ordained."[127] The vote was fifteen to three, with three abstentions.

On October 1, 1967, Phyllis Ingram was ordained in the Congregational Church.[128] The second B.D. woman student, Allison Cheek, waited on the church's action for some time, meanwhile teaching Greek and Hebrew part-time at the seminary.[129] Along with Nancy Hatch Wittig, Mrs. Cheek was one of those irregularly ordained in Philadelphia in 1974. The number of women enrolled in the seminary remained relatively low for some years. Gradually they increased from seven in 1977 to about sixty in 1989–90 in both B.D. and M.T.S. degree programs. Women on the faculty and staff gradually increased also. A major addition was that of Marianne Micks as professor of theology in 1974.

10. ECUMENICAL INVOLVEMENT

The events of the 1950s and 1960s–and especially the civil rights movement and all that it involved–drove the seminaries to pay attention to society in general and to the city in particular in order to prepare pastors to minister in urban America. In part this was viewed as a counterbalance to the emphasis on psychology that was so strong at the seminary in the 1950s. The drive was motivated also by the development of research by the American Association of Theological Schools aimed at publication of a report, "Theological Education for the 1970s." This research stressed the critical importance of an ecumenical setting such as that at the Urban Training Center in Chicago, led from 1964 to 1972 by J.P. Morton. In Washington, D.C., an Urban Training Program was developed, providing opportunities for field work in urban settings. The program, in which the Episcopal Diocese of Washington was heavily involved, was ecumenical and for a time was based at the parish of St. Stephen and the Incarnation. The course was related to one on the city taught by Charles Ellett. In 1966 the seminary had a quota of six middlers and six seniors in the program.[130]

With the advent of John Fletcher as assistant professor of church and society, the seminary began participation in the Institute for Policy Studies, which in turn assisted in the planning of the Interseminary Program in Church and Society, a field program focused in part on government, including work in congressional offices.[131] Virginia Seminary was a charter member of this interseminary program, founded in 1967, along with Union Seminary (Richmond) and Duke University Divinity School. The numbers involved were never large. In May 1968 it was reported that twelve Virginia students were enrolled for the next academic year in the Urban Training Program and five in the Interseminary Program. But the interest of those involved was great and had its effect upon the seminary, if in no other way than in taking students off campus into the city and into the federal government for education that was in numerous ways relevant to the seminary course of study.

When Gordon Charlton arrived at the seminary, he became another strong advocate for such programs. Charlton, as field education director, was also a member of the church and society department, where he offered an elective called "Orientation to the Metropolitan Community." One major outcome of all this was that some members of the Washington Urban Training Program board and staff ventured upon a full scale experiment in an alternative form of theological education that they named Inter-Met. When Fletcher left the seminary, it was to become president of InterMet from 1970 to 1977.

At the same time the seminaries of the Washington area were seeking new ways of cooperation. For some years the faculties of Virginia Seminary, the Divinity School of Howard University, and Wesley Seminary had met occasionally. In 1966 the board granted permission to the faculty to admit non-Episcopalians to its B.D. course.[132] In 1967 representatives of Catholic University, Howard, Wesley, and Virginia met and arranged for an exchange of faculty on a limited basis. They agreed to have Professor Allison teach a course on the Reformation at Catholic University and for a faculty member from there to teach a course on modern Catholic theologians at Virginia.[133] Dr. Dewey Beagle of the Wesley faculty helped out after the retirement of Dr. Kevin by teaching Old Testament at Virginia.

In January 1968 Dr. James Ross, a Congregational Church clergyman, was elected professor of Old Testament, the first full-time non-Episcopalian on the faculty.[134] In May 1968 the dean reported to the board the founding of the Washington Theological Consortium, consisting of Catholic University, Howard, Wesley, Gettysburg, and Virginia.[135] In April of the same year Professor Graham reported on a meeting with representatives from "Wesley and four of the Roman Catholic houses of study: the Josephites, Dominicans, Paulists, and Oblates." These schools, along with Virginia Seminary, agreed to "allow crossregistration at each school with no additional tuition charge, unless there is an unusually heavy load of students coming from one school."[136] From this point on, largely through the subsequent formation of the Washington Theological Consortium, Virginia Seminary was committed to ecumenicity in theological education.

Thus it was that, in response to the societal and ecclesiastical challenges of the 1950s and 1960s, the seminary experienced changes that in various ways were to effect its life. The seminary would henceforth have Afro-American students and women students; it would be involved in urban America, chiefly through supervised field education; and it would be involved in a consortium of Roman Catholic and Protestant theological schools. What suffered as a result? Principally, it would seem, the strong focus on overseas missions. So prominent in the early years, the focus on missions was overshadowed by concerns affecting American society.

In addition to the decline of interest among students in overseas missions, there were other negative results. One involved a growing criticism of the seminary at the very time that it was seeking to change. John Fletcher's departure and the founding of Inter-Met were interpreted by some as a renunciation of Virginia's way of theological education. However, for some this had the effect of a reaction against Fletcher and action-based theological education through Inter-Met. Meanwhile, there were dramatic changes happening on the theological scene, to which we now turn.

11. THE KERYGMATIC/APOLOGETIC THEOLOGY OF C.L. STANLEY

Theology at Virginia Seminary in the 1950s and 1960s was dominated by Paul Tillich, under whom A.T. Mollegen and Clifford L. Stanley had studied, being among Tillich's first students at Union Theological Seminary in the 1930s. Stanley's course in systematic theology followed the main topics in Tillich's system: revelation, God, Christ, Spirit, and the Kingdom of God, using Tillich's method of correlation. Mollegen remained in contact with Tillich, who acknowledged the assistance of the Virginia theologian in shaping the first volume of the *Systematic Theology*.[137] Mollegen also helped Tillich understand his own theology. Responding to Mollegen's essay "Christology and Biblical Criticism in Tillich," the German stated that he had no need to deal with criticisms of his understanding of the historical Jesus, as "an answer by myself has been made unnecessary by the contribution of Mr. Mollegen who has presented a clear exposition of the topic of the historical Jesus." Indeed, he said, Mollegen's explication "has, I confess, a clarity which I have myself found it very difficult to achieve."[138]

Mollegen himself was perhaps more affected by Reinhold Niebuhr than by Tillich. Nevertheless, Tillich and his method of correlation made its impact on Mollegen's thought. Reuel Howe imbibed much from Tillich through Mollegen and Stanley, designing his courses and writing his book *Man's Need and God's Action* (1953) in relation to Tillich's method. In turn, Tillich had an influence on the development of a new church school curriculum, the Seabury Plan, through Howe and others. In this curriculum a teacher was to assist students in defining human needs and discovering God's answers to them.[139]

Stanley, as Charles Price has written, did not simply teach Tillich to his students, however. Stanley used "Scripture more extensively than Tillich." He rejected Tillich's "restitution theory" of the Resurrection, emphasizing the importance of the body: "The body makes it possible for others to recognize us, and for us to communicate with them." He emphasized the doctrine of the Church as Tillich did not, and he respected the laity. Price wrote of Stanley, "He is a theologian of the laos and for the laos, never forgetting that his seminary students were to teach laity." He devoted much energy to Christianity and Modern Man, a program in the "school for laity" that ran from 1946 to 1964 chiefly at Washington National Cathedral.[140] Founded, significantly, by laity and by A.T. Mollegen, Christianity and Modern Man was a forerunner of the Lay School of Theology, now so important a part of the seminary.

Of these emphases, which mark the difference between Tillich and Stanley, the most important was that of the doctrine of the Church. Speaking of this, Price says, "He developed it independently, long before the third volume of Tillich's system appeared. Stanley regards this part of his work as the center. To it all the rest leads." Price concludes, "To the celebration of the grandeur and misery of the Church, Stanley gives himself without stint. It is in many ways the most characteristic part of his work."[141]

In a volume of essays published in 1953 by members of the Frontier Fellowship and dedicated to Reinhold Niebuhr, Stanley wrote on the Church. The title, "The Church, in but not of the World," indicates a dialectic of transcendence and immanence. The dialectic informs the essay and all of Stanley's lectures on the doctrine of the Church. The analogies used to describe the Church ("body, marriage, family, nation") all express the objective truth, which is the Church, and "suggest that this truth is twofold. The Church is the name of *a relation of God and man* which is as close as that of parts of an organism, as intimate as a marriage. Secondly, there is in the Church *a kind of humanity* which is as strongly marked *as a family, as individualized* as a nation."[142]

The new relationships between God and humanity and the new humanity itself "are constituted by Justification and Sanctification." Here Stanley exhibited a strong appreciation for the teachings of the sixteenth-

A.T. Mollegen and Clifford Stanley

century Reformers and especially of Luther. With the conviction that "the problem of existence is insoluble in terms of existence" and that actuality, which is good, is maintained ("It is impossible to destroy it"), he asserted that justification means that sin is overcome, though it "remains on the moral level, remains as a fact, but its ultimate character is changed. Its fangs are drawn."[143]

The Church is humanity thus justified. The Church is also the community of sanctification, of people made holy, "caught up in the divine realm." He acknowledged that, while as sanctified "Christianity brings a new order of possibility into the world," it encounters resistance and must deal with actualities that cannot be negated without destroying actuality itself. Thus: "Just as Justification is a life of holiness in spite of the sinful facts of life, so Sanctification is a life of holiness hampered by and in some sense built upon structures that contradict it. Church life is thus dual. . . ."[144]

Stanley placed great emphasis on the dual nature of the Church. As Price states, Stanley regarded the Church, together with the Bible and the sacraments, as deserving "our utmost reverence. . . . It was the primary continuing medium of God's revelation. . . ." "On the other hand, Stanley is more than a little suspicious of Church and sacraments. . . . This negative attitude is to be explained by his abhor-

287

rence of every idolatry and pretended absolutism."[145] In his essay Stanley wrote of the duality,

> Heaven is the place, as the Lord's Prayer suggests, where God's will is done. Earth is the fallen place where God's will is not done. The two cannot be simply merged, as in mysticism and utopianism. The sinful otherness of earth is the measure of its reality. The holy otherness of heaven is a measure of its inaccessibility. Their coming together hampers heaven's spontaneous obedience, as evidence the allowances of Justification, the limited achievements of Sanctification. Their coming together destroys earth's sinful autonomy, as witness the universal cleansing of Justification, the renovating process of Sanctification.[146]

In a sense the most radical of Stanley's teachings came as extensions of the thought involved in such a description of the Church. Thus, he said, reminiscent of F.D. Maurice's dictum that Christ died for all and that thus all are in Christ, "the Church . . . includes all men. Men do not come into it, because they are in it. The possession of humanity is possession of redeemed humanity, in an age of redemption, in a redeemed world."[147] There is, it follows, to use Edward Farley's words, a "theological given" that is not dependent upon belief. Says Stanley, in a statement worthy to be put alongside Sparrow's "Seek the truth . . .," "Belief does not create that which it believes; it responds to it."[148] Again, he wrote,

> The terms *that which is believed* and *by whom it is believed* are in some sense correlative. Yet belief does not create its object and consequently *that which is believed* is independently and antecedently true. In this case, it is first true that all men are incorporated into the Church, the holy folk. From this point of view, all men are equally in the Church, God's new creation of all mankind; "Church members" are not in any more than non-Church members. No one can take anyone in or put anyone out.[149]

He was willing to admit that "in a limited sense" the Church "is confined to believers,"[150] but he is most concerned to emphasize "the object rather than the subject of faith." The liturgy and preaching, truly understood, proclaim the gospel, creating belief.

Stanley's understanding of the Church extends into his conviction that the Church involves all of "life's activities." Acts of corporate worship recall us to this reality. "In worship, the Church recognizes itself as the people of God, recognizes and rejoices in this wonderful status. In the hour of worship the Church looks at the life which in other hours it lives." He warned against that worship which is self-worship. True worship "is worship of that which grasps man, or of man as grasped by it. It is worship of the grace that enfolds man, of man enfolded by grace."[151] In worship we meet God, "God whose revelation point is the Church."[152]

At the end of his essay Stanley considered this doctrine of the Church in relation to the crises of the late 1940s and early 1950s and, in particular, to "godless communism," "group pretentiousness," such as that exhibited by the Nazis, and by utopianism. He concluded with this stirring affirmation:

> The Church is no less than mankind in redemption, the human enterprise regarded as created anew. It is a conception that is powerful for every time and therefore also for our time. The Church is "there," and all that remains is to point to it and to acknowledge the sight. Inspiring greatness and gentle tenderness meet and balance in this noble reality—the Church.[153]

This essay, which is immediately recognizable as the careful, thoughtful statement of a man of great faith, is representative of the theological work of the man who was the theologian of Virginia Seminary from 1946 to 1970. It was written in 1953 when Professor Stanley was indisputably a theologian of the Church. In 1974 at the time of A.T. Mollegen's retirement, William J. Wolf of the Episcopal Theological School gave a lecture at the seminary on the changing theological landscape during Mollegen's years, beginning in 1936. He spoke of the rise of neoorthodoxy as liberalism waned, the virtual dominance for a time of the neoorthodox in theology. Then he spoke of the challenge of the 1960s, the rise of secularism, the "God-is-dead" theologians, and the publication of Paul van Buren's *The Secular Meaning of the Gospel* (1963).

Linguistic analysis and logical positivism raised serious questions concerning the credibility of that which Stanley regarded as objective givens. Ultimate concern was shrouded in doubt and disbelief. As this occurred, alternative theological positions were emerging from post-Vatican II theologians such as Hans Küng, from process theologians spinning out of the implications inherent in Alfred North Whitehead's philosophy (Kroner and others), and from those who derived theology from the insights of modern science (Teilhard de Chardin). Langdon Gilkey in *Naming the Whirlwind* (1969) was evolving a "secular theology," and liberation theologies (Latin American, black, feminist) were reaching into the American consciousness. As might be expected in a time of theological and religious pluralism where competing theologies were claiming truth for themselves, a reaction on the right set in. The Fundamentalists were heard from anew in a new Fundamentalist theology that turned its back on the theological/cultural ferment.[154] Devotees of a burgeoning movement for charismatic renewal simply ignored the tumult, focusing their attention on religious experiences.

In the midst of this, the theological territory inhabited by Mollegen and Stanley either became a battleground or was deserted. Stanley began to feel that the theology he so carefully taught was no longer being owned by his students. Commenting on Barth and Tillich, Wolf said, "Linguistic analysis has rendered their philosophical way of putting things increasingly vulnerable in a more thoroughly secularized culture."[155] That was said in 1974. In 1993 the theology of Tillich as presented by Stanley does not seem as irrelevant as it appeared to be in 1974. Among the strong abiding features of Stanley's teaching are 1. the Tillichian method of correlation, which takes seriously but not uncritically both the human situation and this world, 2. the careful balance of theology as kerygma and theology as apologetic, 3. the sense of dialectic and the appreciation of tension that prevents simplistic absolutisms and especially those associated with "civic religion," 4. the appreciation of tradition (witness Stanley's course on the history of Christian thought) without the idolization of tradition, 5. a critical understanding of Scripture within the context of a deep and abiding joy in God's Word in and through Scripture. Stanley's students, if they were at all open to his influence, gained from him a vivid sense of joy in the Christian faith, such a joy as opened the possibility for the honest facing of questions and doubts and gained the inspiration to explore without fear of falling into the abyss. He would have his students make known this joy and its hope to those they served.

Indeed, the method of correlation had a very practical outcome. I think here of Krister Stendahl's description of the preacher as fully conversant with the biblical thought-world and also with the thought-world of the present culture, bringing the one to bear on the other.[156] And I think of Douglas John Hall's critique of Tillich's method; its presupposition of harmony, continuity, and permanence; its questionable ontology (questionable in our time); its reduction of the reality and sense of tension, "the central factor in Christian theological method" now; and its insufficient "place-consciousness."[157] But the method of correlation does bear some resemblance to Hall's "contextuality," which requires that the theologian be involved in tradition but also in contemporary events and places. Thinking of tradition, Hall writes of the theologia crucis and its insistence "that what is revealed in the suffering, death, and resurrection of Jesus Christ is God's abiding commitment to this world."[158]

Furthermore, although many persons contrast Barth and Tillich—the one as kerygmatic and the other as apologetic; Barth as conservative, Tillich as liberal—we recognize that Tillich "never lost sight of the kerygmatic dimension of the Christian message."[159] Stanley responded positively to the humanist in Tillich, perhaps as he was influenced by Professor Bell, under whom he studied at Virginia. And he took seriously the philosophic/

290

cultural contexts. But Stanley was profoundly kerygmatic. His description of worship in the Church in terms of God encountering us is likened to the position developed by Stephen Sykes and others—fundamental faith arising in the context of Scripture and liturgy together, the telling of the salvific story, the doing of the sacred drama, which forms and reforms us in faith as fragile humans.

Which way would theology go after Stanley? What combination of kerygmatic and apologetic would develop? Changes there would be. The theology of the 1970s and 1980s as taught at Virginia would reflect the likenesses and differences of the several people who taught it. No longer would there be *a* theologian. Stanley was the last. Theology was to be more kerygmatic with Rodgers and Scott, more Anglican with Price and Hancock. And there would be a woman (Micks) and a black (Eversley) with their particular personal, social, and intellectual interests. The old course on world religions was gone. A specific course in apologetics disappeared with the retirement of Trotter. The big course on the history of Christian doctrine faded away. In their places church history dealt more with doctrine than it had, including seminars on Augustine, Calvin, Luther, and Hooker. The apologetic task was shared, and there was to be a department of Christian ethics and contemporary society. In place of a world religions course, there was to be a department of mission and world religions. A rich curriculum carried on the old traditions in new ways. The teaching in time would reflect more vividly the pluralism so dominant in theology at the end of the twentieth century.

NOTES

1. David Halberstam, *The Next Century* (New York: William Mor row, 1991), 16, 52–53, 57 and elsewhere.
2. Ahlstrom, *Religious History*, 952.
3. Ibid., 952–953.
4. David E. Sumner, *The Episcopal Church's History, 1945–1985* (Wilton, Conn.: Morehouse, 1987), 161.
5. Booty, *Crisis*, 54.
6. Huntington, *American Politics*, 169–77.
7. Booty, *Crisis*, 60–61.
8. Ahlstrom, *Religious History*, 967.
9. Charles R. Feilding, *Education for Ministry* (Dayton, Ohio: AATS, 1966), 10.
10. *Ministry for Tomorrow, Report of the Special Committee on Theological Education* (New York: Seabury, 1967), 128.
11. See Robert W. Prichard, "Virginia Seminary Since World War II," *Seminary Journal*, 37/1 (June 1985): 33.

12. Bd. min., 1939–53, (April 4, 1949), 157. The enrollment figures reported here are mostly derived from board and faculty minutes.

13. Report of dean to board (November 12, 1952) in fac. min. folder no. 5.

14. Bd. min., 1939–53, 80.

15. Ibid., 95.

16. Ibid., 116–17.

17. Ibid., 124 (February 5, 1947).

18. Ibid., 132 (June 4, 1947).

19. Fac. min., 1934–47, 242–43. Others considered at this time for the theology chair were F.W. Dillistone, T.O. Wedel, and Charles Lowry himself. The faculty was in favor of Dillistone and divided over Stanley, Lowry, and Wedel at a meeting on November 8, 1945. There was no majority in favor of Lowry's return. Finally, they indicated that they would take Stanley over Wedel (the vote was four to three).

20. Trotter papers, VTSA. See also "The Trotter Years," an issue of *Virginia Seminary Journal* 21/3 (March 1969).

21. See Kenneth Heim, *Ken: a man on a journey*, selected from letters and writings (Wyncote, Penn.: Arie Heim Lindabury, 1983).

22. This is *England's Earliest Protestants, 1520–1535* (New Haven: Yale, 1964). See his edition of the *Journals of the Protestant Episcopal Church in the Confederate States of America* (Austin, Texas: Church Historical Society, 1962).

23. Bd. min., 1939–53 (June 7, 1950), 179.

24. See fac. min., folder no. 7 (November 9, 1953). The board elected Franklin Young; Graham was second.

25. Ibid. (January 11, 1954).

26. Ibid., folder no. 8 (February 22 and April 12, 1954).

27. Bd. min., 1953–59, 41.

28. Bd. min., 1939–53 (June 1, 1949), 165, 168.

29. Ibid. (June 7, 1950), 179.

30. Ibid. (June 1, 1949), 165.

31. Fac. min., folder no. 6 (December 15, 1952).

32. Bd. min., 1939–53 (November 16, 1949), 172.

33. Ibid., 1953–59 (June 1, 1955), 41.

34. This information was derived from interviews with Professor Kelleran conducted by Margaret R. Woolverton for the Episcopal Women's History Project. My thanks to Mrs. Woolverton for her expert work.

35. Fac. min., folder no. 7 (October 26, 1953).

36. Ibid., folder no. 10 (April 6, 1956).

37. Bd. min., 1939–53 (June 16, 1946), 96.

38. Ibid. (April 26, 1946), report following 102.

39. Ibid. (July 15, 1946), 112.

40. Ibid. (November 13, 1946), 119.

41 Ibid. (June 2, 1948), 143. See "Duties of Bursar" as amended (July 1948), following page 102.

42. Ibid. (June 1, 1949), 163.

43. Ibid., 167. Also see 168.
44. Ibid. (November 16, 1949), 169.
45. Ibid. (June 6, 1951), 198.
46. Fac. min., folder no. 4, sheet following minutes for October 11, 1951.
47. Bd. min., 1939–53 (June 6, 1951), 201; (November 14, 1951), 207.
48. Fac. min., folder no. 9 (March 13, 1956).
49. Communication of Dean Kloman to faculty (March 8, 1956), fac. min., folder no. 9.
50. Bd. min., 1953–59, executive session (May 30, 1956), 12.
51. Ibid., 1959–66, executive committee (April 7, 1960), 57; full board (May 4, 1960), 67. See fac. min., folder no. 12 (May 18, 1960).
52. Appended to Bd. min., 1959–66 (May 23, 1962), 149–52.
53. Ibid., 149.
54. Ibid. (November 6, 1963), 203; (December 12, 1963), 200.
55. Appended to Bd. min. (September 10, 1964), 237–40.
56. Ibid. (September 17, 1964), 242–43.
57. Fac. min., folder no. 11 (February 8, 1957).
58. Joint Conference on the Relation Between Clinical Pastoral Training and Theological Education (November 27 and 28, 1953), 2–3, 4–5. Record set down by Barton Lloyd, fac. min., folder no. 8, item no. 6.
59. Board-faculty meeting (June 2, 1953), in fac. min., folder no. 7.
60. Report of dean to board (June 3, 1953), 1; fac. min., folder no. 7.
60. In fac. min., folder no. 7, dated May 25, 1953. Kloman had this statement distributed to the board.
62. Fac. min., folder no. 8, item no. 5.
63. Ibid., folder no. 5, item no. 7.
64. Ibid., folder no. 8, item no. 14. See rest for further criticisms and also suggestions for remedy without jettisoning CPT.
65. Fac. min., 1963–64, no pagination.
66. Ibid.
67. Ibid., 1964–65 (February 17, 1965), 1–3.
68. Ibid. (May 14–15, 1965), 6.
69. Ibid., 1965–66 (November 3, 1965).
70. Bd. min., 1953–59 (May 30, 1956), 7.
71. Ibid. (June 5, 1957), 2.
72. Fac. min., report of curriculum committee, folder no. 11, item no. 33. See bd. min., 1953–59 (November 13, 1957), 7.
73. Bd. min., 1953–59 (November 13, 1957), 41.
74. Bd. min., 1959–66 (November 10, 1965), 334.
75. Bd. min., 1959–66 (May 21, 1963), 188.
76. Bd. min., 1959–66 (November 6, 1963), 205.
77. His title was changed from assistant professor of church and society, bd. min., exec. comm. (December 3, 1965), 347.
78. See fac. min., folder no. 12 (May 16, 1960), with curricular proposals attached. See also Trotter memo to faculty curriculum committee.

79. See catalogue 1961–62, 22–23, etc., and catalogues for years following.
80. The minutes for the meeting of the committee on faculty and curriculum of the board (May 31, 1960), fac. min., folder no. 12.
81. "Tentative Proposal" (March 15, 1960), fac. min., folder no. 12.
82. Bd. min., 1959–66 (November 9, 1960), 94; (May 24, 1961), 110; (November 14–15, 1961), 128; exec. comm. (March 20, 1962), 142.
83. See fac. min., 1963–64 (January 15, 1964).
84. Catalogue (1966–67), 21. A review of this is still in the catalogue.
85. Fac. min., 1964–65 (February 10, 1965), attached proposal entitled "A Major Study of Theological Education." See also May 14–15, 1965, "Background Material."
86. See his report to the board entitled "Theological Education at the Virginia Seminary," fac. min. (November 15, 1965).
87. "Premises," attached to fac. min. (May 13–14, 1966).
88. See the proposed curriculum attached to fac. min. (December 7, 1966), and catalogue for 1967–68.
89. Bd. min., 1966–72 (May 24, 1967), 51.
90. Fac. min. (April 24, 1968), 2.
91. Ibid. (May 1 and 2, 1968), 6.
92. Ibid. (April 24, 1968), 1.
93. Bd. min., 1959–66 (May 24, 1961), 112–13; (June 27, 1961), 117–18;. (November 14–15, 1961), 126–27, 131.
94. Ibid. (December 13, 1962), 165.
95. Ibid. (May 12, 1964), 221–24.
96. Ibid. (May 26, 1964), 225.
97. Ibid. (September 10, 1964), 239.
98. Ibid. (May 25, 1965), 314.
99. Ibid. and 316–17.
100. Ibid. and 318.
101. Ibid., 1966–72 (November 9, 1966), 12; (February 12, 1968), 90.
102. Ibid. (February 2, 1966), 53, 357.
103. Ibid., 22–24.
104. Ibid. (March 13, 1967), 37; (April 10, 1967), 42.
105. Ibid. (November 14, 1967), 66.
106. Ibid. (November 13, 1968), 144.
107. Ibid., 140, 165.
108. Ibid., 1959–66, 332.
109. Ibid., 1966–72, 65.
110. Ibid., 1939–53, 82.
111. Ibid. (April 4, 1949), 161.
112. Ibid. (November 16, 1949), 170–71.
113. Ibid., 192.
114. Ibid. (June 6, 1951), 204.
115. Ibid., 1953–59 (November 12, 1958), 3; (November 10, 1959), 36–37.
116. Ibid., 1939–53 (June 4, 1952), 212; (June 3, 1953), 224. See the docu-

ment dated 1953 in the library file, "Brief History of Bishop Payne Divinity School and VTS," and Odell Greenleaf Harris, *The Bishop Payne Divinity School, Petersburg, Virginia, 1878–1949* (Alexandria, Va.: VTS, [1980]).
117. Fac. min. (September 3, 1965).
118. Bd. min., 1966–72, exec. comm. (November 14, 1967), 67; (November 15, 1967), 72.
119. Fac. min. (October 25, 1967).
120. Bd. min., 1966–72 (May 21, 1968), 110–11; (October 19, 1968), 127.
121. Fac. min. (April 26, 1951), folder no. 4.
122. Ibid. (January 6, 1960), folder no. 11.
123. Ibid. (January 19, 1956), folder no. 9.
124. See Ibid. (February 1, 1961), folder no. 11.
125. Ibid. (March 10, 1965); bd. min., 1959–66, exec. comm. (March 11, 1965), 281; full bd. (May 25, 1965), 304.
126. Bd. min., 1959–66, 388.
127. Fac. min. (March 16, 1966); (October 5, 1966); bd. min., 1959–66, 393.
128. Fac. min. (September 20, 1967).
129. Bd. in., 1966–72 (May 24, 1967), 54.
130. See fac. min. (November 18, 1964); (May 11, 1966); (February 17, 1965); bd. min. 1959–66, exec. comm. (March 13, 1967), 36.
131. Fac. min. (November 30, 1966); (February 15, 1967); (November 1, 1967); (September 15, 1968); bd. min. (November 14, 1967), 67; catalogue (1970–71), 61.
132. Bd. min., 1966–72, 20.
133. Ibid. (November 15, 1967), 74.
134. Ibid. (January 22, 1968), 66.
135. Ibid. (May 20, 1968), 4.
136. Fac. min. (April 24, 1968), 4.
137. Paul Tillich, *Systematic Theology* (Chicago: University of Chicago, 1950) 1: viii.
138. Charles W. Kegley and Robert W. Bretall, eds., *The Theology of Paul Tillich* (New York: Macmillan, 1952), 348.
139. See Booty, Crisis, 28.
140. Charles P. Price, "Clifford Leland Stanley: Teacher and Theologian," *Theology and Culture: Essays in Honor of Albert T. Mollegen and Clifford L. Stanley*, ed. W. Taylor Stevenson, Supplementary Series, no. 7, *Anglican Theological Review* (November 1976), 23–24.
141. Ibid., 24.
142. Clifford L. Stanley, "The Church, in but not of the World," *Christian Faith and Social Action*, ed. John A. Hutchison, (New York and London: Scribners, 1953), 57–58.
143. Ibid., 58–59.
144. Ibid., 59–60.
145. Price, "Clifford L. Stanley," 24.
146. Stanley, "The Church," 62.

147. Ibid.
148. Ibid., 63.
149. Ibid., 64.
150. Ibid., 69.
151. Ibid., 66.
152. Ibid., 67.
153. Ibid., 73.
154. See William J. Wolf, "The Theological Landscape 1936–1974: An Address," *Theology and Culture*, ed. Stevenson, 31–41.
155. Ibid., 38.
156. Krister Stendahl, sub Biblical Theology, *Interpreter's Dictionary of the Bible* (New York and Nashville: Abingdon, 1962), 1:430.
157. Douglas John Hall, *Thinking the Faith: Christian Theology in a North American Context* (Minneapolis: Fortress, 1989), 357–363.
158. Ibid., 29.
159. Ibid., 351.

CHAPTER NINE

A DECADE OF CHALLENGE AND TURBULENCE: THE 1970s

1. THE HISTORICAL SETTING

In April 1969 a new dean of Virginia Theological Seminary was elected. In May the Presiding Bishop of the Episcopal Church received a letter, an extension of the Black Manifesto, demanding $60 million to fund the program of the Black Economic Development Conference, 60 percent of profits on assets each year, and an accounting of the total assets of the Episcopal Church in all dioceses. This was to constitute reparations to those "victimized by the most vicious, racist system in the world." The Black Manifesto signaled a shift in the civil rights movement from the quest for equality to the assertion of black power. The rage of those who considered themselves the victims of a racist society was evident in rioting, fire, and death in the urban centers, in campus demonstrations, and in sit-ins in venerable academies of learning.

The rage against racism, combined with protest against growing poverty among the disadvantaged, occurred against the background of growing unrest in other areas of concern. There was growing opposition to the war in Southeast Asia, with the burning of draft cards and violent demonstrations on college campuses and elsewhere, made more violent by police and military efforts to control and stop them. There were growing demands on the part of women in American society, spurred by the creation in 1967 of the National Organization for Women (NOW). There was a new radicalism apparent in organizations such as Students for a

Democratic Society, allied with civil rights and antiwar movements largely sexist as women pointed out—challenging the society's morality, indulging in drugs, free sex, and rock music. And at the same time the Cold War continued with periodic confrontations, such as in Southeast Asia.[1]

It was a turbulent time. From a positive point of view, Samuel Huntington regarded the turbulence of the 1960s and 1970s as denoting a period of creedal passion when what he calls the "Ideals versus Institutions gap" produced an awareness of hypocrisy and the demand that the ideals of "liberty, equality, individualism, democracy, and the rule of law under a constitution" be restored and affirmed. Huntington tells of a graduate student at the Harvard commencement of 1969 delivering the English oration and asking, "What is this protest about?" Addressing his elders he said that it was not an effort "to subvert institutions or an attempt to challenge values which you have instilled in us. . . . You have taught us repeatedly that trust and courage were standards to emulate. You have convinced us that equality and justice were inviolable concepts. You have taught us that authority should be guided by reason and tempered by fairness. *And we have taken you seriously.*"[2] From a positive point of view the turmoil was necessary to reform society and return to the ideals on which the nation was founded.

From a negative point of view, the turbulence challenged and at times destroyed that authority necessary to maintain a just society. Many involved in the protests were, in their rage, antinomian. Lives were harmed, some were destroyed, and the alienation of distinctive groups in the pluralistic American society grew to a point where for a time it seemed that orderly government on democratic principles was impossible. The academies were especially affected, their orderly routines of teaching and learning virtually overwhelmed by social activism. Students in a strange attempt to assault the "enemy" boycotted classes, staged sit-ins, vandalized buildings, and intimidated administrations and faculties, with a resulting decline in academic standards as well as in academic discipline.

The churches were tested and many of them severely damaged, especially the mainline churches, including the Episcopal Church, in which conservative elements were alienated as those more liberal sought to involve the churches in the plight of the powerless and disadvantaged, the poor and those discriminated against to empower the powerless. Some young people fled from the churches, regarding them as hopelessly engaged in the mire of hypocrisy. The decline in church membership, already apparent in the 1960s, continued through the 1970s, into the 1980s. It seemed that the more the churches attempted to be relevant to the issues of the day, the more they became politicized and defensive, even self-doubting. In important ways they were seeking to be obedient to the gospel, prophetically, as expressed by Langdon Gilkey, criticizing and luring "long-established notions of justice, obligation, power, and equality into deeper interpretations and so onto higher levels."[3] But to some the churches seemed to be lackeys of radical groups, insensitive to the feelings of others. Pastoral responsibilities were often neglected by those devoted to prophetic witness and the churches suffered as a result.

The response of the Episcopal Church to the Black Manifesto was twofold. The demand for "reparations" was rejected. The need for economic justice was heeded. A special convention met at Notre Dame University from August 31 to September 5, 1969, where, after vigorous and often emotional debate, a special fund of $200,000 was voted for black clergy to dispense to the Black Economic Development Corporation. This response was followed by a backlash, funds being withheld from the national church, resulting in a reduction of personnel and program at the Episcopal Church Center in New York and the departure of Presiding Bishop John Hines. He was replaced by the more conservative, peacemaking John Allin. As reform took place—principally through the growing involvement of blacks in the hierarchies of the church, the ordination of women, and the advent of a new Prayer Book—a shifting occurred in the mood of the church. Those entering seminary seemed to be more conservative, less committed to social action, more concerned for personal spirituality. Charismatic persons became increasingly more evident in parish churches and seminary chapels.

Contributing to the turbulence was the involvement of the mainline churches in liturgical renewal. Liturgical experimentation with implied and often explicit criticism of old ways of worship, together with the advent of the Book of Common Prayer of 1979, disturbed those for whom change—especially change in things held precious—was unwelcome, causing some to leave the church for more conservative churches or no church at all. Viewed positively, however, the liturgical movement reformed the church, helping the churches to regain a sense of identity in relation to Scripture and the early church. Horton Davies, writing of Gabriel Hebert, spoke of the liturgical renewal of the church "'as a way of life for the worshipping community' which was a corporate renewal of faith (through theology proclaimed in Sermon and Sacrament), a commitment and consecration (through the Offertory), and an incentive to serve and transform the fragmented society outside, as the very mission of the Church."[4] The result of liturgical renewal for the Episcopal Church was a Prayer Book that represented the diversity of views of worship in the church. It provided alternatives, required liturgical expertise in its use, and presented the understanding that liturgical revision is an ongoing process.

Deeply affecting the mood of the 1970s was the anxiety caused by the arms race, especially that involving the United States and the Soviet

Union, and the fear of nuclear holocaust. The dangers inherent in abuse of the environment and the pollution of earth's water and soil also caused anxiety. So did business crises, recessions and inflation, and much else. Positively, there was a growing sense of interdependence among the inhabitants of the planet and a growing desire for peace and stability. There were advances in medicine, in manufacturing technologies, and a growing sense that it should be possible for all to have a life-sustaining, life-enhancing standard of living.

All of this affected the Virginia Theological Seminary. In particular, the seminary was challenged by the various movements for civil rights, for women's rights, and for students' rights. It was challenged by the liturgical movement and by those who saw the church to be irrelevant in American society. It was confronted by changing views of theological education, by pressures from without and within to maintain academic standards while diversifying course offerings. Voices were heard on behalf of student power, faculty power, and alumni power. In this turbulent time the institution struggled to remain responsible to the vision of its founders while being responsive to the changing world. One theme of great importance in the society and of significant importance to the seminary as an institution of the Episcopal Church was that of human sexuality (especially whether homosexuality was right or wrong) which gained prominence in 1970 and was still being hotly debated in 1981, the point at which this chapter ends. That it is still a major issue in the church in 1994 indicates how great a problem it is, persons holding very strong opinions in opposition to one another with little indication of any willingness to compromise.

Now we proceed to review first of all the course of the institution *qua* institution during the 1970s and into the 1980s and then to address the issues that demanded much time and energy.

2. THE WOODS ADMINISTRATION

On April 24, 1969, at a special meeting of the board of trustees, the Reverend Granville Cecil Woods, Jr., was elected dean of the seminary. Born in 1922, he received a B.A. degree from Vanderbilt University in 1942, served as an aerial gunner in World War II, did graduate work at Yale University in English literature, and taught for two years in the department of English literature at the University of the South. Having decided to seek ordination, Woods entered Virginia Seminary, graduating in the class of 1953. He was ordained and served churches in the Diocese of Tennessee. In 1958 he was awarded an S.T.M. by Yale Divinity School

Granville Cecil Woods, Jr., Dean (1969–1983)*

and joined the faculty of the School of Theology of the University of the South in Sewanee, Tennessee, as chaplain and as assistant professor of liturgics. During his time at the School of Theology he spent a leave of absence studying at Oxford University. At the time of his election as dean, he was rector of Otey Memorial Church in Sewanee and teaching part-time at the School of Theology.[5]

Upon assuming the deanship, Woods chose from the faculty Richard Reid to be associate dean for academic affairs and CEO when the dean was absent. Reid had been secretary of the faculty and had proven his ability as an administrator as well as an effective professor of New Testament. He was to remain associate dean until Dean Woods' resignation in 1982, when Reid was made acting dean. With the resignation of Frank Pisani, the development office fell vacant. The new dean asked for and was given permission to have two officers, one a director of alumni and public relations and the other a director of development.[6] The first position was filled by the Reverend Dabney J. Carr III, a 1960 graduate of the seminary, and the second by Armistead Boothe, an attorney, a Virginia politician, a financial consultant, and a longtime member of the Education Society and of the seminary board of trustees.[7] The business manager, in succession to Ben Boogher, was the Reverend William W. Blood, a 1962 graduate of the seminary who had been assistant business manager since 1967. In 1969 Philip Smith resigned to be succeeded in 1970 as chaplain and associate dean for student affairs by the Reverend Brice Sidney Sanders.[8] A 1955 graduate of the Episcopal Theological School, Sanders was rector of the Eastern Shore Parish, Virginia Beach, at the time of his election. The administration also included the Reverend Gordon Charlton, assistant dean and professor of field education from 1967 to 1973, and the Reverend Bennett Sims, associate dean and director of the Center for Continuing Education from 1966 to 1972.

This combination of men provided for a strong administration and one that from the outset was answerable to the dean and through the dean to the board. The dean's position was strengthened when in October 1969 the board agreed that only the dean, now dean of the administration and of the faculty, could be present at Board meetings, others being brought in only for special purposes.[9] At the April 1971 meeting of the executive committee of the board it was formally determined that from hence forth the dean should be known as "dean and president" and the head of the board as "chairman."[10] It was subsequently agreed that Richard Reid as associate dean should be vice president of the seminary. All of this was determined early in Dean Woods' administration. The concentration of power in the deanship was to be tested as students, faculty, and alumni demanded greater participation in decision making at every level of the seminary's life, including the board. There were already alumni trustees; there were to be also faculty and student representatives to the board.

During the decade of the 1970s the administrative personnel changed further, but the basic structure remained constant. Armistead Boothe retired in 1976 after a relatively brief but highly successful "second" career at the seminary, at which time Dabney Carr absorbed the development office, combining it with alumni affairs and public relations.[11] In 1974 Sid Sanders resigned to become dean of St. Andrew's Cathedral, Jackson, Mississippi. He was succeeded by John Rodgers, professor of theology, who had been exercising a chaplaincy ministry for some time as a teacher, and who resigned in 1976 to become a professor at Trinity Episcopal School for Ministry.[12] Rodgers was succeeded as chaplain in 1977 by the Reverend Churchill J. Gibson, a 1956 graduate of the seminary who was chaplain of St. Stephen's School, Alexandria, Virginia, at the time of his election.[13]

Gordon Charlton resigned as assistant dean and professor of field education in 1973 to become dean of the Episcopal Theological Seminary of the Southwest in Austin, Texas, where he succeeded the Very Reverend T. Hudnall Harvey. The Reverend William S. Pregnall was elected by the board to the field education position.[14] A 1958 graduate of the seminary, Pregnall was vicar of St. Augustine's Church, Washington, D.C., when chosen. In 1981 he resigned to become dean of the Church Divinity School of the Pacific. The Reverend Edward Morgan III then was elected to the field education post.[15] While rector of St. Luke's Church, Alexandria, Virginia, Morgan had been active in the seminary's field education program and was an adjunct member of the faculty.

In 1971 Bennett Sims was elected Bishop of Atlanta and was succeeded as director of the Center for Continuing Education by the Reverend Robert W. Estill, a 1952 graduate of the Episcopal Theological School and rector of St. Alban's Church, Washington, D.C.[16] In the interim between Sims' departure and Estill's arrival, while the continuing education program was being reviewed, the center was being administered by the Reverend John Porter, a Roman Catholic priest, and the Reverend Christopher Bryan, an English scholar who had been on the seminary faculty for a year teaching New Testament.[17] Estill resigned in 1976 to become rector of St. Michael and All Angels, Dallas, Texas. He was succeeded by his assistant, the Reverend Richard Alan Busch, a 1959 graduate of the Yale Divinity School with a Ph.D. from Claremont Theological School.[18] In the space of twelve years there were numerous administrative changes, but it is to be noted that all of the men were leaders. Those who left the seminary moved on to further leadership roles in the church, leaving behind solid contributions in their fields of expertise. Their elections had been the work of the dean and the board working together, consulting with the faculty, when necessary, as in the case of the positions in student affairs, academic affairs, and field education.

The finances of the seminary improved during the 1970s but not without occasional deficit budgets and the need to impose budgetary restraints. In 1976 it was reported that the budget had doubled every ten years during the past thirty years up to 1970, after which it was increasing 10 percent per year.[19] In 1971 the budget was $1,200,000 with 20 percent coming from student fees, 60 percent from endowed funds, and the balance from annual giving, with an expected 2 percent deficit.[20] In 1972 the budget was $1,197,447 with expected income of $1,149,310; the Center for Continuing Education was budgeted for $78,950 with an expected income of $64,450. In that year, to help balance the budget, tuition was raised from $1,000 to $1,250.[21] For the year 1977–78 the budget was $2,187,000 with a projected deficit of about $70,000.[22] In time the budget was balanced. But for a while an unexpected drop in enrollment, spiraling inflation (especially affecting fuel and utilities), and pressure to increase salaries and provide more subsidies for student housing provided a sense of financial instability. By 1980 there was a slight budget surplus.

During the same time the seminary's portfolio had grown, with some remarkable gains in the corpus. In one year, 1973, almost $1 million was added to the invested funds. In 1974–75 over $2 million was added. The invested funds increased from roughly $2 million in 1957 to $8 million in 1967 and $13 million in 1976 to more than $20 million in 1981.[23] Annual giving increased, bolstered by the concept of 1% of net disposable income from parishes of alumni and friends. The program was generated by the Board for Theological Education. But long before the 1 percent plan was approved by General Convention in 1982, Dean Woods had been proposing that 1.5 percent of net parish disposable income be given to Virginia Theological Seminary. By 1980, 85 to a hundred parishes had been giving on this basis, while at the same time the Theological Education Offering had increased by 16 percent.[24] It is of interest to note that in the year 1977–78 when a substantial deficit was anticipated and budget reductions imposed, including the transition of the refectory to cafeteria-style meals,[25] the financial restraint efforts resulted in a 1978–79 budget without a deficit. The deficit budgets, in other words, were manageable in the long run but only because the administration and the board took them seriously and because the development department labored hard to increase endowment income and annual giving.

During the period from 1969 to 1981 buildings were cared for, including the redecoration of the chapel, and the grounds were enhanced. In 1969 the continuing education building was completed, and Sparrow Hall was remodeled to accommodate a growing number of women students.[26] By 1973 Sparrow was no longer adequate to house the women students, and Wilmer Hall was remodeled for that purpose.[27] By that time the library was much in need of additional space. In 1974 an architect was hired to plan a large extension, and capitol funds were raised under the leadership of Dean Woods and Armistead Boothe. By 1979 $1,175,465 had been raised, and the completed library addition was dedicated in 1980 in honor of Mr. Boothe.[28] From time to time other building projects were discussed. As in the past, consideration was given to building married student housing on the campus, but again the board resisted the idea and chose to increase the housing allowance provided to seminary families. At one point, in 1976, "Maywood," then vacant, was used as a dormitory, the number of single students exceeding accommodations then available. But that expediency was short-lived.

Enrollment fluctuated, as at other seminaries, and as the 1970s progressed there were alarming indications of an overall decline, especially in the M.Div. program. Figures indicating total enrollment took into account those in the M.A.R. (subsequently M.T.S.) program—which enrolled as many as 19 in 1977—S.T.M. students, special students, and others, including D.Min. students when that degree was offered. Thus in 1975 the board was informed that there was a total enrollment of 212 students, although the entering

class dropped to 40 from the "normal" 55 of recent years.[29] Total full-time
enrollment dropped from 179 in 1976 to 127 in 1979,[30] helping to account
for the budget deficits at that time. In August 1979 it was reported to the
faculty that 24 students were entering the junior class in the M.Div. program (eighteen men and six women) and 18 entering the first year of the
M.T.S. program (seven men and eleven women).[31]

In 1980 the dean appointed a committee, chaired by Professor Pregnall,
to study the situation.[32] The committee reported in 1981 and stated that
the reasons for the decline included (1) the founding of the Trinity Episcopal School for Ministry, which enrolled a junior class of 26 in 1980,
compared to 28 at Virginia Seminary, (2) "the perceived high cost of living in the Washington, D.C. area," (3) "desirability of private school education for children," subsidized by General Theological Seminary and not
by Virginia, and (4) a seemingly negative attitude among students at Virginia Seminary.[33] The committee did not recognize in this report the other
factors apparent in the Episcopal Church: the growing number of ordinands
educated elsewhere than at the denomination's own seminaries and the
increasing scarcity of job opportunities in the church, with the decline in
church membership and the accompanying financial problems. The situation brought about efforts at recruitment and, most dramatically, the
removing of restrictions preventing those from entering the M.Div. program who were not postulants or candidates for holy orders.[34] The immediate effect of that was a drop in enrollment in the M.T.S. program. During the next decade enrollment was stabilized, with some fluctuations,
the M.Div. program remaining numerically strong by comparison with
most other seminaries.

The board minutes reflect the high degree to which the board of trustees exercised its authority in responsible ways under the chairmanships of
Bishops Gibson, Rose, and Hall in a period of considerable turmoil. It did
this not only through the two meetings each year of the full board, and
through the regular meetings of the board's executive committee, but also
through sometimes arduous labor in numerous committees related to every phase of the seminary's life.

3. DECISION MAKING:
MEETING FACULTY AND STUDENT DEMANDS

In order better to understand the seminary in the 1970s, it is necessary to
consider the broader issues that had so great an impact on its life. In considering those issues, I do not mean to discount the importance of the
ordinary. Indeed it was the maintenance of the ordinary round of events—

especially in chapel, classrooms, and library—that enabled the institution to weather challenges. But changes in polity, curriculum, the composition of the faculty, and much else must be understood in the light of the conflicts engaged in by the seminary and by the society and the church of which the seminary is a part. In what follows, the issues will be considered one at a time, with awareness that at times they overlap and at times interact. Certainly from the perspective of those involved in running the seminary and, I think, especially of the dean and the chairman of the board of trustees, the events coinciding and crisscrossing compounded the impression of turbulence.

Before the arrival of the new dean, events were set in motion by the faculty and students to secure more representation in the decision-making affairs of the institution. The faculty set about revising its bylaws, working through a committee chaired by Henry Rightor, a lawyer as well as a professor of pastoral theology. The bylaws were dealt with in faculty meetings extending from May 1969 through May 1970 and covered many subjects. The most important and most discussed was article 3 insisting that the faculty be participants with voice if not vote "in all procedures established for formulating policy and making decisions in such areas as appointments, tenure, promotion, and dismissal." With attention directed toward procedures established by the American Association of Theological Schools, the faculty further requested that five faculty elected by the faculty itself be allowed to attend board meetings and that each one be assigned to membership on one or more committees of the board. An exception was to be made for executive sessions of the board, when faculty would not be present.[35]

In the meantime the student body was petitioning for greater participation in decision making. On May 7, 1969, a proposal was sent to the faculty suggesting that student representatives be on the theological education (curriculum), admissions, finance, and scholarship committees of the seminary. The student body also presented a motion by the student council inviting the faculty to appoint three members to join with three students to form "a permanent committee to consider faculty-student relationships and specifically at the present time enlarged student representation in decision-making committees" (such as the curriculum, admissions, scholarship, and worship committees). The faculty accepted this invitation with but two negative votes.[36] On October 1, 1969, the faculty voted to include student representatives on the curriculum, admissions, and scholarship committees.[37] Subsequently, the executive committee of the board agreed to discuss student representation in decision making. In March 1970 two students brought to the dean a petition signed by forty students and three faculty members "making certain demands and requesting a special meeting of the Board of Trustees." The request was granted but not before protest was raised by two professors that they signed only a part of the petition presented.[38] A special meeting of the faculty was held, followed by a seemingly unpleasant meeting of faculty and students.

The executive committee of the board met in a special meeting on May 11, 1970, to deal with both faculty and student representation on the board. There it was decided that the following be representatives on the board with voice but no vote: the dean; two faculty members elected for two-year terms; two students, one elected by the student body for one year and the other the student body president, who upon graduation would be an alumni trustee for one year. On May 26 this action was confirmed by the full board, which ruled that there be one faculty member and one student on each of the standing committees of the board. Provision was made for there to be executive sessions of the board and committees as needed.

All of this was happening simultaneously with planning for, conducting, and then dealing with the consequences of a conference on racism in the church, which in turn focused attention on the seminary itself. The seminary had begun to admit black students in the early 1950s, had merged with the Bishop Payne Divinity School, and was administering the Payne funds for the benefit of black candidates for the ministry of the Episcopal Church. Black clergy were invited to the conference, which was held on May 10, 1970. Some twenty-two proposals were made, including the suggestion that the seminary liquidate all of its assets and give the money to the Center for the Education of Black Clergy in Atlanta, Georgia, and "that all members of the faculty and Board resign and be replaced by Blacks."[39] It should be noted that, under the influence of the Black Manifesto, similar demands were being made elsewhere.

Such proposals were rejected, but others were seriously considered concerning admission and recruitment of black students; the hiring of black faculty and administrators, secretaries and clerical workers, maintenance men (with insistence that policies concerning black personnel be just and fair); the establishment of a black studies department, including a course on racism; the placement of CPE and field education students in black ghetto settings; and much else.[40] Task forces were established to work on the demands as made. At a meeting of the board executive committee, faculty, students, and a committee of "Concerned Persons"—chiefly alumni—were called in and addressed the issues with board members. The faculty representatives urged that the board have an open meeting with students and faculty on the issues. This was scheduled. The student representatives linked the general demands of the students with the issues coming out of the conference on racism. The "concerned persons," led by Thom Blair, made seven proposals: (1) that there be some black faculty, secretaries, etc., (2) that the board sign the Civil Rights Act, (3) that there be required Afro-American studies for seminarians, (4) that the board make public all information concerning the Bishop Payne funds, (5) that all board meetings be open to the public, (6) that the board make public its budget, financial holdings, and investment policies, and (7) that there be faculty and student representatives on the board, with vote.

On April 24, 1970, the board, with Bishop Gibson in the chair, met with the student body and listened to fourteen students (and five faculty) speak on the issues at hand. The board then met in executive session. The Civil Rights Act was signed. A vote of confidence was given to Dean Woods. Work was begun on faculty and student representation on the board, with a committee chaired by Jack Spong charged to examine Afro-American studies, the writing of a racially inclusive employment policy, support for black alumni, recruitment of black students, a review of the use of the Bishop Payne funds, and investment policies to promote the rights and dignity of racial and ethnic minorities. It was agreed to make the treasurer's annual report available in the library. The director of field education was asked to continue seeking placements in black ghetto settings for those assigned to CPE and field education.[41] In short, the board adopted all but the most extreme proposals. In March it had elected John Walker, the first full-time black M.Div. student in the seminary, to be chaplain and associate dean for student affairs, but he declined the election. A black studies program was begun, visiting lecturers who were black were brought in to teach, the library was named for Bishop Payne, and a committee, including Walker, was established to advise on the employment of blacks in the institution.

None of these actions was easily implemented. Recruitment continued to be difficult. The black studies program was in difficulty by 1972. One problem concerned the existence of the Absalom Jones Institute in Atlanta. The seminary board of trustees raised funds to help support the institute. But in 1972 John Walker, now a bishop and member of the board, suggested that the Bishop Payne funds be turned over to the Absalom Jones Institute, something which the seminary's legal counsel ruled that the board could not do. However, it was suggested that the funds could be used for the education of blacks at the institute as well as at Virginia Seminary, and in fact that happened until the institute closed.[42]

In time black scholars began teaching at the seminary, including Henry Mitchell, an alumnus who taught Black Religious Experience in America, and John Davis, a former member of the faculty at the Bishop Payne School who taught a course on Black Muslims and Islam. There were others. In

1977 the board elected the Reverend Lloyd A. Lewis,[43] a 1972 graduate of the seminary who had done his graduate work at Yale. Lewis taught full-time at the seminary as assistant and then associate professor of New Testament until 1991, when he left to become dean of the Mercer School of Theology on Long Island, New York.

There was still much to be done. In 1976 black students expressed unhappiness: there was no full-time black faculty member, people tended to "put them down."[44] In 1979 Marianne Micks, a faculty representative to the board, reported that there was concern over continuing racism and sexism in the community. "Black students continue to express a sense of alienation. . . . Women continue to experience overt discrimination."[45] In spite of continuing problems it is nevertheless fair to say that the seminary had come a long way, dealing realistically and carefully with an issue that was tearing apart other educational institutions.

Professor Micks referred in 1978 to the unhappiness of women students. This, too, was an issue in the life of the seminary during the 1970s. It was a major issue in the life of the Episcopal Church, the churches, and society. In 1969 women students were enrolled in the seminary, and the first M.Div. women students already had graduated. Most of the women were in the M.A.R. program, and some did not think that the seminary took them seriously.[46] But the protests were by-and-large reasonable and mild tempered. The board did seek to improve living conditions by remodeling Sparrow Hall for the use of women.

In 1972 the Board for Theological Education held a conference at the seminary to discuss the "changing role of women in the church," with faculty and students in attendance from various seminaries. In October the faculty met to consider "endorsing a statement by the faculties of the Episcopal Consortium for Theological Education in the North East [ECTENE] on the subject of the ordination of women." The faculty, adding two modifications, endorsed the statement favoring the ordination of women by a vote of eighteen to two with two abstentions.[47] On November 14 women students wrote a letter thanking the faculty and requesting an opportunity for dialogue.[48] The December issue of AMBO, the student publication, was dedicated to the issue of women's ordination, publishing the faculty resolution of October 27, 1972, affirming the ECTENE statement. The faculty resolution included these words:

1. We regard it as a serious matter to deny ordination to the priesthood or consecration [to the episcopate] to a person with a deep sense of vocation, who is otherwise qualified, on the sole basis that she is a woman.

2. While we believe that the possibility of the ordination of women is

rooted in the Gospel, we recognize that it may not now be appropriate in cultural contexts in the world differing from our own.

3. Neither the ordination of women nor the restriction of ordination to men should be an issue which causes cessation of ecumenical dialogues or of attempts to draft proposed plans of union which are already underway or may be initiated in the future, nor should either position cause withdrawal from relationships of intercommunion which are already in effect.

Along with the faculty resolution, *AMBO* contained a strong argument in favor of women's ordination but also some cautionary notes.[49] In March 1973 it was reported that the Student Body supported the ordination of women by a vote in proportion of three to one.[50] Women about to graduate continued to ask for faculty support in seeking ordination to the priesthood. But they were also concerned about sexism in the seminary, wanting to discuss with the faculty "(1) The need for women on the faculty; (2) The possibility of a woman assistant at the Center of Continuing Education; (3) Their impression that some members of this community are ignoring the issue; (4) The need to take into account the material written on the subject of ordination of women; (5) The possibility of having women clergy take part in special services here; (6) The small role given to women at the ecumenical service on Friday, January 25."[51] On February 20, 1974, two women met with the faculty to discuss these and other issues. The disappointment of the women that the General Convention had refused to allow ordination of women exacerbated a troubled situation. Members of the seminary faculty, led by Henry Rightor, began making plans for ways and means to educate the church on the matter.

In May 1974 ninety-two persons representing several seminaries met at the Virginia Theological Seminary for the "Conference on Women for the Ordained Ministry," a conference that was also a meeting to devise strategies to achieve General Convention's approval of the ordination of women to the priesthood and to the episcopate. One strategy was to have the presiding bishop call a special convention to deal with the issue, a move approved by the faculty.[52] Tensions continued to mount at the seminary, a sermon by Professor Trotter advocating women's ordination arousing a strong protest from some male students.[53] The faculty found itself seriously divided over the irregular ordination in Philadelphia on July 29, 1974, of women to the priesthood. They found themselves unable to sign a statement from the Episcopal Divinity School because of its approval of the ordinations.[54] The majority of the faculty, almost two years later, gave their support to the ordinations in Philadelphia and the later ones in Washington, declaring them to be real but deficient, with deficiencies that could be corrected.[55]

At the 1976 General Convention the ordination of women to the priest-hood and to the episcopate was approved. Patricia Park was ordained to the priesthood in the field house at the Episcopal High School on January 2, 1977; the first such ordination in the seminary chapel took place on March 9, 1977, when Georgia Shoberg was ordained. On August 31, 1977, it was reported that Georgia Shoberg would be the part-time assistant chaplain of the seminary, with money provided for this purpose by the Alumni Association.[56] There had already been women on the full-time faculty, beginning with Marian Kelleran and now in 1977 with Marianne Micks. The chief goal had been achieved, but the issue remained alive, with accusations of sexism on campus, offense taken at the sexist lan-guage of the 1979 Book of Common Prayer, the difficulty some women had in finding parish assignments, and protests against Presiding Bishop Allin's opposition to the ordination of women. In the light of Bishop Allin's statement of opposition, the faculty and the board of trustees reaf-firmed their support "of the many women who have been ordered deacons and priests in this Church and those who are preparing for such ordina-tions in this and other institutions."[57]

The fact that there was increased support for student and faculty views on issues such as that concerning race greatly assisted a relatively smooth handling of the issue of women's ordination.

4. THE ALLISON CONTROVERSY: CRITIQUE OF SEMINARY TEACHING

The next issue of concern involving the board, faculty, students, and alumni was also of concern at other seminaries. This was the quality and character of the education provided by the seminary and its relevancy in the contem-porary world. In the last chapter, reference was made to discontented alumni who found the seminary curriculum to be out of touch with present reality. Now at the beginning of a new deanship there was controversy around John Fletcher, whose graduate education was supported by the board and who was brought on to the faculty to teach courses in church and society.

Fletcher did much to organize seminary participation in the Interseminary Program in Church and Society and became increasingly involved in it. He requested a year's leave of absence, without salary, to conduct experiments in new forms of theological education. His project was designed "to demonstrate the effectiveness of on-the-job theological education for parish ministry." In pursuing this project, Fletcher hoped to obtain the cooperation of the Washington Theological Consortium, which as a "cosponsor" would provide faculty to teach on a contract basis. As time passed, it became clear that Fletcher intended to work full-time in what was called Inter-Met. It was also clear that he was very critical of seminaries such as Virginia. In an interview published in the *Virginia Churchman* Fletcher said,

> The problem is that seminaries do not produce ministers who can do the job. . . . Particularly in the congregation. The students are deprived of the fullest potential of their education because they are surrounded and nurtured by academic people who, through process of selection, themselves don't know too much about what it means to lead a congregation or to work in a community. Academic guilds are self selective. When you go to seminary you get rewarded if you go on to graduate school. . . .[58]

In February 1971 Fletcher resigned from his teaching position at the Virginia Seminary, although he continued to lecture in the continuing education program.

In reality the seminary since the 1960s had been actively concerned to bridge the supposed gap between the theological encyclopedia (biblical, historical, and theological) and the so-called practical disciplines. It had established a strong program of supervised field education, with faculty involvement, continued the CPE requirement and field programs for the second summer, hired Fletcher to establish a department of church and society, and participated in field programs fostered by Fletcher. The seminary had founded a continuing education program that regularly brought clergy and others from the field to the seminary. The program had its influence on the seminary, faculty, and students. Indeed, some felt that field programs were being emphasized to the detriment of the classical theological disciplines.

The struggle between those advocating emphasis on Bible, history, and theology and those advocating greater emphasis on on-the-job training was experienced by all seminaries and found focus at Virginia Seminary during the 1970s through the criticism voiced by C. FitzSimons Allison, professor of church history. In 1969 Professor Allison reported that he found students to be "soft."[59] During a discussion of the seminary fostered by Milton Crum, professor of homiletics, Allison expressed his concern that students were "spread all over the place" and talked of the need to provide "some structure of synthesis for the students' theological education."[60]

In 1972 the American Association of Theological Schools visited the seminary for the purpose of reaccreditation. While on the whole making a favorable report, it did note a problem in the relationship between the classical disciplines and pastoral theology.[61] As a faculty representative to the board, Allison, in October 1974, cited in a statement to the executive committee the AATS evaluation as saying, "We would . . . raise questions regarding the core curriculum as it is presently structured. Primarily, we would question its balance. There seems to be too little work in church history and systematic theology in proportion to the required work in other areas—homiletics, pastoral theology, liturgics—as well as the requirements in field education." He went on to speak of "grade inflation" and stated his conviction that many students graduated without the rudiments of a theological education.[62] The faculty agreed that there was a serious problem, but there was also a serious reaction against Allison's taking his criticisms to the board. At some length the faculty discussed Allison's report in relation to a response prepared by Milton Crum. In the discussion there was expressed a strong desire to improve the quality of education at the seminary. But the conviction was expressed that, in addition to laying down stronger requirements and grading more stringently, there must be other "motivation for the students' integrating and appropriating a theological education in faith."[63]

In his report to the board Allison suggested that the board "might recover something of its traditional function" in supervising or monitoring the curriculum. In spite of a formal agreement by the faculty to work on the issues raised, Professor Allison went to the meeting of the full board in November and reported that the faculty had "not moved with any seriousness of purpose to offer solutions to the questions he had raised." Other faculty present expressed agreement with Allison, Charles Price stating that comprehensive examinations might help the faculty to cope with the problem. The board urged the faculty to make improvements.[64]

At this point, attention might shift to consideration of another curriculum change to which the Allison controversy contributed directly. That change, however, will be examined later in this chapter. For the present it is sufficient to note that the Allison protest, made by a sincerely concerned teacher and by one who was involved in the institution and elaboration of a nationwide examination of those preparing for the ordained ministry, seriously affected the seminary community as a whole.

At Virginia Seminary the Allison protest became the basis of what AMBO, the student publication, called the "Great Debate." This occasional paper printed a copy of Allison's report to the board, and a student, Jim Bradley, responded with an article entitled, "VTS' Problems and How to Fitz What's Wrong." Bradley was disturbed by the report, believing that his disagreement with Allison was based on radically different "doctrines of man," Allison believing that "if left to their own devices VTS students are lazy, shiftless, anti-intellectual and set to get whatever they can for nothing. . . . And what is needed, if we are to believe the report, is to whip these students qua niggers into line."[65] The language was partly that of the

MISSION AND MINISTRY

student movement in protesting that universities treat "students as niggers."
Allison replied, arguing that "Jim's thrust" is diametrically opposed to the
reasonable expectation that the seminary give "proper guidance to theological students in what they should have in preparation for ministry." Allison
interpreted Bradley as saying that "the students need no guidance but 'are
in as good a position to decide *what* they should be taught, *how* it should be
taught, and who should teach it.'" Allison admitted that his view of fallen
human nature "prohibits agreement with Bradley."[66]

Following the publication of AMBO, at a meeting of the executive
committee of the board, Allison reported that the faculty was working on
two curriculum revisions to meet his criticisms.[67] At the May board meeting it was announced that Professor Allison was leaving the seminary to
become rector of Grace Church, New York City. He went from there to
become Bishop of South Carolina and continued his efforts to improve
theological education, especially in the classical disciplines.

5. HUMAN SEXUALITY: THE ISSUE

The nature of human sexuality was an issue of importance for both church
and society. It had been discussed in the seminary for some time, but it
surfaced in a more serious way during Dean Woods' first year when he
spoke to the faculty about questions brought to his attention with regard
"to the seminary's attitude to homosexuality." In discussion, faculty members argued that homosexuality is a pathological condition requiring psychiatric care and that they could not recommend for ordination a person
known to have this problem, who resisted therapy.[68] A committee was
appointed and produced a statement that, when amended, was adopted
by the faculty. The statement expressed compassion for homosexuals, the
faculty being concerned to deal pastorally and not moralistically with
Christian homosexuals. The statement provided theological grounds for
heterosexuality whose fundamental expression is "life long monogamous
marriage excluding all premarital and extramarital coitus" and asserted
that homosexuality is "a pathological condition, which if uncorrected,
constitutes a grave disability for the ordained ministry."[69]

This statement was then distributed. The executive committee of the
board wanted the statement clearly to affirm that the seminary would not
knowingly accept an applicant nor retain a student who was a practicing
homosexual.[70] This was done. Student reaction included a paper from
"more than two, but not necessarily all" homosexual students in the seminary in which theological, psychological, and practical considerations were
presented. The seminary policy was found to be theologically faulty, de-

314

nying the freedom assumed by the doctrine of justification "to be myself." It was psychologically wrong and pastorally cruel and practically impossible to administer. Dr. Rodgers responded, saying "that the Doctrine of Justification does not mean that one is free to do just anything."[71] At a subsequent meeting the faculty affirmed the policy statement that the seminary "does not knowingly accept an applicant or retain a student who is a practicing homosexual," but some felt that the faculty document seemed to imply that unmarried persons were less than human. A new statement was prepared, discussed, but not approved, except for a general reaffirmation of the overall policy.[72]

In the meantime, the board meeting on March 14, 1977, added words to the statement so that it read "practicing or professing homosexuals."[73] In May the board at its annual meeting endorsed a resolution passed by its executive committee, setting forth seminary policy:

> . . . that students and faculty are expected to endeavour seriously to order their lives in accordance with the biblical norms with regard to sexual as well as all other ethical questions, that unmarried students and faculty are expected to live celibate lives, that married students and faculty are expected to live in faithfulness to their marriage vows avoiding adulterous relationships; and that the Seminary does not knowingly admit or retain students or employ or retain faculty who do not live in accordance with these norms or who are practicing or professing homosexuals.[74]

This did not put an end to the controversy. One bishop accused the seminary of not taking a stand on homosexuality, evidently because he knew of a homosexual or homosexuals in the seminary. The dean responded by stating that he had no intention of setting up a system of surveillance. There was discussion of the implications of divorce and remarriage. The Alumni Association executive committee urged a reconsideration of the board's policy. The faculty agreed that the policy needed clarification, especially in relation to divorced and remarried persons and the church's canons.[75] A number of suggestions for reworking the policy were made by the Alumni Association, by faculty, by students, and by the dean and Dr. Reid. On November 10, 1981, the board adopted a new policy statement, drafted initially by a two member faculty committee. This then remained the policy, printed in seminary catalogues in succeeding years. This carefully worded statement reads as follows:

1. The area of sexual behavior, as well as other aspects of human behavior, is relevant to a person's entrance into and continued membership in Virginia Seminary.

2. The Bible is the basic resource for norms of Christian sexual behavior and a Christian understanding of human sexuality. This in no way rules out new insights and new understandings from a variety of disciplines, for God is the source of all truth. Neither does it rule out the biblically mandated responsibility to state and attempt to live according to the claims of Christian truth as perceived by significant segments of the historic Christian community.

3. Faculty and students are expected to lead a life which is "a wholesome example to all people" (BCP pp. 517, 532, 544). In addition to all that this includes positively in the specific area of sexual behavior, it excludes at least the following: sexual intercourse outside the bonds of marriage, adulterous relationships, and the practice of homosexuality.

4. The proper Christian approach to cases of sexual immorality, as to all immorality, should be pastoral, not legalistic and merely condemnatory.

5. Seminary policy concerns sexual behavior in contrast to sexual orientation. Furthermore, this policy distinguishes between arguing a particular moral viewpoint in the context of teaching and learning and practicing acts which are contrary to traditional Christian norms and to positions taken by the General Convention of the Episcopal Church.

6. CHANGING WORSHIP:
MODIFYING THE VIRGINIA TRADITION

The last issue to concern us in this chapter is that of worship and is related to the liturgical movement, the introduction of trial worship services, and the Book of Common Prayer as adopted by the General Convention of the Episcopal Church in 1976 and 1979. The request by some students through the years for more frequent celebrations of Holy Communion, for evening prayer in addition to morning prayer, and for the use of more ceremonial combined with the appearance of trial liturgies, the "Zebra Book" and the "Green Book," and finally the 1979 Book of Common Prayer as proposed and as finally authorized—all of this raised questions concerning the liturgical tradition of Virginia Theological Seminary. That tradition had not been static. Changes had occurred, including ceremonial changes and changes in vestments, such as the use of colored stoles. A cross and candles had been placed on the Holy Table, which was part table and part altar. The 1967 Holy Communion was used on a trial basis when it first appeared.

In the first year of Dean Woods' tenure there were numerous proposals for a remodeling of the chapel and for a discussion of the "Virginia Tradition."[76] Such a discussion took place on October 29, 1969 at a faculty meeting devoted to it alone as informed by a paper that had been delivered by Dean Zabriskie about 1953 (intended to form a chapter in the book on Virginia Tradition, as discussed in chapter 7). At the end of a lengthy consideration of the tradition in relation to contemporary needs, it was decided that a new document was needed as a basis for further discussion and that regular, corporate worship in the chapel needed to be supplemented by groups meeting "for more informal kinds of worship." It was also decided that new guidelines for the chapel use and greater efficiency in the conduct of worship were needed and that thought should be given to remodeling the chapel. It was acknowledged along the way that the dean was "rector" of the chapel and that the worship committee was advisory.[77] At a later meeting the dean "suggested that the norm" for liturgical worship "here ought to be the Prayer Book and services approved for trial use with enrichment from other Anglican Prayer Books and authorized collections." At that time it was agreed that services on Thursday mornings might be experimental, but there was some uneasiness about what that meant.[78]

There then occurred extensive discussions concerning experimental worship at the regular chapel services. In May 1970 Dean Woods proposed the following for the next academic year: "Monday, Morning Prayer (possibly with a sermon); Tuesday, Holy Communion; Wednesday and Thursday morning, responsibility turned over to students or groups of students who indicated a desire to conduct experimental or innovative services . . . ; Thursday evening, Holy Communion with sermon; Friday, Morning Prayer or the Litany or some authorized combination of Prayer Book Services." The faculty adopted this schedule with one amendment: that there be but one day—Wednesday—for experimental services each week.[79] Work was done on guidelines. The day for experimentation was changed from Wednesday to Friday, at which time if students "wish to have a communion service with full ceremonial, it is perfectly all right for them to invite an outsider to do it."[80]

In 1971, in response to the demands of some students, the worship committee proposed that there be a daily Holy Communion. The faculty denied the request, for the proposal assumed that the Holy Communion on days when a community celebration was not scheduled would be attended only by a few, not by the community, in violation of the spirit of the liturgy as a corporate event.[81] In 1972 a customary, or guidelines on liturgical use, was presented, amended, and adopted, taking into account variations in the trial use of the time, allowing the use of eucharistic vestments on Fridays, which were days for experimentation.[82]

In 1974 Charles Price had returned to the faculty after an absence of ten years. He presented a paper with six principles, which the faculty adopted as a working paper for the use of the worship committee in preparation for writing "a rationale for the Virginia Tradition." Price wrote, concerning the six principles:

First and foremost has been faithful attention to the Word of God, by hearing the Scriptures read systematically morning by morning according to the Church's lectionary. . . . A second principle has to do with the way the centrality of the Eucharist is established. It is established by intensity rather than frequency. . . . A third principle is that worship is an activity of the entire community. All of us, students and faculty alike, are expected to be in attendance. The absence of each is missed. . . . A fourth principle is careful simplicity of ceremonial. . . . A fifth principle is that Chapel services are conceived primarily as occasions of worship and only very secondarily as opportunities for instruction. . . . A sixth principle is that in Christ we have been made "no longer servants but friends." The spirit of worship in the Chapel has not been so much the meticulous following of a way deemed to be liturgically proper as the expression of a forth-right, direct, and even intimate relationship of a community to the God whom it presumes to address as "Abba."[83]

These principles, drawn out of the Virginia Tradition, were the expression of the concerns of a member of the faculty deeply committed to liturgical revision, who was a member of the Standing Liturgical Commission of the Episcopal Church and who had taught liturgics at the seminary. Returning after ten years he was troubled by the degree to which the principles were being ignored.

In 1977 the new Prayer Book as proposed was in use at the seminary. Services from the 1928 Prayer Book and from the proposed book (both Rites I and II) were scheduled for portions of the year, and detailed instructions were prepared, reflecting the growing enrichment and complexities of the new liturgical practices. Tension continued on various levels as to the frequency of Holy Communion, the use of ceremonial, and experimental or innovative worship. At its annual year-end meeting in 1978, the faculty recognized the extent to which they differed from one another on liturgical matters. The dean

said he believed that there was a deep level of agreement among the faculty about the centrality of worship and its role in the life of the Christian community and of this seminary. He noted, however, that there were some serious disagreements about the particular styles of worship. He noted that for a long time in the history of the seminary there was general agreement about the use of a very simple style of worship. This consensus seems now to have broken down, particularly because of more diversity among the faculty and partly because of changes in the church as a whole and the adoption of the proposed book.[84]

318

The diversity was to increase; on one occasion there was an episode of speaking with tongues in the chapel. The dean remarked, "The charismatic members of the community seem to feel our worship is cold, sterile, and formalistic."[85] In 1980 there was much discussion of "potentially exclusive language," which was to persist as a problem for years to come, especially in relation to the 1979 Prayer Book.[86] At that time small group worship had been instituted on Wednesday mornings in place of a chapel service. Students kept up pressure for more flexibility, while many faculty were concerned to maintain some order and discipline in worship. In a way the issue was that of interpreting the Virginia Tradition anew in the light of great change in the church and with consideration of what it meant to have *corporate* worship. There was the certainty that with every student generation there would be complaints and the need to orient students, as well as new faculty, to the Virginia Tradition.

7. NEW FACULTY, NEW CURRICULUM

Faculty members come and go. During their time at the seminary, whether it be long or brief, they make significant contributions to the life of the institution and, in particular, to the curriculum through their teaching but also through participation in periodic curriculum reviews. In this section our concern shall be focused on the curriculum. But first we must note the changes in faculty between 1969 and 1981.

With Robert Kevin's retirement, the seminary elected the Reverend Robert Bennett to work with Murray Newman and James Ross. Bennett was a scholar finishing work on a Ph.D. at Harvard Divinity School. In January 1969 the faculty had reason to believe that Bennett would accept and that they would have their first full-time black colleague. Bennett, however, took a position offered to him by the Episcopal Theological School in Cambridge. The board then elected the Reverend Frank VanDevelder.[87] Born in Jackson, Michigan, in 1928, VanDevelder earned an A.B. from Pasadena College (1951) and an M.A. in 1953. He graduated from Virginia Seminary in 1963 and went on to Drew University, where he earned a Ph.D. (1967). While working on his doctorate, he was an assistant at Christ Church, East Orange, New Jersey. From there he went to be professor of biblical studies at St. Andres Seminary in Mexico, from whence he was called to Virginia Seminary. An accomplished Old Testament scholar, VanDevelder is the author of *Biblical Journey of Faith: The Road of the Sojourner* (1988).

In 1970 Clifford Stanley retired. While the board had already chosen

Charles Price to succeed Stanley, Price had not yet determined when he would be free to rejoin the Virginia faculty. John Rodgers was to take over the teaching of systematic theology. David Scott, a 1961 graduate of the Episcopal Theological School, having just received his Ph.D. from Princeton University, was hired to fill the gap. It was a short-term appointment then made a permanent one as the dean and faculty saw him becoming a valuable member of the theology department.[88] Born in 1936, Scott wrote a dissertation entitled "Egocentrism and the Christian Life: A study of Thomas Aquinas and Martin Luther" (1968). After a time as principal of a school in Liberia, he was an instructor first at Dartmouth and then at the Episcopal Theological School, where he was teaching at the time of his election.

In 1973 Price returned, and the next year Marianne Micks was elected professor of historical theology.[89] Dr. Micks had had a distinguished career as the professor of religion and dean of the college at Western College in Ohio. Having earned a B.D. at the Church Divinity School of the Pacific and a Ph.D. from Yale University, at the time of her appointment she had published two major books: Introduction to Theology (1964) and The Future Present: The Phenomenon of Christian Worship (1970).

In 1971 Holt Graham, professor of New Testament, resigned for personal reasons. Other members of the department at that time were A.T. Mollegen and Richard Reid. Since Mollegen was due to retire in 1974, the seminary sought for an experienced New Testament scholar and elected the Reverend Reginald Fuller.[90] Fuller, born in England in 1915, had earned B.A. and M.A. degrees from Cambridge University, taught from 1955 to 1966 at Seabury Western Theological Seminary, and was professor of sacred literature at Union Theological Seminary, New York, at the time of his election to the Virginia faculty. Widely regarded for his scholarship, Fuller was the author of many books and articles published in the United States, England, Germany, and elsewhere, including A Critical Introduction to the New Testament (1971) and Historical Criticism and the Bible (1984). Another distinguished scholar, C.W.F. Smith, a graduate of the seminary in the class of 1933, served from time to time during these years as a visiting professor, teaching New Testament and liturgics after his retirement as professor of New Testament at the Episcopal Theological School.

In this time of transition the department of New Testament was bolstered for one year by the Reverend Christopher Bryan. In 1974 Professor Mollegen retired. In 1977 another New Testament scholar was hired. This was the Reverend Lloyd Alexander Lewis, born in 1947, a graduate of the seminary in the class of 1972, who earned his Ph.D. from Yale University with a dissertation entitled "As a Beloved Brother: The Function of Family Language in the Letters of Paul" (1985).

When John Fletcher resigned from the chair in church and society in

1971, the faculty and the board considered various possible successors and eventually chose Allan Mitchell Parrent.[91] Born in Kentucky in 1930, Parrent, a lay theologian, earned an M.A. and an M.Div. from Vanderbilt University and a Ph.D. from Duke University, with a dissertation entitled "Responsible Use of Power: The Cuban Missile Crisis in Christian Perspective" (1969). He had served as a Navy Air Intelligence Officer from 1956 to 1959, was a foreign service officer in the U.S. State Department, 1962–64, and was working in the Washington office of the National Council of Churches Department of International Affairs at the time of his election to the faculty. Parrent, with a perspective influenced by Christian Realism, brought a distinctly different emphasis to church and society from that of John Fletcher and his concern for bioethics. When Professor Mollegen retired in 1974, Professors Parrent and Scott jointly took over the teaching responsibilities for Christian ethics.

With the retirement of Marian Kelleran in 1974, the board once more was searching for someone to teach pastoral theology and (since this person was to succeed Kelleran) to teach Christian education. The choice eventually fell on the Reverend John Whitney,[92] a 1953 graduate of the seminary with a Ph.D. from Pennsylvania State University. Born in Pennsylvania in 1920, Whitney had extensive experience in college work. When Henry Rightor retired in 1978, the board elected the Reverend Howard Hanchey to teach in the pastoral theology department.[93] Born in Richmond, Virginia, in 1941, a graduate of the University of North Carolina (1963) and Virginia Seminary (1967), Hanchey earned a D.Min. from Union Seminary, Richmond, Virginia, in 1975 and brought to the seminary considerable experience in parish ministry, in clinical pastoral education, and in field education supervision. These two men constituted the department until 1982 when Whitney resigned. In 1974 Lowell Beveridge retired as professor of speech and music and was succeeded by the Reverend Sherodd Albritton, born in 1923, a graduate of Furman University, Yale University (M.Mus.), and Virginia Seminary (1965). Albritton was given the title of professor of homiletics and music, continuing in that capacity until his retirement in 1991.

When Professor Allison departed for New York in 1975, the board elected William Sutherland Stafford to be assistant professor of church history. Born in 1947, Stafford was a graduate of Stanford University and had received his Ph.D. from Yale University in 1976, having written his dissertation on the Reformation in Strasbourg. Stafford, who had no seminary degree, was subsequently ordained in 1981. In the 1976–77 academic year, as Stafford arrived, the Reverend William Haugaard, formerly dean of the Episcopal Theological Seminary of the Caribbean and soon to be professor of church history at Seabury-Western Theological Seminary, was visiting professor of church history. These men joined John Woolverton, who was to take a leave of absence in 1980–81 to be a visiting professor at William and Mary College.

The last curriculum revision discussed in this history occurred in 1967 when a quarter system was put into effect, with numerous elective choices and a core of required courses. The emphasis was on flexibility. Almost from the beginning complaints were heard especially concerning the fast tempo involved in the quarter system. Other factors were involved as the seminary became more deeply committed to the Washington Theological Consortium, which exerted pressure to have a uniform calendar for the participating schools.

In 1971 a new curriculum was adopted with two equal semesters and a middle term of brief duration in which students were required to take either one or two courses or projects. The curriculum committee had in mind a variety of possibilities for the middle term, including regular courses, seminars, guided research projects, or the opportunity to study under supervision in special areas. During the three years fifteen elective courses were possible. The core curriculum involved two three-hour courses each in Old Testament, New Testament, church history, and systematic theology; one three-hour course in biblical languages and one in Christian ethics, while the practica accounted for about ten courses.

It soon became apparent that some students were not taking the middle term seriously. In 1974 the middle term (sometimes called the January term) was dropped in order to conform to the Washington Consortium's calendar. Prior to this the departments made presentations to the faculty as a whole concerning their goals and how they were seeking to fulfill those goals in the present curriculum. This task occupied large portions of faculty meetings between October 1973 and April 1974. Such discussion was focused on the M.Div. program. But the M.T.S. program was involved also, as was the S.T.M., so the faculty also discussed the difficulty of meeting AATS standards for that degree, principally courses designed especially for such graduate work. In March 1974 the graduate study committee of the faculty recommended that the S.T.M. degree be discontinued, and the board gave its approval.[94] Eventually the seminary was to award a diploma in theology for international students who had formerly worked for the S.T.M.

In the fall of 1974 the Allison report to the board appeared, and the subsequent discussions led into plans for further curriculum revision. In December 1974 the curriculum committee presented a plan involving two tracks. The first track would modify the present curriculum, providing a better balance between electives and required courses. The second track would involve all electives and comprehensive examinations.[95] The discussions, including further proposals, were continued throughout 1975 and into 1976.

A new curriculum was adopted in December 1975 and approved by the executive committee of the board.[96] It was essentially the first track and did, in fact, increase the emphasis on the classical disciplines, providing two semesters each of required courses for Old Testament, New Testament, and systematic theology with one elective to be chosen in addition from each department's offerings. Church history had three required courses and was to include the history of Christian thought. Ethics had one required course, and students were required to take one elective in either Christian ethics or church and society.

As to the *practica*, pastoral theology had three required courses; homiletics had two. Field education was involved in the middler and senior years: in the middle year were field education and a colloquy, and in the senior year students were to have field education or a field education component in an academic course. The latter might involve working in a parish with the worship committee there while taking liturgics at the seminary. Biblical languages were required for one full course. The second track was postponed for further discussion. In June 1976 the faculty approved a pilot project for three to five students from the junior class each year.[97] In the first year no students elected to pursue track two, and the faculty questioned its need. In 1980 five juniors elected to follow track two, and in 1981 comprehensive examinations were administered.[98]

It should be noted also that toward the end of the 1970s there were the following elective courses: "The Black Religious Experience in America" taught by Professor Carleton Hayden of Howard University; "Eve and Adam" a study of the roles of women and men in Christian tradition taught by Professor Marianne Micks; "Theology and Popular Culture" taught by Professor David Scott; and several courses in Christian social ethics taught by Professor Allan Parrent. Courses taught by Parrent included "Ethics, Economics, and Ecology"; "The Small American City," which focused on Alexandria, Virginia, with field components; and "Twentieth Century Christian Social Thought." There were courses on marriage, human sexuality, and one entitled "Christian Perspectives on Influential Non-Christian World-Views," taught by members of the pastoral theology department. The curriculum emphasized the core classical disciplines but also reflected concern for the issues of the day.

8. THE SEMINARY REACHES OUT

During the 1970s the seminary reached out in a number of directions into new or newly reorganized ventures. Under Bennett Sims the Center for Continuing Education developed as a major element in the seminary's life. Sims insisted on the need for experimentation and freedom from control by the seminary faculty. He also insisted that the program of the center be ecumenical, and he brought non-Episcopalians into it not only as students but as administrators in the program itself. In part due to continuing problems in financing the center, a task force chaired by the Reverend Bradford Hastings went to work, as did the executive committee of the Alumni Association. The result was a suggestion that the work of the seminary be rethought with much more emphasis on continuing education and on the professional retraining of the clergy, many of whom were in transition from parish work to secular work. The latter was an outgrowth of a crisis in the Episcopal Church: the growing number of clergy, the reduced number of parishes and parish situations, and, as a result, the many clergy unable to find jobs in the vocation to which they were called and for which they were educated.

To accomplish this reorientation, it was suggested that one-half of the seminary's resources be devoted "to training personnel for the ministry of the Church, and one-half for the professional development of those already ordained."[99] This dramatic suggestion will concern us further when we consider the Alumni Association. Here it is sufficient to say that the proposal was received and discussed by both board and faculty without approval per se. The basic aim of the center, to "focus both on personal growth of clergy and their professional development," was affirmed and a commitment made to keep the center afloat financially, with the recognition that not everything of value could be done.

The task force completed its work after Bennett Sims resigned to become Bishop of Atlanta. It was during the tenure of his successor, the Reverend Robert Estill, that a D.Min. program was instituted as an integral part of the center's work. Approved in 1974, begun in the summer of 1975, the program was evaluated and accredited after an ATS visitation in December 1979.[100] The Reverend Richard Busch, previously noted, was brought onto the staff to head the D.Min. program in part because of his experience in the pioneering work on the degree done at Claremont in California. In the summer of 1975 seven people were enrolled in the D.Min. program, and from that point on it grew and was widely regarded as successful. Although enrollment fluctuated there was never any doubt as to the feasibility of the D.Min. program. According to a report made in October 1976, the core of the program included

1) a prerequisite experience of at least one term in the V.T.S. Continuing Education program, 2) a series of action/reflection examinations in these four designated dimensions of ministry (a. general pastoral, b. communicative and educative, c. administrative and organizational, and d. theologi-

cal and ethical), 3) two summer workshop sessions of one month each summer, and 4) a thesis project.[101]

By 1980 thirty students were enrolled in a program that had as its purpose "1. To identify, develop and articulate the theological and behavioral assumptions that inform ministry; 2. To demonstrate an understanding of the relationship of those assumptions to the Christian tradition and appropriate behavioral sciences; 3. To demonstrate the ability to analyze and reflect critically upon acts of ministry in the light of the above; 4. To develop a unified theology and model of ministry that will inform and guide the practice of ministry."[102]

The program of supervised field education was begun in the late 1960s, first under Gordon Charlton and then William Pregnall. To succeed, the program needed the cooperation of clergy in the field willing to be trained and to function as supervisors. It also needed the close cooperation of the faculty in affirming the necessity of field education in the overall process of theological education and in participating in the program, especially in colloquies. A colloquy involved one faculty member, one clergy supervisor, and one lay person, with the students. It encouraged students to reflect upon their experiences in the field in the light of their theological studies. In 1969 Charlton acknowledged some as yet unsolved problems in the program but strongly affirmed its value.[103] A major issue concerned faculty involvement. In 1970 the supervisors spoke of their need for a closer relationship with the faculty.[104]

Speaking at a workshop for field education supervisors, Charles Price referred to the tension between academic work and field work, a "built-in tension" not to be escaped or solved. Price went on to say,

I would like to think that this tension can be a creative and not a destructive one. If I could be sure that my academic contribution to theological education would be respected in the field, I could be free from the necessity of taking two minutes at the end of every lecture to demonstrate how relevant it is. That relevance would be tested in the field by a test I trusted. And by the same token, if you could be sure that the problem of living and teaching the Christian faith in a parish were more sympathetically understood, you perhaps could affirm more positively the importance of biblical, historical and theological studies. But it will take a lot of living together to reach that goal.[105]

In saying this Price was identifying a very real issue and pointing to a very possible solution. Still, some faculty continued to complain of the amount of time students spent in field education, and supervisors complained of a lack of understanding, indeed a lack of interest, some said— on the part of faculty.

In 1975 William Pregnall explained the field education program in this way:

Field Education concurrent with other studies academically oriented, provides a tension and dialogue between theory and practice. Field training sites are the laboratories in which the biblical drama, systematic theology, and the history of the Church are experienced in ways that enable them to begin to integrate thought and behavior. Field experience also contributes to and tests the spiritual formation of the future ordained minister and assists in the acquisition of necessary professional skills.[106]

Provision was also made for students to spend an interim year of from nine to fifteen months following the middle year in a variety of settings where the seminary could be assured of adequate supervision. One option was the Interseminary Program in Church and Society, providing an "in-depth involvement in a major social or political institution" as a part of their total theological education. This program was shared originally by Duke Divinity School, Union Seminary of Richmond, and Virginia Theological Seminary. By 1975 Union and Duke had withdrawn. Virginia continued its Capitol Hill Internship Program until 1977. From 1967 when the program began more than eighty interns had taken part, "working in secular jobs to test their own concepts of social ethics, to gain insight into the structures of man's communal life, and to gain a perspective on the requirements of a public ministry."[107]

A major achievement during Dean Woods' tenure was the creation of and participation in the Washington Theological Consortium. This ecumenical venture was organized in 1970. In that year Dr. Charles Taylor was asked to become the full-time coordinator of the consortium. In 1971 Dean Woods was elected acting president and chairman of the executive council of the consortium.[108] Virginia Seminary faculty became involved in the work of consortium committees, teaching in other schools, and attending convocations. Issues were discussed, such as a common calendar and common grading practices.[109] Students began cross-registering, and by October 1971 it was reported that forty-eight students from other consortium schools were enrolled in Virginia Seminary courses, four of which were taught at St. Paul's College, Washington, D.C. Eleven Virginia Seminary students were enrolled in courses given by other schools. By 1975 fourteen schools were involved in the consortium, most of them Roman Catholic, such as the School of Religious Studies, Catholic University of America, Dominican College, and Capuchin College. In addition there were the school of religion at Howard University, Wesley Theological Seminary, the Lutheran Theological Seminary of Gettysburg, and the Virginia Theological Seminary. It was said,

> Students at V.T.S. have found that other schools in the Consortium offer vast and rich faculty, library, and student resources. In some cases the Consortium offers courses not offered at V.T.S., such as Radio and T.V. Evangelism. In other cases students cross register to gain exposure to a theological tradition different from their own. To this end, students in any member school of the Consortium are permitted to take courses for credit in any other member school. In addition, there are opportunities for exchanges of faculty for particular courses and for participation in Consortium seminars led by a faculty team representing two or more member schools.[110]

As was suggested on more than one occasion, involvement in such an ecumenical venture was responsive to the growing concern expressed in the Association of Theological Schools and in the Board for Theological Education (BTE) that theological education occur in ecumenical settings. In 1968–69 Frederick J. Warnecke, Bishop of Bethlehem in Pennsylvania, spent a leave of absence working for the Board of Theological Education to assess the situation in accredited seminaries of the Episcopal Church and in other places where people were being educated for the ordained ministry. In his report to the House of Bishops, Warnecke bemoaned the isolation of many seminaries—their isolation from one another, from the Episcopal Church, and from "life in the world today." Faculties didn't get together; "Boards of Trustees seldom meet each other." He recommended that the BTE do something about that. He also expressed the opinion that too many small, inadequately supported seminaries were all doing the same things. He recommended diversification and a reduction in the number of seminaries.[111]

Throughout the 1970s there was pressure not only to overcome isolation but also to reduce the number of seminaries in the Episcopal Church. Virginia Seminary considered and after much discussion declined participation in ECTENE (the Episcopal Consortium for Theological Education in the North East), involving General Theological Seminary, the Episcopal Theological School, and the Philadelphia Divinity School.[112] The suggestion was made that Virginia Seminary enter into cooperation with some other Episcopal seminary. The School of Theology of the University of the South (Sewanee, Tennessee) was considered but no action was taken. Along the way the seminary became much involved in the work of the BTE, especially in efforts made to raise national funds for the support of theological education. Those efforts culminated in 1982 with the adoption by General Convention of the 1 percent program.

The seminary was also involved in another action, which resulted in part from the ferment of the 1960s. That was the creation in 1970 by General Convention of a General Board of Canonical Examiners and of a General Ordination Examination (GOE). The board, which first met under the chairmanship of Bishop Stephen F. Bayne, agreed that the seminaries were best able to judge the academic competence of their students and that bishops and their advisors could judge best the personal qualifications of candidates for the ordained ministry. They then concluded,

A third area related to, but not coincident with those previously mentioned, involves an individual's ability to focus his faith and learning in a way responsive to the needs and demands of people in the world. It is the purpose of these general examinations to offer to the Church a partial means of assessing a candidate's capability to make this synthesis.[113]

In subsequent attempts at a statement of purpose the board emphasized its responsibility to test candidates in the canonical areas (Bible, church history, theology, pastoral care, ethics, contemporary society, and mission) but not in the way a seminary would test. These new examinations would test a candidate's ability to reflect and to apply what he had learned. At their first meeting the members of the board considered an examination composed of one question on authority, of one question on communication, and of one question on ministry and mission.[114] The first examination was of the third type (relating seminary learning to the needs and demands of people) and was given to 192 persons from January 31 to February 5, 1972.

In time more and more persons of influence regarded the GOE as a means of evaluating, if not controlling, the seminaries. Convinced with C. FitzSimons Allison that the seminaries were not doing their job, members of the Board of Canonical Examiners introduced "objective" examinations, testing students' basic, factual knowledge. Also, in the beginning the GOE was not considered a test to pass or fail but rather a means to demonstrate competency in canonical areas. But more and more people began to regard the GOE as the test for ordinands. The GOE from its inception tended to dominate the attention of students. They prepared for GOEs as if preparing for the most stringent bar examination.

In December 1975 Dean Woods expressed concern over what seemed to be the poor performance of Virginia Seminary students in the GOE taken in January 1975, having procured figures that indicated relatively poor competence in theology, ethics, and church history. He reported adverse criticisms of the seminary based on these results.[115] The faculty expressed concern. Similar concern was expressed in other seminaries.

The effect was, on the one hand, to stimulate greater academic rigor and, on the other hand, to demoralize faculty who were doing their best with the students sent to them by the church. Some faculty in some places became cynical and prepped their students openly for the "objective" parts of the examinations. The problems involved in all of these concerns were not to be solved in the 1970s and 1980s.

9. STUDENTS AND ALUMNI: AGENTS OF CHANGE

The student body was not oblivious to the ferment of the time. As we have noted, students demanded and obtained participation in decision making on the board of trustees and on board and faculty committees. All through the 1970s and 1980s evaluation of students was a major topic of conversation. Elaborate systems of evaluation of personal qualifications for the ordained ministry (the seminary's judgment being required by the church's canons: title III, canon 10, sec. 5(5)) were devised that aroused "anxiety/paranoia" in the student body. Pressure was exerted to involve students themselves more directly in the evaluation process. In return students wanted to have the faculty evaluated and pointed to the ATS procedures for doing so. AMBO printed a "course evaluation form," a very serious exercise involving not only the evaluation of faculty but also of students.[116]

The students were, as we have seen, very much involved in the issues of the time: racism, women's ordination, and the quality of education in the seminary. Some were children of the Age of Aquarius: It was rumored that marijuana was being smoked in the dormitory rooms.[117] Yet as the 1970s wore on, there were signs of growing conservatism in the student body. A report on a 1976 conference on ministry, stated that some visitors objected to the "Fundamentalist" and "anti-intellectual" attitude in leaders of discussion sections.[118] Students began to arrive with renewal and charismatic backgrounds. Personal religion began to eclipse social concern.

In 1980 a student life questionnaire was distributed; 113 students returned the completed forms. The results indicated a very high degree of satisfaction with the seminary as it was, a high level of trust in the faculty, approval of the seminary's worship tradition, and acceptance of the evaluation process. To the statement "I was fearful of and reluctant to express my feelings and opinions openly in the confines of the VTS community," 61 percent of the new students and 67 percent of returning students answered, no. The problem areas seemed to Churchill Gibson, who conducted the survey, to be communications and student evaluation.[119] By 1980 the students had accomplished much to enhance their situation and had become less demanding, less angry than their predecessors in the early 1970s.

On the other hand it appears that the Alumni Association was in the same mood in 1980 as it had been in 1970. In 1970 the executive committee of the board received a report of growing dissatisfaction with the seminary on the part of its graduates in the field. One board member believed that it came especially from those in special ministries who tended to write off seminary education as they had received it. In response the board agreed to maintain the seminary's "commitment to the classical Christian faith while at the same time [being] open to changes in many areas of education."[120] In 1981 the Alumni Association asked that the seminary's "policy on sexual behavior be abrogated," an indication of persistent dissatisfaction with their alma mater. In between, in 1971, the graduates had proposed, as we have observed, a redistribution of the institution's assets to benefit continuing education and retraining. The board had refused, after considerable debate. A positive result of that confrontation was a meeting between the executive committee of the association and the faculty, resulting in a lessening of tensions between the two bodies.

The association promoted the D.Min. program; sought for and obtained a promise of career counseling and attention to deployment; supported the hiring of a woman priest as assistant to the chaplain; continued to give serious attention to the seminary's sexual behavior policy, with consequent modifications to that policy; and sponsored a ministerial competence survey.[121] The Alumni executive committee met again with faculty members in 1979 to discuss "Managing Conflict between the Traditional Church and Renewal Movements."[122] In 1981 they met again with the faculty to discuss the sexual behavior policy.[123] In 1978 a member of the association had proposed that there be but one tenured member in each department, others coming from parishes on term appointments. But the board rejected that proposal.[124] Specific requests were denied more often than accepted, but clearly an active and outspoken Alumni Association was being heard.

In 1979 the association published this statement of purpose:

Working with the Dean and Faculty, students and trustees, the Alumni Association Executive Committee seeks to provide resources, concerns and insight into issues of theological education which reflect the perspectives of those involved in the church's ministry beyond the Seminary; and to that end to involve alumni/ae in initiating and funding programs of significant value to the Virginia Seminary; and to represent the same on and in the work of the Board of Trustees; and to communicate the work, goals and decisions of the Seminary to the graduates.[125]

This statement of purpose indicated the high goals set by alumni for the support of the seminary and a level of commitment that was quite extraordinary. Although some might express their disagreement with the seminary on one issue or another, the vast majority were loyal overall to the institution.

10. THE THEOLOGICAL PERSPECTIVES OF MICKS AND PRICE

In the 1970s the Virginia Theological Seminary possessed two theologians who strove to present theology systematically not only through their teaching but also through their writings. Each had distinctive emphases that tended to complement one another.

Marianne Micks described herself as a "historical theologian." In her *Introduction to Theology* (1964, revised 1983) she makes clear the truth of this statement. The structure of the book is based upon the three "resources for the thinking Christian," the three authorities in theology: "Scripture, tradition, and reason."[126] She treats the Bible as history, "remembered history," with "meaning today to men and women who have made this history their own internal history and who call the events into the present through remembering, to participate in their meaning and power."[127] In this way of regarding the Bible, the reading of Scripture in public worship is of vital importance. Indeed, corporate worship is both the locus of remembering and the setting in which those who hear the Word of God respond.[128]

Tradition, as a resource for Christian thinking, concerns historical theology and the history of Christian thought. "The sphere of tradition in the Christian Church involves the total thought and practice of the Church through the centuries—the whole experience of the living, ongoing community."[129] Of prime interest here are the teachings of the Church's theologians on matter and spirit, the deity of Christ, the seriousness of sin, reason and revelation, and faith and works.

This leads to the third resource, reason, defined by Micks in terms of "the apologetic task of communicating the Christian gospel in a world that respects reason more readily than it respects either Scripture or tradition."[130] Here she concentrates on apologetic theology, saying, "Each generation of Christians is called upon to express the gospel in the language of its own time and place."[131] This involves "the search for effective theological language," dealing with demythologizing and re-mythologizing, the human predicament, the nature of faith, and the church and the world. She ends her book with a chapter, new in the 1983 edition, entitled "Toward an Ecumenical Theology." There Professor Micks states,

Christian theology today stands open, then, on two fronts. It is engaged in a dialogue within the Christian family. Each part of the family is contributing to

this dialogue. The whole Church is stimulated by it toward creative, fresh thinking about the revelation of God in Jesus Christ. At the same time, Christian
theology is engaged in a dialogue with the world of which it is a part. If it is to
speak the truth of Christ with relevance to that world, it must speak as a united
Church. But it need not speak in a monotone. Even as it calls all people into
unity, an ecumenical theology can praise God for diversity.[132]

As a professor of historical theology, defined in relation to Scripture,
tradition, and reason, Marianne Micks has written a book *The Future
Present: The Phenomenon of Christian Worship* (1970), that takes seriously
"remembered history." She also has written a book on Christian anthropology, *Our Search for Identity: Humanity in the Image of God* (1982). It is
an exercise in apologetic theology with two chief purposes: (1) "to re-
think Christian anthropology in dialogue with contemporary thought"
and (2) "to remain in active dialogue with biblical and historical anthropology so that our present understanding of humanity is stretched and
deepened by our theological tradition." She presupposes "that any answers to the question of being and becoming fully human today are both
enriched and judged by the humanity of the one long called 'perfect man'—
Jesus of Nazareth."[133] Thus we find her standing as it were between tradition (including the remembered history of Scripture) and the present crises in society, looking back in order to draw upon the wisdom of the ages
in addressing, with attention to contemporary insights, the issues of this
age, in which the quest for understanding what it means to be human is of
critical importance. Over all there is the image of God revealed in Jesus
Christ (2 Cor. 4:3–6). Reflecting on the Epistle to the Hebrews (in connection with Paul's teaching on the *imago dei*) Micks writes,

> Jesus is the pioneer of true humanity, the one who delivers the children of
> God from the power of death and brings them to glory. To that end, he
> shared our flesh-and-blood nature, our state of being a little lower than the
> angels. To that end, he became like us "in every respect" (Heb. 2:17). He
> suffered and he died.
>
> This same Jesus, according to Hebrews, "reflects the glory of God and
> bears the very stamp of his nature" (1:3). The destiny of faithful women
> and men is to share God's holiness (12:10). Lest we grow weary in the life
> of faith, we are exhorted to look to Jesus and what he endured for the sake
> of the joy that was set before him (12:2).[134]

In 1977 in India Charles Price published a survey of Christian faith
and practice. Called *Principles of Christian Faith*, it was included in a series
on world religions initiated by the Islam and the Modern Age Society in

New Delhi.[135] The book, as Price reports in his preface, originated in a seminar at the Center for the Study of World Religions at Harvard Divinity School in which Price participated while Preacher to the University and Plummer Professor of Morals at Harvard. The result was a full-scale systematic theology, largely descriptive, reflecting its author's wide knowledge and experience not only as a theologian but also as a student of Scripture, liturgy, and the history of Christian doctrine. It is learned, with careful word studies and incisive comments on the relations between ancient teachings and modern problems. While it is obviously the work of an Anglican, it is consistently ecumenical. Indeed, one of the exciting aspects of the book is to be found in Price's awareness of the teachings of other world religions and in his concern to set forth Christian faith and practice in relation to Islam, Buddhism, and Hinduism. The theological description thus points toward the future in which the dialogue among the world religions will be increasingly important.

Price takes as his basic principle Friedrich Schleiermacher's statement that "Christianity is a monotheistic faith, belonging to the teleological type of religion, and is essentially distinguished from other such faith by the fact that in it everything is related to the redemption accomplished by Jesus of Nazareth."[136] While the book ranges widely and systematically through the major topics of Christian theology, the emphasis falls on revelation as communicating that reality which "is *ultimate* reality, the touchstone by which all other reality is to be measured,"[137] focused on the revelation of God in Jesus Christ as found in Scripture in the context of the worshiping community.

In discussing redemption, Price says that of all the applicable metaphors the "language of *love* (Greek *agape*) is the most characteristic of the Christian religion, Christ's reconciling life and death is the work of love, and reveals that 'God is love.'"[138] In an important discussion of authority, Price asserts that "in the Christian religion, Christ himself is authority. The Bible is an empirical reality. Reading and hearing it have the power to reveal Christ to those who search it with obedience and expectancy and *the Christ who is so revealed judges the scripture, which in many passages falls below his standards of justice and compassion*. It is he who has authority, not the scripture."[139] At the heart of this book is redemption by God through Christ, which in the epilogue is identified as the basis of Christian hope for the church, for individuals, and for the world.[140]

Of particular interest, given the concern for Christianity in the midst of world religions inherent in this study, is Price's discussion of the doctrine of the Incarnation. There he wrote, in part,

On the one hand, it allows Christians to recognize the revelations embod-

333

ied in other religions as revelations of the one true God. . . . The belief that the Logos was incarnate in the man, Jesus of Nazareth, can give Christians a basis for recognizing the Logos wherever it appears. . . . But to confess that in Jesus Christ alone was "all the fullness of God pleased to dwell," does in the end sharply distinguish the Christian religion from other faiths.

The Christian might point out to the Hindu "that to hold that only one man has been the full incarnation of the Word does not mean that there have not been reflections of God in other times and at other places, but it does establish a basis of judgment by which other revelations can be evaluated as more or less adequate to what one holds most important and real."[141] Thus did Price engage in dialogue with other world religions.

There is in Price's theology as presented in *Principles of Christian Faith* a strong affirmation of fundamental belief in redemption by God through Christ and a charitable attitude toward the various ways in which that redemption is described in fragile, finite human language, as in the various doctrines of the Atonement. Another conviction that runs through the book is that, with this fundamental affirmation, important relationships demand that we see things in connection and not in separation—as in the relationship of worship as service to God and worship as service to the world (litourgia in all its breadth of meaning) and as in the relationship of liturgy to Christian ethics as transforming process.

In this insistence upon interrelationships and interdependence, Price is following a venerable Anglican (but not exclusively Anglican) tradition, seeing all things in relation to origins and ends. In an address given at the University of the South in 1980, in the presence of Archbishop Ramsey and others, Price addressed the question of Anglican tradition and spoke of the attitude toward authority as one of the salient features of Anglicanism.[142] This attitude informs all of Price's theological reflections. He said, in part,

In the Christian community authority belongs finally and ultimately only to the one who comes out of Being itself, who liberates us from our enemies, including our final enemies, sin and death.

God's authority is like that of a commanding general, and thus all other authorities are like the authority of legates, all other authorities are subordinate.

Thus only those ecclesiastical structures which mediate the creative and liberating power of God can have and should have authority. Only those doctrines which communicate a deeper understanding of that creating and liberating love can have and should have authority. Such authority is freely and gladly accorded to those structures and persons and doctrines by those who experience the release they mediate. . . . Until it is both claimed and granted, one cannot properly speak of authority at all.[143]

NOTES

1. On all of this see my *The Episcopal Church in Crisis* (Cambridge, Mass.: Cowley, 1988), especially chap. 2.
2. Huntington, *American Politics*, 2.
3. Langdon Gilkey, *Through the Tempest: Theological Voyages in a Pluralistic Culture*, ed. Jeff. B. Pool (Minneapolis: Fortress, 1991), 173.
4. Horton Davies, *Worship and Theology in England* (Princeton, N.J.: Princeton University, 1965), vol. 5, *The Ecumenical Century, 1900–1965*, 40.
5. See Armentrout, *Quest for the Informed Priest*, 337–38.
6. Bd. min., 1966–72 (September 15, 1969), 220.
7. Ibid. (December 8, 1969), 248.
8. Ibid. (May 27, 1970), 291.
9. Ibid. (October 9, 1969), 233–34.
10. Ibid. (April 19, 1971), 374.
11. Ibid., 1972–77 (May 18, 1976), 211.
12. Ibid. (January 13, 1975), 156.
13. Elected May 18, 1976, but did not begin until 1977.
14. Bd. min., 1972–77 (May 22, 1973), 40.
15. See fac. min. (May 11, 1981).
16. Bd. min., 1972–77 (May 23, 1973), 55.
17. Ibid., 1966–72 (May 24, 1972), 466.
18. Ibid., 1972–77 (May 19, 1976), 220.
19. Ibid. (May 19, 1976), 221.
20. Ibid., 1966–72, 407.
21. Ibid. (May 23, 1972), 454–55.
22. Loose file, bd. min. (November 15, 1978).
23. See bd. min., 1972–77 (November 9, 1976), 241, and (May 13, 1981).
24. Fac. min. (December 1, 1980).
25. Ibid. (May 30, 1978).
26. Bd. min., 1966–72 (June 23 1969), 218.
27. Ibid. (November 14, 1972), 497, and 1972–77 (May 22, 1973), 43.
28. Ibid. (May 21, 1974), 118; dean's file (May 16, 1979).
29. Ibid., dean's file (November 9, 1977).
30. Ibid. (November 14, 1979).
31. Fac. min. (August 29, 1979).
32. Ibid. (September 3, 1980).
33. See report attached to fac. min. (February 23, 1981).
34. Bd. min., dean's file (November 14, 1979).

35. See fac. min. (May 9–10, 1969); (October 1, 1969); (December 17, 1969).
36. Fac. min. (May 8–9, 1969) with attached documents.
37. Fac. min. (October 1, 1969).
38. Ibid. (March 18, 1969); see (March 19, 1969), special meeting.
39. Bd. min., 1966–72 (May 11, 1970), 275–76; (May 26, 1970), 279–80.
40. Fac. min. (February 18, 1970); (April 9, 1970).
41. Bd. min., 1966–72 (April 24, 1970), 271–74.
42. Ibid. (May 23, 1972), 451; see (May 24, 1972), 464; and (November 14, 1977); fac. min. (May 28, 1971); (December 1, 1971).
43. Bd. min., dean's file (November 9, 1977).
44. Fac. min. (November, 15, 1976).
45. Bd. min., dean's file (May 17, 1978).
46. Fac. min. (May 14, 1969).
47. Ibid. (October 26–27, 1972) with the ECTENE statement appended.
48. Fac. min. (November 29, 1972).
49. AMBO 8/3 (December 1972).
50. Bd. min., 1972–1977 (March 19, 1973), executive committee. See (May 12, 1973), full board.
51. Fac. min. (February 6, 1974).
52. Ibid. (September 16 and 23, 1974).
53. Ibid. (October 4, 1974).
54. Ibid. (October 14, 1974).
55. Ibid. (June 2, 1976).
56. Ibid. (August 31, 1977).
57. This is the faculty statement, adopted October 3, 1977. The board statement of November 9, 1977, is in agreement with it.
58. Fac. min. (January 6, 1971), article attached.
59. Ibid. (January 8, 1969).
60. Ibid. (March 18, 1970), edited tape of discussion appended.
61. Ibid. (May 19, 1972).
62. Bd. min., 1972–77 (October 2, 1974), 137.
63. Fac. min. (October 21, 1974), with appended materials.
64. Bd. min. (November 13, 1974), 146–47.
65. AMBO (March 1975), 8.
66. Ibid., 13–14.
67. Bd. min., 1972–77, 163.
68. Fac. min. (September 8, 1970).
69. Ibid. (November 18, 1970), with statement appended.
70. Bd. min., 1966–72 (January 11, 1971), 362.
71. Fac. min., special meeting (April 4, 1971), with student paper appended.
72. Ibid. (June 2, 1976); (May 2, 1977).
73. Bd. min. (March 14, 1977), 266.
74. Ibid., 1972–77 (May 17 and 18, 1977), 268ff. For the statement see fac. min. (May 31, 1977).
75. Fac. min. (March 30, 1981); see minutes for May 27, 1980.

76. Fac. min. (May 9–10, 1969).
77. Ibid. (October 22, 1969), with portions from Zabriskie's paper appended.
78. Fac. min. (November 19,1969).
79. Ibid. (May 8–9, 1970).
80. Ibid. (November 9, 1970); see October 6, 1970.
81. Ibid. (February 3, 1971).
82. Ibid. (June 6, 1972).
83. Ibid. (June 5, 1974), Price's paper appended.
84. Ibid. (May 30–31, 1978).
85. Ibid. (December 18, 1978); see January 29, 1979.
86. See report of the worship committee (March 31, 1980), and fac. min. (October 6, 1980).
87. See bd. min., 1966–72 (May 28, 1969), 200.
88. Ibid. (December 8, 1969), 249; (February 9, 1970), 253–54; (March 8, 1971), 366; and elsewhere.
89. Ibid., 1972–77 (January 14, 1974).
90. Ibid., 1966–72 (November 10, 1971), 424.
91. Ibid. (May 24, 1972), 465.
92. Ibid., 1972–77 (November 14, 1973), 88.
93. Ibid., dean's file (May 17, 1978).
94. Fac. min. (March 6 and 20, 1974); bd. min., 1972–77 (May 22, 1974), 120. See fac. min. (December 6, 1972).
95. Fac. min. (December 9, 1974).
96. Ibid. (December 15, 1975); see June 19, 1976.
97. Ibid. (June 1, 1976).
98. Ibid. (January 14, 1980); (April 13, 1981); see December 8, 1980.
99. See the executive committee proposal in a letter from the Very Reverend Thom Blair to the Alumni, (April 10, 1971).
100. Bd. min, 1972–77 (May 22, 1974), 116–17; (January 13, 1975), 157.
101. Fac. min. (October 4, 1976), report appended.
102. Bd. min., dean's file (November 12, 1980).
103. Fac. min. (March 12, 1969).
104. Ibid. (April 1, 1970).
105. "The Significance of Field Education for Theological Education Seen from the Point of View of a Seminary Teacher: Four Observations," *Seminary Journal* 26/2 (March 1974): 4.
106. Catalogue (1975–76), 36.
107. Ibid., 40.
108. Bd. min., 1966–72 (March 9, 1970), 259–60; (May 26, 1971), 392.
109. See, for instance, fac. min. (December 10, 1979).
110. Catalogue (1975–76), 42.
111. Fac. min. (April 16, 1969), appendix A, letter dated April 14, 1969.
112. See fac. min. (April 21, 1975); (June 4, 1975).
113. Stephen F. Bayne to all bishops (January 11, 1971), Bayne Archives, General Theological Seminary, drawer 3, 400.

114. See the minutes of the first meeting (December 2–4, 1970), and "Interim Report to the House of Bishops" (October 24, 1971).
115. Fac. min. (December 1, 1975); see April 2, 1979.
116. AMBO 8/4 (January-February 1973): 3.
117. Fac. min. (November 18, 1970).
118. Ibid. (February 9, 1976); see bd. min. (October 13, 1975).
119. Ibid. (January 19, 1981), questionnaire and results appended to minutes. See student objections to pastoral theology, bd. min. (April 19, 1971); (May 14, 1980); (November 12, 1980).
120. Bd. min., 1966–72 (September 14, 1970), 315.
121. Ibid., dean's file (May 13, 1981).
122. Fac. min. (January 15, 1979).
123. Ibid. (January 12, 1981).
124. Bd. min., dean's file (May 17, 1978); see fac. min. (November 20, 1978).
125. Bd. min., dean's file (May 16, 1979).
126. Marianne H. Micks, Introduction to Theology rev. ed. (New York: Seabury, 1983), xv. First published 1964.
127. Ibid., 11.
128. Ibid., 52–54.
129. Ibid., 58.
130. Ibid., xv.
131. Ibid., 115.
132. Ibid., 162.
133. Marianne H. Micks, Our Search for Identity: Humanity in the Image of God (Philadelphia: Fortress, 1982), 2.
134. Ibid., 15.
135. Charles P. Price, Principles of Christian Faith (New Delhi: Islam and Modern Age Society, 1977).
136. Ibid., xiii.
137. Ibid., 37.
138. Ibid., 110.
139. Ibid., 43.
140. Ibid., 295.
141. Ibid., 129–30.
142. The address was published first by St. Luke's Journal of Theology 23/4 (September 1980) and then by Forward Movement Publications, with the title The Anglican Tradition. What is it? Can it last? (Cincinnati: Forward Movement, 1984).
143. Price, Anglican Tradition, 10.

CHAPTER TEN

THE SEMINARY
PREPARES
FOR
THE FUTURE

1. THE SETTING: THE CHALLENGE

The decade from 1982 to 1993 has seen many dramatic developments on planet earth. Such events include the disintegration of the USSR and the end of the Cold War; the growth in prominence and horror of ethnic conflicts; economic recession; environmental catastrophes; and a shifting of political and economic power causing sometimes painful realignments and an increasingly active role for the United Nations. In the United States there has been an intensifying of concern for domestic issues such as crime, unemployment, a sagging economy, the health-care crisis, the spread of HIV/AIDS, and much else. Looming as a growing dark, menacing cloud is the burgeoning national debt, the interest of which consumes an ever-growing portion of the nation's wealth with dire consequences not only to needful individuals but to the commonwealth.

The seeming inability of the members of the government to solve such problems, compounded by mismanagement and corruption, has resulted in what E.J. Dionne, Jr., has called a loss of faith in democratic institutions on the part of the electorate and a widespread cynicism where political parties and elections are concerned.[1] David Halberstam has pointed to another factor: the tendency on the part of many not only to yearn for a romanticized past but to live as though the past were present, the Cold War still a reality, the Soviets still seeking the overthrow of democracy. His message is that we cannot ignore change, cannot live as though the

Cold War was still our chief concern. Nor can we ignore the dangers of a burgeoning national debt. "History punishes those who come late to it."[2]

Thomas Cranmer in the sixteenth century understood that change and the effort required to address the challenges accompanying change must be taken seriously. He demonstrated his genius and political acumen in producing the Book of Common Prayer that reformed the worship tradition of the Western church in the light of Scripture and the example of the early church. He recognized the need for worship in the vernacular, not the language of the illiterate villagers but the language then emerging as that of the nation. He did this while retaining a eucharistic prayer reminiscent of the Roman canon missae, insisting upon continuity where such was permissible but also at times requisite. Such reform, recognizing the just claims of Christian humanism, continental reforms, and reasoned traditionalism, required that restraint be imposed on radical reformers, restraint which in an age of violence often led to unjust and cruel measures. But restraint was necessary in order to achieve that reform which was faithful to the truth once delivered to the saints and responsive to changing circumstances in which the gospel was to be transmitted. This element of Cranmer's genius has informed the development of worldwide Anglicanism, but is by nature frail, itself in need of renewal in each generation.

The Episcopal Church (U.S.A.) during the last decade has been struggling, not always successfully, with change necessitated by historical events while maintaining continuity with its essential past, that which faithfully transmits the foundation without which its identity is blurred if not lost. The complexity of the changes occurring and the reality of human finitude and sin mitigate against success as the world judges success. But a high degree of responsiveness to change regulated by fidelity to the essentials of faith is not only possible but necessary. "History punishes those who come late to it." History also punishes those who act as though there has never been a past.

The remarkable story of the Virginia Theological Seminary through the 1980s and into the 1990s is the story of an institution that has faced the future, adjusting to changing circumstances while adhering to the essentials of its own particular tradition and the greater tradition of catholic Christianity. This has not been done perfectly, but it has been done. Previous administrations from Dean Zabriskie through Dean Woods prepared the way, as did the many administrations that preceded them. But the story of the past decade reflects most clearly the personality and vision of Dean Richard Reid, together with board and faculty, with the support of alumni, students, and staff, and the many friends and donors who have participated in the vision of a faithful, lively, creative, outreaching seminary.

Richard Reid taught New Testament at the Virginia Theological Seminary beginning in 1958. He had served as associate dean for academic affairs and vice president of the seminary and was acting dean at the time of his election. To many he seemed the obvious choice to succeed Dean Woods. He was a proven scholar-theologian, an able administrator, and had worked closely with the board of trustees on many matters. There were others considered, but by the time the board assembled to elect a new dean, four of the five finalists had withdrawn. On November 10, 1982, Reid was unanimously elected.[3]

The election process was methodical and elaborate, in keeping with modern selection processes in the church. It began with the resignation of Dean Woods and the appointment of a search committee, chaired by Robert Atkinson, Bishop of West Virginia. Board, faculty, alumni, and students were represented on the committee. Barbara Wheeler, president of Auburn Seminary, New York, a highly regarded expert on theological education, was appointed to be a consultant. At a special meeting of the board of trustees the report of the search committee was heard and three documents approved: (1) the profile of the dean and president, (2) the job description of the office of dean and president, and (3) the hopes statement.

The profile mentioned the many facets of belief and personality, experience and expertise that were expected in the ideal dean for Virginia Seminary. These ranged from commitment "to the evangelical heritage of VTS" (involving as it did the promotion of missions and evangelism) to the pursuit of "broad intellectual interests" and "theological insight." Most importantly for the coming decade, the profile named "vision, imagination, the security to take risks" and an understanding of "the demands of institutional leadership: how to work with a board and others to develop plans for the use of the institution's resources, how to manage, recruit, and supervise a strong administrative team." The job description, among many other things, described the dean's function "as principal planner, leading the board in the establishment of goals—both short and long range." As to planning for the future, the hopes statement was clear. First, it reaffirmed the basic task of the seminary as that of serving "God through the preparation of the best qualified lay and ordained ministers for the Church and World." It then specified as hopes for the future development of the seminary "an increased engagement with the Church and the world," involving the responsible use of the "Seminary's total resources in ways that will model Christian stewardship"; "an increased emphasis on mission," involving the development of a seminary international in character as regards both faculty and students; and "an increased emphasis on the Seminary as a center for theological reflection," involving the encouragement of faculty research and publishing and also the preparation of "graduates better prepared to teach the Christian faith in local Church settings."[4]

On April 6, 1983, Robert Hall, Bishop of Virginia and chairman of the board of trustees, installed Richard Reid as dean and president of the Virginia Theological Seminary in the presence of a great throng in the Flippen Field House of the adjacent Episcopal High School. In his address at the dinner held later that day the new dean emphasized the fundamental task of the seminary:

> ... to provide those who come a chance to encounter God in Christ through the Scriptures, through disciplined and serious reflection on the way Christians have responded to the revelation of God in their thinking and their living and in their ministry of service to one another and to the world. This seminary, I believe, exists to serve the Church by making available careful, disciplined, faithful study of Scripture, History, Theology, Ethics, Worship, Preaching, and Pastoral Care which will prepare men and women as leaders in the ministry of the Church.[5]

He then proceeded to speak of the importance of mission and evangelism, of the need to be open to learn about the issues concerning people at home and abroad, to begin "at least to understand the issues at stake in dialogue with other religions," and to be willing to engage in dialogue with secular culture, "not in order to be won over by it, but in order to understand how best to present the truth of the Christian faith in ways that can be heard and understood." In tune with all of this Dean Reid spoke specifically of a new commitment to Christian education. "He said that it is time for the Episcopal Church to renew its commitment to Christian Education and that he hoped Virginia Seminary can 'help lead the way.'"[6]

Taken together, the board's hopes statement and the Dean's inaugural address pointed the way to the future and thus to (1) a strengthening of the basic foundation of the seminary in preparing men and women for ministry, (2) a fresh approach to mission and evangelism both locally and worldwide, and (3) the enabling of the Episcopal Church to renew its commitment to Christian education.

2. THE NEW ADMINISTRATION PLANS FOR THE FUTURE

As he began, Dean Reid called upon Dr. Allan Parrent, a prominent member of the faculty, to be associate dean for academic affairs and invited the Reverend Frederick Stair, former president of Union Theological Seminary, Richmond, to consult with him on the administrative structure of the seminary.[7] At the annual board meeting in May 1983 a concrete beginning was made for the realization of the hopes statement and the dean's chal-

Richard Reid, Dean (1983–1994) *center,*
with Verna Dozier and Bishop Robert Atkinson

lenge in his inaugural address. First, the dean introduced the idea of a capital funds campaign, and a beginning was made in the creation of a long-range planning committee, which would soon begin work under the chairmanship of Mrs. James S. Lacy, a member of the search committee and of the board. Then the Reverend Locke E. Bowman, Jr., an ordained Presbyterian moving toward ordination in the Episcopal Church, was elected professor of Christian education and pastoral theology, filling the chair left vacant by the departure of the Reverend John R. Whitney.

It is evident from the board minutes that Professor Bowman was being hired not only to teach but also to found the "Center for Christian Education." It is apparent that the Center for the Ministry of Teaching, as it was to be called, was in mind from the beginning of Dean Reid's administration.[8] That Bowman was highly qualified for the realization of Dean Reid's vision was acknowledged by experts such as Sara Little and Campbell Wyckoff.[9] For many years he had been an educator, editor, and executive for Christian education in the United Presbyterian Church. At the time of his election by Virginia Seminary, Bowman was executive director of the National Teacher Education Project, Scottsdale, Arizona, and editor and publisher of *Church Teacher* magazine. His arrival at the seminary in the autumn of 1983 was of considerable significance for the future, as we shall have cause to note later in this chapter.

The long-range planning committee began its work by drafting and

343

circulating a mission statement. This was done in consultation with the Reverend William Baumgartner, head of the seminary division of the National Catholic Education Association. The faculty discussed the first draft in March 1984. In the course of its discussion it emphasized the traditional function of the seminary in educating persons for the ministry of the church (lay as well as ordained), the importance of the ministry of teaching for the future, and a recommitment to mission and the study of world religions.[10] The faculty shared the hopes and the vision of the board and the new dean. The final version of the statement was adopted by the board in November 1984 and read as follows:

> Virginia Theological Seminary is a seminary of the Episcopal Church accredited by the Association of Theological Schools. It seeks to further the universal mission of Christ's Church by providing graduate theological education and serving as a theological resource for the church.
>
> The Seminary's primary mission is to prepare men and women for the ordained ministry, particularly for service in the parish ministry and leadership in the church. Out of its evangelical heritage and its missionary tradition, it emphasizes the ministries of preaching, teaching, pastoral care and social justice. It seeks to prepare its students as servants of Jesus Christ to equip the people of God for their vocation and ministry in the world. It also provides continuing education for clergy of all denominations and theological education for laity.
>
> This Seminary believes that theological education leading to a degree requires full-time study and full participation in its common life and worship. It also believes that theological education is greatly enhanced when it is done within an ecumenical context.[11]

Next came the discussion of long-range planning goals. The committee, according to its minutes of September 20–21, 1984, developed goals in six areas: internal governance, a Center for the Ministry of Teaching, continuing education, student services, including child care and married student housing, world mission, and curriculum development. These goals were discussed by the faculty in October, the dean asking for a consideration of priorities. In the course of discussion emphasis fell on (1) "world mission," expansion of activities that "may eventually require a new member of the faculty in this area," (2) "church and community (including emphasis on urban affairs and minorities)"—one faculty member suggested adding "rural-ministry"—and (3) "a capital funds drive for the following four items, a) A Center for the Ministry of Teaching, b) Increased endowment for continuing education, c) Student scholarships, and d) Married housing."[12]

At the semiannual meeting of the board in November 1985 the follow-ing goals were set forth for the next three years:

I. To improve the students' understanding of and commitment to mis-sion, establish a teaching post in missiology and world religions, and to develop new cross-cultural opportunities.
II. To improve the program for international students.
III. To improve the students' understanding of and commitment to the mission of the Church in the metropolitan area.
IV. To consider a program for students who wish to serve as church school chaplains and teachers of religion.
V. To serve student needs for child care.[13]

A committee had been established to work on married student housing.

By 1986 the long-range planning committee was working with Walton-Madden-Cooper, Inc., to develop a land-use master plan.[14] Much needed, new facilities were considered. By 1987 the building of a child-care center was authorized to accommodate the already existing child-care program, temporarily located in the Mollegen Gymnasium. Other specified build-ing programs, viewed as necessary to the achievement of the board's goals, were a new classroom-auditorium building, consolidation of office space in Bohlen and Aspinwall halls, a student activity center, and some resolu-tion of the married student housing issue, which might or might not re-quire new buildings on campus. At the same time endowment funds were to be sought to provide more scholarship funds, more support for continu-ing education, support for the new Center for the Ministry of Teaching, and additional faculty "chairs," specifically for a new chair in world mis-sion.[15] It was becoming more and more apparent that, if the basic program and the new possibilities were to be accommodated adequately, a major new academic center was needed. The means for financing such a facility were already emerging as a result of a few major gifts. The Addison Aca-demic Center was opened for use in February 1993.

3. NEW VENTURES IN EDUCATION: THE CENTER FOR THE MINISTRY OF TEACHING AND THE INSTITUTE IN SCHOOL MINISTRY

The seminary began in the early nineteenth century with the single in-tent of preparing men for the ordained ministry of the Episcopal Church. Not long after its founding it was recognized that the seminary's basic purpose would benefit by providing preparation for the men entering the

Photograph Courtesy of Alexandra Dorr

The Addison Academic Center

seminary, and thus the seminary board founded the Episcopal High School. In time it added the preparatory department within the seminary itself. The first became independent of the seminary, and the second was discontinued as the need for it waned. In the 1960s the seminary sought to meet the need for postseminary education, viewed as an extension of the basic purpose, and the Center for Continuing Education was founded with, in time, a doctor of ministry degree program. It continues as one of the vital components of the institution, fully accredited and widely acclaimed.

At the beginning of Dean Reid's administration, attention returned to preseminary education with the founding of the Center for the Ministry of Teaching. Nearing the end of the twentieth century, Virginia Theological Seminary has major programs for preseminary, seminary, and postseminary education—all supportive of the basic purpose.

The initial impetus for the Center for the Ministry of Teaching came from a growing awareness of the need for emphasis on education in the church—for the youngest members of the church and also for the members of all ages. According to the perceptions of many people, the Episcopal Church had neglected such education to its own great peril. In February 1984 Locke Bowman drafted a proposal for the attention of the board. In this proposal he related the idea of the center to the seminary's evangelical and missionary commitments. His focus from the beginning was on the "effort to train and equip the laity for effective teaching of the gospel."[16] In an interview conducted in May 1984, Bowman summarized his philosophy of Christian education.

My "philosophy" is profoundly simple. I believe there is no such thing as "education" without teaching. . . . If we begin with the teacher, helping him/her to do the best possible job, then all the rest will follow. Curricular resources will be the tools of the teacher, not the teacher's master. Schools and organizational structures will be shaped to make the teachers' roles more prominent. Innovation will proceed from teachers' insights, worked out with their students in an atmosphere of mutual respect.[17]

This new addition to the seminary was thus named the Center for the Ministry of Teaching. It was designed to provide courses and library resources for faculty and students in the seminary's basic programs; to provide resources and services to parish leaders, both lay and clergy; and to promote "research and development that will foster improved teaching practices and curricula in the Episcopal Church."[18]

At the board's annual meeting in May 1984, approval was given to implement the proposal in three phases.

Phase I: Establishing a Library of Resources in Christian Education, and a Calendar of Events for Church Teachers/Educators—operative by January 15, 1985.

Phase II: Developing an innovative Laboratory for Parish Leaders—with first course offerings beginning September 1, 1985.

Phase III: Establishing a Department of Research and Development, to begin its work January 15, 1986.[19]

Toward the realization of these goals, Packard-Laird Hall was remodeled to accommodate a library, staffed by a librarian/consultant; a model classroom and program of courses, in time supervised by the assistant director of the center; and space for research and development, staffed by a professional. All of these things were accommodated. Qualified staff was hired, including Amelia J. Gearey, with a doctorate in early childhood education, who joined the center staff in 1987 and became assistant professor of Christian education and assistant director of the center in 1990.

In 1986 the center's publications program began with the production of a tabloid newspaper entitled *Episcopal Teacher*. It is issued ten times a year and distributed to about 3,500 paid subscribers in fifty states and six countries other than the United States. The paper provides resources on Christian education to all age groups. In 1987 the center prepared a confirmation course, "Encountering Christ in the Episcopal Church." In 1988 the center began developing a nine-year curriculum from preschool through grade 6. This is a major venture of national importance, involving Dr. Judith Seaver as managing editor, Professor Bowman as editor-in-

347

chief, and Dr. Gearey as associate editor. The curriculum, being produced jointly with Morehouse Publishing, is scheduled for completion in 1995 and is in use in about 2,500 Episcopal churches.

The curriculum was preceded by a "foundation paper" that explained that "the aim of Christian Education in Episcopal parishes and congregations is to assist every member in living out the covenant made in Holy Baptism." Its foci are faith and practice, participation and explanation; it takes seriously the church's teaching and practice, God's revelation to us and our worship of God. There is a strong evangelical emphasis in this understanding. "The Church's ministry of teaching is an urgent endeavor undertaken by God's faithful people who renounce sin and evil, who turn to Christ as Savior, and who put their trust in the grace and love of God, living together as redeemed sinners in the community of the thankful." There is also an intent to take the contemporary scene seriously. "We are set down in the world's midst and must learn its language systems in order to communicate and interpret our faith within it. The insights and wisdom of every available discipline devoted to the pursuit of truth about our human situation offer valuable resources for our endeavor."[20] In this paper we find reflected much that was of primary concern to Meade and Sparrow and to all who contributed to the making of the seminary's theological heritage. In particular there is a commitment to the faith once given to the saints and a responsiveness to all who seek for truth.

In addition to publications, the Center for the Ministry of Teaching began planning for a new degree program, that of the master of arts in Christian education (M.A.C.E.).[21] First formally considered in 1988, the board approved the new program in May 1989,[22] and the first students were enrolled in 1990. Patterned after the program of the Presbyterian School of Christian Education, the two-year program includes basic courses in the traditional areas of theological studies as offered to M.Div. and M.T.S. students, and it includes special courses in Christian education. Such traditional studies are supplemented by work in the center's teaching laboratory and in relevant field education. By 1992 four degrees had been awarded.

Finally, the center's staff assists in the conducting of the summer four-week sessions of the Virginia Seminary Institute in School Ministry. Independent of the center, the institute is another entity in the seminary's efforts to provide for the educational needs of the church. It began with the arrival of the Reverend Edward Stone Gleason as director of development at the seminary.[23] Gleason, a graduate of the seminary in 1960, had extensive experience in secondary schools as a teacher and as headmaster of Noble and Greenough School, Dedham, Massachusetts, where he was located at the time of his election in 1987. In December 1987 Dean Reid, at one time a teacher of classics at St. John's School, Houston, Texas, convened a planning group consisting of himself; Gleason; Ann Gordon, director of the National Association of Episcopal Schools; Dan Heishman, director of the Council for Religion in Independent Schools; representatives of the seminary faculty and graduates involved in secondary school education. The group enthusiastically endorsed the formation of an institute. Gleason, as director of the institute, in reflecting upon its role, has said, "School ministry requires theological understanding, a philosophy of education, skills in developing curriculum, liturgical knowledge and understanding, counseling expertise, and much more, all bound together by a lively life of prayer."[24] The institute is designed to assist teachers of religion and chaplains in schools to gain more of the knowledge and skills required by their vocations and, incidentally but importantly, to do so in a program that affirms their ministries and provides means of mutual support. Twelve were enrolled in the program as it began in 1989 and nineteen in 1990.

4. FACULTY AND CURRICULUM

The basic program for preparing men and women for ministry in the Episcopal Church underwent significant changes during the decade, chiefly in relation to changes in the faculty but also in course offerings. As previously mentioned, in 1981 the Reverend Edward Morgan III succeeded the Reverend William Pregnall as professor of field education and director of field work. In 1983 Professor Woolverton resigned to become rector of Trinity Church, Portland, Maine, and was succeeded in the church history department by the Reverend Robert W. Prichard. A graduate of Princeton University and Berkeley Divinity School at Yale, Prichard earned his doctorate from Emory University. He served churches in Virginia before arriving at the seminary to teach American church history. He is author of *Readings from the History of the Episcopal Church* (1986) and *A History of the Episcopal Church* (1991). In the same year, 1983, Professor Bowman arrived. Professor Fuller retired in 1985 and was succeeded by B. Barbara Hall as Professor of New Testament. Professor Hall earned her A.B. degree from Bucknell University, her M.A. as well as her B.D. from Yale University, and her S.T.M. and Ph.D. degrees from Union Theological Seminary, New York. Formerly a missionary to Brazil, she came to Virginia Seminary from General Theological Seminary, New York, where she had been professor of New Testament.

In 1987 Professor Micks retired, followed by Professor Price in 1989, making Professor Scott the senior member of the theology department. To replace Professors Micks and Price, two new faculty members were hired in 1988. The first was the Reverend Walter Eversley, born in Guyana,

349

a graduate of Moravian College, Bethlehem, Pennsylvania, with a Ph.D. from Harvard University and a J.D. from Columbia University School of Law. With broad experience in pastoral ministry, chiefly in the Moravian Church, and teaching experience at the New York Theological Seminary and elsewhere, Eversley was ordained in the Episcopal Church before coming to the seminary. The second new member, the Reverend Christopher David Hancock, was born in England. He graduated from Oxford University and earned a Ph.D. in theology from Durham University. Having gained pastoral experience, Hancock was chaplain of Magdalene College, Cambridge, and lecturer in the faculty of divinity at Cambridge prior to his arrival at Virginia Seminary. We shall consider the theological importance of these two appointments later in this chapter.

With the retirement of Professor Crum in 1989, followed in 1991 by the retirement of Professor Albritton, who had had responsibilities in both homiletics and church music, the homiletics department was restaffed. First came the Reverend Judith M. McDaniel in 1990 to be assistant professor of homiletics. A graduate of the University of Texas and of General Theological Seminary, Mrs. McDaniel is at this writing a Ph.D. candidate in rhetoric from the University of Washington, Seattle. In 1991 the Reverend William H. Shepherd, Jr., was hired as an assistant professor of homiletics. A graduate of the University of Georgia and of Berkeley Divinity School at Yale University, he left the faculty in 1993. On Albritton's retirement as professor of speech and music, Raymond F. Glover was elected in 1991 professor of music and seminary organist. A distinguished church musician, general editor of The Hymnal 1982 and The Hymnal 1982 Companion, Glover was graduated from the University of Toronto (B.M.), Union Theological Seminary, New York, School of Sacred Music (M.S.M.), and has honorary doctorates from Virginia Seminary and Berkeley at Yale.

It should be noted here that Dr. Gearey, who came on the staff of the Center for the Ministry of Teaching in 1987, was made assistant professor of Christian education in 1990. In 1991, after thirty-seven years of service, Jack Goodwin retired as seminary librarian with rank of professor in the faculty. He was succeeded by Mitzi M. Jarrett Budde, elected librarian and assistant professor in 1991. She is a graduate of Lenoir-Rhyne College, North Carolina; Lutheran Theological Southern Seminary (M.A.R.), South Carolina; and the University of South Carolina (M.L.S.). Ms. Jarrett was library director and assistant professor at Lutheran Theological Southern Seminary prior to arriving at Virginia Seminary.

In 1991 Professor Lloyd Lewis resigned to become deputy for education and dean of the George Mercer, Jr., Memorial School of Theology in the Diocese of Long Island. His place in the New Testament department was

Hebrew Class

taken in the next year by the Reverend David R. Adams, a graduate of Yale (B.A., B.D., Ph.D.). Elected associate professor of New Testament, Adams held the same position at Princeton Theological Seminary from 1976 to 1986. Formerly a Presbyterian, Adams was ordained in the Episcopal Church and served churches in New Jersey.

In 1987 an appointment was made heralding an important shift in curricular emphasis, one very much in keeping with the seminary tradition. For some years the seminary had been involved in the Seminary Consultation on Mission (SCOM) with Professor VanDevelder, himself a former missionary, as a key leader in the effort to inspire and reform seminary involvement in mission, especially overseas missions and the care of those from overseas studying in the seminaries of the Episcopal Church. There had been international students at the seminary from early in its history. In the autumn of 1992 the International Student Forum at the seminary, begun by Professor VanDevelder, listed seventeen members, most from Africa but with representatives from Jerusalem, Vietnam, Germany, and England. With the assistance of SCOM, the seminary had worked hard during the past decade to provide for the actual needs of the international students. Symbolic of this was the provision of a diploma in theology, awarded for the successful completion of a course lasting one year. Each year in May the seminary sent an average of fifteen students to St. George's College, East Jerusalem, for a course called "The Bible and Its Setting." The Missionary Society continued its work, major efforts being missionary emphasis week and the dispersal of chapel offerings through grants made for mission work at home and abroad. A course in missiology was offered regularly, taught by adjunct professors such as the Reverend Dr. Paul Clasper.

It was clear to Dean Reid and the long-range planning committee that, if the seminary was to do justice to its missionary heritage, such activities, while laudable, were insufficient. As previously noted, the board in 1985 endorsed as one of its goals for the next three years the establishment of a teaching position in missiology and world religions.[25] A search committee was established,[26] and a profile was presented and discussed at the year-end meeting of the faculty in 1986. The professor of mission and world religions was to be "an evangelical Christian. A person committed to an evangelical understanding of the Christian faith, and to the extension of the Christian Church to all the world." This professor was to be socially committed (for the transformation of society), ecumenical, knowledgeable about the world, and possess cross-cultural experience. He or she was to be a scholar, a theologian, a teacher, a "church person," and a pastor/diplomat. The job description called for this professor to teach two courses each semester in the fields of history of missions, theology of mission, evangelism, world religions, and the dialogue of Christianity with other religions; develop a seminar for international students and convene the committee on international programs; assist in the admission and support of international students and be an adviser to the council of the seminary's Missionary Society; and "take a regular part in the work of the faculty and its committees and serve as an adviser to a group of students."[27]

The search ended with the choice of the Reverend Richard J. Jones.[28] A native of Washington, D.C., born in 1943, Jones was graduated from Oberlin (B.A.), the Johns Hopkins University School of Advanced International Studies (M.A.), Virginia Theological Seminary (M.Div.), and the University St. Michael's College, Toronto (Ph.D., 1988). His overseas experience included Vietnam and Ecuador. He began teaching in 1988, and in a short time there was an increased interest in missions at the seminary.

Not only had a new department been created and the activities specified in the job description begun, but by 1992 a new cross-cultural requirement had been added to the M.Div./M.T.S. curriculum. Candidates for these degrees had to complete satisfactorily one course in the department of mission and world religions or one course of like nature at another Washington Theological Consortium school or one semester in the Overseas Seminary Internship Program or one cross-cultural program (academic or nonacademic) approved by the committee on summer intern grants. As the catalogue description states:

> This requirement of significant exposure to a culture other than one's own is intended to equip graduates to contribute to the ongoing mission of the church. Mission may be distinguished from, yet is intimately related to, the passing on of tradition and the renewal of our common life within the church. Participation in the mission of the church includes educating parishes about appropriate modes of global mission, including assisting in the development of indigenous leadership, contextual theologies, and interdependence in the Body of Christ. Mission includes participating in the current challenge to Christian theology to consider and assess the revelatory and possible salvific value of other religions.[29]

Closely related to the new emphasis on mission was a response to the Lambeth Conference of Bishops' designation in 1988 of the 1990s as the "Decade of Evangelism." In 1990 a required quarter-course (half semester) in evangelism was added to the M.Div. program. Beside the pastoral theology department's core courses in administration and pastoral care, a core area in evangelism, listing seven courses, was instituted. The courses were taught by various members of the faculty, but primary responsibility rested with Howard Hanchey, professor of pastoral theology and author of *Church Growth and the Power of Evangelism, Ideas that Work* (1990).

In 1984–85 there had been a review of the curriculum, as a result of which the basic structure of the previous curriculum was retained with a required core curriculum, beginning with a strongly biblical emphasis. There were, as a result of the review, sixty-three required hours and twenty-four elective hours. Some adjustments were made, especially in liturgics, music, theology, church history, and pastoral theology. Alongside the M.Div. program and relying upon it were the M.T.S. program designed for the laity and the M.A.C.E. program just beginning. It should be noted that track two, discussed in the last chapter, was discontinued, and in the autumn of 1991 an honors thesis was instituted. A diploma in Anglican studies was offered beginning in 1989. This is a post-M.Div. diploma designed for those entering the Episcopal Church's ordained ministry from non-Episcopal seminaries. It involves a one-year program, drawing on courses from various departments. During the past decade the curricular offerings were enriched through new courses and new faculty at Virginia Seminary as well as in the Washington Theological Consortium, in which the seminary continued as an active participant. Students in the M.Div.

and M.T.S. programs were required to take at least one course in another consortium school.

Supporting faculty and curriculum has been the Bishop Payne Library. Under librarian Jack Goodwin it continued to grow. In 1983 the library collection contained 106,000 items and 550 periodical subscriptions. In 1992 there were 126,076 items and 865 subscriptions. The staff grew from two library professionals and two assistants to six professionals and three support staff. Among those added was Mrs. Julia Randle, the first professional archivist of the seminary, working on a part-time basis. Of great significance has been the computerization of the library catalogue with all that that entails. Mitzi (Jarrett) Budde, the current librarian, is building on the work done by her predecessor and is concerned to increase library holdings and facilities in relation to new ventures such as the International Research Center for Anglican Studies.

5. THE FUNCTIONING OF THE INSTITUTION: ADMINISTRATION AND FINANCE

Throughout the past decade the seminary has been ably governed by its forty-two-member board of trustees. It was chaired until 1985 by Robert Hall, Bishop of Virginia, and from 1985 until 1993 by Robert Atkinson, Bishop of West Virginia, who had chaired the committee to select the new dean. The board was composed of bishops and other representatives of the seven dioceses in Maryland, Virginia, West Virginia, and the District of Columbia, along with at-large and alumni trustees. They were joined by representatives of the faculty and the student body. The board continued to meet twice a year with most of the preparatory work being done by executive, faculty and theological education, and finance committees, which also had delegated responsibilities to perform between board meetings.[30]

The administration has been led by the dean and president, who serves at the pleasure of the board. At the time of his resignation, Dean Woods urged the board "that for the well-being and effective functioning of the Seminary as a whole, the office [of Dean and President] not be weakened in relation to the Alumni Executive Committee, the Student Body, the Faculty, or the Board itself."[31] The search committee kept this in mind in developing the profile and the job description, which guided them and continues to provide an appropriate basis for a strong executive officer of the seminary.[32]

During the past decade the executive officer has been provided with additional assistance at the senior staff level. The associate dean for academic affairs and vice president, Allan Parrent, is in many ways second in command, being in charge of the seminary when the dean is absent. There continues to be an associate dean for student affairs and chaplain, the Reverend Churchill Gibson, who serves as the dean's representative in pastoral matters involving faculty, students, staff, and their families. Since 1987 the Reverend Edward Stone Gleason has been director of development, responsible for both annual and capital fund-raising programs. Also he is now in charge of alumni relations and publications and is involved in future planning for the seminary. In 1984 David Charlton, who had been assistant vice president for business affairs of William and Mary College, was hired to succeed the Reverend William Blood as business manager of the seminary.[33]

In 1986 the dean spoke of changes in administration necessitating the addition of a new member of the staff, an assistant to the dean, to assist him in a number of areas "including admissions, work with student spouses, Conference on Ministry, Orientation, and other areas." He spoke of the "need for an additional faculty adviser, colloquy mentor, and minister of the week." If possible, this person would be an ordained woman.[34] The person chosen was the Reverend Martha Johnston Horne,[35] a graduate of the seminary (1983) with expertise in counseling psychology. In 1988 David Charlton resigned as business manager to become president of church schools in the Diocese of Virginia. However, he continued to live on campus and was designated an assistant to the dean, providing consultation services, "especially concerning buildings and grounds, insurance and personnel policies."[36] At that time a new position was created, and Martha Horne was made associate dean for administration, assuming "some of the major responsibilities of the Business Manager as well as being chief admissions officer and working with spouses." As this new office developed, it became clear that the seminary comptroller, Mrs. Mary Hix, was assuming greater responsibilities, was being heavily involved in budget preparation and control, and was working closely with the seminary treasurer and the board finance committee.

The financial resources of the seminary have kept pace with the growth in plant, program, and personnel. The annual budget has risen from $2,743,000 in 1981–82 to a projected budget of $6,040,315 for 1992–93. Revenue in 1981–82 amounted to $2,743,000 and to $6,301,338 in 1991–92. This latter fiscal year ran a deficit of $26,668. The necessary revenue came first and foremost from income on investments, endowment, estates, and trusts, which provided roughly 60 percent of revenues during the decade. In 1983 the seminary had nearly $30,000,000 in endowment. By 1991–92 the value of the endowment was $47,563,131 and the market value was $54,918,435. Total assets in the latter year were $64,034,162, an increase of $16,000,000 over 1987–88. Also of importance was annual giving, largely composed of income from the 1 percent program, which rose from about $375,000 in 1980 to over $850,000 in 1991–92. The financial condition fluctuated as the financial markets fluctuated and interest rates dropped. Modest deficits were not surprising, and the financial health of the seminary was maintained.[37]

One issue effecting financial investments called for especially careful judgment on the part of the board. It was related to pressure put on the board to disinvest in companies doing business in South Africa, as an action in opposition to the South African government policy of apartheid. At a special meeting of the board in January 1986 the matter was debated with presentations made by two members of the faculty. Charles Price urged total disinvestment and Allan Parrent argued for a policy of selective disinvestment.[38] The board eventually voted for selective disinvestment, specifically disinvestment in corporations doing business in South Africa that "are not signatories to the Sullivan principles [concerned for just treatment of blacks] and have not achieved a performance rating of I or II as determined by the A.D. Little Corporation, which evaluates the performance of all signatories."[39] This action did not satisfy everyone. The debate concerning disinvestment continued in AMBO, the student publication, in classrooms, and in hallways.

In October 1988 an article by student Leon Spencer appeared in AMBO, printing the July resolution of General Convention supporting Archbishop Tutu's appeal for "comprehensive economic and diplomatic sanctions against South Africa." Spencer urged the seminary to adopt a policy of total disinvestment. Allan Parrent responded, arguing on behalf of selective disinvestment and reminding readers of the moral ambiguities involved in the South African situation.[40] The debate continued,[41] and as a result the board at its annual meeting in 1989 voted twenty-two to eleven by secret ballot to revise and strengthen its disinvestment policy, directing "its investment managers to sell by May 31, 1990, all securities of corporations doing business in South Africa." It was added that the seminary would show interest in and concern for the situation in South Africa after its financial relationship with South Africa ended.[42] By one estimate the disinvestment and reinvestment in other securities would cost the seminary about $43,840.40.[43]

The board successfully dealt with the costs involved in the realization of long-range planning goals. Possible financial requirements for doing so were discussed from 1988 until 1990, when it was decided to proceed with the building plans: the construction of a new classroom building with auditorium and the redoing of Aspinwall and Bohlen halls, chiefly for administrative purposes.[44] The other costly possibility—married student housing with buildings constructed on the campus or purchased in the vicinity—was put aside in favor of the long-standing policy of subsidies for married students living off campus. In 1991 a capital funds drive was launched.[45] Dr. Henry St. George Tucker of Richmond was named honorary chairman and the Reverend Dr. Charles Price, professor emeritus, and Mr. Edgar Woolard, trustee, were named cochairmen. A goal of $9,386,000 was set to build ($5.3 million) and endow ($2.5 million) the academic center, as it was called now, and to renovate Aspinwall and Bohlen halls ($1.5 million). The board designated three major bequests for the campaign, and by the end of 1992, $8,645,533 had been given or pledged.[46] By then the successful conclusion of the campaign was within sight, including the cost of a new bookstore in the academic center.

It was decided that the new construction should be named the Addison Academic Center. The person being honored was Edmund B. Addison (1883–1922) whose grandfather, the Reverend Walter Delaney Addison, had been William Meade's mentor and guide as Meade prepared for ordination. Edmund Addison had been an executive officer in the Virginia Carolina Chemical Company and from 1866 to his death was a vestryman at St. James' Church, Richmond.[47] In February 1993 the Center was completed. The first classes were held in it, with some nostalgic remembrances of classes in Aspinwall but with excitement as the seminary prepared for greater service in the future.[48]

6. STUDENTS: NUMBERS AND CONCERNS

At any given time a great number of people are studying at Virginia Seminary. In 1982 Acting Dean Reid reported a total of 223 students in degree programs; 137 M.Div., 12 M.T.S., 22 special students, 10 auditors, and 42 D.Min. In addition there were about 300 in the Lay School of Theology, 250 in continuing education programs (including the yearly refresher course during the summer), for a grand total of 773 students during the year.[49] Entrance into the master's level programs (M.Div., M.T.S., and, after 1990, M.A.C.E.) has remained steady; between 46 (1984) and 59 (1986) with the notable exception of 1990, when the number was 35 with 23 entering M.Div. students. This was a low point due to many factors external to the seminary, including the decreasing number of persons being admitted to postulancy in the dioceses. The next year the total was 56 with 45 entering the M.Div. program. But even in 1990 the total number of all entering students, including those entering the three master's level programs along with one-year full-time students and transfers into the middler and senior classes totaled 65, the same number as in the previous year. The number of women in the student body has been between one-third and one-half of the total.

Continuing Education, D.Min. group, 1982

There have been about 10 international students each year, and in 1992 5 African American students entered the M.Div. program, a large number by comparison with other seminaries.

In 1983 10 faculty members met with 18 senior students to discuss their experience in seminary. The general tenor of the meeting was positive. The students expressed appreciation for the core curriculum; for the faculty and their genuine concern for students, their studies and their personal growth; for the sense of community; for the balance between structure and freedom; and much else. There were negative comments, including protests about too heavy a workload, not enough time given to instruction in Christian ethics and contemporary ethical issues, the need for greater stress on lay ministry, and the appearance of the seminary as "primarily a White, middle class, suburban ghetto." Numerous recommendations were made, including concrete suggestions to facilitate more discussion of social issues, more emphasis on Christian education, "greater balance between foundational (theory) courses and issue-oriented courses," and much else.[50]

There was constant concern during this decade for married student housing. As we have seen, serious consideration was given to this matter by the

Board and the Long Range Planning Committee. The faculty devoted much of its meeting on November 5, 1985 to the issue seeking for concrete solutions, discussing in particular possible sites for such housing on the Seminary campus.[51] That this planning was put aside did not indicate a lack of concern but rather the divided opinion among students and others concerning on-campus housing and the financial and legal difficulties involved in carrying through the project as some desired. As a result, the resolution to provide greater housing grants and to use any and all available means to care for the families of students was strengthened. One of the means of assisting families was being met by the organization of a childcare program on campus in 1986 and the construction of Butterfly House to accommodate the program, the building being completed in 1990.

Discussion of the ordination of women continued during the decade. Due to the expression of objections to such ordination on the part of some students in 1987, the faculty asked Professor Prichard to prepare a brief history of the faculty's actions concerning the ordination of women. The faculty issued a statement affirming their continuing support of such ordination, at the same time emphasizing the freedom of the opposition to express their contrary views.

> We tolerate these opinions on the grounds of academic freedom. We mean this to be a place where questions can be asked and struggles for growth go on in an honest and decent way. That tolerance, however, should not create the slightest doubt about our position and the position of this church.[52]

The board joined the faculty in this reaffirmation and in the affirmation of academic freedom or tolerance for those in disagreement with board and faculty.[53] In a related issue, the seminary sought to meet the call of its women and others for the use of inclusive language, not only in liturgy, but in the classroom, in seminary publications, and generally.[54]

Another major concern among students was mentioned in the report of a meeting of twenty-eight graduating students and sixteen faculty on April 26, 1984. First among the list of areas needing attention was that of "spiritual development." All three of the discussion groups meeting during this session emphasized spiritual development, the need for more classes on the subject, the feeling that those involved in Cursillo and other programs of spiritual renewal were treated as "second class" students, and the need for a more devotional approach in biblical studies. Positively, it was said, "The spiritual life here is very healthy. . . . Some of the most meaningful moments came as professors shared their faith" with students in the classroom. There was affirmation of the importance of small group worship, such as that conducted in advisee groups one morning each week.[55]

In 1984 the Reverend Dabney Carr, then director of development and alumni affairs "entered the Shalem Institute's Spiritual Guidance Program in Washington, D.C. From then until his retirement this summer [1990]," Dean Reid wrote, "Dabney served part-time and then nearly full-time as the Seminary's first spiritual director, listening on a regular schedule to as many as thirty to forty-five individuals per year."[56] In 1986 Carr indicated his intention to resign as director of development and to continue as director of alumni affairs, at the same time assuming further duties in spiritual direction.[57] This happened with the election of the Reverend Edward Stone Gleason as director of development in 1987.[58] At his retirement in 1990 Carr became one of several spiritual directors made available to students on a regular basis.

In 1990 the Spiritual Formation Group, led by Dean Reid and Chaplain Gibson, issued a booklet containing a statement "Some Assumptions About Spiritual Direction at the Seminary." It also contained a list, with personal descriptions, of ten available spiritual directors, including Gibson and Carr, various qualified clergy and laity in the vicinity, as well as the Reverend Paul Wessinger, S.S.J.E. Specific reference was made to the Shalem Institute and to Sr. Rosemary Dougherty, director of spiritual guidance of the institute. The book was presented as a means by which the seminary "is offering students an opportunity for individual or group spiritual direction as one possible way to help deepen their spiritual relationship with God."[59] The intention was to provide this additional means of spiritual formation, supplementing the routine of worship in chapel, in advisee groups on Tuesday mornings, prayer and Bible student groups of various kinds, as well as the continuous effort made as faculty and students together "seek to deepen their knowledge and understanding of the Christian life."[60]

In this way Virginia Seminary sought to maintain that emphasis on personal piety that was of such great importance to the founders, exemplified by Prayer Hall, the daily family worship and weekly faculty meetings held in it, and by the chapel and the regular round of public worship there—in so many ways the heart of the school. There was also the great weight attached to serious disciplined learning through reading and recitations, the writing of essays and examinations, the preparation and preaching of sermons. This was done in such a way that the learning became a chief means of spiritual formation and growth. This is so in part because the subject matters treated in the classroom were the sum and substance of faith. And finally, there was field education, in the earliest days an evangelistic adventure preaching the gospel, ministering to the needs of people, organizing prayer meetings, and gathering people for formal worship.[61] While modern field education differs and is considered a part of the core curriculum, many students find that their field activities as well

The Seminary at Prayer, 1986
Churchill Gibson, Dean Reid, John Pitts (student) serving

as participation in the related colloquy provide means of spiritual formation and growth.

The education of students in the field, concurrent with course work at
the seminary, involves the exercise of practical skills. "Growth in personal and professional identity is crucial—the deep discovery of 'who I
am.' 'Is this truly my calling' is the level of testing a vocation to the ordained ministry. The integration of academic and field work occurs when
the student reflects theologically on the practice of ministry 'How is God
present and active in all this?'" Working with the field education advisory
committee, the Reverend Edward Morgan III developed further the colloquy for weekly small group discussion—including students, a faculty
member, a lay person, and a parish priest—where reflective learning can
take place, relating field work and academic work to the benefit of both.[62]

While emphasis here is placed on M.Div. students, all students of the
seminary—full-time and part-time, continuing education, the Center for
the Ministry of Teaching, the Institute of School Ministry, and the Lay
School of Theology—are involved in an atmosphere of academic rigor
and spiritual growth. Admittedly, all this requires dedication and effort

on the part of everyone involved. For as people come and go, circumstances change, the heritage is reinterpreted, and the tradition established
in 1823 is reclaimed again and again.

7. THE THEOLOGICAL ETHOS

With the retirement of Professors Micks and Price and the growth of the
theology department around Professor Scott (joined by Professors Hancock
and Eversley), the theological ethos of the seminary emerged ever more
clearly in contradistinction to the theology of Paul Tillich and the method
of correlation. Tillich and his method exemplified for Professor Scott a
utilitarian view of God as the God who provides answers to human needs
and who perfects both individual personality and human society. As influenced by Thomas Aquinas, Karl Barth, the Caroline divines, and Scott's
mentor at Princeton, Professor Arthur McGill, Scott replaces the utilitarian view of God with a vision of God and the transfiguration of individual
life through the glory of God's triune being. The focus in this theology is
on God and God's glory and on participation in God's glory. "Through
Christ, through the Holy Spirit, in the Christian community, God draws
us into community with Himself and shapes us, whom He created in His
image, into the structure and dynamics of His threefold life of love."[63]
Scott finds this theology eloquently expressed in the theology of seven-
teenth-century Anglicans such as Joseph Hall and Jeremy Taylor.[64]

Professor Scott located this position early in his theological career as
he made his personal journey from Tillichianism to what he now calls
dynamic orthodoxy. In his 1968 doctoral dissertation, arguing against that
destructive egocentrism prevalent in American society and exemplified
by the teaching of Norman Vincent Peale, Scott wrote "that the egocen-
tric person intends the magnification of his own glory, i.e., the glory of his
ego as the center of his selfhood in isolation from God and the neighbor."[65] In contrast the student of Jesus, as Jesus is found in the New Testament, discovers that there is a

> greater glory than the glory of one's own ego as reflected in one's accom-
> plishments, and that is the glory of God. In Jesus it appears that man can
> be transfigured with the glory of divinity; he is not limited to the hope of a
> merely human glory. . . . Jesus also shows men how they may possess God's
> glory. Men become the inheritors of God's glory when they love God and
> their fellow men with the whole heart, mind and strength. That is, they
> receive God's glory when they do God's will and thus are seeking the mani-
> festation of God's glory among men. In their participation in God's will

through their obedience to it, they are transformed with the same glory that shines through their works. . . . In "seeking" God's glory they are themselves being covered with it and transfigured by it.[66]

This focus on God's glory and our participation in it saves us from the disappointment and despair of egocentrism, such disappointment and despair as inevitably comes when the expected divine utility is not evident. It is God's glory, not ours, that is the focus of dynamic orthodoxy.

Professor Walter Eversley represents a somewhat different perspective. He does not regard himself as Barthian, urges his students to seek the truth come whence it may, and stresses the doctrine of creation. Nevertheless, in his doctoral dissertation of 1975, done under the supervision of Professor Richard R. Niebuhr at Harvard, Eversley also places emphasis on God's glory.

He argues against views of the doctrine of the Atonement that understand God as initiating the Atonement solely on account of human sin and affirms that God initiates Atonement on his own accord, not because of sin but because of his love for his creation. Atonement is "a showing forth" of the divine glory "through Jesus Christ, the brightness of his glory." Eversley went on to say in his thesis:

This manifestation of glory is a continued demonstration of creative-preservative love for the entire cosmos and includes man's salvation from sin. All of creation comes to its true self in Jesus Christ, hence Jesus Christ is also the glory of creation.[67]

This glory of God (*kabod, doxa*) inspires, calls forth praise of God. Thus this theology could aptly be called a doxological theology whereby, for instance, the mission of the church is not ours but Christ's mission in which we share. As R.K. Orchard writes, "To share in Christ's Mission is to join the whole choir of heaven in adoration of His Father and our Father, His God and our God. It is to share by faith in His ascension. It is to join in a doxology. . . ."[68] The focus is on God and God's glory, on participation in that glory. To do so in obedience is to witness to it in the world through words and deeds of love. Thereby we "possess" a glory beyond all human possibility. The vision is immense, as immense as God's glory, and involves all of creation.

For David Scott and Christopher Hancock, the vision is all important and finds expression in an organization begun in 1990 called Scholarly Engagement with Anglican Doctrine (SEAD). The "Theological Foundation" set forth by SEAD is a reflection not only of classic Anglicanism of the sixteenth and seventeenth centuries but of classic Christianity, that of the Scriptures and the first four general councils. On this foundation SEAD seeks

> to promote a creative engagement between the "faith once delivered to the saints" and the modern world, in which both the historic faith and its contemporary appropriation are essential to its task. Its members believe that faithfulness to Christian/Anglican identity requires Christians to be lovingly and truthfully engaged with the complex and controversial moral and justice issues of our time within the framework afforded by the Anglican church's historic authorities.[69]

Christopher Hancock understands this theological position as "dynamic orthodoxy." Born in England into a strictly (he has called it neo-Benedictine, Hasidic) evangelical family, Professor Hancock's spiritual journey led him out of rigidity into creativity. His study of history prompted him to question the finality of human achievement and to gain an awareness that "God's grace works in spite of the condition of people in the church." His study of theology led him to an awareness of Christian identity transcending any particular expression of it. Beyond and above all he discerned mystery, one might say, *doxa*. Thus for him dynamic orthodoxy involves spirit and spirituality and, as he has said, the integration of "the best of spiritual energy to the wisest of Christian strategy."[70]

Such orthodoxy calls for the exercise of humility in worship and involves obedience to God's will. In his doctoral dissertation of 1984, Christopher Hancock reflected deeply upon the impact in Anglicanism of the *lex orandi* on the *lex credendi* as he explored Anglican teaching between 1827 and 1899 on the priesthood of Christ. Quite clearly, to focus on God's glory as do Scott and Eversley is to transcend the modern dissociation of sensibility, to acknowledge that theology begins with the contemplation of God—and is in its way prayer—and that primary theology occurs when the people of God gather for the worship of God, there to be overwhelmed by God's glory.

To refer to a theological ethos is not to say that the seminary is without diverse points of view. There is diversity within the theological department itself. But there is a shared perspective, generally if not universally acknowledged. Some might not choose to call it "dynamic orthodoxy," but almost all would agree that they ground themselves, their faith, and what they teach in Scripture. One example of a broader consensus is to be seen in a joint publication that is also reflective of the dynamism in "dynamic orthodoxy," engagement "with the complex and controversial moral and justice issues of our time within the framework afforded by the Anglican church's historic authorities." This is *A Wholesome Example: Sexual*

Morality and the Episcopal Church (1991) edited by Professor Prichard. Prepared for distribution among delegates to the General Convention that met in Phoenix, Arizona, in 1991, it contains contributions by Dean Reid and Professors Murray Newman, William Stafford, Robert Prichard, David Scott, and Adjunct Professor Joseph Trigg. In addition there is reprinted an article by Stanton L. Jones and Don E. Workman called "Homosexuality: The Behavioral Sciences and the Church." The book sets forth the case against the ordination of homosexual and lesbian persons and argues against the blessing of same-sex unions. In a clear statement made in the chapter by Newman and Reid, it is said that the New Testament "affirms that heterosexual marriage is the only proper locus of sexual intercourse. That assertation derives primarily from the intention of God in creation itself. All other forms of sexual intercourse are wrong."[71]

This conclusion is based upon an exposition of Anglican authority that, while acknowledging the ultimate authority of God, acknowledges the mediate authorities of Scripture, tradition, reason, and experience (if the latter is to be included). "The Bible is first and primary." Newman and Reid state,

> The Bible is the Word of God in the words of the faithful people of God and (as all Episcopal clergy declare at the time of ordination) contains all things necessary for us and our salvation. For the church, therefore, the Bible is the first and primary authority in regard to the nature and activity of God, the nature of humanity, and God's will for humanity and the world.[72]

Therefore what the Scriptures have to say on such a subject as human sexuality must be taken with the utmost seriousness, interpreted carefully, with each particular interpretation "ultimately subject to reevaluation in the light of new study of Scripture."[73] What these writers find in their research is that only two positions on sexuality are permissible on the basis of Scripture: faithful heterosexual marriage or celibacy.[74]

Writing in defense of the doctrine in nineteenth-century England of Christ's priesthood, Professor Hancock said,

> In an age when the nature of priesthood, of the Church, of Christ, and the role of the Christian as a social and spiritual being are again under particular scrutiny, it is, perhaps, necessary and appropriate that solutions for these questions be sought for both in the pew, in prayer and in doctrine, in studied reflection on individual doctrinal questions and careful sensitivity to the historic, conservative witness to the interrelatedness of Christian doctrine, believing in the living Christ, the eternal priest, to bring us in Himself to the Father and to empower us by His Spirit to continue His work of priestly mediation of Divine grace and life to the world.[75]

This is another way of defining something of what is meant by the theological ethos of Virginia Seminary in the past few years. That it preserves continuity with the Evangelical tradition beginning with Keith and Meade, Sparrow and Packard, is evident. That it contains certain tensions, as between so-called conservative and liberal elements, is also a witness to continuity with the past when such tensions were also evident. The great truth is that the present theological ethos is imbued with what I choose to call dynamic evangelicalism.

8. FACING THE FUTURE:
AN INTERNATIONAL RESEARCH CENTER
FOR THE ANGLICAN COMMUNION

The Virginia Theological Seminary made great strides in the past decade. But as this review of the history of the institution and its people comes to a conclusion, it must be recognized that there will be challenges and changes will be ahead. In 1994 Dean Reid's tenure as dean and president came to an end and another phase of the history of the Seminary began with the election of the Very Reverend Martha J. Horne as the fourteenth dean of the Seminary. She is the first woman to head a seminary of the Episcopal Church. In addition, another major project on the agenda of the long-range planning committee is still in the planning stages. That is the founding of an International Research Center for the Anglican Communion. The idea for this grew in the mind of Dean Reid initially as he talked with Stephen W. Sykes, then Regius Professor of Divinity at Cambridge University, now Bishop of Ely. The dean reported that Sykes

> expressed the concern that Episcopal seminaries in this country need to assume a stronger leadership role in the academic life of the Anglican communion. In the past the communion has tended to look to England for academic leadership, and in particular to the major universities. With changes going on in England, the ability of universities to fill this role will become less.[76]

Dean Reid also mentioned a conversation "with a clergyman from the Anglican Church in Nigeria." This man indicated that African theologians were beginning to write "serious works of theology from an African perspective." He was concerned that this writing not take place "in total isolation from theological work being done in other parts of the world, including the West."[77]

The board of trustees considered the idea of such a center at its semiannual meeting in 1989 and commended it with enthusiasm to the consideration of the long-horned planning committee.[78] In April 1990 Dean Reid drafted a proposal for discussion by the faculty, describing "a 'think tank' for the Anglican Communion" in which a few fellows at the postdoctoral level would be gathered each year under the direction of a prominent theologian of the Anglican Communion to work on their own projects. These would be "projects of concern to the Anglican Communion." The fellows would share their insights through seminars, conferences, and publications.[79] The faculty discussed the proposal, shared ideas, and expressed enthusiasm for the center.[80]

The proposal was further refined and presented to the board at its annual meeting in 1990, where it was decided to form a committee for further planning.[81] Bishop Peter James Lee of Virginia was to be the chairman of the committee. At the annual meeting the next year the board approved the proposal as then presented and agreed to begin searching for a director.[82] At this point the board and the seminary administration became occupied by the building of the Addison Academic Center. The International Research Center of necessity had to await the completion of that project and the associated capital funds drive.

The proposal as presented in 1991 contained this explanation:

The Virginia Theological Seminary proposes to establish an International Research Center for the Anglican Communion as a catalyst for thought, dialogue and scholarship in Anglican encounter with a multi-cultural world. This Center is an outgrowth of the Seminary's long standing commitment to world mission and ecumenism and its belief that the unique and historic contribution of Anglicanism lies in its theological balance and its capacity for being comprehensive. It will seek to serve and enhance the intellectual and ministerial life of the international Anglican Communion.[83]

It was understood that the center should serve three purposes:

first, to coordinate and nurture scholarly engagement among Anglicans worldwide;
second, to house Anglican materials and host Anglican scholars,
third, to devote time, money and energy towards assisting individuals and groups around the world to reflect creatively upon the historic nature and contemporary possibilities of the Anglican Christian tradition.[84]

The realization of this center has been in the minds of those creating the Addison Academic Center, remodeling Aspinwall and Bohlen halls, expanding library holdings, and further planning for more conference housing facilities. The initial funding of the center has been given serious consideration by the director of development and the board. The estimate of the amount required in 1991 was set at $6,000,000, mostly in endowment to support the director, the fellows, staff, and program. Such funds were to be raised in a worldwide campaign.

9. CONCLUSION

It was the intention of the founders of the Virginia Theological Seminary that it should be "a school of prophets," that is, a school in which sound learning combined with sincere piety produced messengers of the gospel of God's saving work through Jesus Christ, ministers of the gospel for the ordained ministry of the Protestant Episcopal Church. There is no question that the purpose expressed by Meade in his circular of 1822, in the Rules and Regulations of 1825, and by the early teachers—Keith and Wilmer, Sparrow and Packard—involved both learning and piety, not apart from one another, but such learning as bred piety and such piety as bred learning.

That purpose also involved certain theological presuppositions. Joseph Packard discussed this in 1873 at the semicentennial observance. He spoke of the seminary's theological tradition, its Protestantism in "holding in purity all the articles of the Christian faith" against all those who through idolatry and superstition—and one might add now, error and atheism—denigrate that faith. He also spoke of its episcopal character, observing the forms and rubrics of our church, not making exclusive claims for this church, not judging the validity of the ministries of other churches, in the tradition of Richard Hooker and William White. And he spoke of its Evangelicalism in emphasizing "a doctrine of a complete justification by the sole merits and death of our Lord and Savior Jesus Christ." He noted that this tradition involves "a warm and fervent spirit of piety."[85]

Packard said that it was the conviction of the founders

> that religious feeling here should not grow cold; that we should breathe here an atmosphere not too rarefied for the breath of life; that the power of Christ in the souls should here be experienced in fuller and deeper measure; and that spirituality, not spurious, should be cultivated here. They hoped that Christian lives here would rise as high as a Missionary temperature.[86]

Professor Packard warned that should the spirit of the founders be negated, "when another Gospel shall be preached and another theology taught here; when, though the symbols of the Divine presence are here, that presence shall be withdrawn," then "the fingers of a man's hand shall come forth and write upon this Pulpit, and yonder Lecture-rooms and Halls: The glory is departed!"[87]

While thus acknowledging the importance of what Packard had to say then, we must know now, as the founders surely knew, that there will be changes. Changes will occur as they have occurred in the past. If we are to be obedient to our Lord and be faithful to the founding purpose of the institution, we and it must change. This is so because while the originating purpose remains the same, the world is not the same, is ever changing, and requires the rethinking of the originating purpose in the light of the present, for the sake of the future.

At the seminary's centennial observance in 1923, George Bartlett, the dean of the Philadelphia Divinity School, spoke of "the demand that our Gospel be thought through afresh." He said,

> I am not pleading for a Modernist Gospel. I do not believe that there is or can be any such thing. The one Gospel is that of Jesus Christ, the same yesterday, today and forever. Nor do I believe that any restatement will or can change that eternal Gospel by one jot or tittle. But God Himself could not reveal Himself powerfully to mankind until in the fullness of time He sent His only begotten Son to take our flesh upon Him, to live, as one of us, among us. So, in a sense, the Gospel of Christ must become incarnate once again, must, that is, restate itself in language understanded of the people, in thought terms that are theirs and not their fathers',—must adapt itself in its application and interpretation to the actual problems, perplexities, and conditions of the world it seeks to save.[88]

It is important to realize that in so speaking Dean Bartlett was not primarily focusing on contemporary issues but on the gospel and that reinterpretation did not involve changing the gospel but understanding how the gospel speaks to this time as well as former times.

Dean Bartlett's statement, while concerned with theological foundations, is also pertinent in its spirit to the institutional embodiment of the purpose as formulated by the founders. This is so and is of importance to us on two levels. First, the originating purpose cannot be expected to live on and be realized by the seminary without reinterpretation. This requires an attitude not of triumphalism but of humility, of a willingness to examine and reexamine the functioning of the seminary in the light of the originating purpose and also in the light of the church's mission (Christ's mission) and message not only as they were but as they are and must be today. Change has occurred. The institution's purpose has been reinterpreted with fidelity to its originators and with responsiveness to the challenges of the postmodern world, not always, not consistently, not perfectly, but actually again and again.

The governance of the seminary has evolved with the gradual emergence of a larger, more complex administrative structure and more efficient, skillful personnel. The faculty has grown with increasingly specialized, more professional additions so that, for instance, where there was one teacher of Scripture in 1923, in 1993 there are six. The curriculum has evolved with greater richness and variety in offerings around a solid core of courses representing the very heart of the theological encyclopedia. The understanding of education for the ministry of the church has changed to take into account the ministry of the laity, to educate women and African Americans in a more and more multicultural setting, including a diverse cross-cultural gathering of students and teachers.

The basic purpose—to educate men for the ordained ministry of the Episcopal Church—has been so reinterpreted as to include not only admission of laity but provision for lifelong education for ministry, from cradle to grave, and for the education of women as well as men. In line with this, a Center for the Ministry of Teaching was founded to accompany the already existing degree programs serving those preparing for ministry per se, lay and ordained, and the Center for Continuing Education, an ecumenical enterprise with multifaceted programs for lifelong education. In addition there are the Lay School of Theology and the Institute in School Ministry. Other efforts at education have been made from time to time, including lecture series and elderhostels.

The seminary was, from the beginning, loyal in its basic commitment to mission and evangelism. That aspect of its purpose has been reinterpreted so that it includes, not only the education of men and women preparing for foreign and domestic mission service, but also the creation of a department of mission and world religions, the addition of courses on evangelism, requirements in both areas, the development of field education in such ways as to foster mission and evangelism, engagement in overseas programs, support for the seminary consultation on mission, and much else. The International Research Center for the Anglican Communion is an important expression of this commitment to mission and evangelism, reinterpreted in the light of a great need in the changing Anglican Communion.

The founders insisted upon sound learning, and that has been fostered through building a professional, highly trained faculty with a rich curriculum, dedicated to a core of necessary learning, with new, exciting facilities for teaching and learning. The founders also insisted upon fostering piety, and that has been accomplished through the curriculum, the regular round of worship in the chapel, small group worship, and most recently in provisions made for spiritual direction. In this we note change from the way things were done in the beginning. Most significantly, family devotions and Thursday evening faculty meeting in Prayer Hall are no more. There is no place called "Prayer Hall." But personal and corporate devotions are prominent in the life of Virginia Theological Seminary and maintain continuity with the originating purpose, providing for sincere piety in relation to sound learning.

Second, the originating purpose is grounded and rooted in the gospel. The Virginia Theological Seminary would not have been founded and would not now exist without the gospel of Jesus Christ. It is upon that gospel, and fidelity to it, that attention must be fixed and our judgments concerning the seminary's history must be based. Fidelity to the gospel forbids idolatry, the idolatrous worship of this or any institution, including the church itself as an institution. The originating purpose is not to be idolized. But it is to be cherished and honored to the degree that it promotes the gospel of Jesus Christ and not some other gospel. What matters finally is that God be praised and that God blesses this institution, its life and work; and that its board of trustees, its administration, its faculty, its students, and its alumni are faithful ministers of God's Word and sacraments.

Toward the end of his sermon on 1 Tim. 1:15, William Sparrow called out to all who heard him and calls out to us now:

> Let us . . . arise, one and all, and address ourselves to an earnest study and right appreciation of the *"faithful saying, so worthy of all ACCEPTA-TION that Christ Jesus came into the world to save sinners."* It is both faithful and gracious. It has been ratified by the word and oath of God, that by two immutable things in which it is impossible God should lie, we might have strong consolation. It has been sealed with the blood of God's own Son, who loved us unto death, even the death of the cross. It has been confirmed by long continued and varied signs in heaven above, and on the earth beneath, that we might know the certainty of this merciful announcement. The heralds of the cross are abroad in the world, proclaiming from one end of it to the other, deliverance to the captive and the opening of the prison doors to them that are bound, and giving the invitation in the words of him that sent them, *"Turn ye to your strongholds, O ye prisoners of hope."*[89]

The ultimate measure of an institution such as the Virginia Theological Seminary, as rooted in a great purpose, grounded in the gospel, is revealed not by its institutional success, as the world understands such success, nor by buildings, money, and numbers, but by the degree to which it witnesses to the gospel in all of its life and sends forth heralds of such a hope.

371

NOTES

1. E.J. Dionne, Jr., *Why Americans Hate Politics* (New York: Simon and Schuster, 1991), 9.
2. Halberstam, *Next Century*, chap. 1.
3. Bd. min., dean's file (November 10, 1982).
4. Ibid. (April 19, 1982), attachments II–IV.
5. *Virginia Seminary Journal* 35/1 (May 1983): 6.
6. Ibid.
7. Richard Reid, memorandum to faculty and staff (March 17, 1983).
8. Bd. min., dean's file (May 18, 1983).
9. Fac. min. (May 16, 1983).
10. Ibid. (March 30, 1984). The first draft of the mission statement is attached to the minutes.
11. Bd. min., dean's file (November 14, 1984). Printed in subsequent issues of the seminary catalogue.
12. Fac. in. (October 30, 1984). There was further discussion at the faculty meeting of January 29, 1985.
13. Bd. min., dean's file (November 13, 1985).
14. Ibid. (November 12, 1986).
15. Ibid. (November 11, 1987).
16. *Proposal* (February 27, 1984), 2.
17. "An Interview with the Reverend Locke E. Bowman, Jr.," *Virginia Seminary Journal* 36/1 (June, 1984): 8.
18. Ibid., ii.
19. Bd. min., dean's file (May 16, 1984).
20. Quotation from the *Foundation Paper*, adopted January 1990, no pagination. See Bd. min., dean's file (November 14, 1990).
21. Bd. min., dean's file (November 16, 1988).
22. Ibid. (May 17, 1989).
23. *Virginia Seminary Journal* 38/3 (June, 1987): 11.
24. Edward S. Gleason, "The Seminary Institute in School Ministry," *Virginia Seminary Journal* 41/3 (November, 1989): 7.
25. Bd. min., dean's file (November 13, 1985).
26. Fac. min. (November 26, 1985; March 25, 1986).
27. Ibid. (May 27, 1986), and appended papers.
28. Ibid. (January 13, 1987; February 24, 1987; March 17, 1987).
29. Virginia Theological Seminary catalogue (1992–93), 19.
30. See *Report of the Self Study of the Protestant Episcopal Theological Seminary in Virginia for the Association of Theological Schools* (1993), sec. VI, 1–3.
31. Bd. min., dean's file (November 11, 1981).
32. See *Report of the Self Study* (1993), sec. IV, 4.
33. Fac. min. (October 17, 1984); bd. min., dean's file (November 14, 1984).
34. Fac. min. (April 15, 1986); bd. min., dean's file (May 14, 1986).

35. Bd. min., dean's file (November 12, 1986).
36. *Report of the Self Study* (1993), sec. III, 5.
37. The data here are derived from board minutes and from the Report of the Self Study (1993).
38. Both presentations were published in the *Virginia Seminary Journal* 37/2 (July 1986): 2–10.
39. Ibid., 10, see the resolution.
40. *AMBO* (October 1988): 3–4, 20–21. And see Parrent's paper dated October 1988.
41. See Spencer, *AMBO* (November 1988), and Parrent, *AMBO* (February 1989): 15–19.
42. Bd. min., dean's file (May 17, 1989).
43. Dean Reid to the board (April 26, 1989), appended item number 16.
44. Bd. min., dean's file (May 16, 1990).
45. Ibid. (May 15, 1991).
46. *Report of the Self Study* (1993), sec. XVII, 4.
47. See Addison (Edmund B.), VTSA.
48. See *Virginia Seminary Journal* 45/1 (May 1993).
49. Bd. min., dean's file (November 10, 1982).
50. Report on the meeting between faculty and seniors held on May 5, 1983.
51. Fac. Min., November 5, 1985, 2–5, and appended report.
52. See fac. min. (November 3, 1987; November 24, 1987), and attached documents.
53. Bd. min., dean's file (November 9, 1987.
54. See memorandum from the VTS women's group to the faculty (February 11, 1986); the fac. min. (March 11, 1986); and the statement "Policy and Guidelines on Inclusive Language" (March 21, 1986).
55. Report on the meeting of the faculty with graduating students (April 26, 1984).
56. Dean Reid in *Virginia Seminary Journal* 42/1 (July 1990): 9.
57. Fac. min. (May 27, 1986.)
58. Bd. in., dean's file (May 13, 1987).
59. "Spiritual Formation at Virginia Seminary," catalogue (Fall 1990), 1.
60. See the statement "Spiritual Formation at Virginia Seminary," catalogue (1992–93), 13.
61. See the trustees' report to the Virginia Convention in 1826, *Virginia Seminary Journal* 43/4 (December 1991): 22.
62. Catalogue (1992–93), 17.
63. David Scott, "Anglican Moral Theology," opening lecture, photocopy.
64. See Scott's book, *Christian Character: Jeremy Taylor and Christian Ethics Today* (Oxford: Latimer House, 1991).
65. David Scott, "Egocentrism and the Christian Life: A Study of Thomas Aquinas and Martin Luther and an Attempted Reformulation" (Unpublished Ph.D. diss., Princeton University, 1968), 246.
66. Ibid., 247.

67. Walter Eversley, "*Christus Gloria*: An Aesthetic, Teleological Investigation of Atonement" (Unpublished Ph.D. diss., Harvard University, 1975), 216.
68. R.K. Orchard, *Missions in a Time of Testing* (London: Lutterworth, 1964), 197.
69. The "Theological Foundation" and this explanation are found in the brochure "SEAD: Scholarly Engagement with Anglican Doctrine."
70. Refer to the tape recording *SEAD 1993: Renewing Anglicanism, 4. The Quest for Dynamic Orthodoxy*, Professors David Scott and Christopher Hancock (Truro Tape Ministry, 1993), no. 5004.
71. *A Wholesome Example*, ed. Robert W. Prichard, (Alexandria, Va., 1991), 7.
72. Ibid., 2.
73. Ibid.
74. Ibid., 67.
75. Christopher David Hancock, "The Priesthood of Christ in Anglican Doctrine and Devotion: 1827–1899" (Unpublished Ph.D. diss., University of Durham, 1984), 1:468.
76. Draft proposal for an Institute for Anglican Studies (1990), 1.
77. Ibid.
78. Bd. min., dean's file (November 15, 1989).
79. See draft proposal for Institute of Anglican Studies, 1–3.
80. Fac. min. (April 24, 1990).
81. Bd. min., dean's file (May 16, 1990).
82. Ibid. (May 15, 1991).
83. "International Research Center for the Anglican Communion, Virginia Theological Seminary, A Proposal," for the May 1991 meeting of the board, 1.
84. Ibid., 7.
85. *Semi-Centennial Celebration* (Baltimore, 1873), 19–20.
86. Ibid., 20.
87. Ibid., 35.
88. Goodwin, *History* 2:560–61.
89. Sparrow, *Sermons*, 341–42.

APPENDIX

The author is grateful to Julia E. Randle, archivist of Virginia Theological Seminary, and to her staff, for the lists that follow. We are also grateful to Mark Duffy, archivist of the Episcopal Church, for his assistance.

VTS BOARD OF TRUSTEES
CHAIRMAN AND PRESIDENT*

Rt. Rev. Richard C. Moore
(1822–1841)
Rt. Rev. William Meade (1842–1862)
Rt. Rev. John Johns (1862–1876)
Rt. Rev. Francis M. Whittle
(1876–1902)
Rt. Rev. Robert A. Gibson
(1903–1919)
Rt. Rev. William C. Brown
(1919–1927)
Rt. Rev. Henry St. G. Tucker
(1927–1944)

Rt. Rev. Frederick D. Goodwin
(1944–1960)
Rt. Rev. Robert F Gibson, Jr.
(1960–1974)
Rt. Rev. David Rose (1974–1977)
Rt. Rev. Robert B. Hall (1977–1985)
Rt. Rev. Robert P. Atkinson
(1984–1993)
Rt. Rev. Peter James Lee (1993–2009?)

VTS BOARD OF TRUSTEES
TREASURER

Col. Hugh Mercer (1822) pro tem
John Gray (1822–1842)**
William Pollock (1842–1865)***
Cassius F. Lee (1865–1890)
Col. Arthur Herbert (1890–1911)
Julian T. Burke (1911–1916)

Arthur Herbert, Jr. (1917–1940)
Taylor Burke (1940–1951)
Benton T. Boogher (1951–1964)
Millard West (1964–1978)
Laurance Redway (1978–   )

* President of the Board Before 1971. Chairman of the Board after 1971.
** Board of Trustees minutes missing for this time period. Change documented in VTS Catalogue 1842–43 and "The Trustees of the Theological Seminary . . . Annual Report," Journal of the Convention of the Diocese of Virginia, 1842, p. 28
*** Listed as treasurer in the Journal of the Convention of the Diocese of Virginia, 1842–1865.

VTS BOARD OF TRUSTEES
SECRETARY

Edward C. McGuire (1822–1858)
Charles B. Dana (1858–1860?)
Records lost
Cornelius Walker (1866–1872)
Henderson Suter (1872–1876)
T.F. Martin (1876–1879)
Julius Grammer (1879–1907)
S. Scollay Moore (1907–1933)

Helen Tighe (1933–1935)
John J. Gravatt (1934–1939)
Carleton Barnwell (1939–1954)
Chisman Hanes (1957–1959)
John N. McCormick (1959–1960)
T. Hudnall Harvey (1960–1964)
John O'Hear (1964–1986)
James M. Green (1986–)

DEANS OF VIRGINIA THEOLOGICAL SEMINARY

Reuel Keith ("Senior Professor")
(Chairman of the Faculty)
(1823–1842)
William Sparrow c. (1842–1874)
Joseph Packard (1874–1895)
Cornelius Walker (Acting Dean)
(1895–1898)
Angus Crawford (1898–1916)
Berryman Green (1916–1931)
Wallace Eugene Rollins (1931–1940)

Alexander Clinton Zabriskie
(1940–1950)
Stanley Brown-Serman (1950–1952)
Edward Felix Kloman (1952–1956)
Jesse McLane Trotter (1956–1969)
Granville Cecil Woods, Jr.
(1969–1982)
Richard Reid (1982–1994)
Martha J. Horne (1994–2007)

VTS ASSOCIATE DEANS

T. Hudnall Harvey (1965–1968)[1]
A. Grant Noble (1960–1962)[2]
Philip Smith (1962–1969)[2]
Frank Pisani (1962–1969)[4]
Bennett J. Sims (1966–1972)[5]
Richard Reid (1969–1982)[1]

B. Sydney Sanders (1970–1974)[2]
John Rodgers (1975–1976)[2]
Churchill J. Gibson (1976–)[2]
Allan M. Parrent (1983–)[1]
Martha J. Horne (1986–1994)[3]

[1] Associate Dean for Academic Affairs
[2] Associate/Assistant Dean for Student Affairs and/or Chaplian
[3] Associate Dean for Administration
[4] Associate Dean for Development
[5] Associater Dean for Continuing Education

VTS BURSARS, BUSINESS MANAGERS

Harrison Fiddeso (1946–48)
Benton T. Boogher (1948–1968)
William Blood (1968–1985)
David H. Charlton (1984–1988)

Ivan Boone (1988)*
Martha J. Horne (1988–1994)**
Mary Lewis Hix (1994–)

OTHER VTS ADMINISTRATORS

John N. McCormick (1956–1962)[1]
Gordon T. Charlton, Jr. (1967–1973)[3]
Armistead L. Boothe (1969–1975)[5]
Dabney Carr (1969–1990)[1]
Robert W. Estill (1973–1976)[2]
William Pregnall (1973–1981)[3]
Richard A. Busch (1976–)[2]
Edward Morgan III (1981–1993)[3]

Locke E. Bowman, Jr. (1983–1994)[3]
Edward S. Gleason (1987–1995)[1]
David H. Charlton (1989–)[5]
Jacques B. Hadler, Jr. (1994–)[3]
Amelia J. Gearey (1995–)[4]
Margaret McNaughton-Ayers
(1995–)[6]

VTS FACULTY

Keith, Reuel (1823–1842)
Wilmer, William H. (1823–1826)
Norris, Oliver (1825)
Lippitt, Edward Russell (1826–1842)
Packard, Joseph (1836–1895)
Sparrow, William (1841–1874)
May, James (1842–1861)
Walker, Cornelius (1866–1898)
McElhinney, John J. (1872–1887)
Nelson, Kinlock (1876–1894)
Grammer, Carl E. (1887–1898)
Crawford, Angus (1887–1920)
Wallis, Samuel A. (1894–1920)
Massie, Robert K. (1898–1913)
Micou, Richard W. (1898–1912)

Green, Berryman (1902–1933)
Kennedy, Paca (1907–1931)
Bell, Cosby (1911–1933)
Rollins, Wallace E. (1913–1940)
Nelson, Thomas Kinloch (1920–1940)
Tucker, Beverly Dandridge
(1920–1923)
Tucker, Henry St.George
(1923–1926)
Zabriskie, Alexander C. (1925–1956)
Stanley, Clifford M. (1930–1936,
1946–1970)
Mitchell, James A. (1931–1933)
Brown-Serman, Stanley (1931–1952)
Lowry, Charles W. (1933–1943)

* Acting Business Manager
** Associate Dean for Administration
[1] Director of Development, Publications, Alumni/Alumnae Affairs
[2] Director of the Center for Continuing Education
[3] Director of Field Education
[4] Director of the Center for the Ministry of Teaching
[5] Special Counsel/Assistant to the Dean (part-time)
[6] Assistant Dean for Admissions and Community Life

Mollegen, Albert T. (1933–1934, 1936–1974)
Ball, C. Sturgis (1934–1941)
Kevin, Robert O. (1940–1967)
Gibson, Robert F. (1942–1947)
Howe, Reuel (1943–1958)
Trotter, Jesse M. (1946–1978)
Heim, Kenneth L. (1946–1952)
Boogher, Benton T. (1948–1968)
Clebsch, William A. (1949–1955)
Goodwin, Robert A. (1949–1956)
Kloman, E. Felix (1949–1956)
Cox, Robert E. (1950–1955)
Kelleran, Marian W. (1950–1973)
Bowie, W. Russell (1950–1955)
Lloyd, Barton M. (1950–1956, 1960–1968)
Beveridge, Lowell P. (1952–1974)
Goodwin, Jack H. (1954–1991)
Graham, Holt (1955–1971)
Newman, Murray (1955–)
Soleau, John (1955–1964)
Beckwith, John Q. (1955–1974)
Frank, William C. (1956–1960)
McCormick, John N. (1956–1962)
Price, Charles (1956–1963, 1972–1989)
Booty, John E. (1958–1967)
Woolverton, John F. (1958–1983)
Reid, Richard (1958–1994)
Smith, Philip (1959–1970)
Noble, A. Grant (1960–1962)
Harvey, T. Hudnall (1960–1968)
Pisani, Frank (1962–1969)
Rodgers, John (1963–1978)
Fletcher, John C. (1966–1971)
Sims, Bennett J. (1966–1972)
Crum, Milton (1966–1989)
Rightor, Henry (1966–1978)
Charlton, Gordon T., Jr. (1967–1973)
Allison, C. FitzSimons (1967–1975)
Ross, James (1968–)
Blood, William (1968–1985)

Carr, Dabney (1969–1990)
Van Develder, Frank R. (1969–1994)
Woods, G. Cecil, Jr. (1969–1981)
Scott, David A. (1970–)
Sanders, B. Sydney (1970–1974)
Fuller, Reginald (1972–1985)
Parrent, Allan M. (1972–)
Estill, Robert W. (1973–1976)
Pregnall, William (1973–1981)
Micks, Marianne H. (1974–1987)
Albritton, Sherrod (1974–1991)
Whitney, John (1974–1982)
Gibson, Churchill J. (1976–)
Busch, Richard A. (1976–)
Stafford, William S. (1976–)
Lewis, Lloyd A. (1978–1991)
Hanchey, Howard (1978–)
Newman, Burton J. (1978–)
Morgan, Edward III (1981–1993)
Prichard, Robert W. (1983–)
Bowman, Locke (1983–1994)
Hall, Barbara (1985–1993)
Charlton, David H. (1985–1988; 1989–)
Horne, Martha J. (1986–)
Gleason, Edward S. (1987–1995)
Geary, Amelia J. (1987–)
Eversley, Walter (1988–)
Jones, Richard J. (1988–)
Hancock, Christopher (1988–1994)
McDaniel, Judith (1990–)
Shepherd, William H., Jr. (1990–1993)
Glover, Raymond F. (1991–)
Budde, Mitzi M.J. (1991–)
Adams, David E. (1992–1994)
Hix, Mary Lewis (1993–)
Grieb, A. Katherine (1994–)
Morse, Jane (1994–1995)
Hadler, Jacques B. (1994–)
McNaughton-Ayers, Margaret (1995–)

FACULTY OCCUPANTS OF ENDOWED CHAIRS

THE DAVID J. ELY CHAIR OF CHURCH HISTORY—EST. 1897

The Rev. Robert K. Massie, M.A., D.D., (1899–1912)
The Rev. Wallace E. Rollins, A.B., B.D., D.D., (1912–1930)
The Rev. Alexander C. Zabriskie, B.A., B.D., (1930–1940)
The Rev. Robert F. Gibson, Jr., B.A., M.A., B.D., (1940–1946)
The Rev. C. FitzSimons Allison, M.Div., Ph.D., (1970–1975)
The Rev. William S. Stafford, B.A., M.A., M.Phil., Ph.D., (1983–)

THE JAMES MAXWELL CHAIR IN CHRISTIAN EDUCATION AND PASTORAL THEOLOGY—EST. 1928

The Rev. Romilly F. Humphries, D.D., (1928–1931)*
The Rev. James A. Mitchell, M.A., B.D., (1931–1934)+
The Rev. C. Sturges Ball, M.A., S.T.D., (1934–1942)**
The Rev. Reuel L. Howe, S.T.D., (1945–1957)++
Mrs. H.C. Kelleran, B.A., (1970–1973)++
The Rev. John R. Whitney, A.B., M.Ed., M.Div., Ph.D., (1974–1982)
The Rev. Locke E. Bowman, Jr., B.A., M.Div., L.H.D., (1987–1994)

Dr. Elizabeth M. Kimball (? -   )

THE HOWARD CHANDLER ROBBINS CHAIR IN HOMILETICS—EST. 1952

The Rev. W. Russell Bowie, M.A., D.D., S.T.D., (1954–1955)
The Rev. John Q. Beckwith, B.D., (1955–1974)
The Rev. G. Milton Crum, Jr., B.S., M.Div., (1974–1989)

THE ARTHUR LEE KINSOLVING CHAIR IN PASTORAL THEOLOGY—EST. MAY 1966

The Rev. Henry H. Rightor, M.Div., J.D., D.D., (1970–1978)
The Rev. Howard Hanchey, B.A., M.Div., D.Min., (1987–)

THE ARTHUR CARL LICHTENBERGER CHAIR FOR CONTINUING EDUCATION—EST. MAY 1966

The Rev. Bennett J. Sims, M.Div., D.D., (1970–1972)
The Rev. Robert W. Estill, S.T.M., (1974–1976)
The Rev. Richard A. Busch, B.A., B.D., Ph.D., (1976– ?)

Dr. Mitzi Jarrett Budde [? -   ]

---

* James Maxwell Chair in Reading and Pulpit Delivery
+ James Maxwell Chair in Reading and Speaking
** James Maxwell Chair in Practical Theology and Homiletics
++ James Maxwell Chair in Pastoral Theology

THE ARTHUR LEE KINSOLVING CHAIR
IN CHRISTIANITY IN AMERICA—EST. 1967

The Rev. John F. Woolverton, M.Div., Ph.D., (1970–1983)
The Rev. Robert W. Prichard, B.A., M.Div., Ph.D., (1988–)

THE CLINTON S. QUIN CHAIR IN CHRISTIAN ETHICS—EST. JAN. 1967

The Rev. Albert T. Mollegen, S.T.M., D.D., S.T.D., (1970–1974)
The Rev. Allan M. Parrent, B.A., M.A., M.Div., Ph.D., (1983–)

THE CATHERINE N. MCBURNEY CHAIR IN OLD TESTAMENT—EST. MAY 1978

The Rev. Murray L. Newman, B.A., M.A., B.D., Th.D., (1978– ?)

Dr. Stephen Cook (? –)

THE WILLIAM MEADE CHAIR IN SYSTEMATIC THEOLOGY—EST. MAY 1978

The Rev. Charles P. Price, B.A., B.D., S.T.D., (1978–1989)
The Rev. David A. Scott, B.A., B.D., M.A., Ph.D., (1989–)

THE MOLLY LAIRD DOWNS CHAIR OF NEW TESTAMENT—EST. 1983

The Rev. Reginald H. Fuller, B.A., M.A., S.T.D., (1983–1985)
The Very Rev. Richard Reid, A.B., A.M., B.D., Th.D., (1987–1994)

The Rev. John Yieh Han Yen, Ph.D. (? –)

GRADUATES OF VIRGINIA THEOLOGICAL SEMINARY
WHO SERVED AS MISSIONARIES IN FOREIGN FIELDS

This lists expands upon the list of seminary missionaries found in Volume II of W.A.R. Goodwin, ed., *History of the Theological Seminary in Virginia*, 1923. He implicitly defined foreign missionaries as those serving in fields designated as foreign as well as Alaska and Hawaii. This list has included those who served in Alaska and Hawaii, provided their service can be documented in the records of the National Council of the Episcopal Church. (Asterisks indicate non-American graduates who returned to their native countries as official paid missionaries of the Episcopal Church.) Sources for this list include: Archives of the Episcopal Church, RG 40, National Council, Minutes, Church Hymnal Corporation, *Episcopal Clerical Directory*, 1898–1993, Domestic and Foreign Missionary Society of the Protestant Episcopal Church, *Annual Report of the National Council*, 1872, 1874, 1891, 1898, 1907, 1910–1938, Episcopal Church Annual, 1980–1994, A.R. Goodwin, ed., *History of the Theological Seminary in Virginia and Its Historical Background*, 1923, Margaret Larom, ed. *Missionary Directory*, 1989, Virginia Theological Seminary, *Catalogs*, 1923–1994, Virginia Theological Seminary Chapel, Overseas Graduates File.

Special thanks are due to the Mr. Mark Duffy, Mr. Donald Firsching, and the staff of the Archives of the Episcopal Church Austin, Texas, for the provision of materials from the National Council Minutes; the Revs. Churchill J. Gibson, Richard

J. Jones, and Robert W. Prichard of Virginia Theological Seminary for unpublished missionary lists; and Donna L. Foughty and Kenneth Kroohs, V.T.S. '95 for
endless hours of research in the *Episcopal Clerical Directory*.

Paul Norborn Abe, 1916—Japan
Nolan Akers, 1952—Costa Rica,
   Colombia, Panama
John Cary Ambler, 1888—Japan
Benjamin Lucius Ancell, 1899—China
*Jesse Krebs Appel, 1933—Brazil
George Hough Appleton, 1882—China
Henry Lee Atkins, Jr., 1964—
   Dominican Republic
Benjamin Axleroad, Jr., 1944—Brazil
Langford Baldwin, 1951—India
Frank Carter Bancroft, Jr., 1930—India
*Orlando Baptista, 1933—Brazil
William Charles Baxter, 1930—
   Philippine Islands
John Boyd Bentley, 1921—Alaska
David Echols Bergesen, 1958—
   Uruguay, Ecuador, Costa Rica
Norman Spencer Binstead, 1915—
   Philippine Islands, Japan
David Bell Birney, 1955—Uganda
Covy Edward Blackmon, 1960—Hawaii
Henry Arthur Blake, 1973—Panama
Alexander Hugo Blankingship, 1924—
   Cuba
Mark Alan Boesser, 1951—Alaska
William Jones Boone, 1835—China
William Jones Boone, 1868—China
Paul Roger Bowen, 1968—Polynesia,
   Tonga, others
Randolph Merritt Bragg, 1973—
   South Africa, others
Alanson Brown, 1951—Mexico
Francis Craighill Brown, 1925—China
William Cabell Brown, 1891—Brazil
George Daniel Browne, 1964,—Liberia
Robert Evans Browning, 1907—China
Harry Taylor Burke, 1934—Philippine
   Islands
Thomas Bowyer Campbell, 1913—
   China

Robert John Carlson, 1956—Guyana,
   Guatemala, Honduras,
   Nicaragua, West Indies
Courtney Lynn Carpenter, 1954—
   South Africa, New Zealand
Anselmo Carral-Solar, 1951,—Cuba,
   Guatemala, Panama
Sergio Carranza-Gomez, 1967—Mexico
Francis de Sales Carroll, 1906—Cuba
Robert Douglas Carter, 1976—Japan
Harry L. Casey, 1962—Ecuador
Bruce Coker Causey, 1951—Brazil
Kochukaleekal John Chacko, 1977—
   India
James Jeffries Chapman, 1899—Japan
Gordon Taliaferro Charlton, Jr., 1949—
   Mexico, Alaska
William Parish Chilton, 1966—
   Nicaragua
Guy Douglas Christian, 1906—Alaska
Charles Halsey Clark, 1952—
   Singapore, Philippine Islands
Thomas Grover Cleveland, 1954—
   Alaska
John Thompson Cole, 1883—Japan
Robert Henry Coleman, 1950—Japan
Emmanuel Gye Collins, 1966—Liberia
Henry Clinton Collins, 1890—Japan &
   China
James Wilver Conner, 1940—Puerto
   Rico
Francis Augustus Cox, 1921—China
Lloyd Rutherford Craighill, Jr., 1952—
   Japan, Okinawa
Lloyd Rutherford Craighill, 1915—
   China
Peyton Gardner Craighill, 1954—
   Japan, Taiwan, Okinawa
James Alleb Dator, 1958—Japan
*Robert Main Demery, 1958—
   Nicaragua, Belize

*Kimber Hsu K. Den, 1927—China
Herbert Alcorn Donovan, 1923—
 Liberia
Peter Reese Doyle, 1958—Liberia
James T. Doyen, 1859—China
Richard Thorp Draper, 1973—Japan
Claude Francis Du Teil, 1949—Hawaii
Edward Ryant Dyer, 1911—China
Charles Harrey Eddy, 1966—Alaska
William David Eddy, 1950—Mexico,
 Japan
Linda Jean Eggleston-Tyree, 1979—
 Kenya
Richard Douglas Eggleston-Tyree,
 1961—Kenya
Norman Henry Victor Elliott, 1951—
 Alaska
Theodore Hubbard Evans, Jr., 1961—
 Hong Kong, Singapore
William A. Fair, 1874—Africa
James Peter Farmer, 1949—Canal Zone
Martin Samuel Firth, 1933—Brazil
Wilfred Collison Files, 1939—Alaska
Custis Fletcher, Jr., 1939—Brazil
John Seymour Flinn, 1954—Uganda
Thomas L. Franklin, 1844—China
Raymond Eugene Fuessle, 1933—Brazil
Henry Dymoke Gasson, 1926—Brazil
Robert Fisher Gibson, Jr., 1942—
 Mexico
Nelson Davis Gifford, Jr., 1926—
 Hankow
John Monro Banister Gill, 1906—
 China
William Anderson Glenn, 1951—Costa
 Rica
Jose Agustin Gonzalez, 1943—Cuba
Conrad Harrison Goodwin, 1913—
 China
Robert Archer Goodwin, Jr., 1910—
 China
William Jones Gordon, Jr., 1943—
 Alaska
Richardson Graham, 1844—China
Allen Jones Green, 1953—Mexico

Robert Barringer Greene, 1949—
 Alaska
Roger Harlan Greene, 1956—Canal
 Zone, PZ
Robert Albert Greisser, 1904—China
Alfred Leslie Griffiths, 1931—Philip-
 pine Islands
William Ranck Grosh, 1950—Hawaii
Curtis Grubb, 1878—Africa
Robert Grumbine, 1951—Alaska
Sumner Guerry, 1921—China
Francis R. Hanson, 1833—China
Bravid Washington Harris, 1922—
 Liberia
Edwin Edward Harvey, 1958—Fiji,
 Polynesia
George Fugio Hayashi, 1957—Hawaii
Samuel Hazelhurst, 1842—Africa
William Clancy Heffner, 1950—
 Okinawa, Hawaii
Edmund W. Hening, 1844—Africa
John Hervey, 1985—Chile
Charles Ashley Higgins, 1937—China
John H. Hill, 1830—Greece
Jennings Wise Hobson, Jr., 1945—
 Alaska
C. Colden Hoffman, 1848—Africa
Hugh Hamilton Holcumb, 1855—
 Africa
Robert Paul Holdt, 1945—Alaska
Kenneth Leigh Houlder, 1910—Cuba
John P. Hubbard, 1851—China
John Edward Huhn, 1902—Alaska
Richard Herbert Humke, 1956—
 Hawaii
Frederick DuBois Huntington, 1979—
 Guatemala
Edward H. Ingle, 1864—China
James Addison Ingle, 1891—China
Roderick Humes Jackson, 1924—Japan
Solomon Napoleon Jacobs, BPDS
 1948—PC, Nicaragua
Robert Longacre Jacoby, 1935—British
 Virgin Islands
Albert Newton Jones, 1943—Alaska

John Robert Jones, 1952—Hawaii, Mexico
Richard John Jones, 1972—Ecuador
Alexander Dubose Juhan, 1943—Cuba
Cleveland Keith, 1850—China
Patterson Keller, 1956—Alaska
Leicester Foulke Kent, 1925—Alaska
Lucien Lee Kinsolving, 1889—Brazil
Michael Joseph Kippenbrock, 1928—Alaska
Richard Ainslie Kirchhoffer, Jr., 1948—Hawaii
Edward Felix Kloman, 1925—Liberia
*Jacob Kikogoro Kobayashi, 1894—Japan
Alfred Coleman Krader, 1955—Hawaii
Keith Kreitner, 1952—Hawaii
Samuel Knox Kreutzer, Jr., 1952—Hawaii
*Graham Kwei, 1949—China
Richard Tippen Lambert, 1950—Alaska
John Dominque LaMothe, 1894—Hawaii
Edmund Jennings Lee, 1900—China
Milton Reese LeRoy, 1950—Cuba
Hunter Merriwether Lewis, 1932—Japan
*Graham Yu Ling Lieo, 1927—China
John Liggins, 1855—China and Japan
Richard Burrus Lindner, Jr., 1957—Brazil
James Hubard Lloyd, 1942—Japan
John Janney Lloyd, 1947—Japan
Charles Henry Long, Jr, 1946—Hong Kong & Far East, Switzerland
Arthur Adams Lovekin, 1954—Liberia
Richard Martin Lundberg, 1940—Hawaii
Arthur Lyon Lyon-Vaiden, 1941—China
Arthur James Mackie, 1923—Cuba
Cameron Farquhar MacRae, 1899—China
Robert Alexander Magill, 1921—China
Edmund Lucien Malone, Jr., 1940—Virgin Islands

Myron Barraud Marshall, 1907—Philippine Islands
Hugh McDonald Martin, 1895—Canal Zone
Richard Knott Martin, 1964—Tanzania, Liberia
Lawrence Walker Mason, 1960—Hong Kong
Robert Kinlock Massie, 1891—China
*Go Matsubara, 1934—Japan
Nathan Mathews, 1900—Africa
George William McCammon, 1980—Ukraine
John Sherwood McDuffie, 1952—Panama
Moultrie Hutchinson McIntosh, 1950—Nicaragua, Panama
John Hamilton McNabb, 1876—Africa
John Gaw Meem, 1891—Brazil
Arthur Hallet Mellen, 1892—Cuba
Erasmus J. P. Messenger, 1845—Africa
Mason Faulconer Minich, 1966—Costa Rica
Launcelot Blackford Minor, 1836—Africa
Arthur Rutherford Morris, 1870—Japan
James Kenneth Morris, 1925—Japan
James Watson Morris, 1889—Brazil
Frank Hazlett Moss, Jr., 1934—Japan
Charles Allen Moya, 1959—Brazil
Joel Williams Murchison, 1952—Central America
*Paul Nagata, 1924—Japan
*Takeshi Naide, 1922—Japan
Yasutaro Naide, 1904—Japan
Robert Nelson, 1845—China
Thomas Kinloch Nelson, 1910—China
Arthur Francis Nightengale (B.P.D.S.), 1915—Panama
Catherine Bukeni Obokech, 1982—Uganda
John M. Obokech, 1982—Uganda
Packard Laird Okie, 1942—Liberia
Lloyd Lein Olsen, Jr., 1984—South Africa, Venezuela

Franklin Thorpe Osborne, 1916—Brazil
George Elden Packard, 1974—
Colombia
Henry Deane Page, 1882—Japan
Henry M. Parker, 1859—China
Henry M. Parker, 1877—Africa
William Barclay Parsons, Jr., 1950—
Japan
Theodore Hall Partrick, 1949—Haiti,
Mexico
James Lindsay Patton, 1890—Japan
John Payne, 1836—Africa
Mark Andrew Pearson, 1974—Kenya,
Philippine Islands
Louis Ashby Peatross, 1913—Japan
Jordan Brown Peck, Jr., 1963—Guam
Charles Clifton Penick, 1869—Liberia
Edward Monroe Pennell, Jr., 1927—
Hawaii
Frank Stanford Persons, II, 1916—Cuba
John Louis Peterson, 1992—Jerusalem
Sally Suzanne Peterson, 1972—South
Africa
Richard Roscoe Phelps, 1906—Brazil
Claude Leon Pickens, Jr., 1926—China
Henri Batcheller Pickens, 1937—
China, Hawaii
George Preble Pierce, 1956—Southwest
Africa
Tak Yue Pong, 1978—Taiwan
Thomas Morgan Prichard, 1978—
SAMS, Colombia
Henry Purdon, 1859—China
Jacob Rambo, 1848—Africa
James Thomas Ramsey, 1972—Malawi
David Benson Reed, 1951—RP,
Colombia
Walter Josslyn Reed, 1925—Liberia
Robert Huie Reid, Jr., 1948—Alaska
Alwin Reiners, Jr., 1954—Alaska
George Wallace Ribble, 1899—Brazil
Watkins Leigh Ribble, 1927—Brazil
Noel David Rich, 1979—Chile
Albert Northrup Roberts, Sr., 1923—
Brazil

Edgar Bolling Robertson, 1943—Liberia
Minor Lee Rogers, 1958—Japan
John Gollan Root, 1964—Uganda
Henry Roble Sanborn, 1921—Alaska
Robert Jordan Sanders, 1976—
Honduras
Jose Guadalupe Saucedo, 1949—
Mexico
Melchor Saucedo-Mendoza, 1945—
Mexico
Thomas S. Savage, 1836—South Africa
Richard William Scheer, 1980—Kenya
Thomas Carson Schmidt, 1955—
Colombia
Hugh Roy Scott, 1852—Africa
Warren Armstrong Seager, 1921—
China
Robert Stuart Seiler, 1952—Philippine
Islands
Caludius Parlett Shelton, 1930—
Alaska
Lemuel Barnett Shirley, 1941—Panama
Charles Philip Shulhafter, 1956—
Guatemala, Costa Rica
Carl Douglas Simmons, 1965—Mexico
Bennett Jones Sims, 1949—Japan
Thomas Lowry Sinclair, 1907—China
Dudley D. Smith, 1859—China
Joshua Smith, 1840—Africa
Robert Smith, 1853—Africa
Robert Macleod Smith, 1950—Japan
Lamar Pound Speier, 1952—Guam,
Hawaii
Leon Pharr Spencer, 1989—Kenya
Robert Lapsley Stevenson, 1943—
Hawaii
Harry A. Stirling, 1924—Virgin Islands
Allen Maxwell Stuhl, 1957—Canal
Zone & Panama
Edward W. Syle, 1844—China
Matilda L. Syrette, 1947—Nicaragua
Charles William Stuart Tait, 1961—
Uganda
*Saburo Takiguchi, 1934—Japan
Owen P. Thackara, 1845—Africa

Harris Bush Thomas, 1899—Puerto Rico

William Matthews Merrick Thomas, 1904—Brazil

Stanley Searing Thompson, 1913—Philippine Islands

Elliot H. Thomson, 1859—China

John Richard Nunnamaker Tinklepaugh, 1974—Rwanda

Iver John Torgerson, Jr., 1959—Hawaii

Todd Hubbard Trefts, 1961—Uganda

Philip Lindell Tsen, 1924—China

Robert Tao Hung Tsu, 1957—Malaysia

Beverley Dandridge Tucker, 1952—Japan

Henry St. George Tucker, 1899—Japan

James Lydell Tucker, 1952—Liberia

William Ryland Downing Turkington, Jr., 1931—Liberia

Philip Williams Turner, III, 1961—Uganda

Samuel Van Culin, Jr., 1955—England, Hawaii

Frank Radcliff Van Develder, 1963—Mexico

Roger Atkinson Walke, 1904—Japan

Edwin Montague Walker, 1961—Costa Rica, Ecuador, Colombia

John Thomas Walker, 1954—Uganda

Laurance Washington Walton, Jr., 1958—Nicaragua

Marvin Leo Wanner, 1927—Alaska

William Thomas Warren, Jr., 1945—Alaska

Richard Armistead Watson, 1958—Virgin Islands

Willian Robert Webb, 1943—Alaska

Stephen Condict Webster, 1926—Liberia

William Howard Weigel, 1923—China

John Armistead Welbourn, 1899—Japan

David Deadrick Wendel, Jr., 1959—Brazil

Philip Eugene Wheaton, 1952—Dominican Republic, Costa Rica

Elijah Brockenbrough White, III, 1968—Fiji

Robb White, Jr., 1902—Philippine Islands

Channing Moore Williams, 1855—China, Japan

Philip Howard Williams, 1913—Alaska

Donald Farlow Winslow, 1956—Japan

Joseph Chandler Wood, 1925—China

Henry W. Woods, 1844—China

Edmund Lee Woodward, 1910—China

William Wright, 1853—Africa

Edward Pinkney Wroth, Jr., 1950—Cuba, Mexico

*Leighton T. Y. Yang, 1938—China

Thomas S. Yocum, 1859—China

Isaac K. Yokoyama, 1877—Japan

William Abbott Yon, 1955, Namibia

Alexander Clinton Zabriskie, 1956—Alaska, Puerto Rico

George Zabriskie, II, 1954—Philippine Islands

BIBLIOGRAPHY

PRIMARY SOURCES

MANUSCRIPTS

The most important primary sources used in this history are located in the Virginia Theological Seminary archives (VTSA), Julia E. Randle, archivist. In this repository are papers of Richard Channing Moore, William Meade, William Wilmer, Joseph Packard, William Sparrow, and many others from 1823 (and before) to the present. Autobiographies of Angus Crawford and Henry St. George Tucker as well as the historical reflections of A.C. Zabriskie have been especially valuable. In the Gibson family papers are to be found notes taken at lectures by Reuel Keith, used here for the first time. The archives contain board and faculty minutes. The board minutes covering the entire history of the seminary (with the exception of the years 1840 to 1866) are invaluable and are in the archives, except for those of recent years that are in the dean's office (referred to in the notes as dean's file). The faculty minutes are complete for the years 1896 (the first year for which we have minutes) to the present. The early minutes were discovered and rescued from destruction by Jack Goodwin, assisted by his library staff. The faculty minutes are in the seminary archives, except for those of recent years, which are in the office of the associate dean for academic affairs. These vary in their usefulness, depending upon who kept the minutes and what was expected of them. There are also minutes of the Alumni Society and its executive committee (incomplete) and of the Society for the Education of Pious Young Men. Various other papers have been used either in their original form or in transcripts made of manuscripts on deposit in other institutions.

PRINTED SOURCES

Periodical literature

Of the printed sources used in this history, note should be made of the *Washington Theological Repertory*, especially from its beginning in 1819 through 1823, and of the *Southern Churchman*, which in its early years was closely associated with the seminary. The latter was consulted in incomplete runs at the library of the School of Theology, the University of the South, and at the VTSA. Other rich sources of information were the yearly *Journals* of the Diocese of Virginia, the triennial *Journals* of the General Convention of the Protestant Episcopal Church, and the *Jour-*

nals of the Confederate States of America, researched at the libraries of the University of the South, the General Theological Seminary, the Episcopal Divinity School-Weston College, and the Virginia Theological Seminary library. Occasional periodic publications of the seminary, most especially the *Virginia Seminary Journal*, and student publications, such as *AMBO*, provided essential details and background information.

Books and articles

The 1923 history of the seminary, edited by W.A.R. Goodwin, listed below, was a major source. Most works by faculty members used in this history are considered as primary materials and are listed here.

Allen, Alexander V.G. *Life and Letters of Phillips Brooks.* 2 vols. New York: Dutton, 1900. Substantial chapters on Brooks as a VTS student.
Atwood, Lt. Col. Thomas W.W. "Life in a U.S. Army Hospital, 1862: From the Private Diaries and Letter of Pvt. Tobie." *Army* (January 1988): 52–57. On VTS as a Union hospital.
Bell, W. Cosby. *If a Man Die.* New York and London: Scribners, 1954). Contains a reminiscence of Bell by W. Russell Bowie.
———. *The Making of Man.* Bishop Paddock Lectures, 1929–30. New York: Macmillan, 1931.
———. *The Reasonableness of Faith in God.* Alexandria, Va.: VTS, 1937. Classroom lectures, edited by Annie Lee Bell.
———. *Sharing in Creation: Studies in the Christian View of the World.* Bohlen Lectures, 1925. New York: Macmillan, 1925.
Booty, John E. "The Law of Proportion: William Meade and Richard Hooker." In *Grace and Obedience, Papers in Honor of John Maurice Gessell,* edited by Donald S. Armentrout. *St. Luke's Journal of Theology* 34/2 (March 1991): 19–31.
———. "William Meade: Evangelical Churchman." *Seminary Journal* 14/2 (December 1962): 9–18. This issue of the *Journal* contains a transcription of Meade's manuscript autobiography and a bibliography of Meade's published works.
Bowie, Walter Russell. *Learning to Live.* Nashville: Abingdon, 1969. Contains reminiscences of a student who became a trustee and then a faculty member of VTS.
Clebsch, William A., ed. *Journals of the Protestant Episcopal Church in the Confederate States of America.* Centenary edition in facsimile. Austin: Church Historical Society, Texas, 1962.
———. "The Reverend Doctor William Holland Wilmer (1782–1827): His Life, Work, and Thought." Unpublished S.T.M. thesis, Protestant Episcopal Theological Seminary in Virginia, 1951.
Eversley, Walter. "*Christus Gloria*: An Aesthetic, Teleological Investigation of the Atonement." Unpublished Ph.D. diss. Harvard University, 1975.
Goodwin, W.A.R., ed. *History of the Theological Seminary in Virginia and Its Historical Background.* 2 vols. New York: Gorham, 1923. The second volume contains

early minutes of the board and of the Society for the Education of Pious Young Men.

Hancock, Christopher David. "The Priesthood of Christ in Anglican Doctrine and Devotion: 1827–1899." Unpublished Ph.D. diss. University of Durham, 1984.

Harris, Odell Greenleaf. *The Bishop Payne Divinity School, Petersburg, Virginia, 1878–1949. A History of the Seminary to Prepare Black Men for the Ministry of the Protestant Episcopal Church.* Alexandria, Va.: VTS, 1980.

Heim, Kenneth E. *Ken: a man on a journey.* Selected from letters and writings of Kenneth E. Heim. Wyncote, Pa.: Arie Heim Lindabury, 1983.

Henshaw, J.P.K. *Memoir of the Life of the Rt. Rev. Richard Channing Moore.* Philadelphia, Pa.: Stavely, 1843. Contains many letters to and from Moore and a selection of his sermons.

Howe, Reuel. *Man's Need and God's Action.* Greenwich, Conn.: Seabury, 1953.

Johns, John. *A Memoir of the Life of the Right Rev. William Meade.* Baltimore: Innes, 1867. Contains many letters to and from Meade and a commemorative sermon by William Sparrow.

Johnson, Ludwell. "How Not to Run a College." Chap. 2 in *The College of William and Mary: A History,* edited by Susan H. Godson Williamsburg: College of William and Mary, 1993. This essay is valuable for information concerning Keith's tenure at William and Mary and the early history of VTS.

Krumm, John. "A.T. Mollegen." In *Theology and Culture: Essays in Honor of Albert T. Mollegen and Clifford L. Stanley.* Supplementary Series, no. 7. *Anglican Theological Review* (November 1976): 9–18.

Lowry, Charles Wesley. *Communism and Christ.* New York: Morehouse-Gorham, 1952.

[Maryland] *Address of the Board of Trustees of the Protestant Episcopal Theological Seminary of Maryland, to the Members of the Church in this Diocese.* Georgetown, D.C.: n.p., 1822.

May, James. *The Advantage of Church Membership with Reference to some Errors, Historically Viewed. A Sermon, Delivered at the Opening of the Diocesan Convention of the Protestant Episcopal Church of Virginia, in Winchester, May 10, 1847.* Philadelphia: Stavely and McCalla, 1847.

———. *The Proper Office and Spirit of the Ministry. A Sermon Preached Before the Society of the Alumni of the Theological Seminary of Virginia.* Washington: Willism Q. Force, 1844.

McElhinney, John L. *The Doctrine of the Church: A Historical Monograph, with a full bibliography of the subject.* Philadelphia: Claxton, Remsen and Haffelfinger, 1871.

———. *"Eternal Hope" Reviewed. A Lecture: Read in Prayer Hall, Theological Seminary of Virginia, May 1st, 1878.* Philadelphia: James A. Moore, 1878.

———. *Regeneration and Baptism: A Paper Read at a Conference Held at Columbus, O., September 13, 1871.* Columbus: Nevins & Myers, 1871.

McKim, Randolph H. *A Soldier's Recollections: Leaves from the Diary of a Young Confederate.* New York: Longmans, Green, 1911. Recalls studying under Sparrow while the seminary was in exile during the Civil War.

Meade, William. "Autobiography," edited by J.E. Booty. *Seminary Journal* 14/2 (December 1962): 30–43. Originally printed in the *Historical Magazine of the Protestant Episcopal Church* 31/4 (December 1962).

―――. *The Law of Proportion in the Church of God: Considered in a Pastoral Address . . . to the Ministers and Members* [of the Diocese of Virginia] *in compliance with the 27th canon of the General Convention.* Alexandria: Southern Churchman Office, 1843. The substance of this address is contained in Meade's *Lectures on the Pastoral Office.* See Booty, above.

―――. *Lectures on the Pastoral Office, delivered to the Students of the Theological Seminary at Alexandria, Va.* New York: Stanford and Swords, 1849.

―――. *Old Churches, Ministers, and Families of Virginia.* 2 vols. Philadelphia: J.B.Lippincott, 1861. Valuable for information concerning Meade himself as well as of the seminary and the diocese.

―――. "The Wisdom, Moderation, and Character of the English Reformers, and of the Fathers of the Protestant Episcopal Church in the United States [An address to the students of our Theological Seminary at Alexandria]." *Southern Churchman* 6/13 (April 3, 1840).

Micks, Marianne H. *Introduction to Theology.* New York: Seabury, 1983. This is a revised version of the book originally published in 1964.

―――. *Our Search for Identity: Humanity in the Image of God.* Philadelphia: Fortress, 1982.

Micou, Richard W. *Basic Ideas in Religion, or Apologetic Theism,* edited by Paul Micou. New York and London: Association Press, 1916. Derived from Micou's lectures.

―――. *Manual of Fundamental Theology and Christian Apologetics.* Louisville: Brewers Printing House, 1907. Lecture notes.

―――. "The Re-discovery of Faith." *Alumni Bulletin of the Protestant Episcopal Theological Seminary in Virginia, for the year 1903,* 9–20. Alexandria, Va.: VTS, 1903.

Mollegen, Albert T. *Christianity and Modern Man: The Crisis of Secularism.* Indianapolis: Bobbs-Merrill, 1961. Based upon the first course of lectures delivered in the Christianity and Modern Man series at Washington Cathedral.

―――. "Christology and Biblical Criticism in Tillich." In *The Theology of Paul Tillich,* edited by Charles W. Kegley and Robert W. Bretall, 230–45. New York: Macmillan, 1952.

―――. "Evangelicalism and Christian Social Ethics." In *Anglican Evangelicalism,* edited by A.C. Zabriskie, 229–61. Philadelphia: Church Historical Society, 1943.

Newman, Murray Lee, Jr. *The People of the Covenant: A Study of Israel from Moses to the Monarchy.* New York: Abingdon, 1962.

Packard, Joseph. *Recollections of a Long Life.* Edited by Thomas J. Packard. Washington, D.C.: Byron S. Adams, 1902. Valuable source material.

Price, Charles P. "Clifford Leland Stanley: Teacher and Theologian." In *Theology and Culture: Essays in Honor of Albert T. Mollegen and Clifford L. Stanley,* edited by W. Taylor Stevenson. Supplementary Series, no. 7. *Anglican Theological Review* (November 1976): 19–30.

———. *Principles of Christian Faith*. New Delhi: Islam and Modern Age Society, 1977. Based on lectures given at Harvard University.

———. *The Anglican Tradition. What is it? Can it last?* Cincinnati: Forward Movement, 1984. A lecture given at the University of the South, first published in *St. Luke's Journal of Theology* 23/4 (September 1980).

———. "The Significance of Field Education for Theological Education as seen from the Point of View of a Seminary Teacher: Four Observations." *Seminary Journal* 26/2 (March 1974).

Prichard, Robert W. *A History of the Episcopal Church*. Harrisburg, Pa.: Morehouse, 1991.

———. "Virginia Seminary Since World War II." *Seminary Journal* 37/1 (June 1985).

Prichard, Robert W., ed. *A Wholesome Example*. Alexandria, Va.: privately printed, 1991.

Protestant Episcopal Theological Seminary in Virginia. *Semi-Centennial Celebration of the Theological Seminary of the Protestant Episcopal Church in the Diocese of Virginia, held on the 24th and 25th Days of September, 1873*. Baltimore: privately printed, 1873).

Scott, David A. *Christian Character: Jeremy Taylor and Christian Ethics Today*. Oxford: Latimer House, 1991.

———. "Egocentrism and the Christian Life: A Study of Thomas Aquinas and Martin Luther and an Attempted Reformulation." Unpublished Ph.D. diss., Princeton University, 1968.

Shiras, Alexander. *Life and Letters of the Rev. James May, D.D.* Philadelphia: Protestant Episcopal Book Society, 1865. Especially valuable for letters to and from May.

Sparrow, William. *The Christian Ministry. An Address Delivered at the Annual Commencement of the Theological Seminary of the Protestant Episcopal Church of the Diocese of Virginia, June 24, 1869*. New York: American Church Press, 1869.

———. "The Right Conduct of Theological Seminaries. An Address delivered at the Twenty-first annual commencement of the Theological Seminary of the Protestant Episcopal Church, in the Diocese of Virginia, July 13, 1843." *Southern Churchman* 9/31 (August 25, 1843). This is of major importance.

———. *Sermons*. New York: Thomas Whitaker, 1877.

———. *Our Times and Our Duties. An Address Delivered at the Annual Commencement of the Theological Seminary of the Protestant Episcopal Church of the Diocese of Virginia, June 27, 1872*. Philadelphia: Leighton, 1872.

Stanley, Clifford L. "The Church, in but not of the World" In *Christian Faith and Social Action*, edited by John A. Hutchison, 53–73. New York and London: Scribners, 1953. Vintage Stanley.

Stevenson, W. Taylor, ed. *Theology and Culture: Essays in Honor of Albert T. Mollegen and Clifford L. Stanley*, edited by W. Taylor Stevenson. Supplementary Series, no. 7. *Anglican Theological Review* (November 1976).

Stone, John S. *A Discourse, Commemorative of the Life and Character of the Rev. James May, D.D., Late Professor of Ecclesiastical History in the Divinity School of* the *Protestant Episcopal Church in Philadelphia*. Delivered in the Church of the Epiphany. Philadelphia: J.S. McCalla, 1864.

Trotter, Jesse M., et al. *Alexander Clinton Zabriskie, 1898–1956*. A special issue of *Seminary Journal* 3/2 (December 1956).

———. *The Trotter Years*. An issue of *Seminary Journal* 21/3 (March 1969).

Walker, Cornelius. *Lectures on Christian Ethics*. New York: Thomas Whitaker, 1895. Based on classroom lectures.

———. *The Life and Correspondence of Rev. William Sparrow, D.D.* Philadelphia: James Hammond, 1876. An invaluable source for understanding Sparrow.

——— *Outlines of Christian Theology*. New York: Thomas Whitaker, 1894. Based on classroom lectures.

Wilmer, William H. *The Episcopal Manual. Being intended as a summary explanation of the Doctrine, Discipline and Worship of the Protestant Episcopal Church, as taught in her public formularies, and the writings of her approved divines. To which are added, observations on family and public devotion, and Directions for a devout and decent attendance on Public Worship, with Prayers, suitable to several occasions: The whole being designed to illustrate and enforce Evangelical Piety*. Baltimore: E.J. Coale, 1822. Of great importance for an understanding of the viewpoint of a man who served the seminary in its earliest days, a founder and professor of theology. Another edition with added materials was provided by John Coleman in 1841.

Wolf, William J. "The Theological Landscape 1936–1974: An Address." In *Theology and Culture: Essays in Honor of Albert T. Mollegen and Clifford L. Stanley*, edited by W. Taylor Stevenson. Supplementary Series, no. 7. *Anglican Theological Review* (November 1976): 31–41.

Zabriskie, Alexander Clinton, ed. *Anglican Evangelicalism*. Philadelphia: Church Historical Society, 1943.

SECONDARY WORKS (BOOKS AND ARTICLES)

Addison, James Thayer. *The Episcopal Church in the United States, 1789–1931*. New York: Scribners, 1951.

Ahlstrom, Sidney E. *A Religious History of the American People*. New Haven and London: Yale, 1972.

Albright, Raymond W. *Focus on Infinity: A Life of Phillips Brooks*. New York: Macmillan, 1961.

———. *A History of the Protestant Episcopal Church*. New York and London: Macmillan, 1964.

Armentrout, Donald Smith. *The Quest for the Informed Priest: A History of the School of Theology*. Sewanee, Tenn.: The School of Theology, The University of the South, 1979.

Bennett, Robert A. "Black Episcopalians: A History from the Colonial Period to the Present." *Historical Magazine of the Protestant Episcopal Church* 43/3 (September 1974): 231–45.

Blackman, George L. *Faith and Freedom. A Study of Theological Education and the Episcopal Theological School.* New York: Seabury, 1967.

Booty, John E. *The Episcopal Church in Crisis.* Cambridge, Mass.: Cowley, 1988.

Bradley, Ian. *The Call to Seriousness. The Evangelical Impact on the Victorians.* London: Cape, 1976.

Brown, Lawrence L. "1835 And All That: Domestic and Foreign Missionary Society Membership and The Missionary Spirit." *Historical Magazine of the Protestant Episcopal Church* (1971).

———. "Richard Channing Moore and the Revival of the Southern Church." *Historical Magazine of the Protestant Episcopal Church* (1966): 3–63.

Clebsch, William A. "Christian Interpretations of the Civil War." *Church History* 30 (June 1961).

———. *England's Earliest Protestants 1520–1535.* Yale Publications in Religion, no. 11. New Haven and London: Yale, 1964.

Davies, Horton. *Worship and Theology in England.* Vol. 5, *The Ecumenical Century, 1900–1965.* Princeton: Princeton University Press, 1965.

Dawley, Powel Mills. *The Story of the General Theological Seminary. A Sesquicentennial History, 1817–1967.* New York: Oxford, 1969.

Dionne, E.J., Jr. *Why Americans Hate Politics.* New York: Simon and Schuster, 1991.

Donovan, Mary Sudman. *A Different Call: Women's Ministries in the Episcopal Church, 1850–1920.* Wilton, Conn.: Morehouse-Barlow, 1986.

Eastlake, Charles. *A History of the Gothic Revival* (1872), edited by J. Mordaunt Crook. Leicester and New York: Humanities Press, 1970.

Feilding, Charles R. *Education for Ministry.* Dayton, Ohio: AATS, 1966.

Gewehr, Wesley M. *The Great Awakening in Virginia, 1740–1790.* Durham, N.C.: Duke, 1930.

Gilkey, Langdon. *Through the Tempest: Theological Voyages in a Pluralistic Culture,* edited by Jeff B. Pool. Minneapolis: Fortress, 1991.

Giltner, John H. *Moses Stuart: The Father of Biblical Science in America.* Society of Biblical Literature, Centennial Publications. Atlanta: Scholars Press, 1988.

Goodrich, Wallace, et al. *The Parish of the Advent in the City of Boston, 1844–1944.* Boston: n.p., 1944.

Halberstam, David. *The Next Century.* New York: William Morrow, 1991.

Hall, Douglas John. *Thinking the Faith: Christian Theology in a North American Context.* Minneapolis: Fortress, 1989.

Holmes, David Lynn, Jr. "William Meade and the Church of Virginia, 1789–1889." Unpublished Ph.D. diss. Princeton University, 1971.

Hopkins, Charles Howard. *The Rise of the Social Gospel in American Protestantism, 1865–1915.* New Haven: Yale, 1940.

Hopkins, Hugh Evans. *Charles Simeon of Cambridge.* Grand Rapids, Mich.: Eerdmans, 1977.

Huntington, Samuel P. *American Politics: The Promise of Disharmony.* Cambridge, Mass.: Harvard, 1981.

Kasson, John F. *Civilizing the Machine: Technology and Republican Values in America, 1776–1900.* Harmondsworth: Penguin, 1976.

Knapp, George Christian. *Lectures on Christian Theology.* Translated by Leonard Woods. 2 vols. New York: Carville, 1831.

Lynn, Robert Woods. "Notes Toward a History: Theological Encyclopedia and the Evolution of Protestant Seminary Curriculum, 1808–1968." *Theological Education* 17/2 (Spring 1981): 118–44.

McAdoo, H.R. *The Structure of Caroline Moral Theology.* London: Longmans, Green, 1949.

McLoughlin, William G. *Revivals, Awakenings, and Reform. An Essay on Religion and Social Change in America, 1607–1977.* Chicago and London: University of Chicago Press, 1978.

McPherson, James M. *The Battle Cry of Freedom: The Civil War Era.* New York: Ballantine, 1989.

Meacham, Standish. *Henry Thornton of Clapham, 1760–1815.* Cambridge, Mass.: Harvard, 1964.

Meyer, Donald B. *The Protestant Search for Political Realism.* Berkeley and Los Angeles: University of California Press, 1960.

Miller, J. Barrett. "The Theology of William Sparrow." *Historical Magazine of the Protestant Episcopal Church* 46/4 (December 1977): 443–54.

Mowry, George E. and Blaine A. Brownell. *The Urban Nation, 1920–1980.* Revised. The Making of America, American Century Series. New York: Hill and Wang, 1981.

Neill, Stephen. *A History of Christian Missions.* Grand Rapids, Mich.: Eerdmans, 1965.

Nevins, Allan, and Henry Steele Commager. *A Pocket History of the United States,* 7th ed. New York: Pocket Books, 1981.

Newsome, David. *The Wilberforces and Henry Manning. The Parting of Friends.* Cambridge, Mass.: Harvard, 1966.

Niebuhr, H. Richard. *The Social Sources of Denominationalism.* New York: Meridian, 1960.

Nye, Russel B. *William Lloyd Garrison.* Boston: Little, Brown, 1955.

Orchard, R.K. *Missions in a Time of Testing.* London: Lutterworth, 1964.

Potter, D.M. "National and Sectional Forces in the United States." *The Cambridge Modern History.* Vol. 10, *The Zenith of European Power, 1830–1870.* edited by J.P.T. Bury, 603–630. Cambridge: At the University Press, 1960.

Pusey, Nathan, and Charles Taylor. *Ministry for Tomorrow. Report of the Special Committee on Theological Education.* New York: Seabury, 1967.

Romaine, William. *The Life, Walk, and Triumph of Faith.* New ed. London: G. Routledge, 1856.

Rose, Anne C. *Transcendentalism as a Social Movement, 1830–1850.* New Haven and London: Yale, 1981.

Rowe, Henry K. *History of Andover Theological Seminary.* Newton, Mass.: n.p., 1933.

Simeon, Charles. *The Excellency of the Liturgy.* New York: Eastburn, Kirk, Co., 1813.

Smith, H. Shelton, Robert T. Handy, and Lefferts A.Loetscher, eds. *American Christianity: An Historical Interpretation with Representative Documents.* New York: Scribners, 1960.

Spielmann, Richard M. *Bexley Hall: 150 Years. A Brief History* Rochester: Colgate Rochester, 1974.

Steiner, Bruce E. *Samuel Seabury, 1729–1796, A Study in the High Church Tradition.* Columbus, Ohio: Ohio University Press, 1971.

Sumner, David E. *The Episcopal Church's History, 1945–1985.* Wilton, Conn.: Morehouse-Barlow, 1987.

Sykes, Stephen W. and John E. Booty, eds. *The Study of Anglicanism.* London and Philadelphia: SPCK, Fortress, 1988.

Temple, William. *Personal Religion and the Life of Fellowship.* London: Longsmans, Green, 1926.

Tillich, Paul. *Systematic Theology.* Vol 1. Chicago: University of Chicago Press, 1950.

Tyler, Alice F. *Freedom's Ferment: Phases of American Social History.* Minneapolis: Augsburg, 1944.

White, James F. *The Cambridge Movement: The Ecclesiologists and the Gothic Revival.* Cambridge: At the University Press, 1962.

Wilberforce, William. *A Practical View of the Prevailing Religious System of Professed Christians, in the Higher and Middle Classes in this Country, Contrasted with Real Christianity.* Boston: Crocker and Brewster, 1829.

Williams, Daniel Day. *The Andover Liberals: A Study in American Theology.* New York: King's Crown Press, 1941.

Woolverton, John Frederick. *Colonial Anglicanism in North America.* Detroit: Wayne State University Press, 1984.

Zabriskie, Alexander C. *No Mean Inheritance.* (MS VTS).

———. "The Seminary's Aim." *Living Church.* (January 22, 1941).

INDEX

The symbol (ph.) indicates a photo.